KAZUKI TAKAHASHI

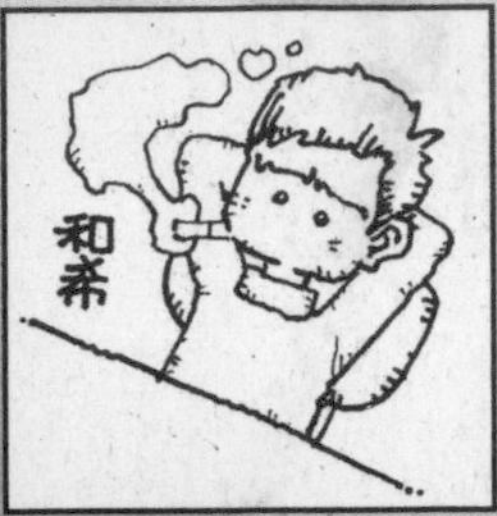

和希

I'M REALLY BAD WITH MACHINES, BUT MR. ITO IS A COMPUTER EXPERT. IN THE ORIGINAL *YU-GI-OH!* SERIES, HE HANDLED ALL THE DIGITAL WORK ON THINGS LIKE SPECIAL EFFECTS AND CARD COMPOSITION. WHEN HE'S IN FRONT OF A COMPUTER, MR. ITO BECOMES MY GURU.

Artist/author Kazuki Takahashi first tried to break into the manga business in 1982, but success eluded him until *Yu-Gi-Oh!* debuted in the Japanese *Weekly Shonen Jump* magazine in 1996. *Yu-Gi-Oh!*'s themes of friendship and fighting, together with Takahashi's weird and imaginative monsters, soon became enormously successful, spawning a real-world card game, video games and four anime series (two Japanese *Yu-Gi-Oh!* series, *Yu-Gi-Oh! GX* and *Yu-Gi-Oh! 5D's*). A lifelong gamer, Takahashi enjoys shogi (Japanese chess), mahjong, card games and tabletop RPGs, among other games.

AKIRA ITO

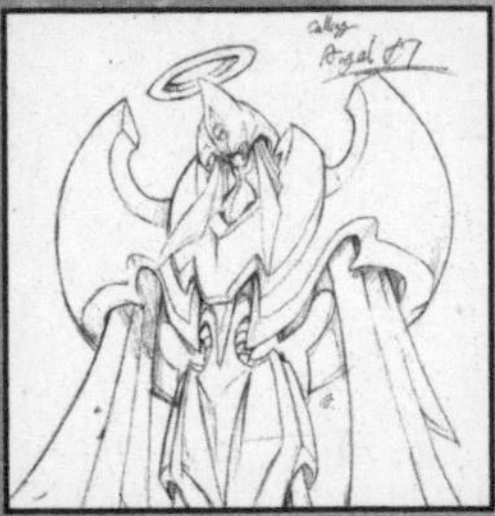

I DESIGNED ALL THE NEW MONSTERS THAT APPEAR IN *YU-GI-OH! R*. IT OFTEN TAKES ME A WHOLE DAY JUST TO DESIGN ONE MONSTER... BUT MR. TAKAHASHI IS REALLY FAST AT DESIGNING THEM, AND THEY ALL LOOK AMAZING! I ENJOY DESIGN WORK, BUT IT'S STRESSFUL.

Akira Ito worked on the original *Yu-Gi-Oh!* manga as an assistant to Kazuki Takahashi. He also assisted in the creation of *Yu-Gi-Oh! GX*. *Yu-Gi-Oh! R* is his first work as lead creator.

Volume 4
SHONEN JUMP Manga Edition

Original Concept/Supervised by **KAZUKI TAKAHASHI**
Story and Art by **AKIRA ITO**

Translation & English Adaptation **TAYLOR ENGEL and IAN REID, HC LANGUAGE SOLUTIONS**
Touch-up Art & Lettering **ERIC ERBES**
Cover Design **COURTNEY UTT**
Interior Design **DANIEL PORTER**
Editor **JASON THOMPSON**

VP, Production **ALVIN LU**
VP, Sales & Product Marketing **GONZALO FERREYRA**
VP, Creative **LINDA ESPINOSA**
Publisher **HYOE NARITA**

YU-GI-OH! R © 2004 by Kazuki Takahashi, Akira Ito. All rights reserved. First published in Japan in 2004 by SHUEISHA Inc., Tokyo. English translation rights arranged by SHUEISHA Inc.

The stories, characters and incidents mentioned in this publication are entirely fictional.

Printed in the U.S.A.

Published by VIZ Media, LLC
P.O. Box 77010
San Francisco, CA 94107

10 9 8 7 6 5 4 3 2 1
First printing, April 2010

Yu-Gi-Oh! R

遊戯王R

VOLUME 4
RETURN OF THE DRAGON

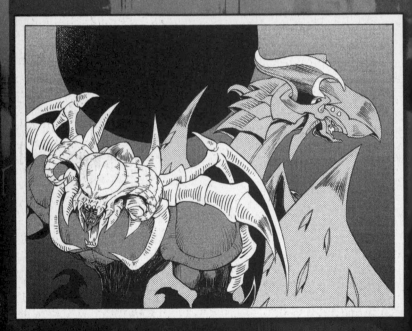

Original Concept/Supervised by KAZUKI TAKAHASHI
Story & Art by AKIRA ITO

CAST & STORY

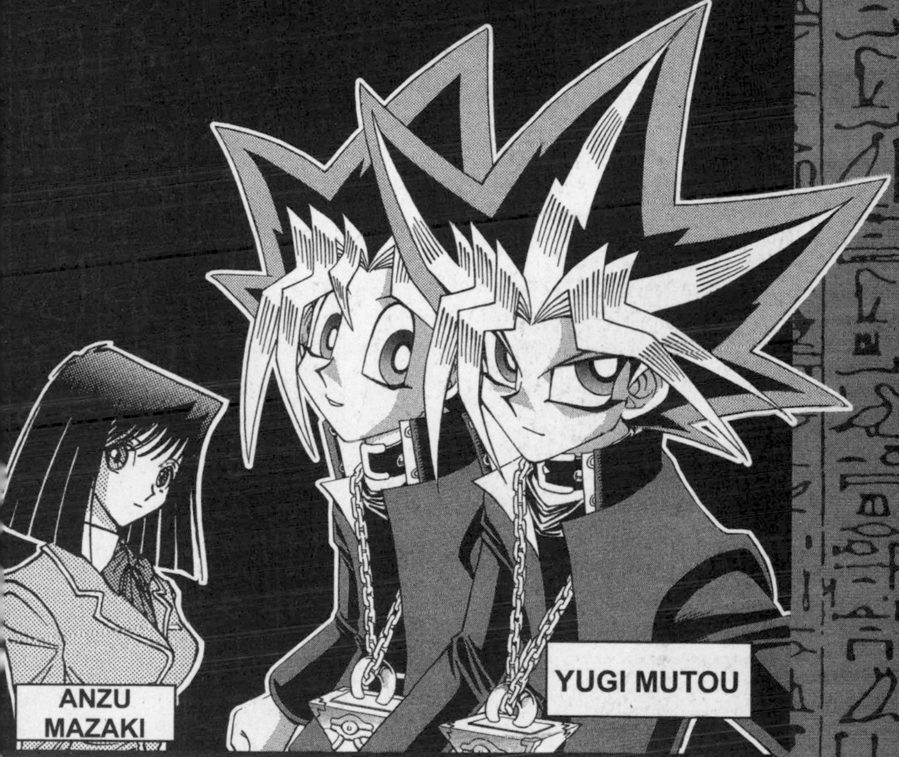
YUGI MUTOU
ANZU MAZAKI

But now a new enemy has appeared. Yako Tenma of Industrial Illusions, Pegasus's company, has made a hostile takeover of Kaiba Corporation and challenged Yugi to a duel. To ensure Yugi's participation, he has kidnapped Yugi's friend Anzu, intending to use her for the diabolical "R.A." Project... resurrecting Pegasus's spirit in Anzu's body! To rescue their friend, Yugi and his friends rush to the Kaiba Corporation skyscraper, where they must battle Tenma's duelist henchmen. But Gekko Tenma, Yako's brother, has joined forces with Yugi to stop his brother... and Kaiba himself has returned to take back his skyscraper from the invaders!

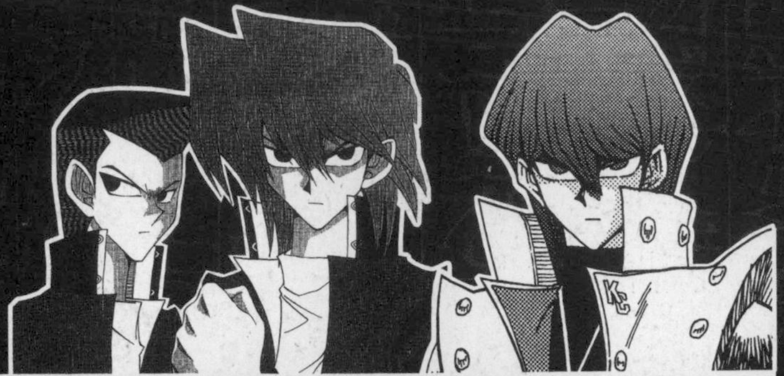

HIROTO HONDA KATSUYA JONOUCHI SETO KAIBA

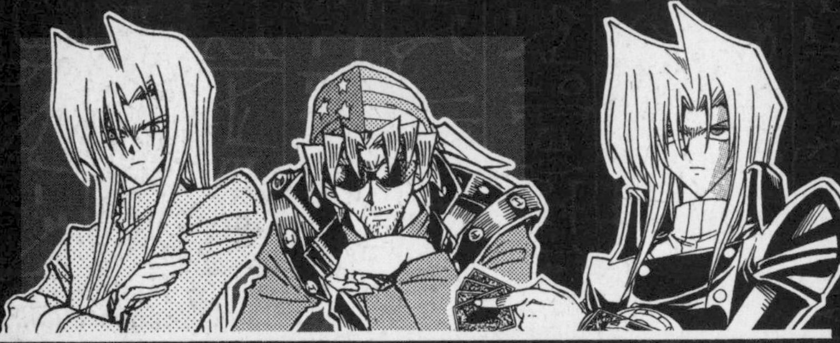

YAKO TENMA BANDIT KEITH GEKKO TENMA

When tenth grader Yugi solved the Millennium Puzzle, another spirit took up residence in his body… Yu-Gi-Oh, the King of Games! Using his gaming skills, Yugi fought ruthless adversaries like Maximillion Pegasus, multimillionaire creator of the collectible card game Duel Monsters, and Seto Kaiba, the teenage president of Kaiba Corporation. After winning the Battle City tournament, Yugi acquired the most powerful cards in the world: the three Egyptian God Cards "Slifer the Sky Dragon," "Obelisk the Tormentor" and "The Winged Dragon of Ra," which were created by Pegasus based on a mysterious ancient Egyptian card game.

VOLUME 4
RETURN OF THE DRAGON

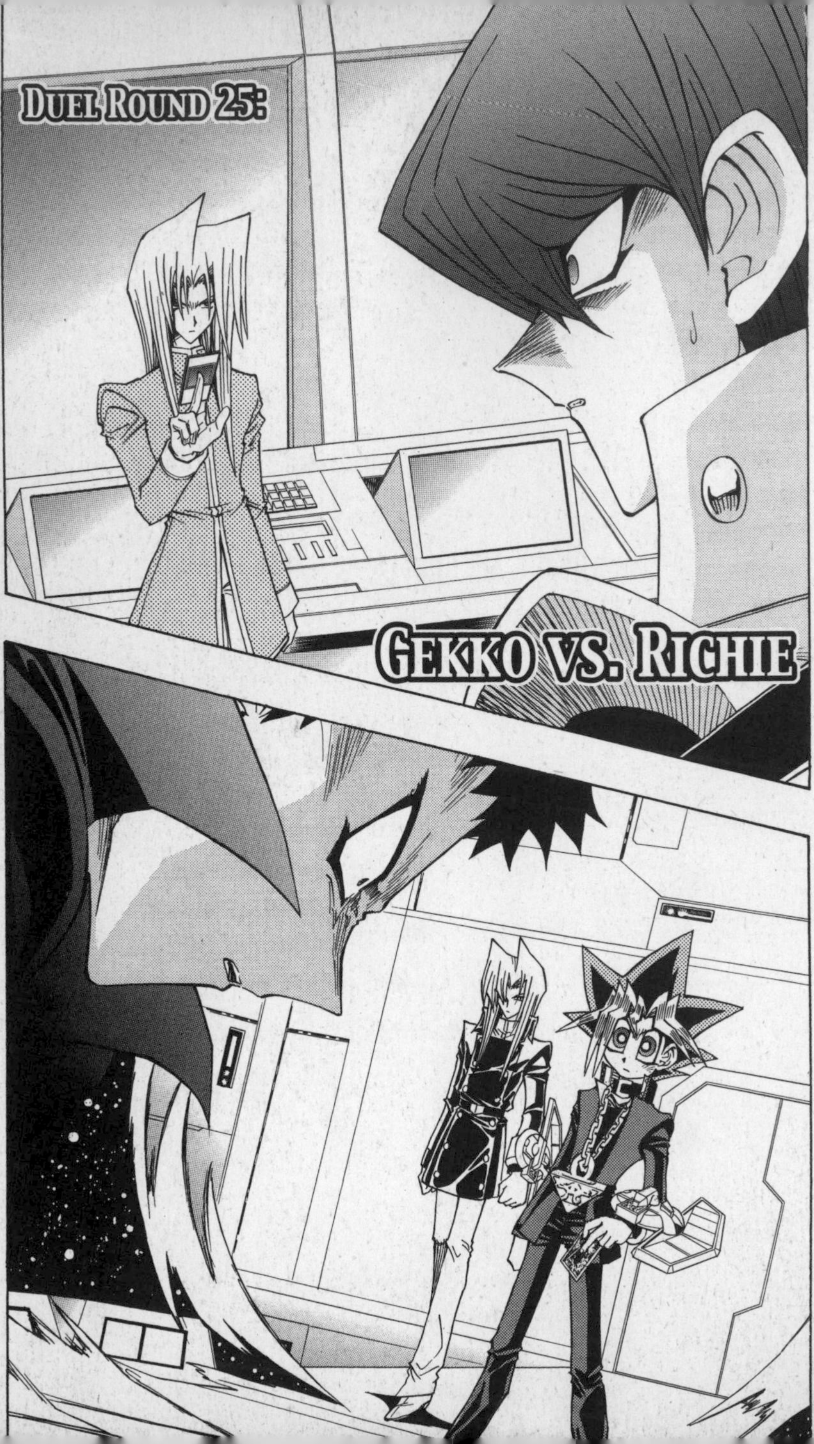
Duel Round 25:
Gekko vs. Richie

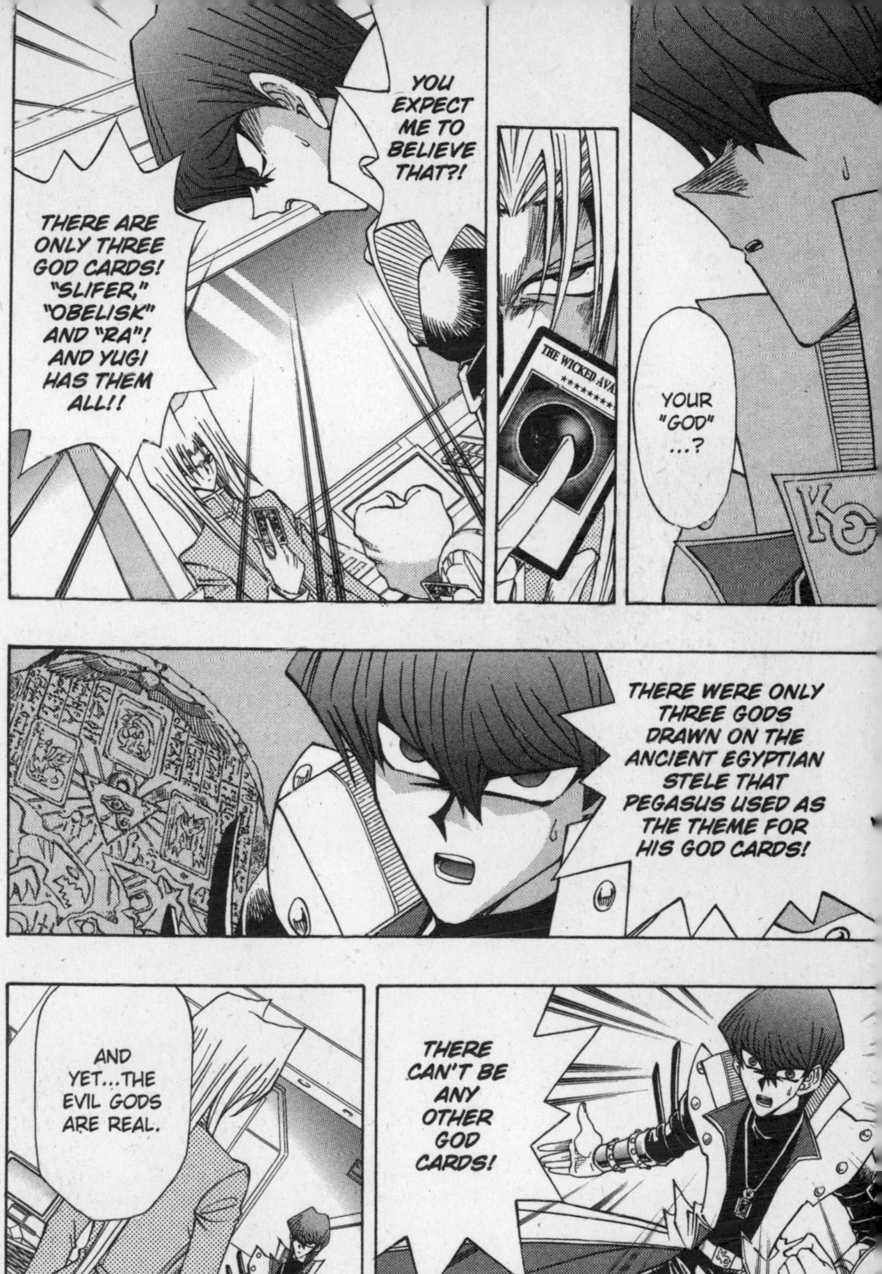
YOUR "GOD" ...?
YOU EXPECT ME TO BELIEVE THAT?!
THERE ARE ONLY THREE GOD CARDS! "SLIFER," "OBELISK" AND "RA"! AND YUGI HAS THEM ALL!!
THERE WERE ONLY THREE GODS DRAWN ON THE ANCIENT EGYPTIAN STELE THAT PEGASUS USED AS THE THEME FOR HIS GOD CARDS!
THERE CAN'T BE ANY OTHER GOD CARDS!
AND YET...THE EVIL GODS ARE REAL.

READ THIS WAY

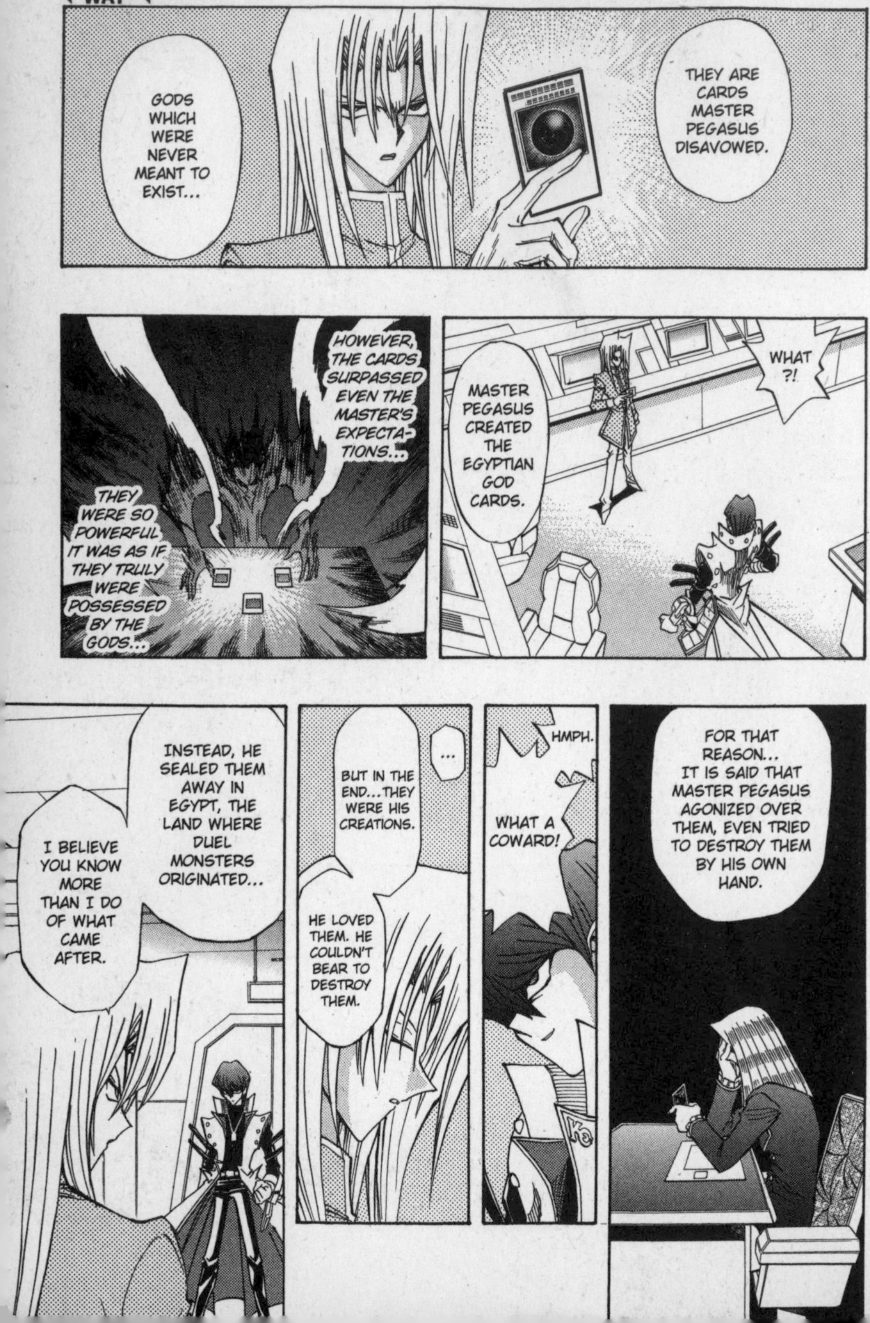
THEY ARE CARDS MASTER PEGASUS DISAVOWED.
GODS WHICH WERE NEVER MEANT TO EXIST...
WHAT ?!
MASTER PEGASUS CREATED THE EGYPTIAN GOD CARDS.
HOWEVER, THE CARDS SURPASSED EVEN THE MASTER'S EXPECTATIONS...
THEY WERE SO POWERFUL IT WAS AS IF THEY TRULY WERE POSSESSED BY THE GODS...
FOR THAT REASON... IT IS SAID THAT MASTER PEGASUS AGONIZED OVER THEM, EVEN TRIED TO DESTROY THEM BY HIS OWN HAND.
HMPH.
WHAT A COWARD!
...
BUT IN THE END...THEY WERE HIS CREATIONS.
HE LOVED THEM. HE COULDN'T BEAR TO DESTROY THEM.
INSTEAD, HE SEALED THEM AWAY IN EGYPT, THE LAND WHERE DUEL MONSTERS ORIGINATED...
I BELIEVE YOU KNOW MORE THAN I DO OF WHAT CAME AFTER.

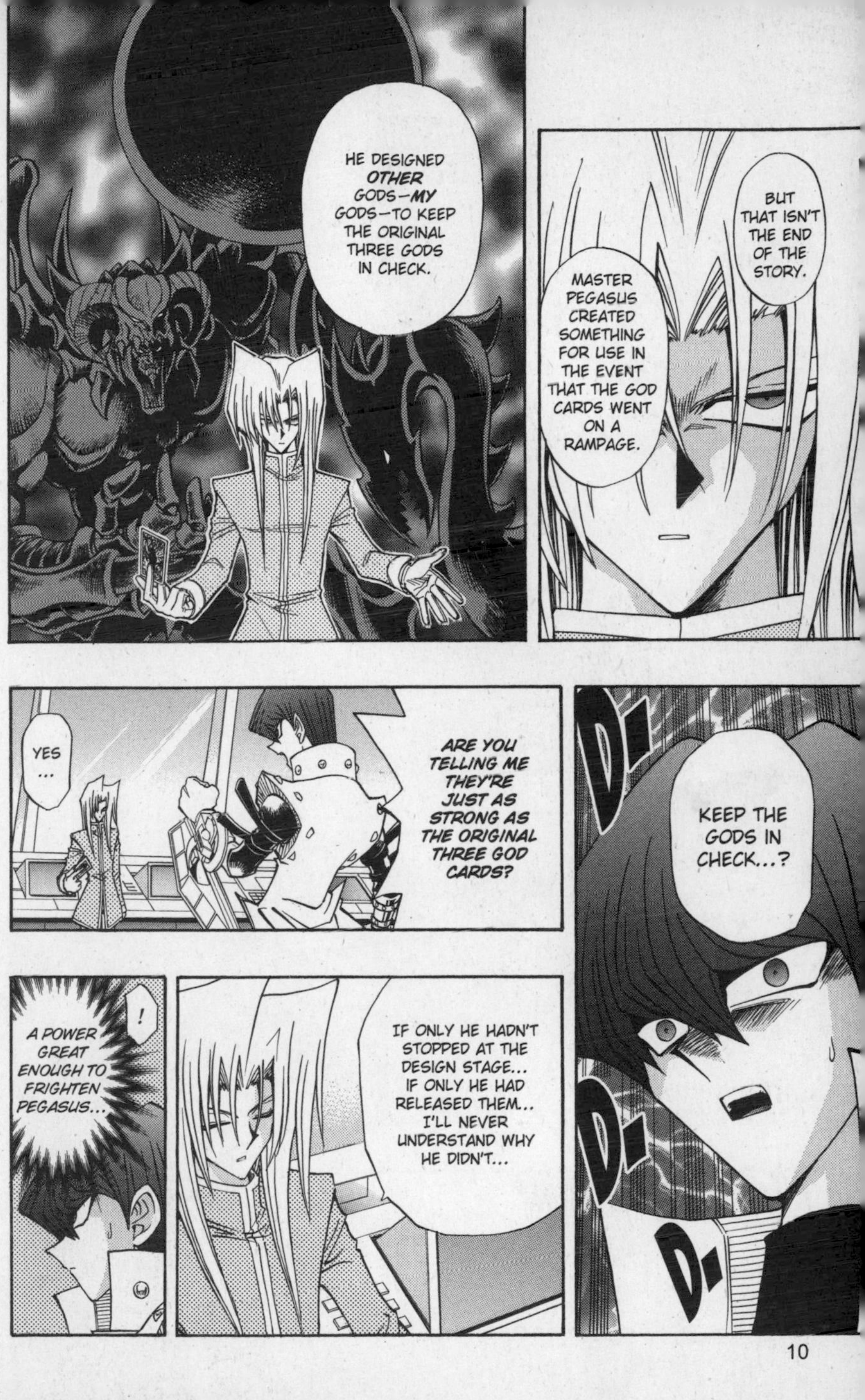
BUT THAT ISN'T THE END OF THE STORY.
MASTER PEGASUS CREATED SOMETHING FOR USE IN THE EVENT THAT THE GOD CARDS WENT ON A RAMPAGE.
HE DESIGNED *OTHER* GODS—*MY* GODS—TO KEEP THE ORIGINAL THREE GODS IN CHECK.
D.
KEEP THE GODS IN CHECK...?
D.
D.
D.
ARE YOU TELLING ME THEY'RE JUST AS STRONG AS THE ORIGINAL THREE GOD CARDS?
YES ...
IF ONLY HE HADN'T STOPPED AT THE DESIGN STAGE... IF ONLY HE HAD RELEASED THEM... I'LL NEVER UNDERSTAND WHY HE DIDN'T...
!
A POWER GREAT ENOUGH TO FRIGHTEN PEGASUS...

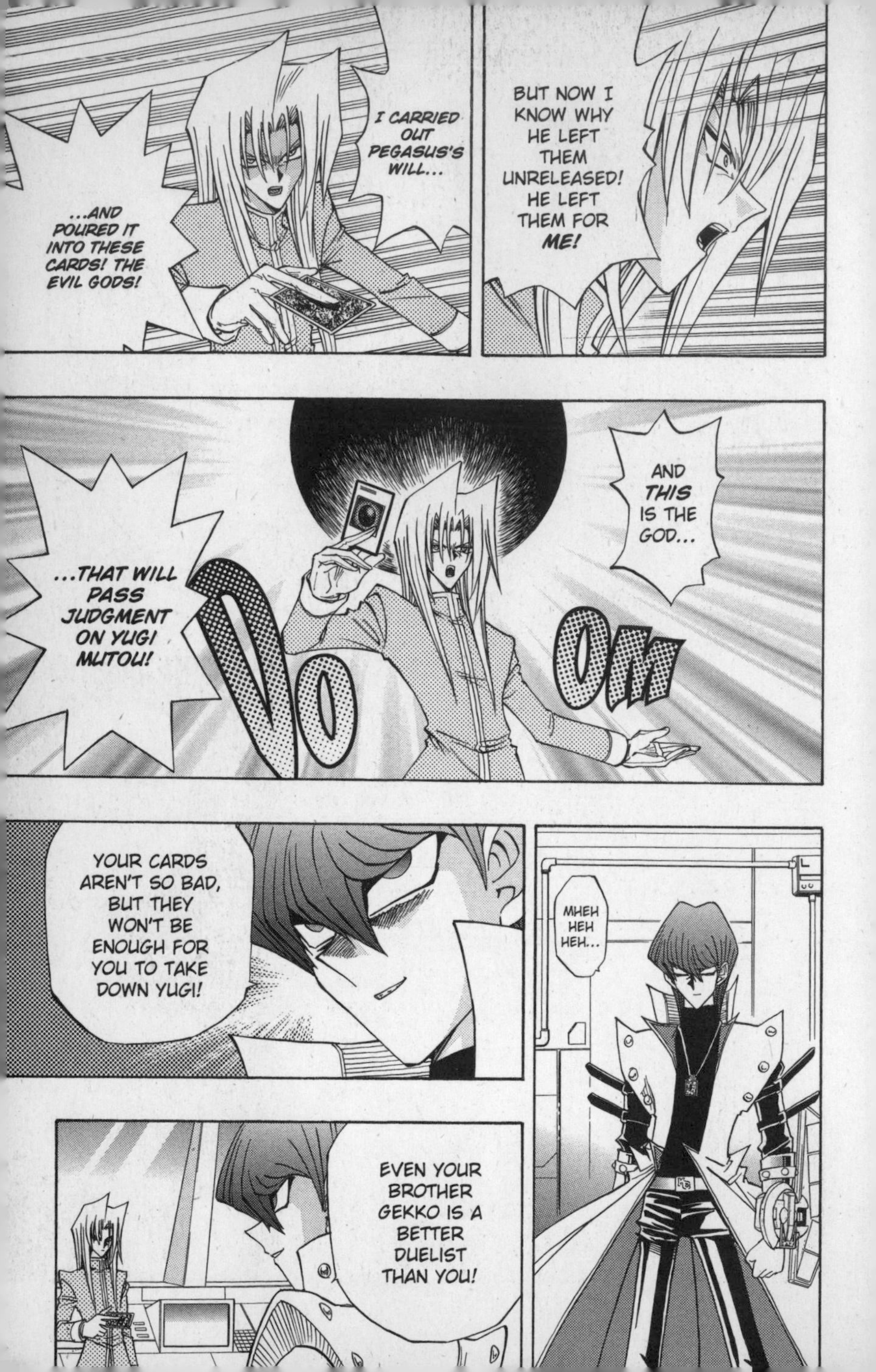

BUT NOW I KNOW WHY HE LEFT THEM UNRELEASED! HE LEFT THEM FOR *ME!*
I CARRIED OUT PEGASUS'S WILL...
...AND POURED IT INTO THESE CARDS! THE EVIL GODS!
AND *THIS* IS THE GOD...
DOOM
...THAT WILL PASS JUDGMENT ON YUGI MUTOU!
MHEH HEH HEH...
YOUR CARDS AREN'T SO BAD, BUT THEY WON'T BE ENOUGH FOR YOU TO TAKE DOWN YUGI!
EVEN YOUR BROTHER GEKKO IS A BETTER DUELIST THAN YOU!

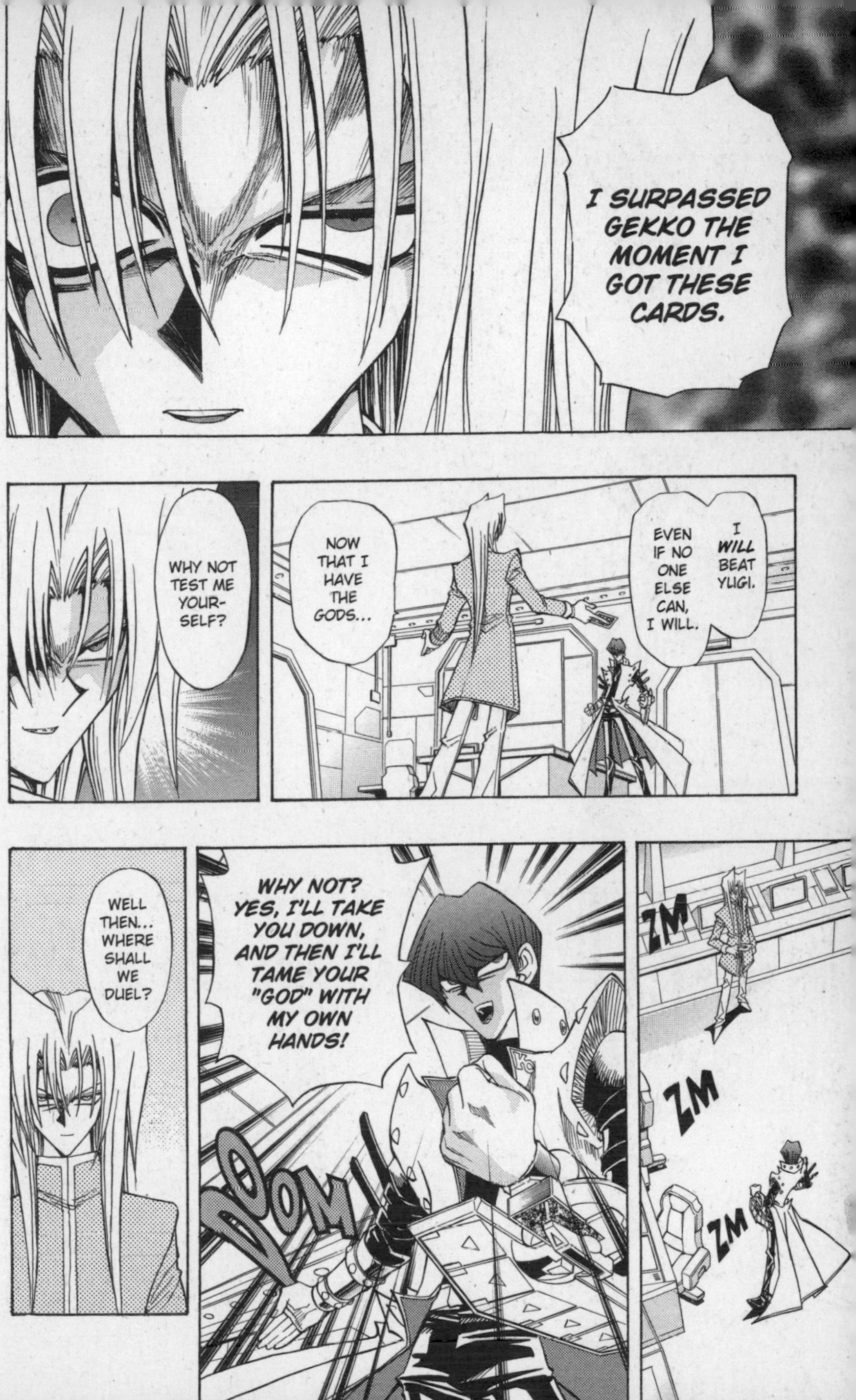
I SURPASSED GEKKO THE MOMENT I GOT THESE CARDS.
I WILL BEAT YUGI.
EVEN IF NO ONE ELSE CAN, I WILL.
NOW THAT I HAVE THE GODS...
WHY NOT TEST ME YOURSELF?
ZM
ZM
ZM
WHY NOT? YES, I'LL TAKE YOU DOWN, AND THEN I'LL TAME YOUR "GOD" WITH MY OWN HANDS!
DOOM
WELL THEN... WHERE SHALL WE DUEL?

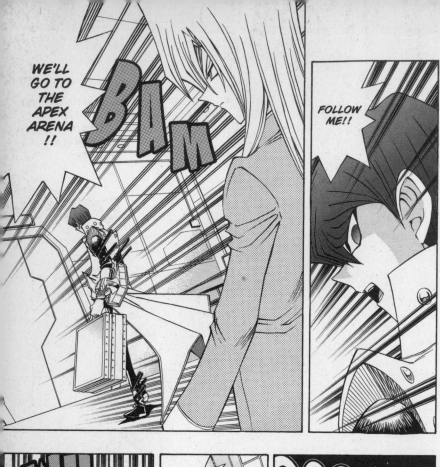

WE'LL GO TO THE APEX ARENA!!

FOLLOW ME!!

WHAM

NNH... UHH... NGG...

DOOOOM

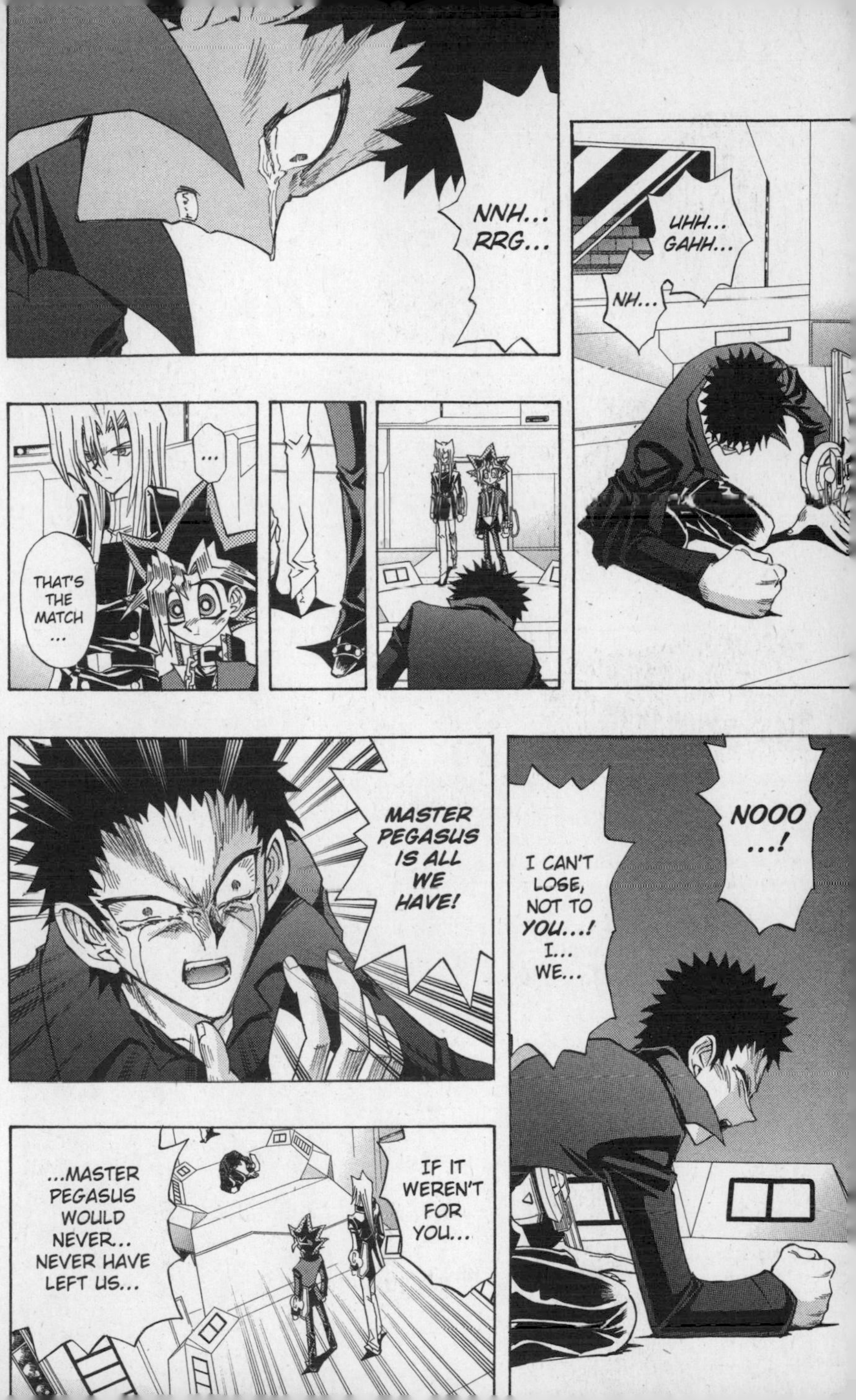
UHH... GAHH...
NH...
NNH... RRG...
...
THAT'S THE MATCH...
NOOO...!
I CAN'T LOSE, NOT TO YOU...! I... WE...
MASTER PEGASUS IS ALL WE HAVE!
IF IT WEREN'T FOR YOU...
...MASTER PEGASUS WOULD NEVER... NEVER HAVE LEFT US...

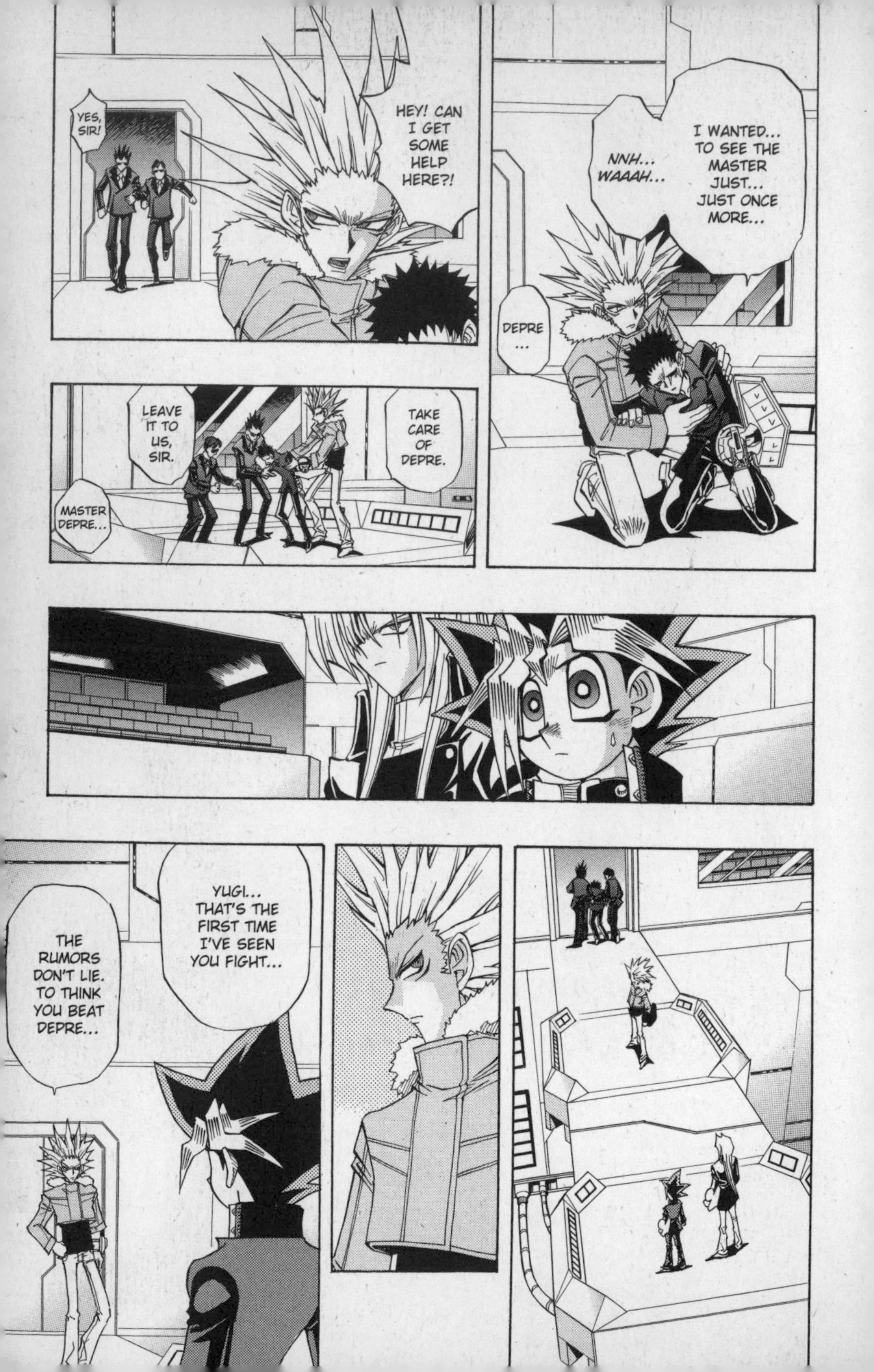
I WANTED... TO SEE THE MASTER JUST... JUST ONCE MORE...
NNH... WAAAH...
DEPRE...
HEY! CAN I GET SOME HELP HERE?!
YES, SIR!
TAKE CARE OF DEPRE.
LEAVE IT TO US, SIR.
MASTER DEPRE...
YUGI... THAT'S THE FIRST TIME I'VE SEEN YOU FIGHT...
THE RUMORS DON'T LIE. TO THINK YOU BEAT DEPRE...

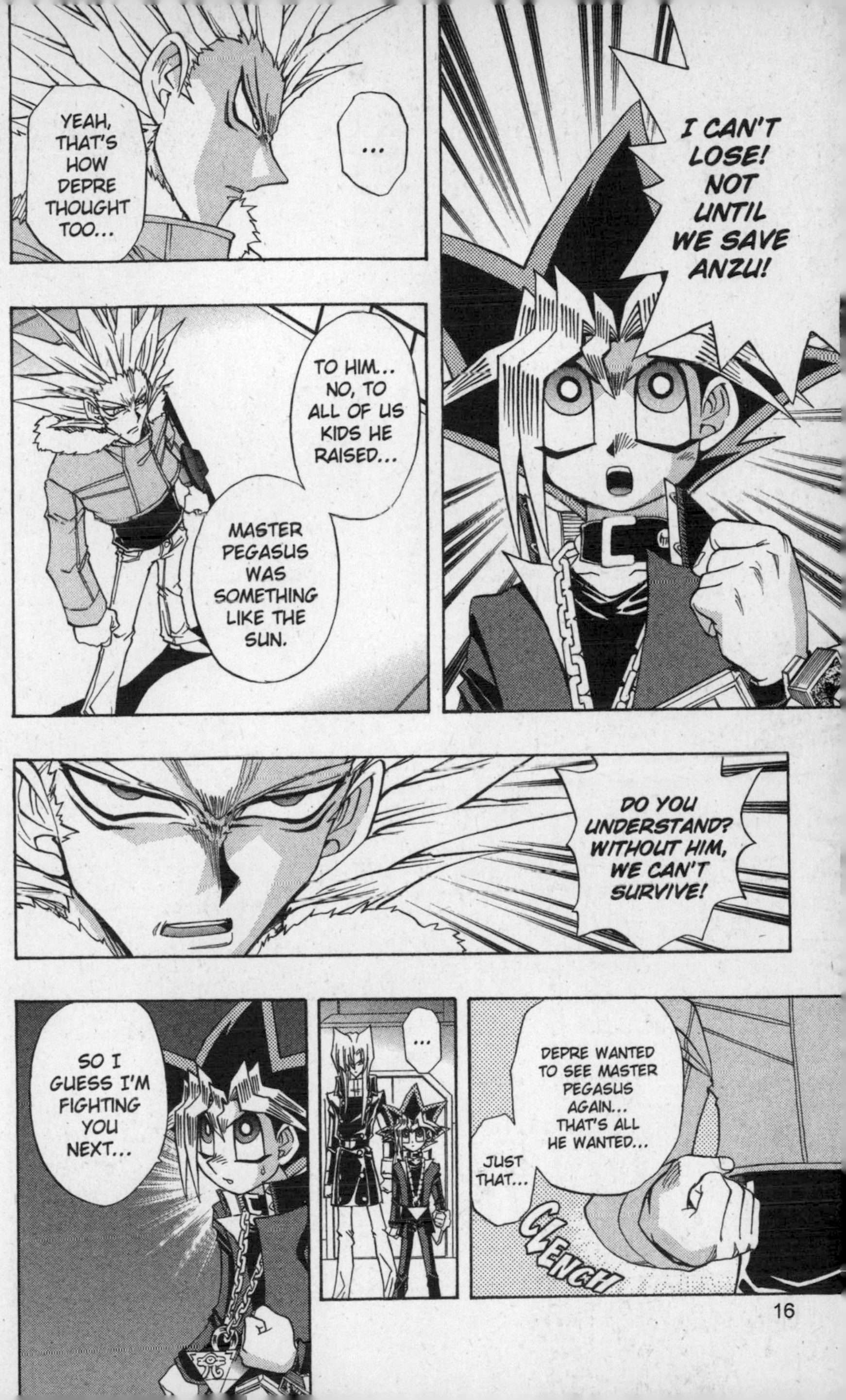
I CAN'T LOSE! NOT UNTIL WE SAVE ANZU!
...
YEAH, THAT'S HOW DEPRE THOUGHT TOO...
TO HIM... NO, TO ALL OF US KIDS HE RAISED...
MASTER PEGASUS WAS SOMETHING LIKE THE SUN.
DO YOU UNDERSTAND? WITHOUT HIM, WE CAN'T SURVIVE!
DEPRE WANTED TO SEE MASTER PEGASUS AGAIN... THAT'S ALL HE WANTED...
JUST THAT...
CLENCH
...
SO I GUESS I'M FIGHTING YOU NEXT...

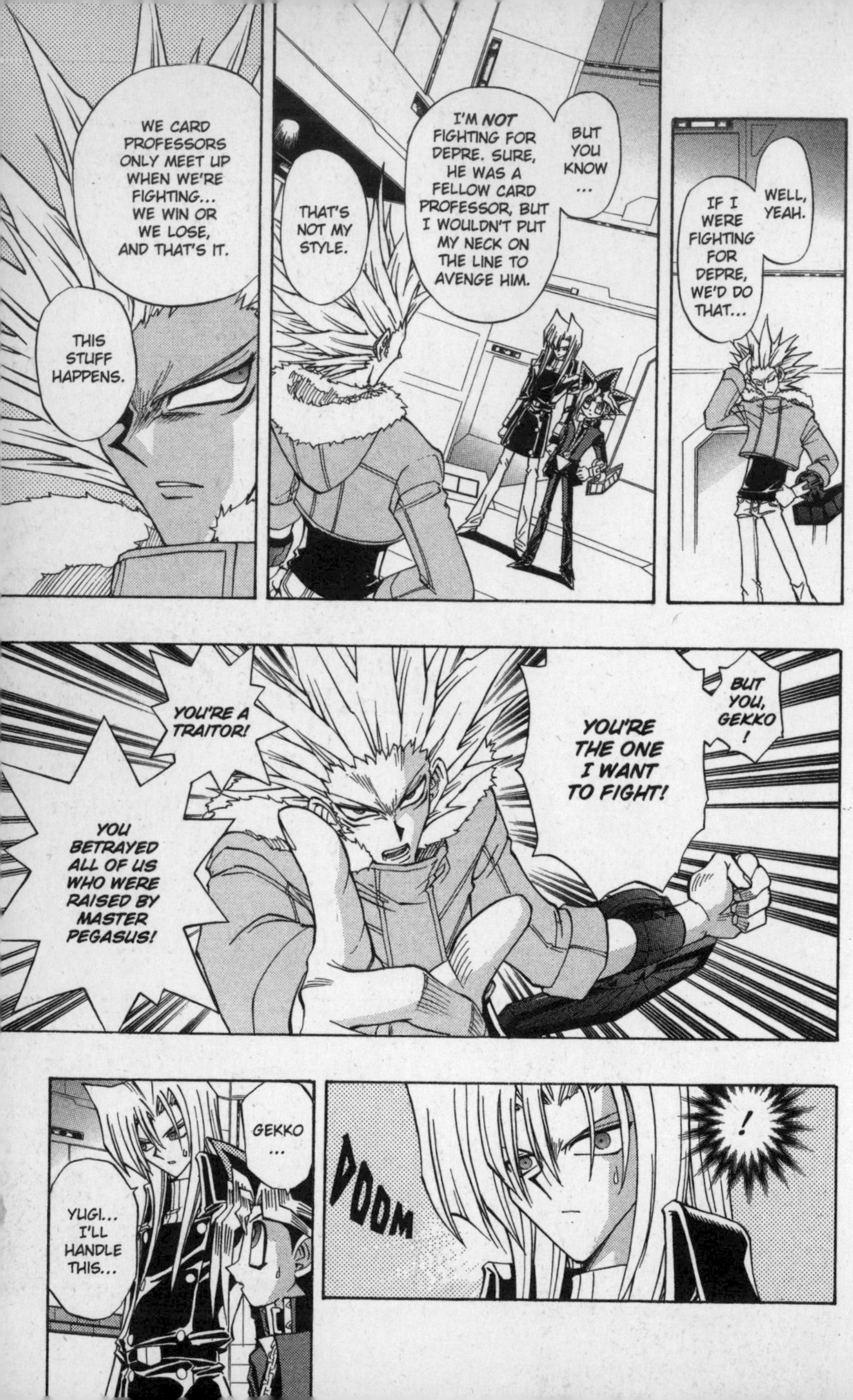
WELL, YEAH.
IF I WERE FIGHTING FOR DEPRE, WE'D DO THAT...
BUT YOU KNOW ...
I'M *NOT* FIGHTING FOR DEPRE. SURE, HE WAS A FELLOW CARD PROFESSOR, BUT I WOULDN'T PUT MY NECK ON THE LINE TO AVENGE HIM.
THAT'S NOT MY STYLE.
WE CARD PROFESSORS ONLY MEET UP WHEN WE'RE FIGHTING... WE WIN OR WE LOSE, AND THAT'S IT.
THIS STUFF HAPPENS.
BUT YOU, GEKKO !
YOU'RE THE ONE I WANT TO FIGHT!
YOU'RE A TRAITOR!
YOU BETRAYED ALL OF US WHO WERE RAISED BY MASTER PEGASUS!
!
DOOM
GEKKO ...
YUGI... I'LL HANDLE THIS...

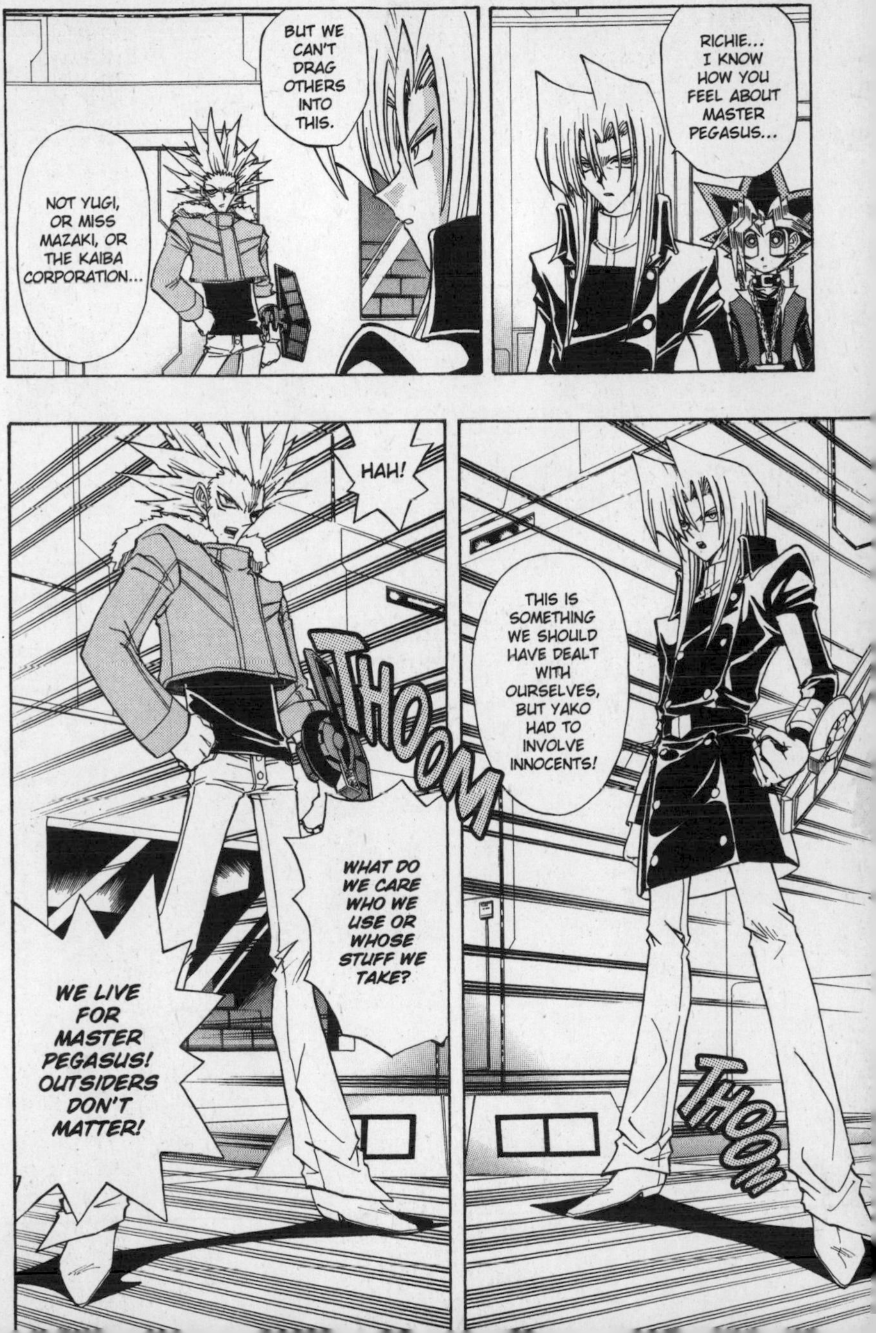
RICHIE... I KNOW HOW YOU FEEL ABOUT MASTER PEGASUS...
BUT WE CAN'T DRAG OTHERS INTO THIS.
NOT YUGI, OR MISS MAZAKI, OR THE KAIBA CORPORATION...
THIS IS SOMETHING WE SHOULD HAVE DEALT WITH OURSELVES, BUT YAKO HAD TO INVOLVE INNOCENTS!
THOOM
HAH!
THOOM
WHAT DO WE CARE WHO WE USE OR WHOSE STUFF WE TAKE?
WE LIVE FOR MASTER PEGASUS! OUTSIDERS DON'T MATTER!

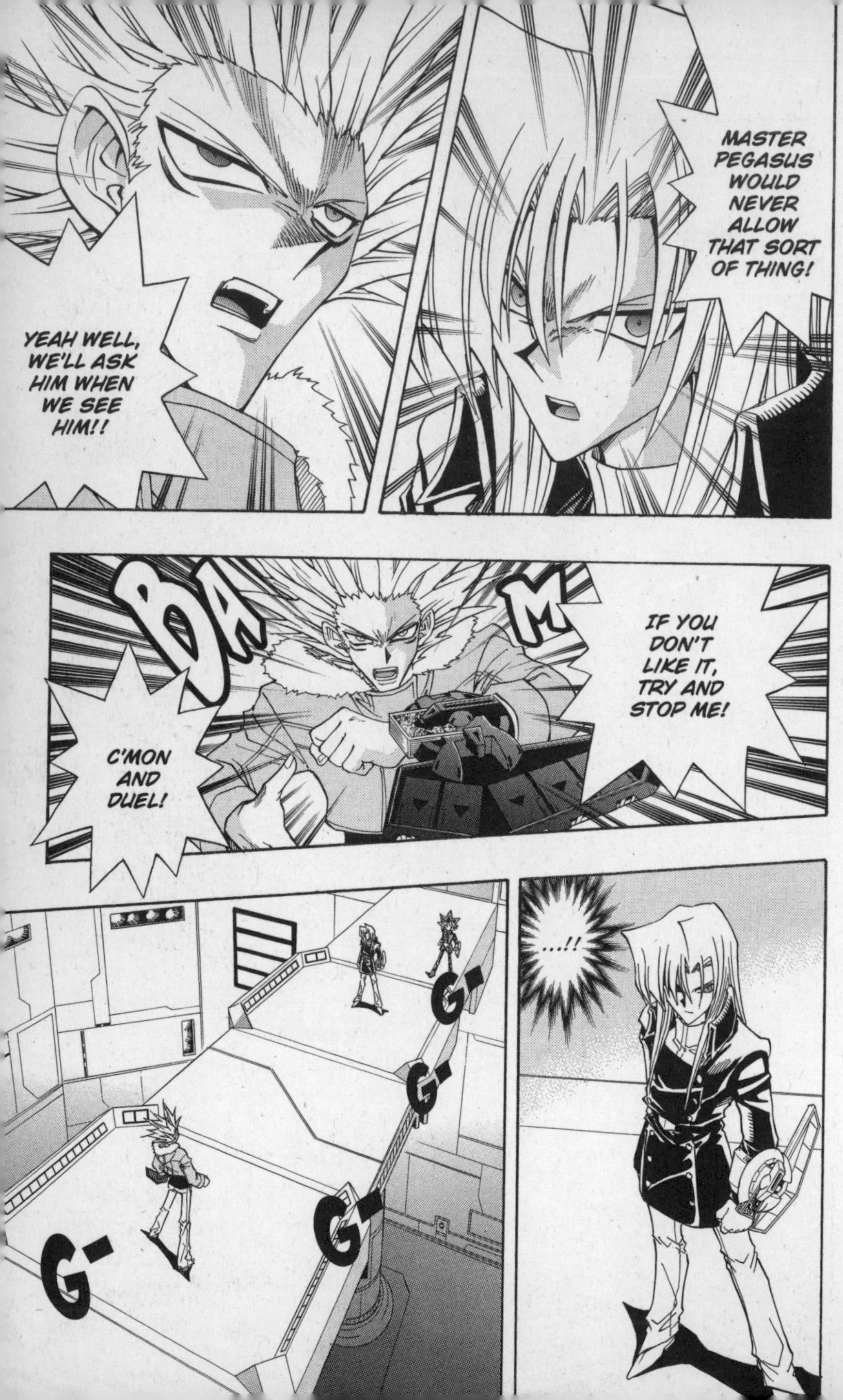
MASTER PEGASUS WOULD NEVER ALLOW THAT SORT OF THING!
YEAH WELL, WE'LL ASK HIM WHEN WE SEE HIM!!
BAM
IF YOU DON'T LIKE IT, TRY AND STOP ME!
C'MON AND DUEL!
...!!
G-
G-
G-
G-

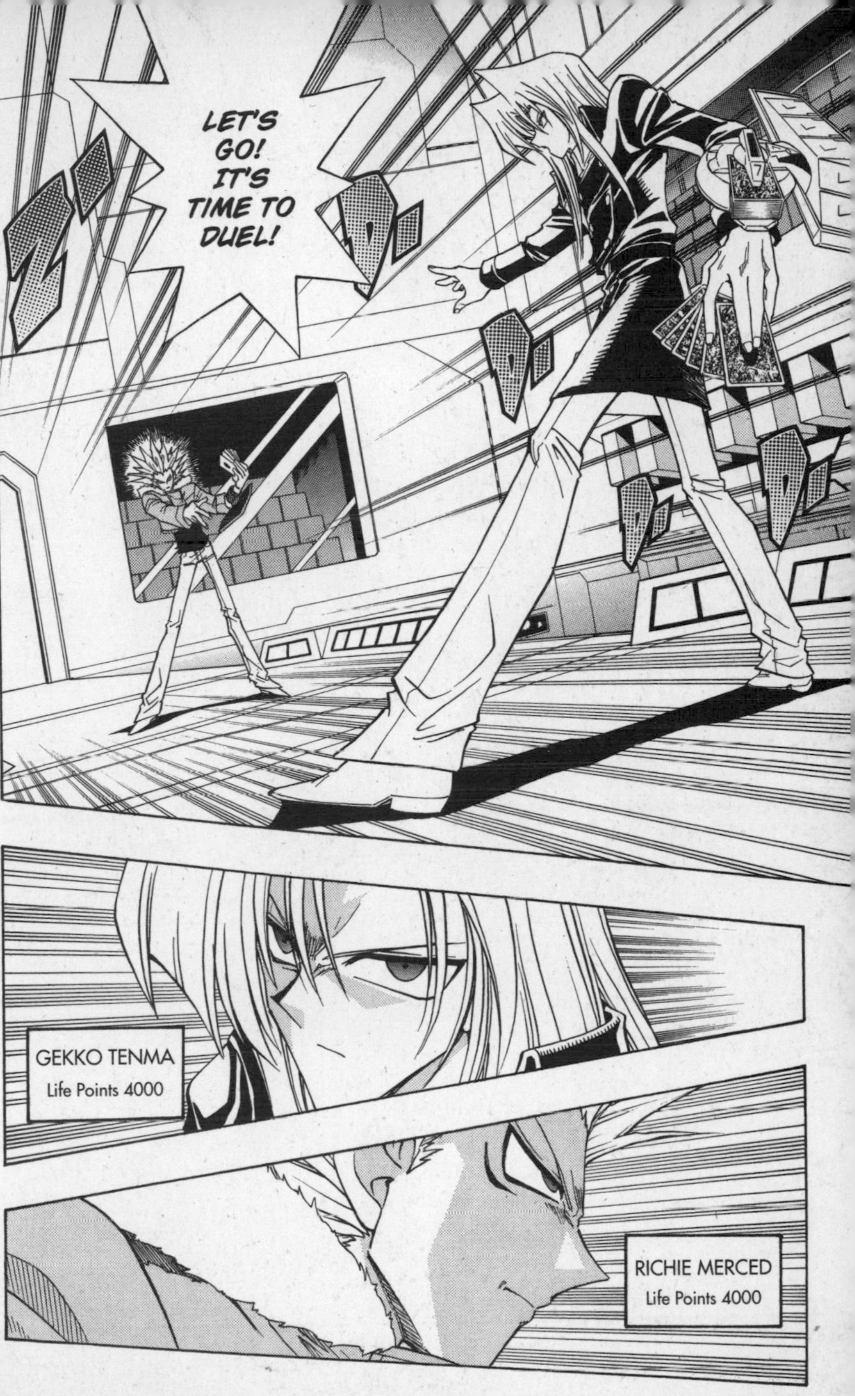
LET'S GO! IT'S TIME TO DUEL!
GEKKO TENMA
Life Points 4000
RICHIE MERCED
Life Points 4000

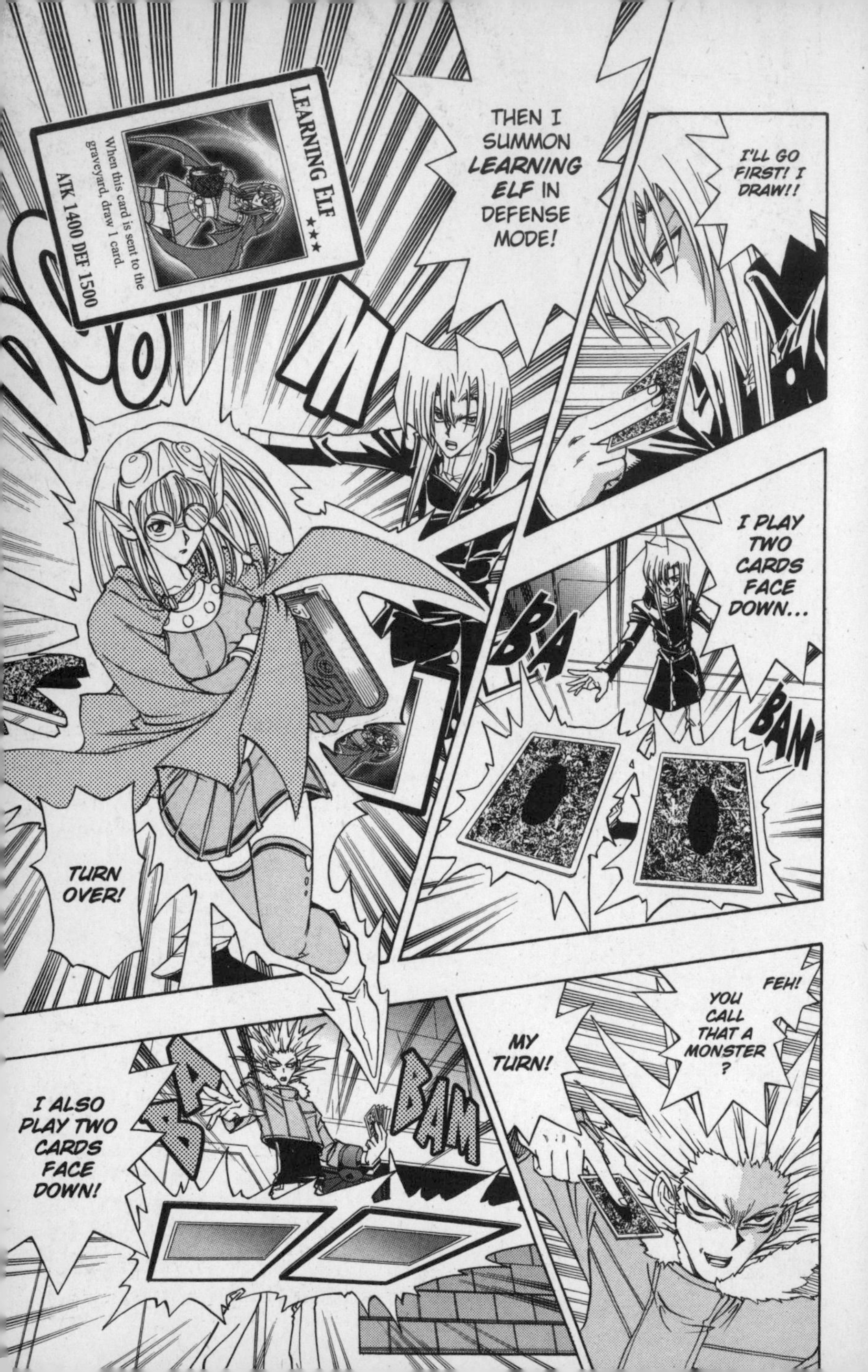
I'LL GO FIRST! I DRAW!!
I PLAY TWO CARDS FACE DOWN...
BAM
BA
THEN I SUMMON LEARNING ELF IN DEFENSE MODE!
LEARNING ELF
When this card is sent to the graveyard, draw 1 card.
ATK 1400 DEF 1500
TURN OVER!
FEH!
YOU CALL THAT A MONSTER?
MY TURN!
BAM
BA
I ALSO PLAY TWO CARDS FACE DOWN!

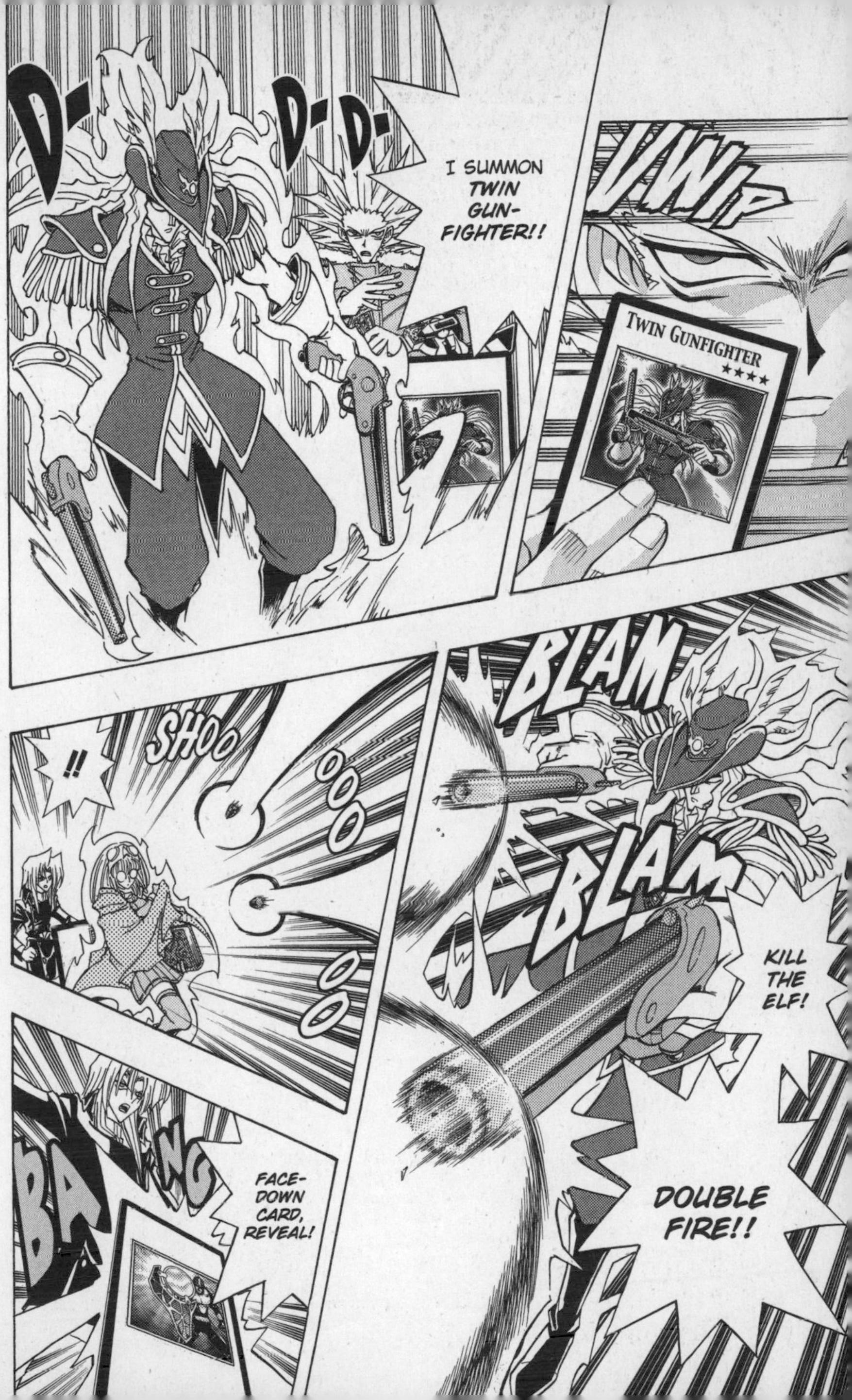
VWIP
TWIN GUNFIGHTER
D-
D-D-
I SUMMON TWIN GUN-FIGHTER!!
BLAM
BLAM
KILL THE ELF!
DOUBLE FIRE!!
SHOOOOOOO
!!
BANG
FACE-DOWN CARD, REVEAL!

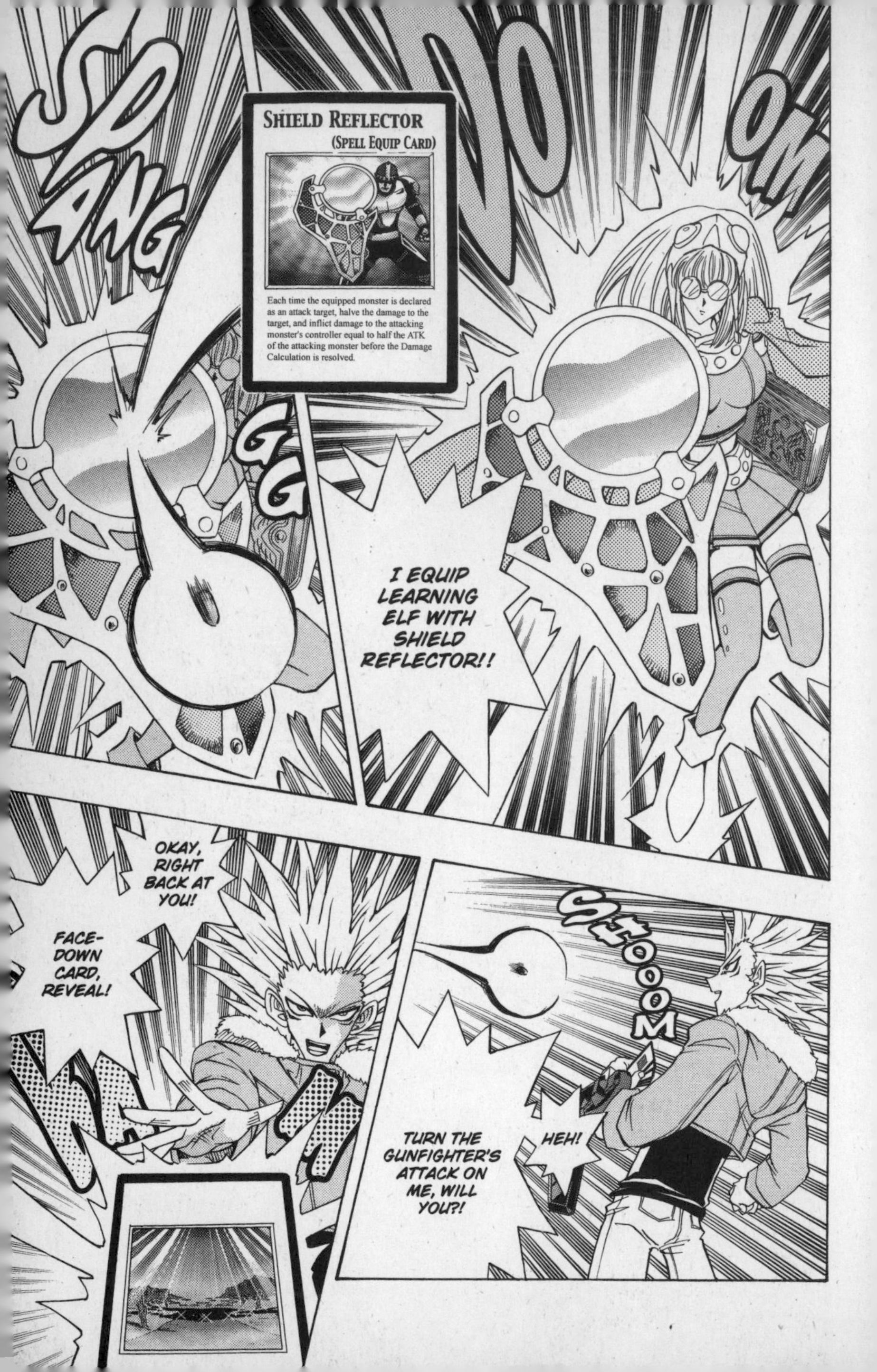
DOOOM
SHIELD REFLECTOR
(SPELL EQUIP CARD)
Each time the equipped monster is declared as an attack target, halve the damage to the target, and inflict damage to the attacking monster's controller equal to half the ATK of the attacking monster before the Damage Calculation is resolved.
I EQUIP LEARNING ELF WITH SHIELD REFLECTOR!!
SPANG
GG
STOOOM
HEH!
TURN THE GUNFIGHTER'S ATTACK ON ME, WILL YOU?!
OKAY, RIGHT BACK AT YOU!
FACE-DOWN CARD, REVEAL!

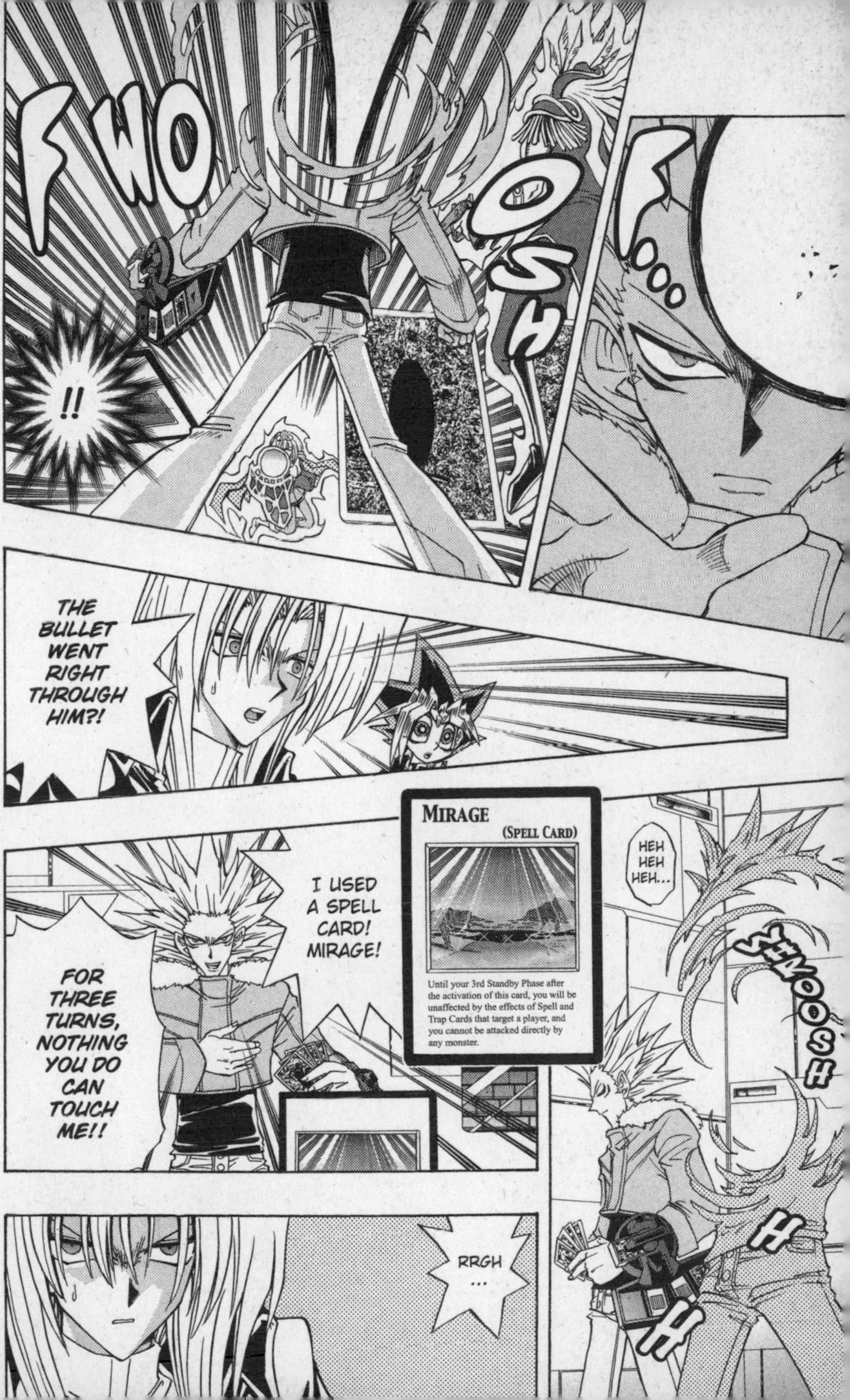

FWO
OSH
!!
THE BULLET WENT RIGHT THROUGH HIM?!
HEH HEH HEH...
SWOOSH
H
H
MIRAGE
(SPELL CARD)
Until your 3rd Standby Phase after the activation of this card, you will be unaffected by the effects of Spell and Trap Cards that target a player, and you cannot be attacked directly by any monster.
I USED A SPELL CARD! MIRAGE!
FOR THREE TURNS, NOTHING YOU DO CAN TOUCH ME!!
RRGH ...

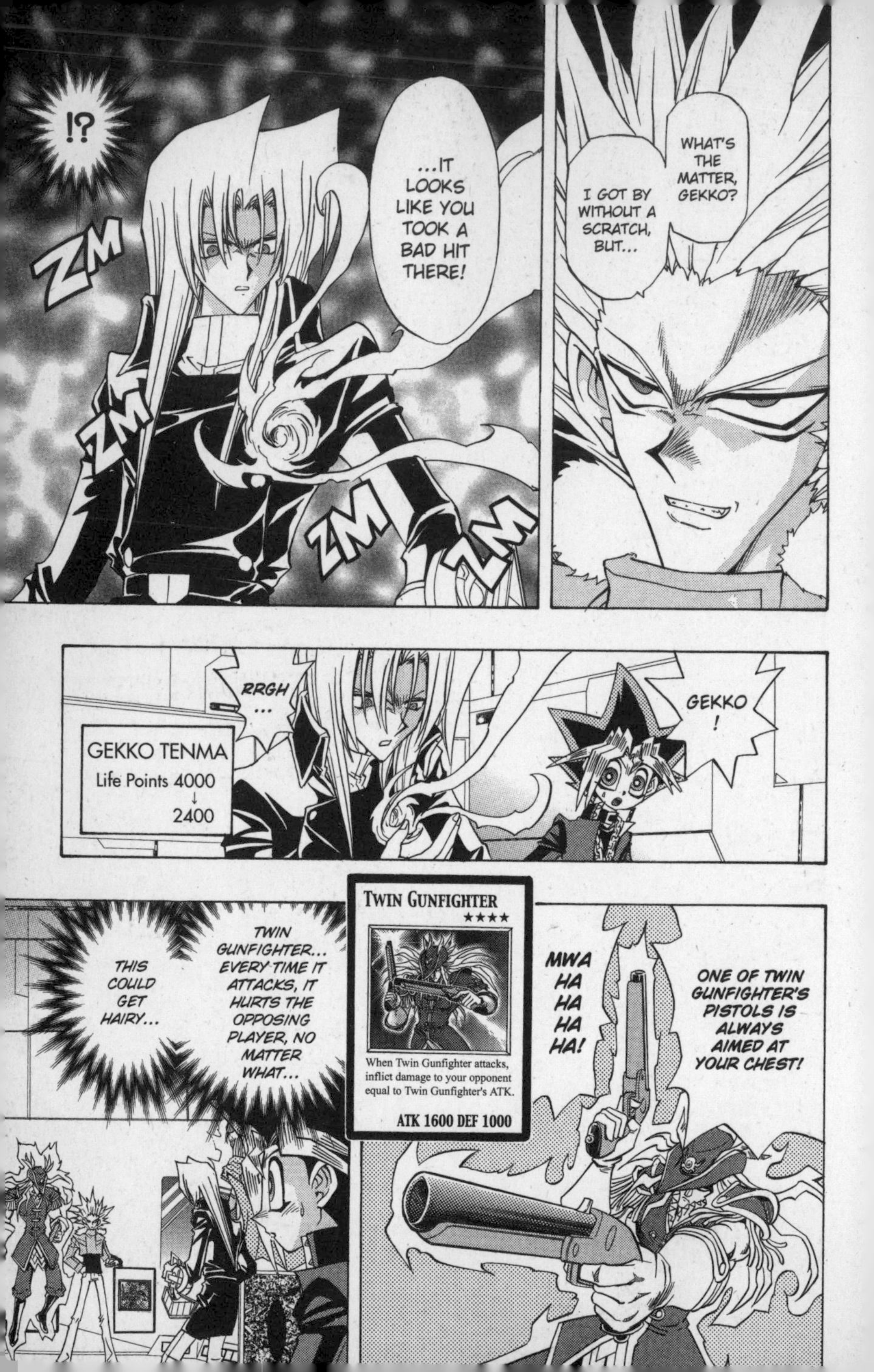
WHAT'S THE MATTER, GEKKO?
I GOT BY WITHOUT A SCRATCH, BUT...
...IT LOOKS LIKE YOU TOOK A BAD HIT THERE!
!?
ZM
ZM
ZM
ZM
GEKKO!
RRGH...
GEKKO TENMA
Life Points 4000 ↓ 2400
ONE OF TWIN GUNFIGHTER'S PISTOLS IS ALWAYS AIMED AT YOUR CHEST!
MWA HA HA HA HA!
TWIN GUNFIGHTER ★★★★
When Twin Gunfighter attacks, inflict damage to your opponent equal to Twin Gunfighter's ATK.
ATK 1600 DEF 1000
TWIN GUNFIGHTER... EVERY TIME IT ATTACKS, IT HURTS THE OPPOSING PLAYER, NO MATTER WHAT...
THIS COULD GET HAIRY...

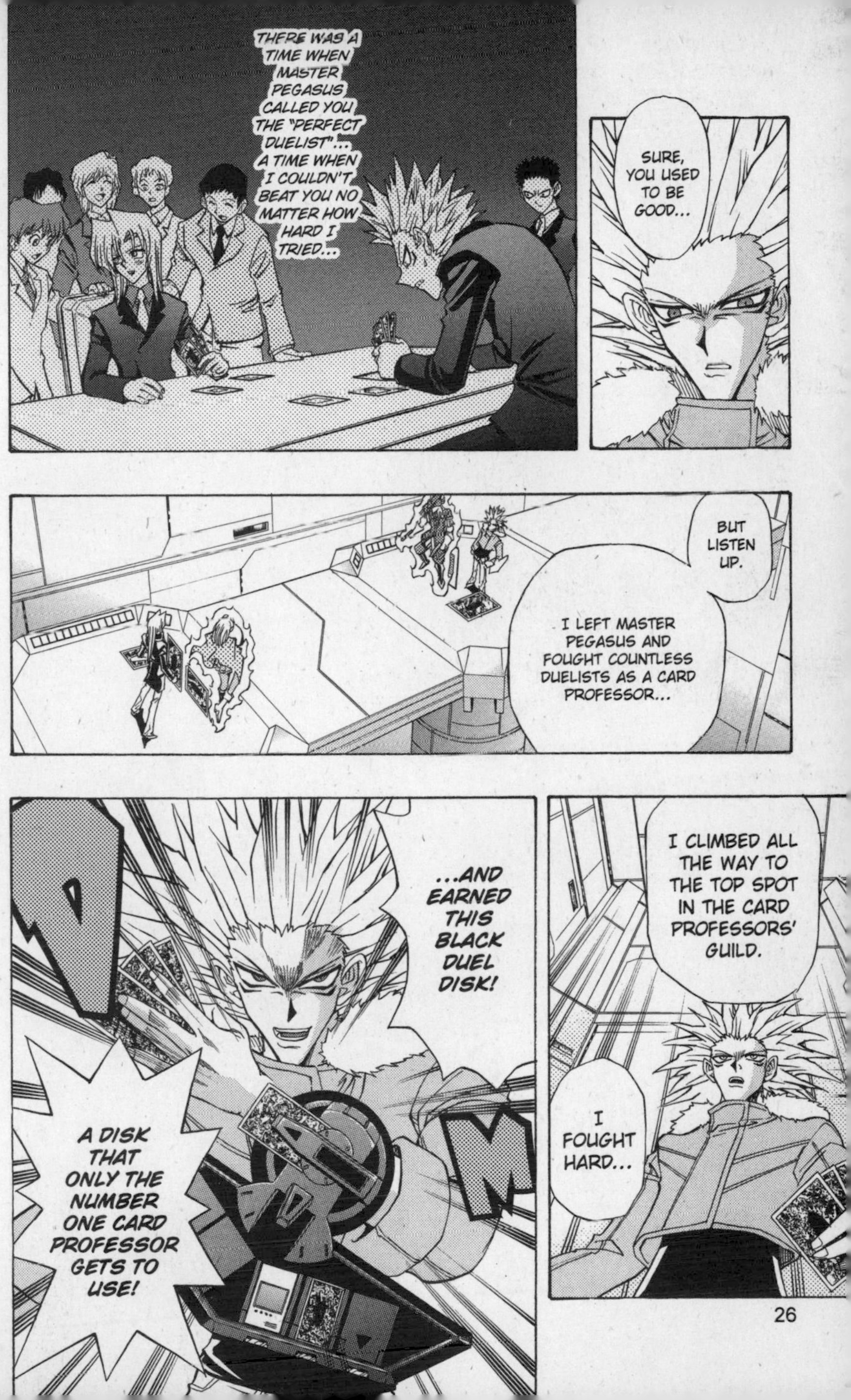
SURE, YOU USED TO BE GOOD...
THERE WAS A TIME WHEN MASTER PEGASUS CALLED YOU THE "PERFECT DUELIST"... A TIME WHEN I COULDN'T BEAT YOU NO MATTER HOW HARD I TRIED...
BUT LISTEN UP.
I LEFT MASTER PEGASUS AND FOUGHT COUNTLESS DUELISTS AS A CARD PROFESSOR...
I CLIMBED ALL THE WAY TO THE TOP SPOT IN THE CARD PROFESSORS' GUILD.
I FOUGHT HARD...
...AND EARNED THIS BLACK DUEL DISK!
A DISK THAT ONLY THE NUMBER ONE CARD PROFESSOR GETS TO USE!

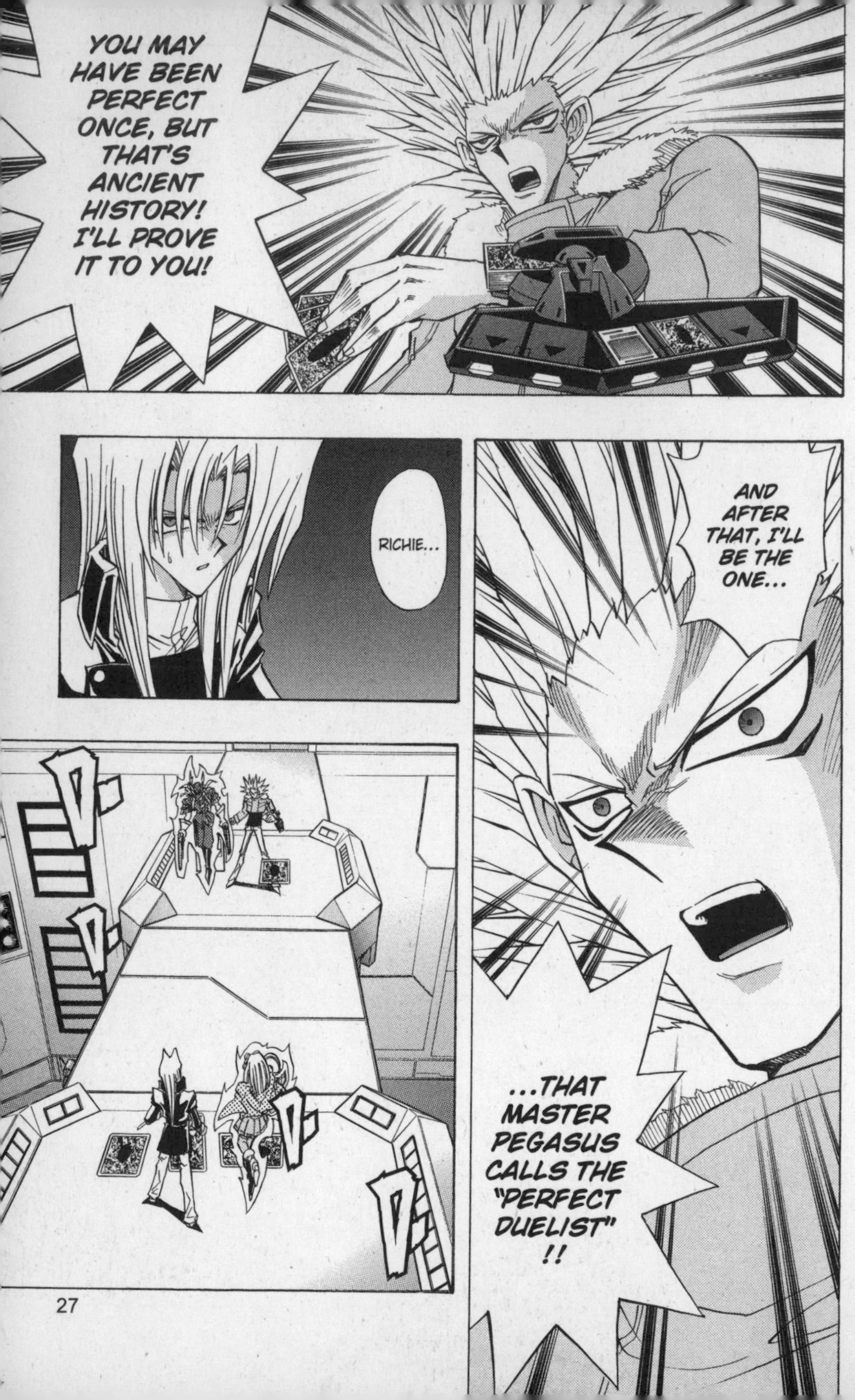
YOU MAY HAVE BEEN PERFECT ONCE, BUT THAT'S ANCIENT HISTORY! I'LL PROVE IT TO YOU!
AND AFTER THAT, I'LL BE THE ONE...
...THAT MASTER PEGASUS CALLS THE "PERFECT DUELIST" !!
RICHIE...

Duel Round 26: Pegasus's Prodigies!!

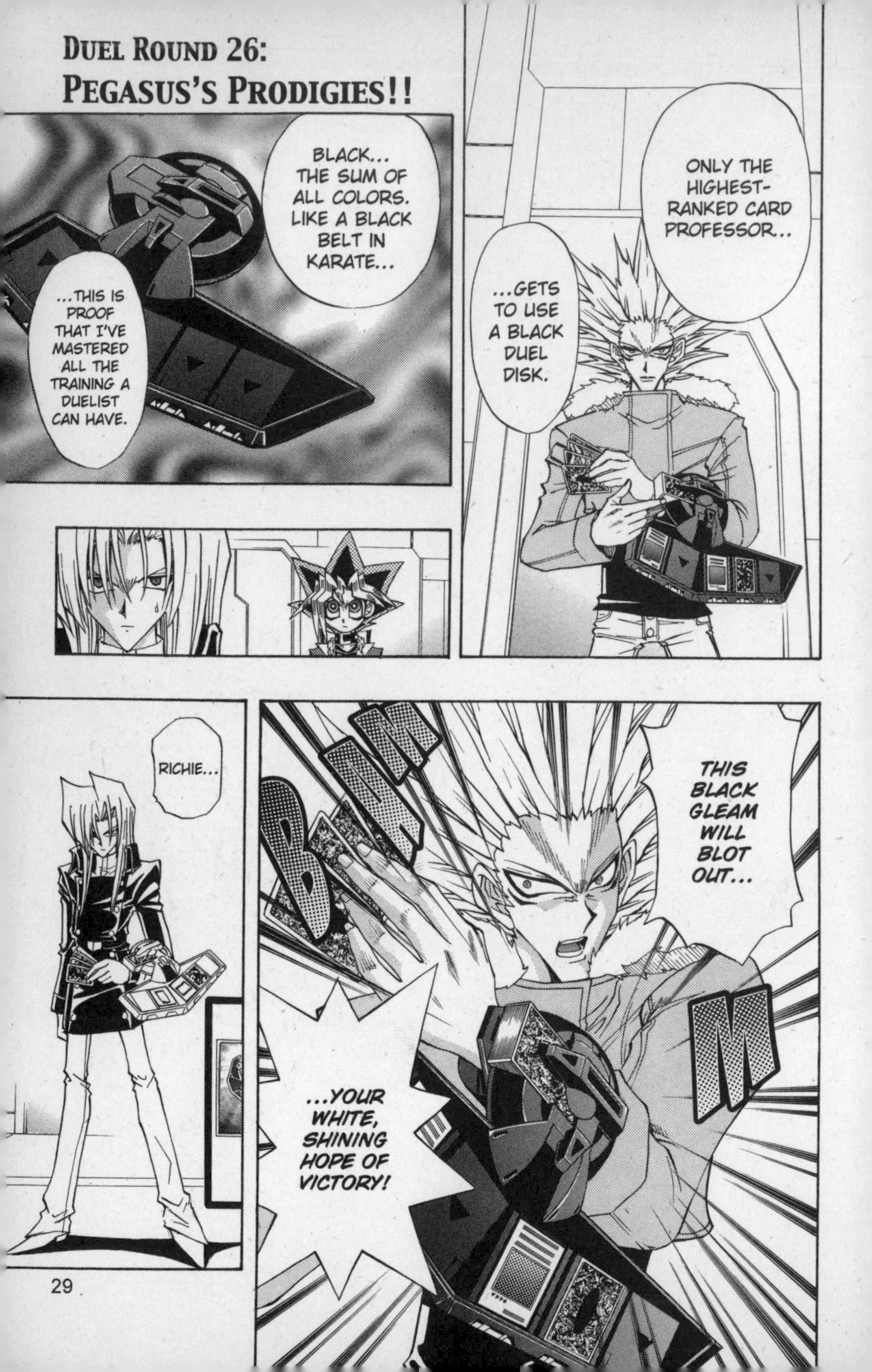
ONLY THE HIGHEST-RANKED CARD PROFESSOR...
...GETS TO USE A BLACK DUEL DISK.
BLACK... THE SUM OF ALL COLORS. LIKE A BLACK BELT IN KARATE...
...THIS IS PROOF THAT I'VE MASTERED ALL THE TRAINING A DUELIST CAN HAVE.
THIS BLACK GLEAM WILL BLOT OUT...
...YOUR WHITE, SHINING HOPE OF VICTORY!
RICHIE...

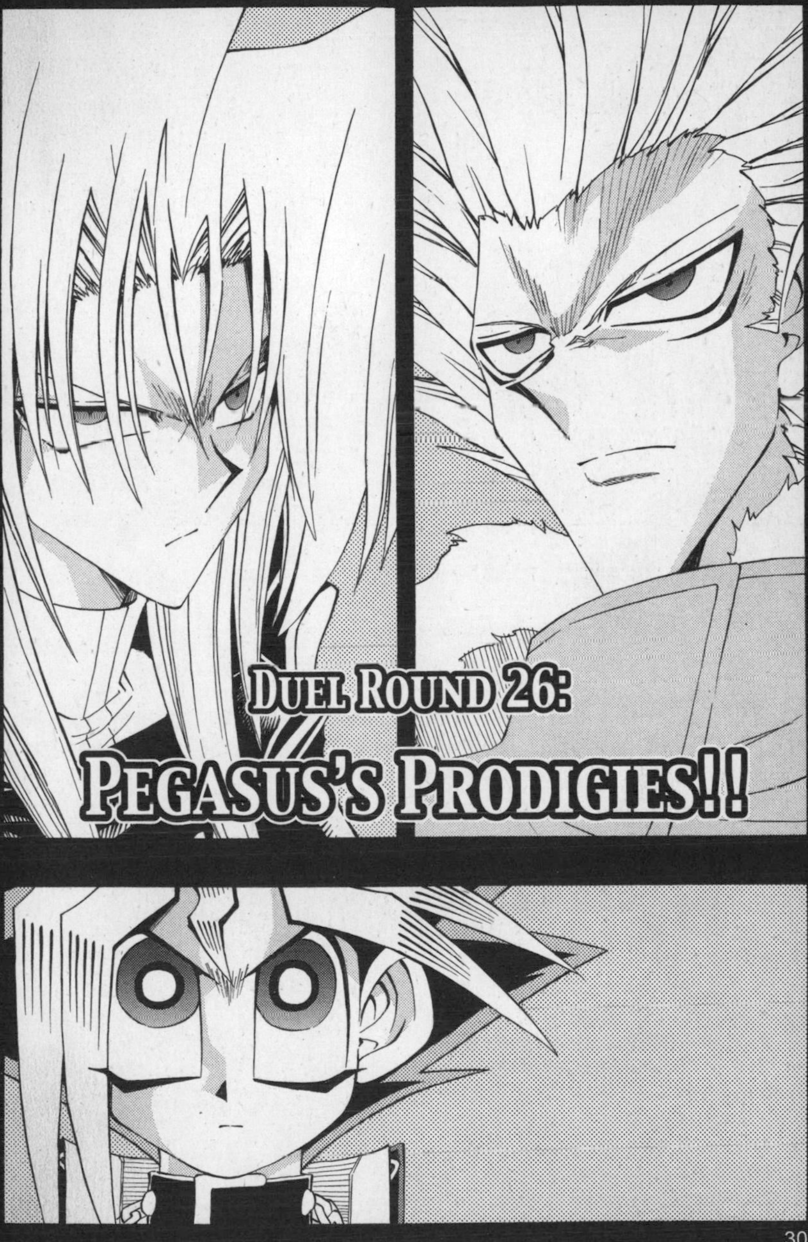
DUEL ROUND 26:
PEGASUS'S PRODIGIES!!

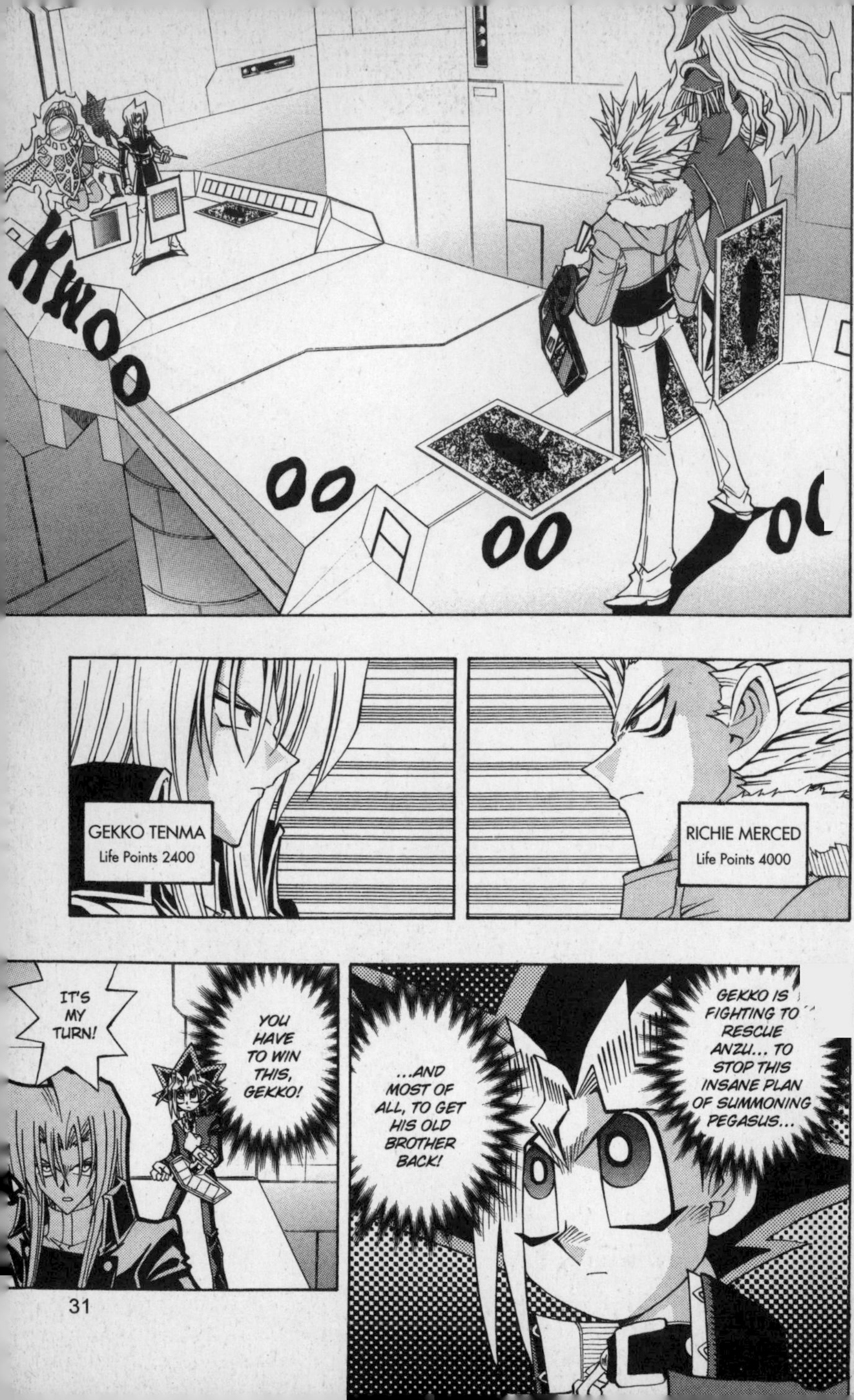
HWOOOOOOOOO
RICHIE MERCED
Life Points 4000
GEKKO TENMA
Life Points 2400
GEKKO IS FIGHTING TO RESCUE ANZU... TO STOP THIS INSANE PLAN OF SUMMONING PEGASUS...
...AND MOST OF ALL, TO GET HIS OLD BROTHER BACK!
YOU HAVE TO WIN THIS, GEKKO!
IT'S MY TURN!

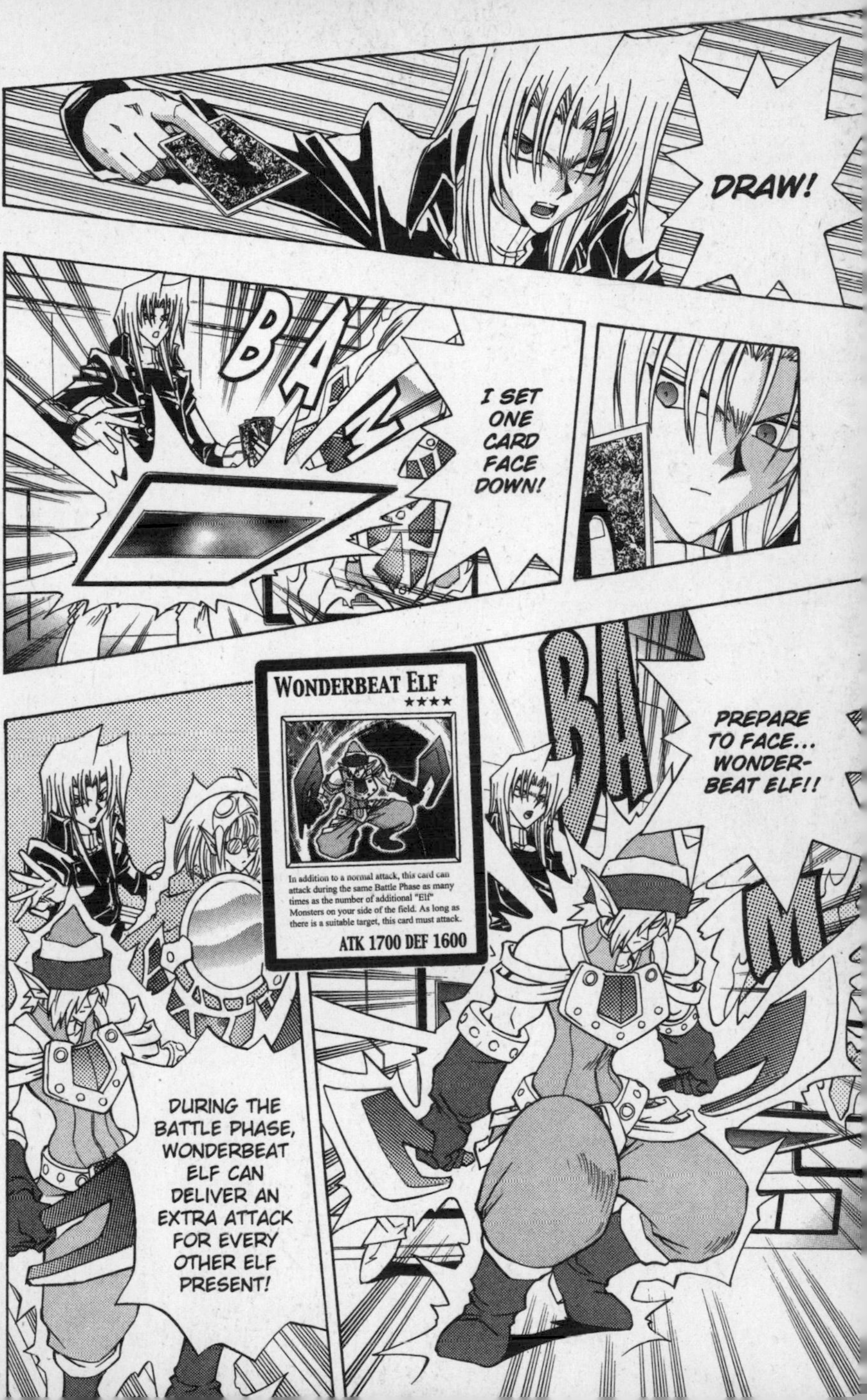
DRAW!
BAM
I SET ONE CARD FACE DOWN!
BAM
PREPARE TO FACE... WONDER-BEAT ELF!!
WONDERBEAT ELF
★★★★
In addition to a normal attack, this card can attack during the same Battle Phase as many times as the number of additional "Elf" Monsters on your side of the field. As long as there is a suitable target, this card must attack.
ATK 1700 DEF 1600
DURING THE BATTLE PHASE, WONDERBEAT ELF CAN DELIVER AN EXTRA ATTACK FOR EVERY OTHER ELF PRESENT!

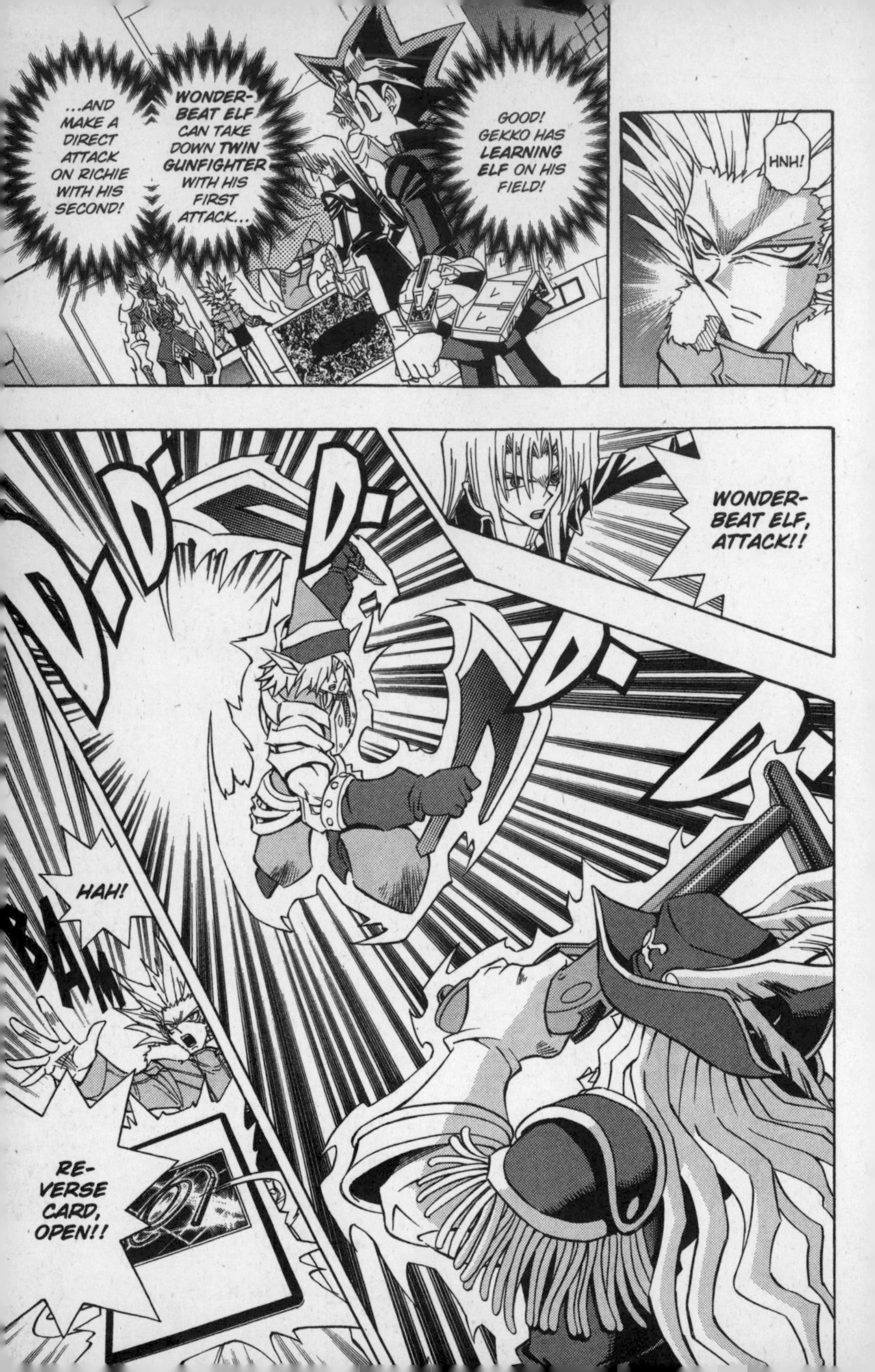
HNH!
GOOD! GEKKO HAS LEARNING ELF ON HIS FIELD!
WONDER-BEAT ELF CAN TAKE DOWN TWIN GUNFIGHTER WITH HIS FIRST ATTACK...
...AND MAKE A DIRECT ATTACK ON RICHIE WITH HIS SECOND!
WONDER-BEAT ELF, ATTACK!!
D- D- D- D- D-
HAH!
BAM
RE-VERSE CARD, OPEN!!

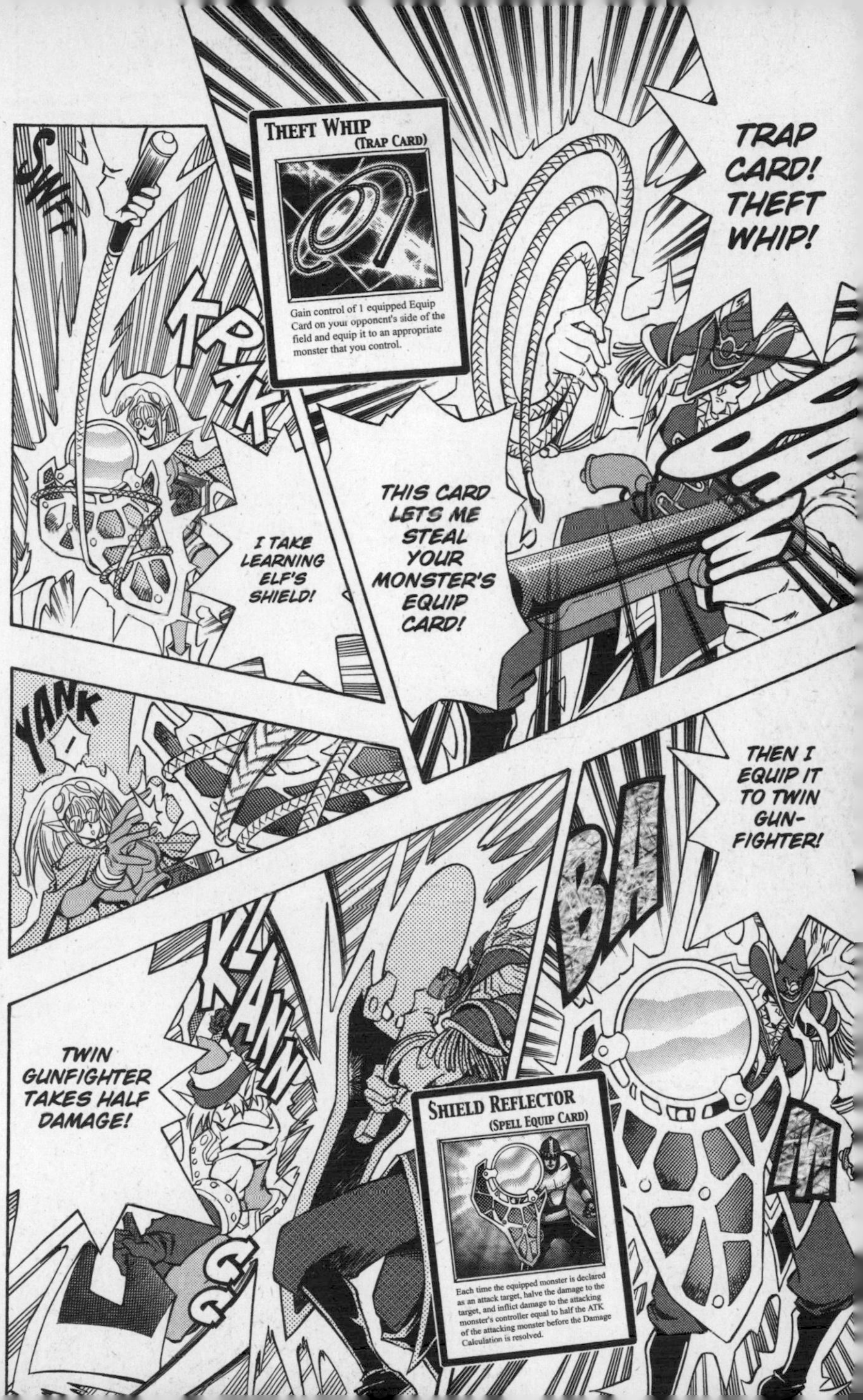
TRAP CARD! THEFT WHIP!
THEFT WHIP
(TRAP CARD)
Gain control of 1 equipped Equip Card on your opponent's side of the field and equip it to an appropriate monster that you control.
THIS CARD LETS ME STEAL YOUR MONSTER'S EQUIP CARD!
SWFF
KRAK
I TAKE LEARNING ELF'S SHIELD!
YANK
!
THEN I EQUIP IT TO TWIN GUN-FIGHTER!
BA
M
SHIELD REFLECTOR
(SPELL EQUIP CARD)
Each time the equipped monster is declared as an attack target, halve the damage to the target, and inflict damage to the attacking monster's controller equal to half the ATK of the attacking monster before the Damage Calculation is resolved.
KLANNN
TWIN GUNFIGHTER TAKES HALF DAMAGE!
GG

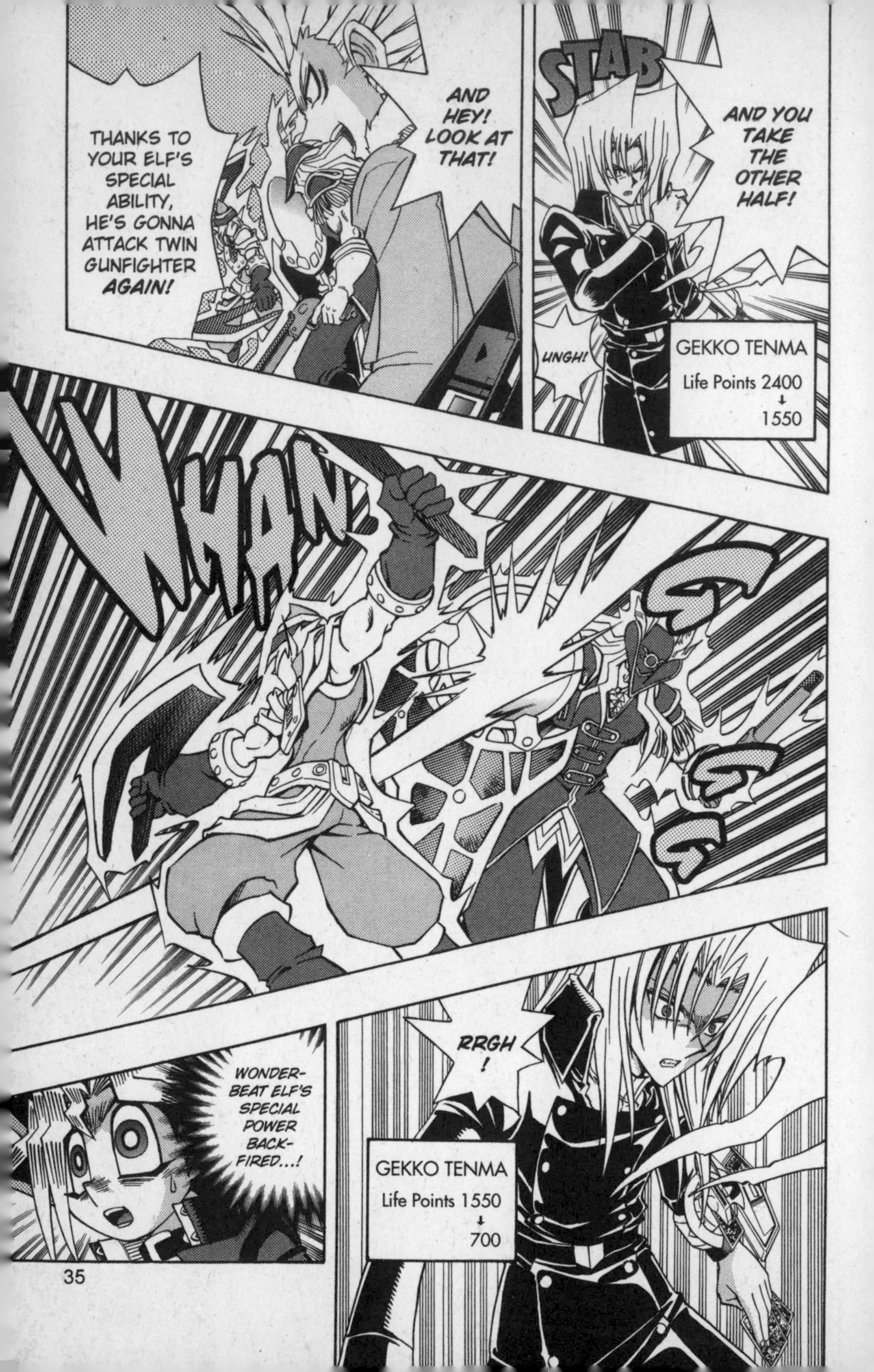
STAB
AND YOU TAKE THE OTHER HALF!
UNGH!
GEKKO TENMA
Life Points 2400 ↓ 1550
AND HEY! LOOK AT THAT!
THANKS TO YOUR ELF'S SPECIAL ABILITY, HE'S GONNA ATTACK TWIN GUNFIGHTER AGAIN!
WHAN
G G G
RRGH!
GEKKO TENMA
Life Points 1550 ↓ 700
WONDER-BEAT ELF'S SPECIAL POWER BACK-FIRED...!

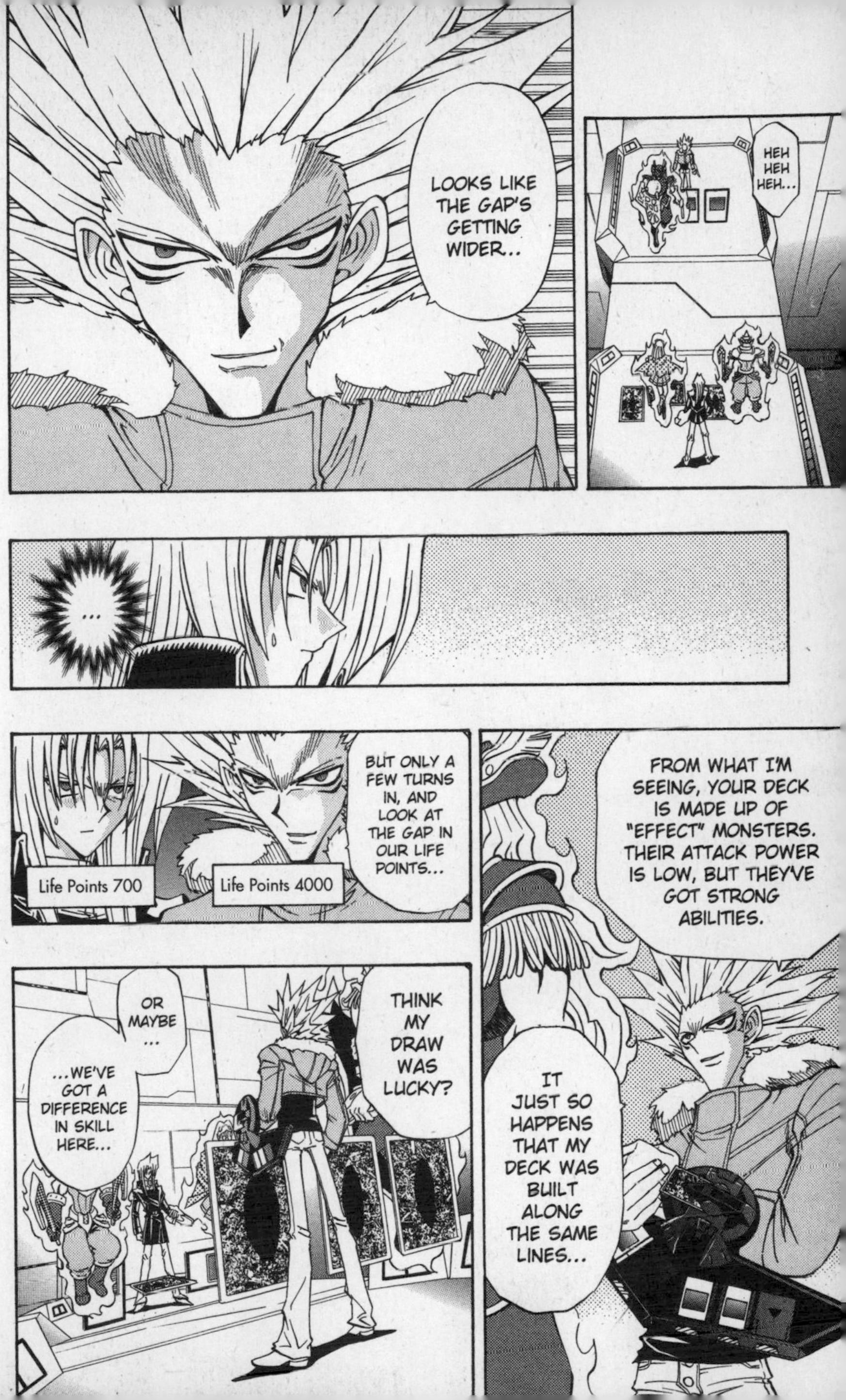
HEH HEH HEH...
LOOKS LIKE THE GAP'S GETTING WIDER...
...
FROM WHAT I'M SEEING, YOUR DECK IS MADE UP OF "EFFECT" MONSTERS. THEIR ATTACK POWER IS LOW, BUT THEY'VE GOT STRONG ABILITIES.
IT JUST SO HAPPENS THAT MY DECK WAS BUILT ALONG THE SAME LINES...
BUT ONLY A FEW TURNS IN, AND LOOK AT THE GAP IN OUR LIFE POINTS...
Life Points 4000
Life Points 700
THINK MY DRAW WAS LUCKY?
OR MAYBE...
...WE'VE GOT A DIFFERENCE IN SKILL HERE...

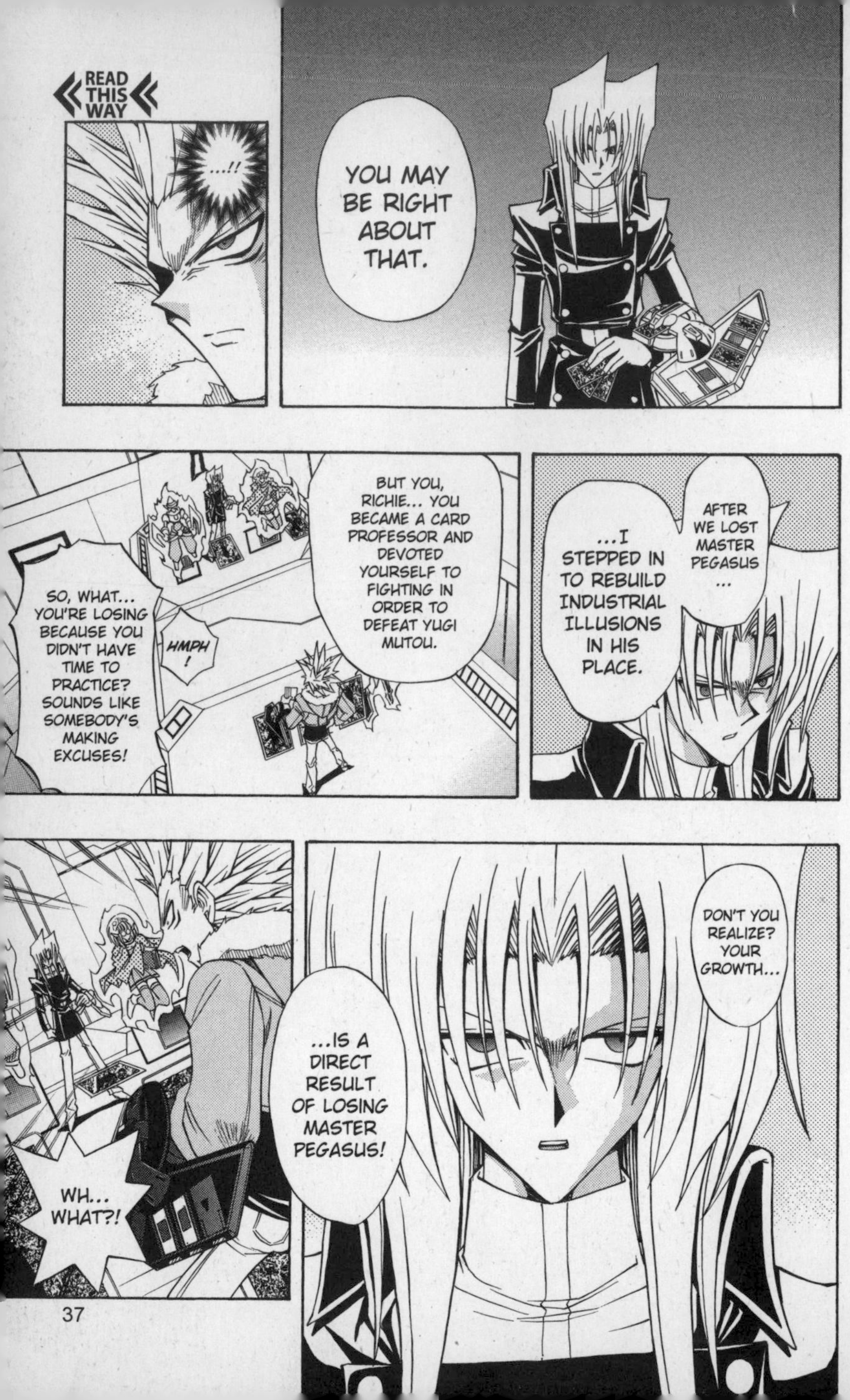
READ THIS WAY
YOU MAY BE RIGHT ABOUT THAT.
...!!
AFTER WE LOST MASTER PEGASUS...
...I STEPPED IN TO REBUILD INDUSTRIAL ILLUSIONS IN HIS PLACE.
BUT YOU, RICHIE... YOU BECAME A CARD PROFESSOR AND DEVOTED YOURSELF TO FIGHTING IN ORDER TO DEFEAT YUGI MUTOU.
HMPH!
SO, WHAT... YOU'RE LOSING BECAUSE YOU DIDN'T HAVE TIME TO PRACTICE? SOUNDS LIKE SOMEBODY'S MAKING EXCUSES!
DON'T YOU REALIZE? YOUR GROWTH...
...IS A DIRECT RESULT OF LOSING MASTER PEGASUS!
WH... WHAT?!

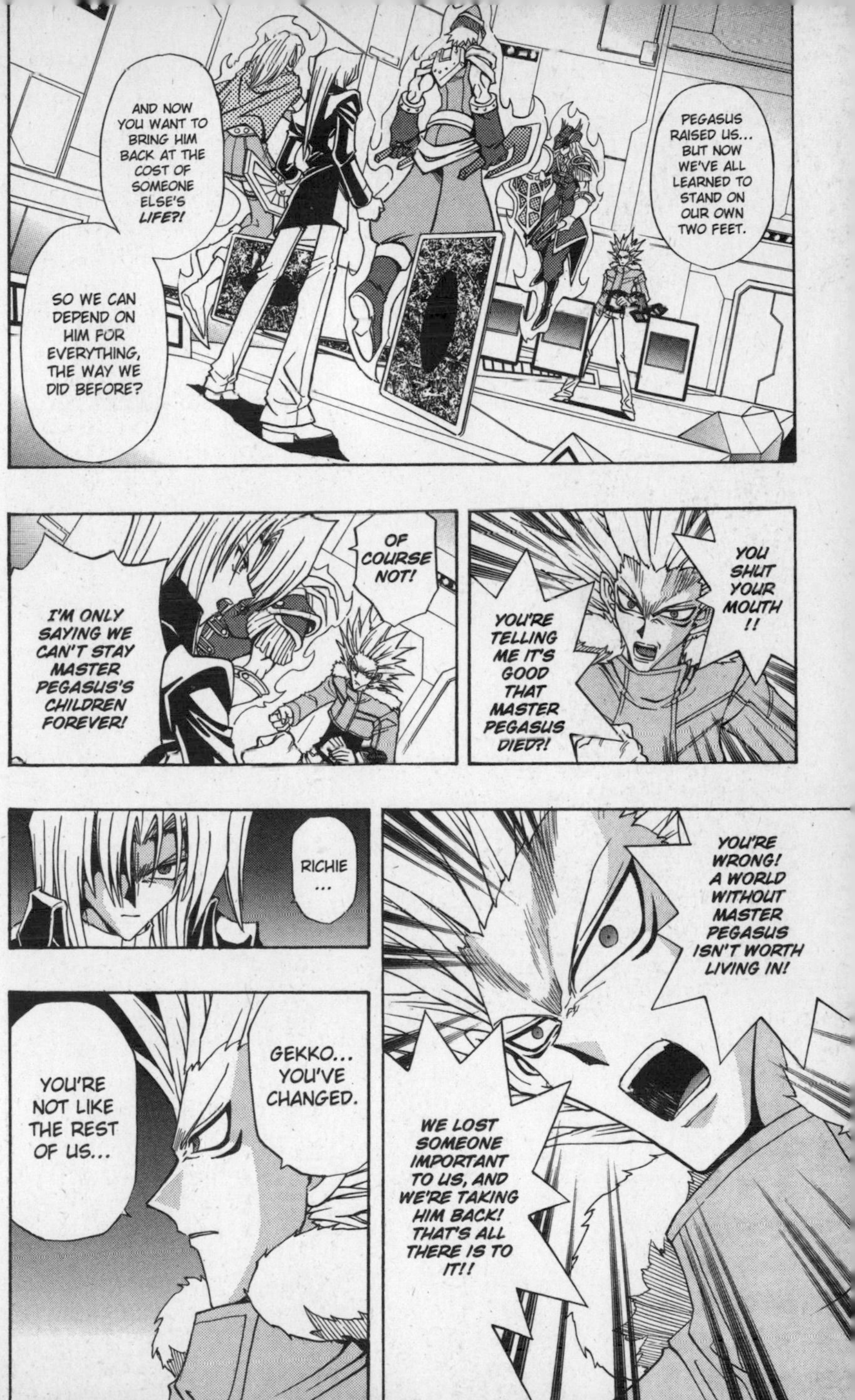
PEGASUS RAISED US... BUT NOW WE'VE ALL LEARNED TO STAND ON OUR OWN TWO FEET.
AND NOW YOU WANT TO BRING HIM BACK AT THE COST OF SOMEONE ELSE'S *LIFE?!*
SO WE CAN DEPEND ON HIM FOR EVERYTHING, THE WAY WE DID BEFORE?
YOU SHUT YOUR MOUTH!!
YOU'RE TELLING ME IT'S GOOD THAT MASTER PEGASUS DIED?!
OF COURSE NOT!
I'M ONLY SAYING WE CAN'T STAY MASTER PEGASUS'S CHILDREN FOREVER!
YOU'RE WRONG! A WORLD WITHOUT MASTER PEGASUS ISN'T WORTH LIVING IN!
WE LOST SOMEONE IMPORTANT TO US, AND WE'RE TAKING HIM BACK! THAT'S ALL THERE IS TO IT!!
RICHIE...
GEKKO... YOU'VE CHANGED.
YOU'RE NOT LIKE THE REST OF US...

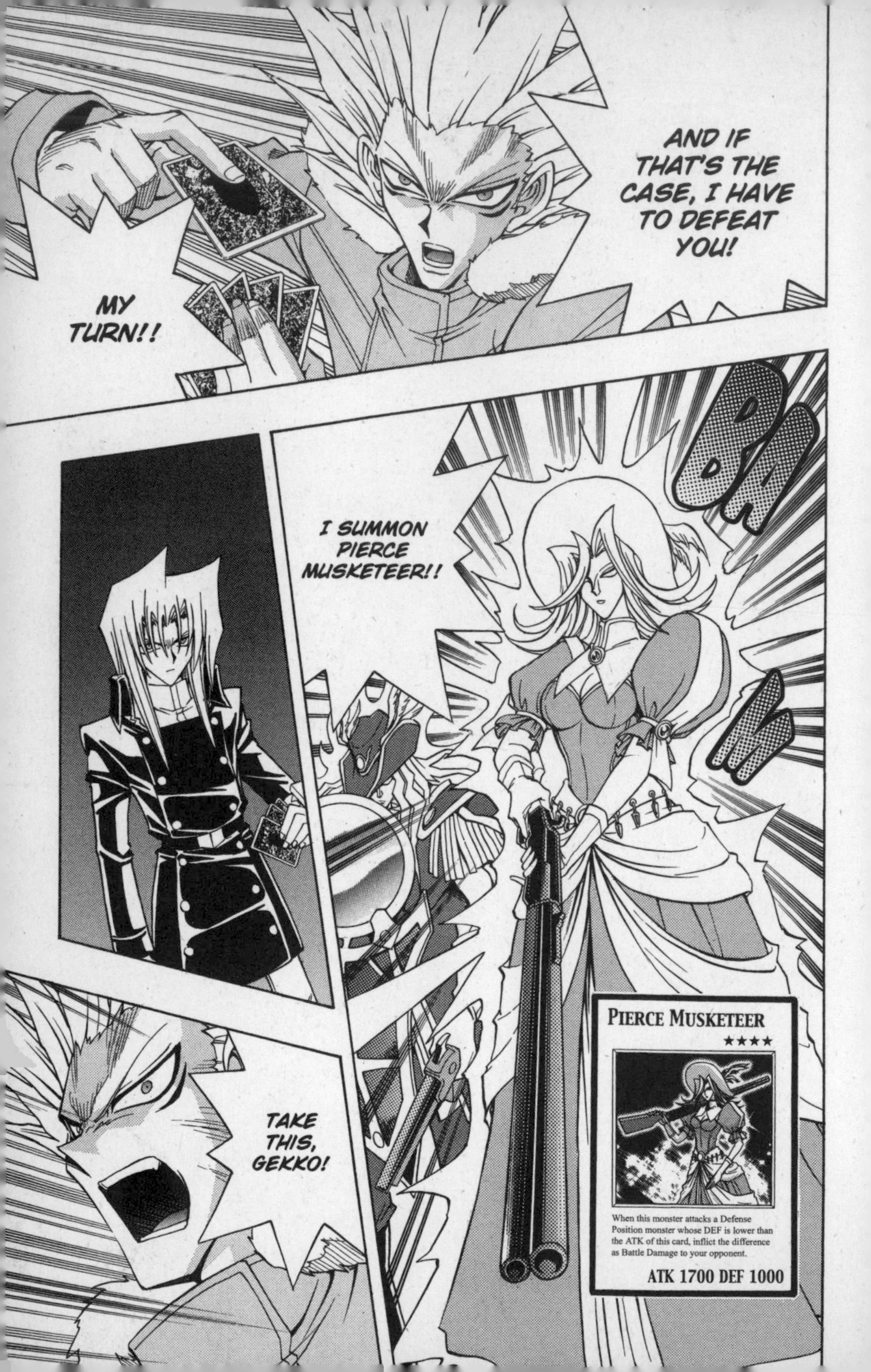
AND IF THAT'S THE CASE, I HAVE TO DEFEAT YOU!
MY TURN!!
I SUMMON PIERCE MUSKETEER!!
PIERCE MUSKETEER
★★★★
When this monster attacks a Defense Position monster whose DEF is lower than the ATK of this card, inflict the difference as Battle Damage to your opponent.
ATK 1700 DEF 1000
TAKE THIS, GEKKO!

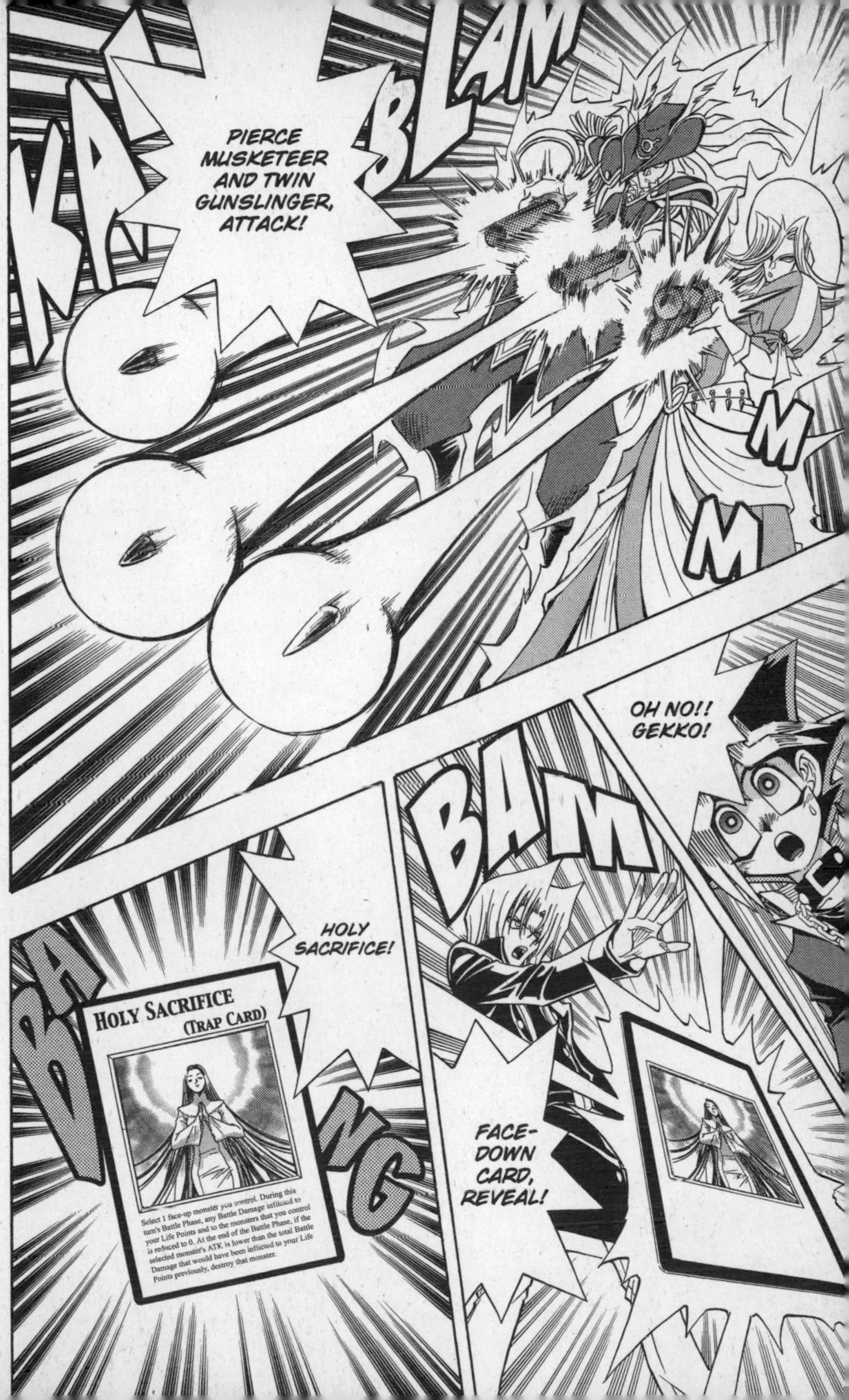
KA-BLAM
PIERCE MUSKETEER AND TWIN GUNSLINGER, ATTACK!
MM
OH NO!! GEKKO!
BAM
FACE-DOWN CARD, REVEAL!
HOLY SACRIFICE!
HOLY SACRIFICE
(TRAP CARD)
Select 1 face-up monster you control. During this turn's Battle Phase, any Battle Damage inflicted to your Life Points and to the monsters that you control is reduced to 0. At the end of the Battle Phase, if the selected monster's ATK is lower than the total Battle Damage that would have been inflicted to your Life Points previously, destroy that monster.
BANG

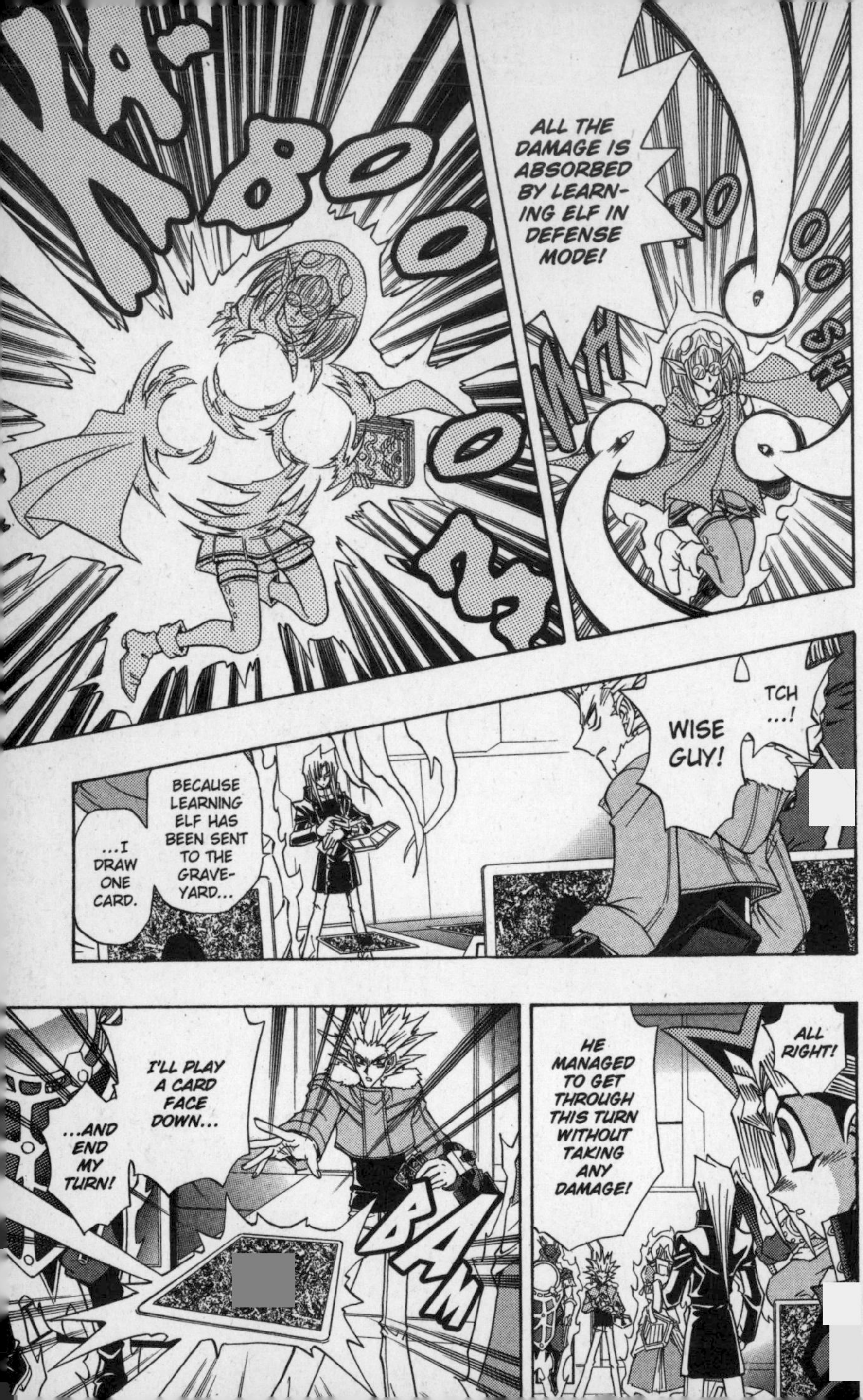
ALL THE DAMAGE IS ABSORBED BY LEARN-ING ELF IN DEFENSE MODE!
TCH ...!
WISE GUY!
BECAUSE LEARNING ELF HAS BEEN SENT TO THE GRAVE-YARD...
...I DRAW ONE CARD.
ALL RIGHT!
HE MANAGED TO GET THROUGH THIS TURN WITHOUT TAKING ANY DAMAGE!
I'LL PLAY A CARD FACE DOWN...
...AND END MY TURN!
BAM

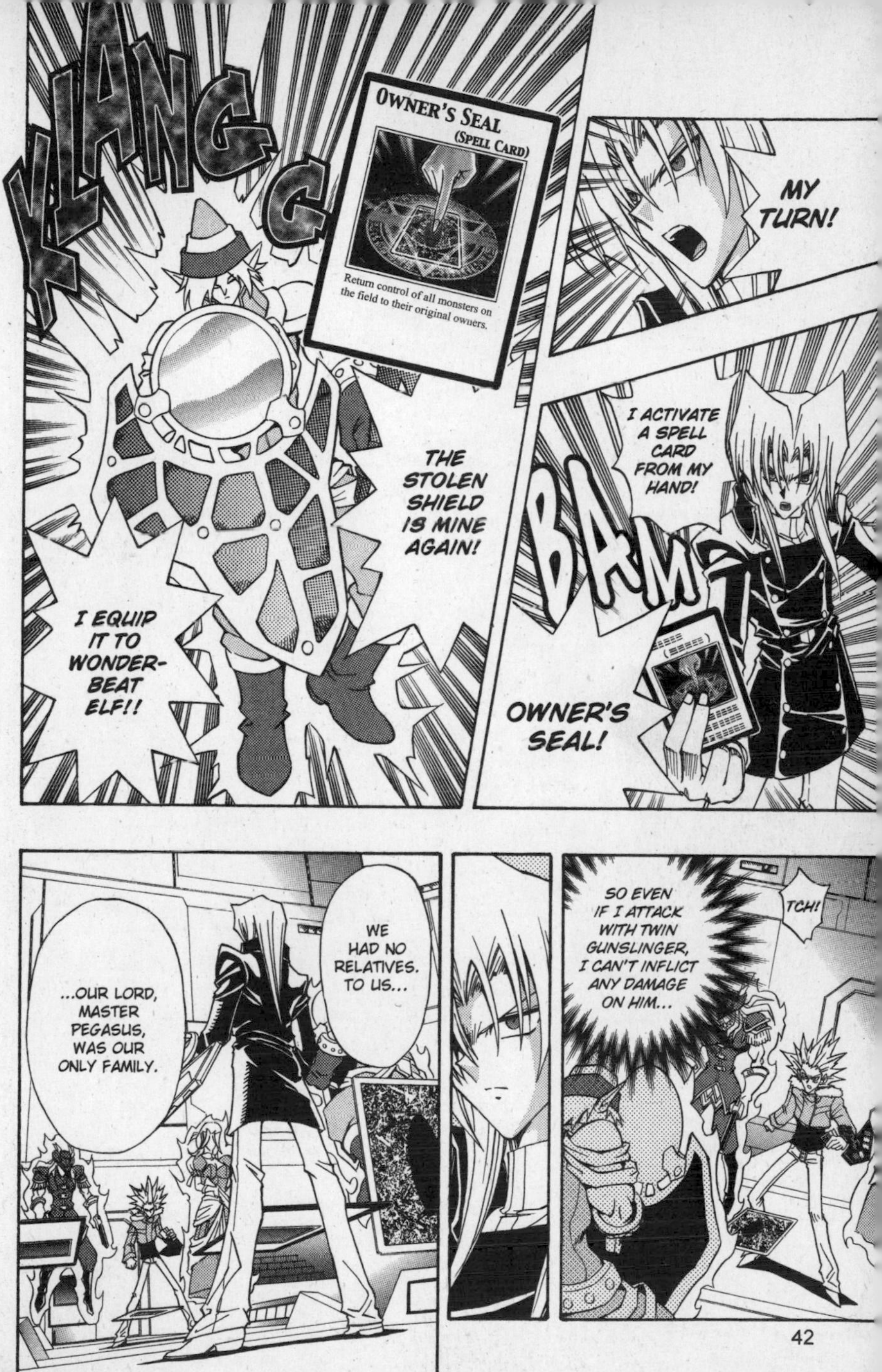
MY TURN!
I ACTIVATE A SPELL CARD FROM MY HAND!
BAM
OWNER'S SEAL!
KLANG
OWNER'S SEAL
(SPELL CARD)
Return control of all monsters on the field to their original owners.
THE STOLEN SHIELD IS MINE AGAIN!
I EQUIP IT TO WONDER-BEAT ELF!!
TCH!
SO EVEN IF I ATTACK WITH TWIN GUNSLINGER, I CAN'T INFLICT ANY DAMAGE ON HIM...
WE HAD NO RELATIVES. TO US...
...OUR LORD, MASTER PEGASUS, WAS OUR ONLY FAMILY.

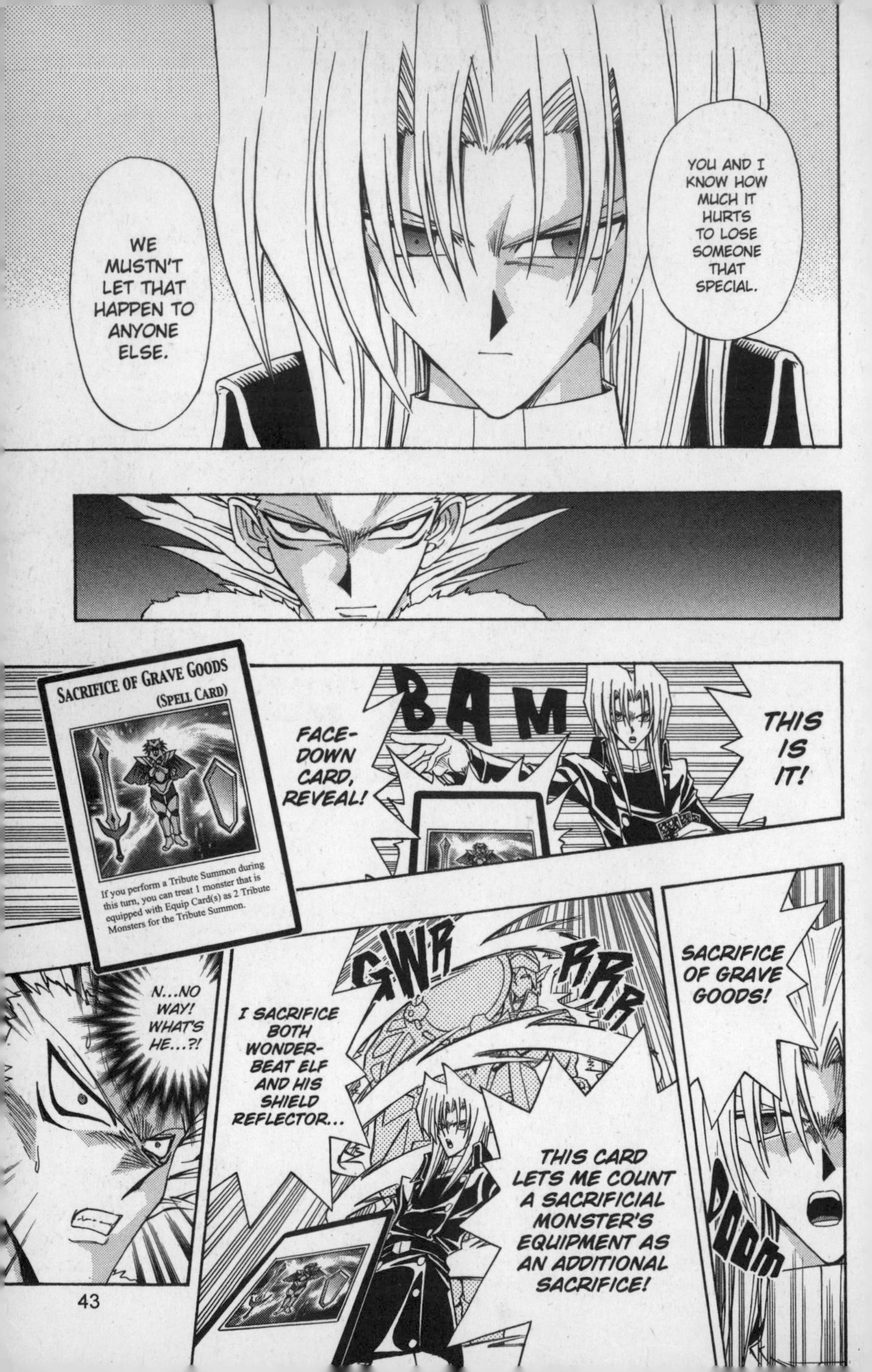
YOU AND I KNOW HOW MUCH IT HURTS TO LOSE SOMEONE THAT SPECIAL.
WE MUSTN'T LET THAT HAPPEN TO ANYONE ELSE.
THIS IS IT!
BAM
FACE-DOWN CARD, REVEAL!
SACRIFICE OF GRAVE GOODS
(SPELL CARD)
If you perform a Tribute Summon during this turn, you can treat 1 monster that is equipped with Equip Card(s) as 2 Tribute Monsters for the Tribute Summon.
SACRIFICE OF GRAVE GOODS!
DOOM
GWRRRR
I SACRIFICE BOTH WONDER-BEAT ELF AND HIS SHIELD REFLECTOR...
THIS CARD LETS ME COUNT A SACRIFICIAL MONSTER'S EQUIPMENT AS AN ADDITIONAL SACRIFICE!
N...NO WAY! WHAT'S HE...?!

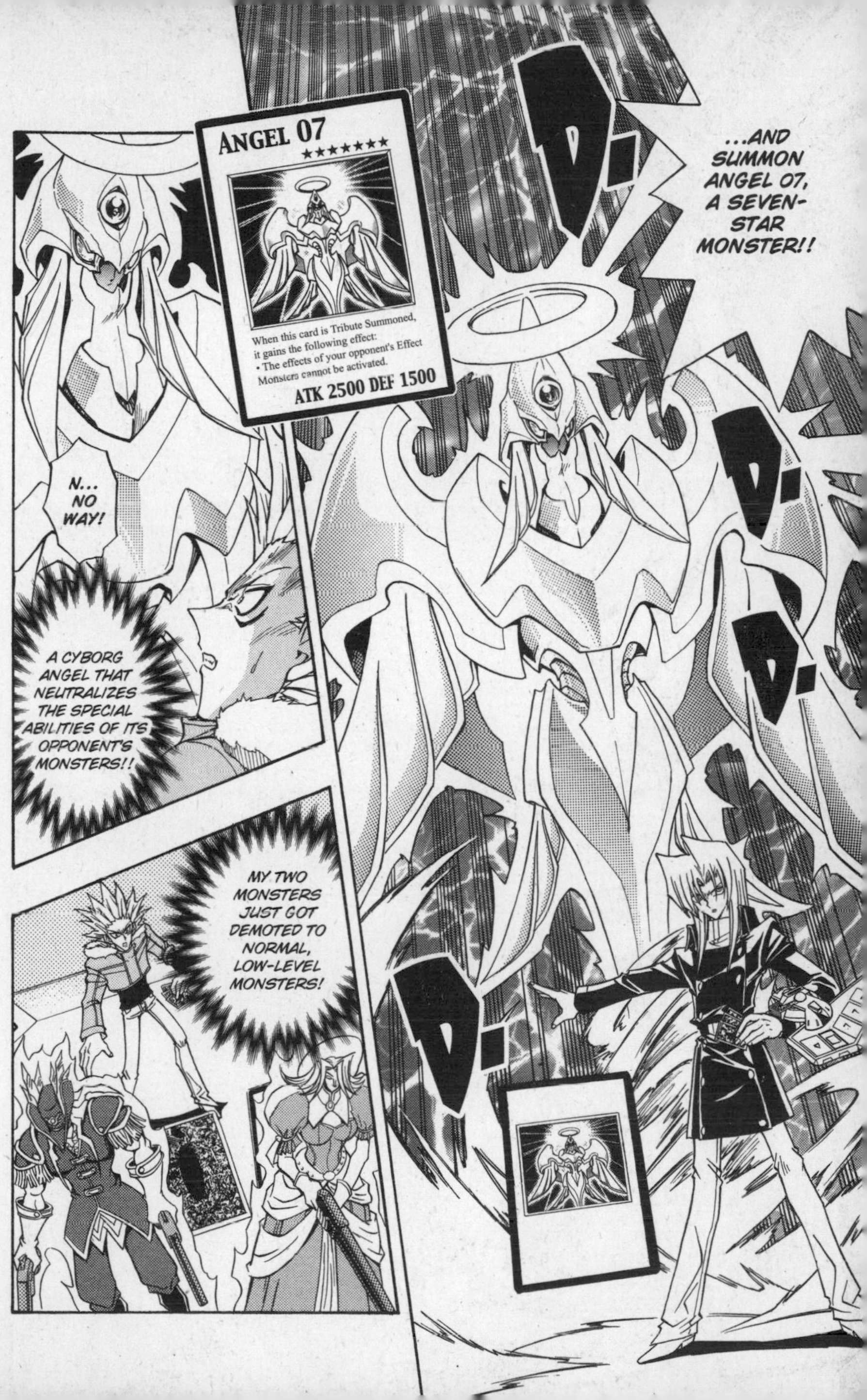
...AND SUMMON ANGEL 07, A SEVEN-STAR MONSTER!!
D.
D.
D.
D.
D.
ANGEL 07
★★★★★★★
When this card is Tribute Summoned, it gains the following effect:
• The effects of your opponent's Effect Monsters cannot be activated.
ATK 2500 DEF 1500
N... NO WAY!
A CYBORG ANGEL THAT NEUTRALIZES THE SPECIAL ABILITIES OF ITS OPPONENT'S MONSTERS!!
MY TWO MONSTERS JUST GOT DEMOTED TO NORMAL, LOW-LEVEL MONSTERS!

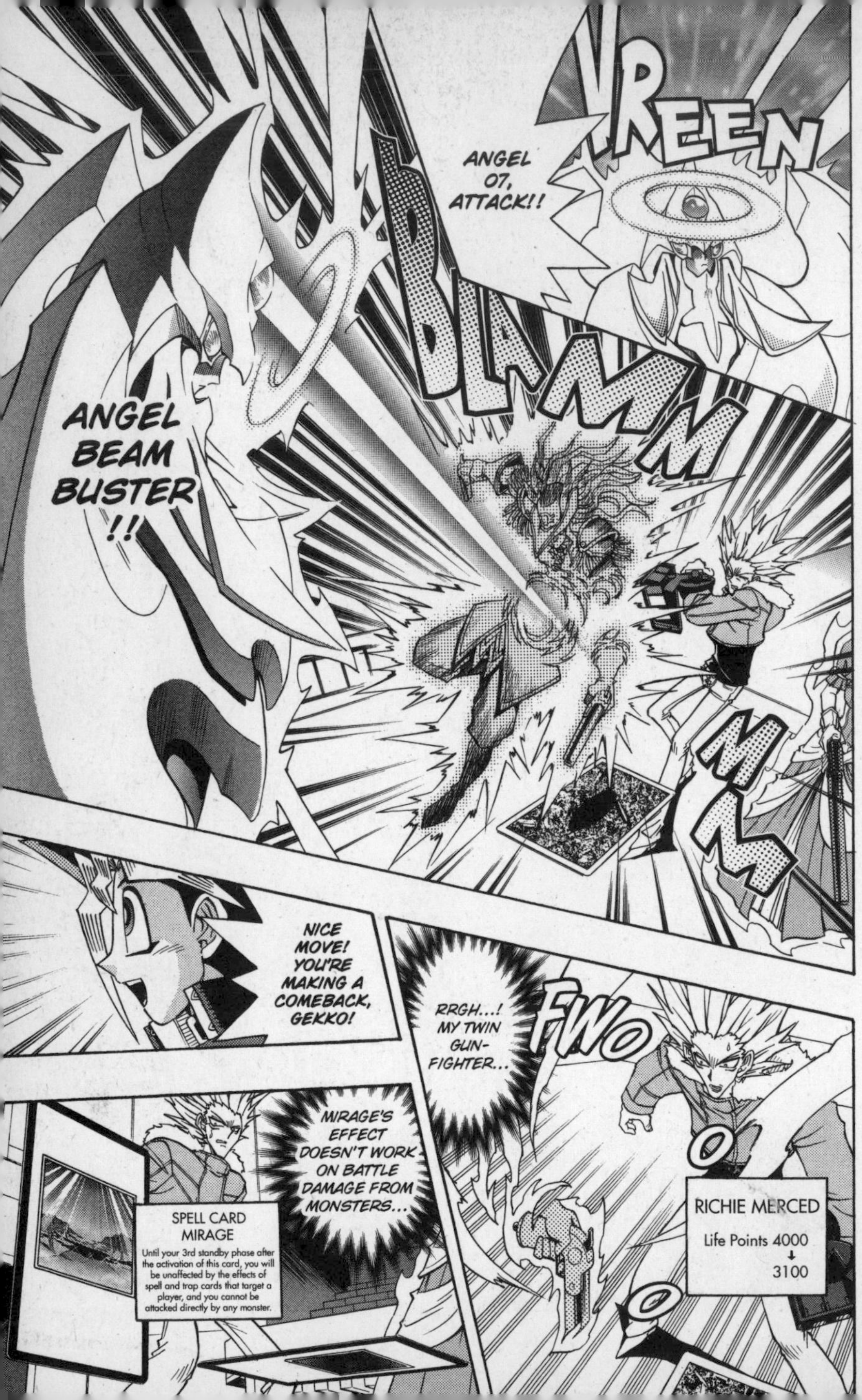
VREEN
ANGEL 07, ATTACK!!
BLAMMM
ANGEL BEAM BUSTER!!
MMM
RRGH...! MY TWIN GUN-FIGHTER...
FWOOO
NICE MOVE! YOU'RE MAKING A COMEBACK, GEKKO!
RICHIE MERCED
Life Points 4000 ↓ 3100
MIRAGE'S EFFECT DOESN'T WORK ON BATTLE DAMAGE FROM MONSTERS...
SPELL CARD MIRAGE
Until your 3rd standby phase after the activation of this card, you will be unaffected by the effects of spell and trap cards that target a player, and you cannot be attacked directly by any monster.

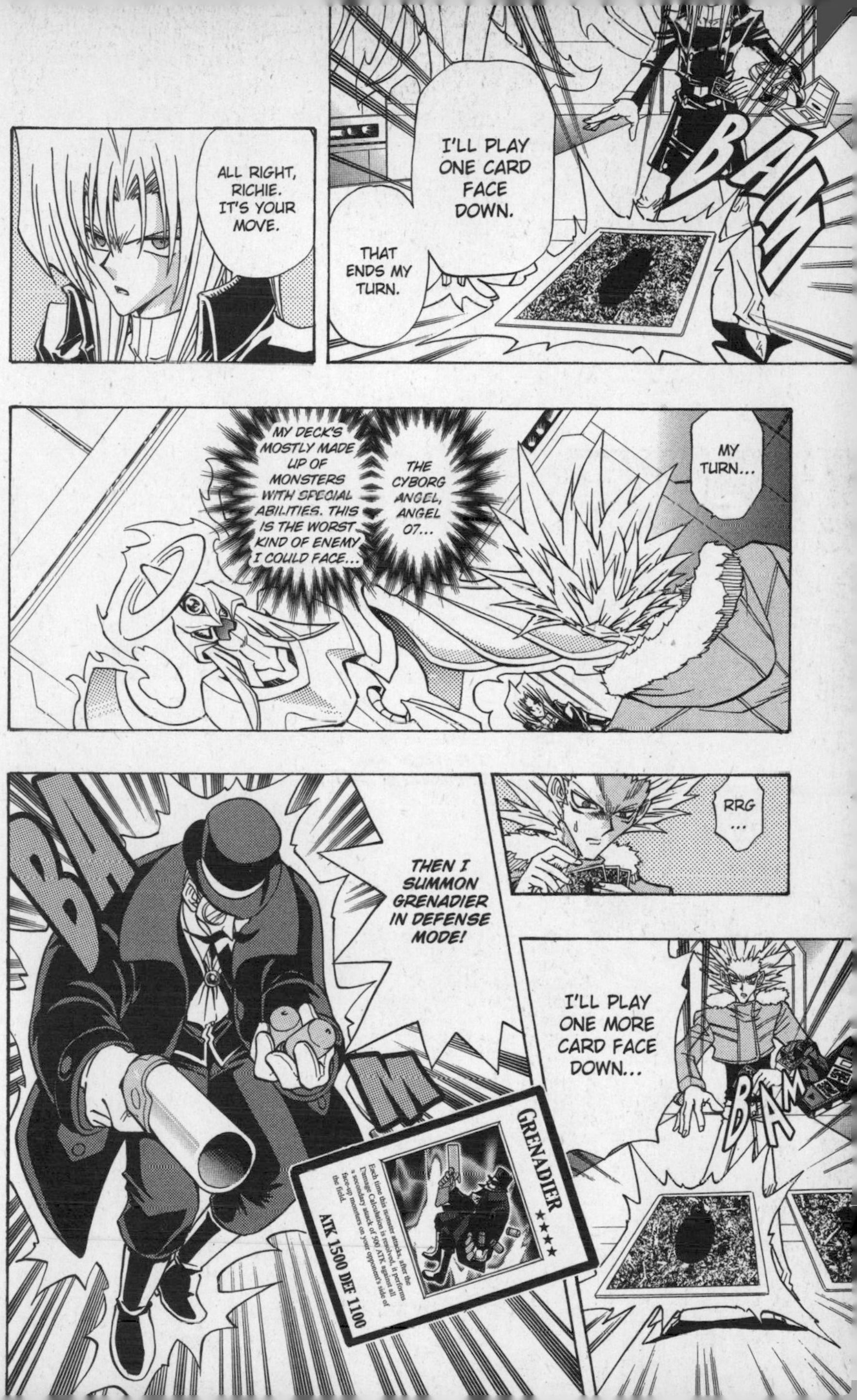
BAM
I'LL PLAY ONE CARD FACE DOWN.
THAT ENDS MY TURN.
ALL RIGHT, RICHIE. IT'S YOUR MOVE.
MY TURN...
THE CYBORG ANGEL, ANGEL 07...
MY DECK'S MOSTLY MADE UP OF MONSTERS WITH SPECIAL ABILITIES. THIS IS THE WORST KIND OF ENEMY I COULD FACE...
RRG ...
I'LL PLAY ONE MORE CARD FACE DOWN...
BAM
THEN I SUMMON GRENADIER IN DEFENSE MODE!
BAM
GRENADIER
Each time this monster attacks, after the Damage Calculation is resolved, it performs a secondary attack of 500 ATK against all face-up monsters on your opponent's side of the field.
ATK 1500 DEF 1100

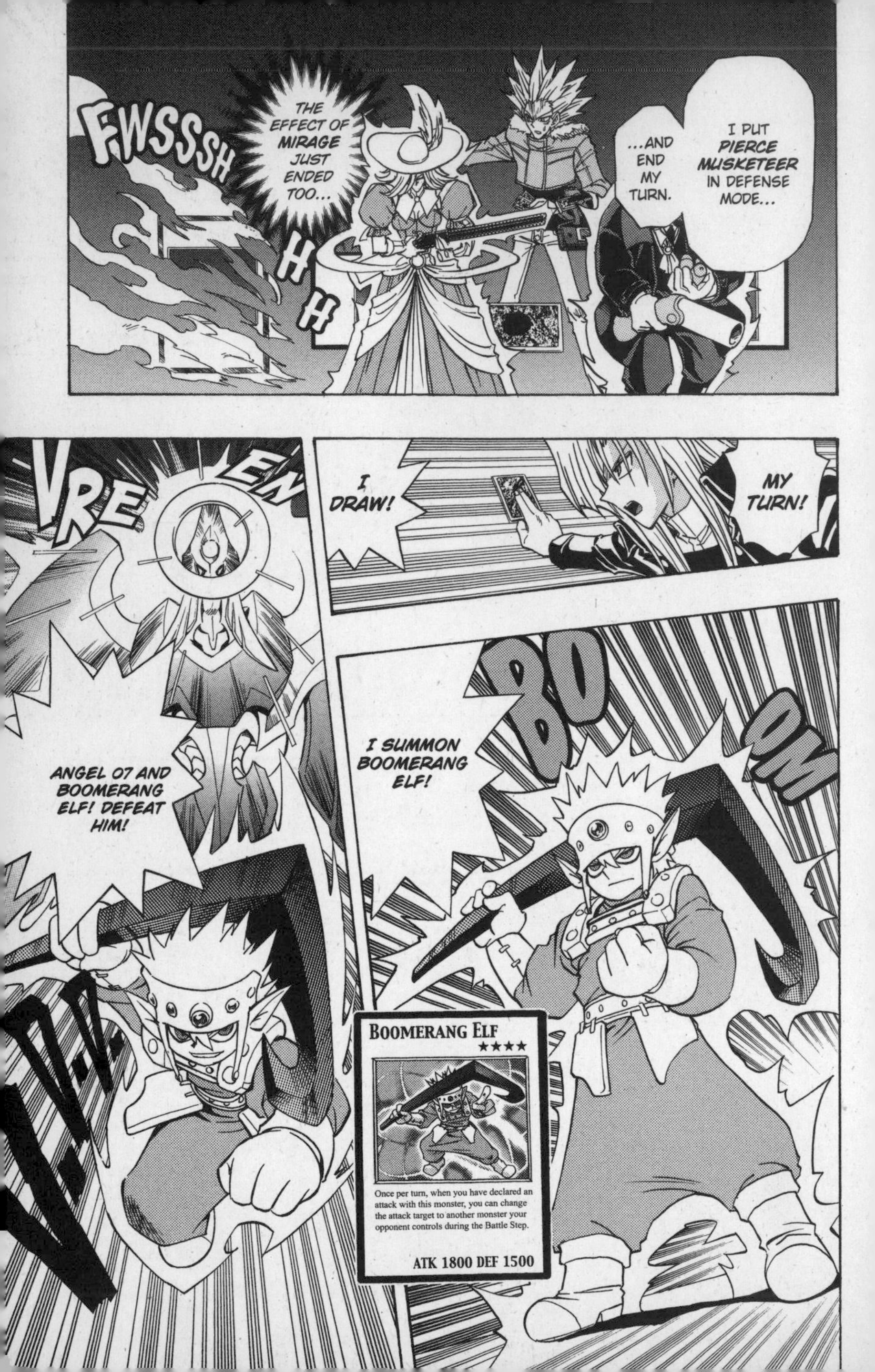
I PUT PIERCE MUSKETEER IN DEFENSE MODE...
...AND END MY TURN.
THE EFFECT OF MIRAGE JUST ENDED TOO...
FWSSSH
HH
MY TURN!
I DRAW!
BOOM
I SUMMON BOOMERANG ELF!
BOOMERANG ELF
Once per turn, when you have declared an attack with this monster, you can change the attack target to another monster your opponent controls during the Battle Step.
ATK 1800 DEF 1500
ANGEL 07 AND BOOMERANG ELF! DEFEAT HIM!

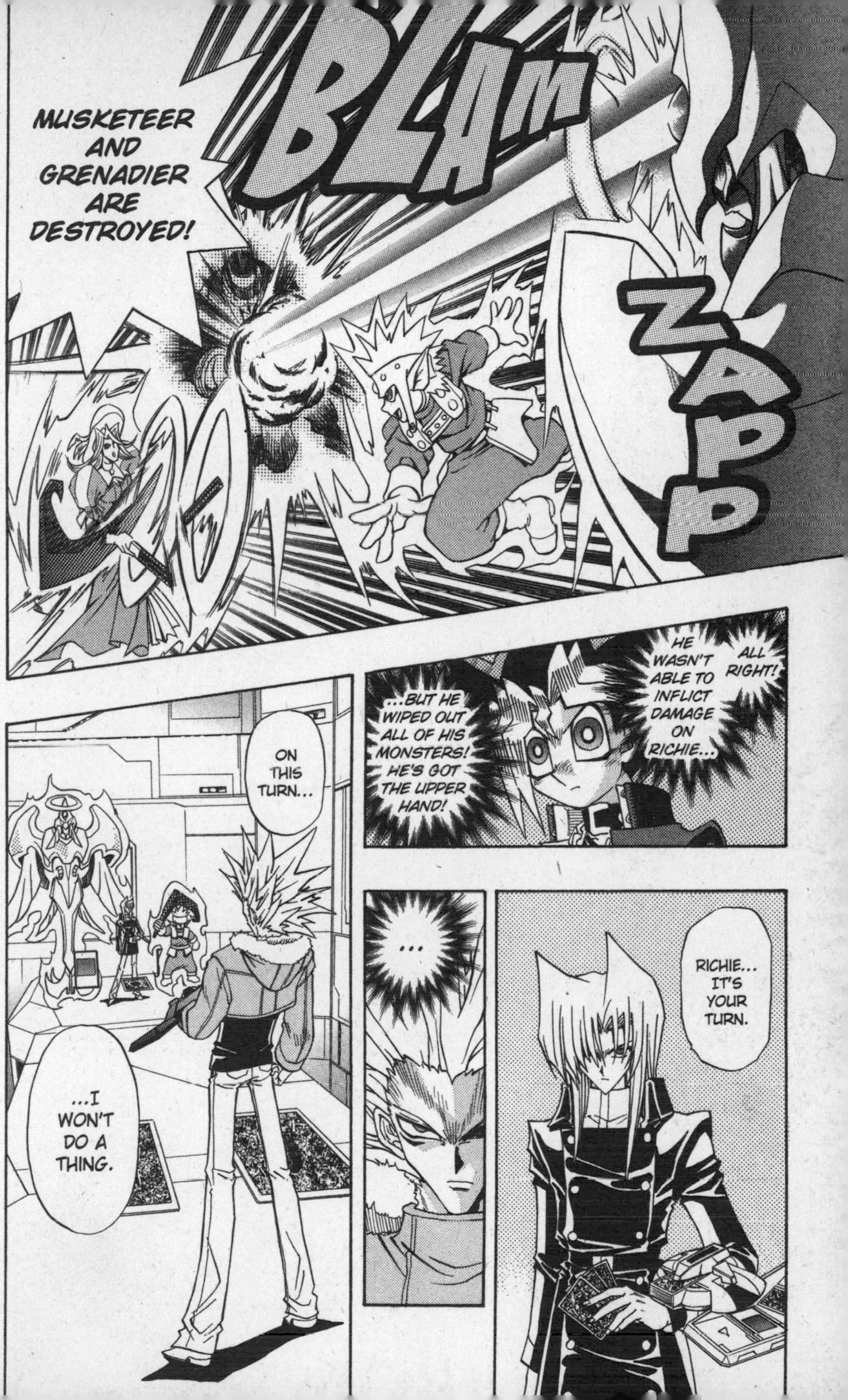
BLAM
MUSKETEER AND GRENADIER ARE DESTROYED!
ZAPP
ALL RIGHT!
HE WASN'T ABLE TO INFLICT DAMAGE ON RICHIE...
...BUT HE WIPED OUT ALL OF HIS MONSTERS! HE'S GOT THE UPPER HAND!
RICHIE... IT'S YOUR TURN.
...
ON THIS TURN...
...I WON'T DO A THING.

READ THIS WAY

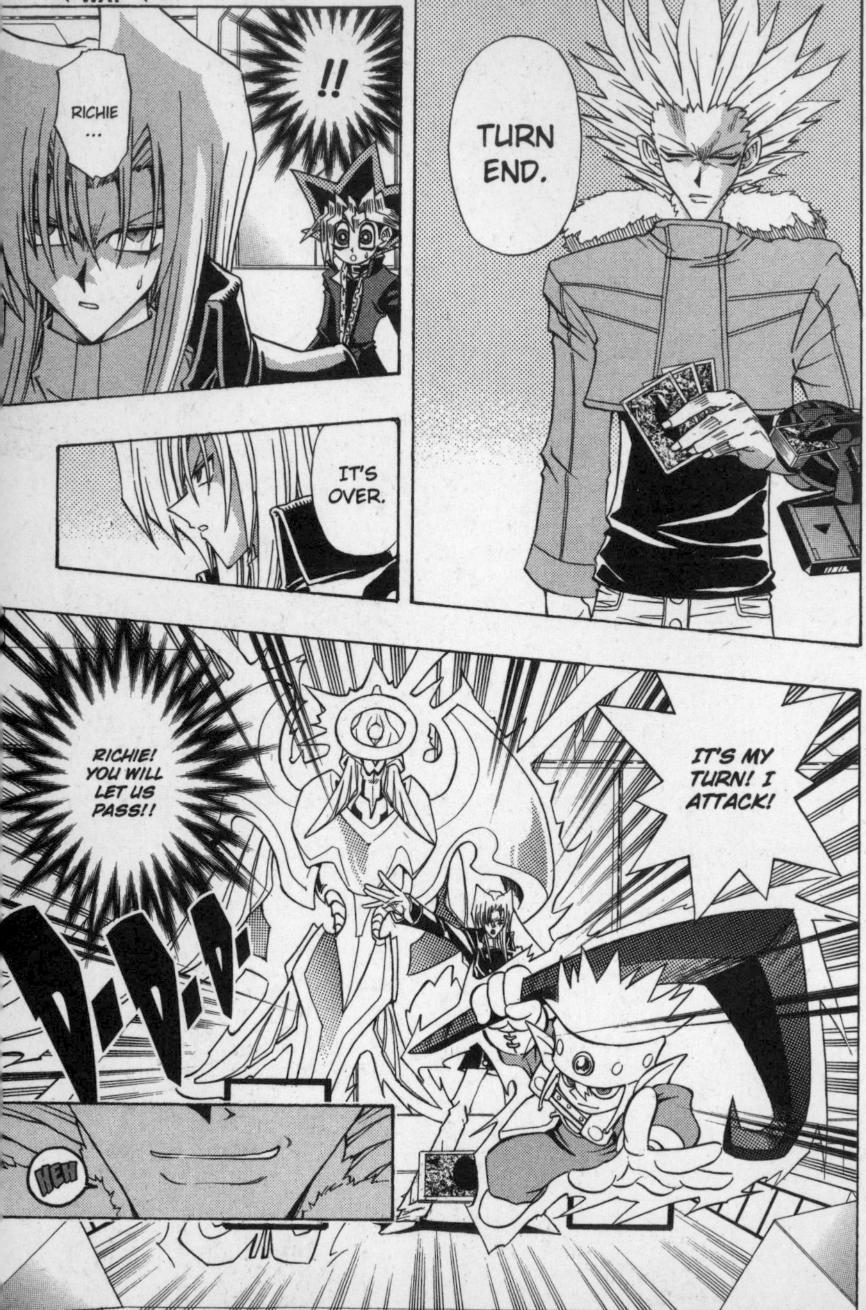
TURN END.
!!
RICHIE ...
IT'S OVER.
IT'S MY TURN! I ATTACK!
RICHIE! YOU WILL LET US PASS!!
HEH

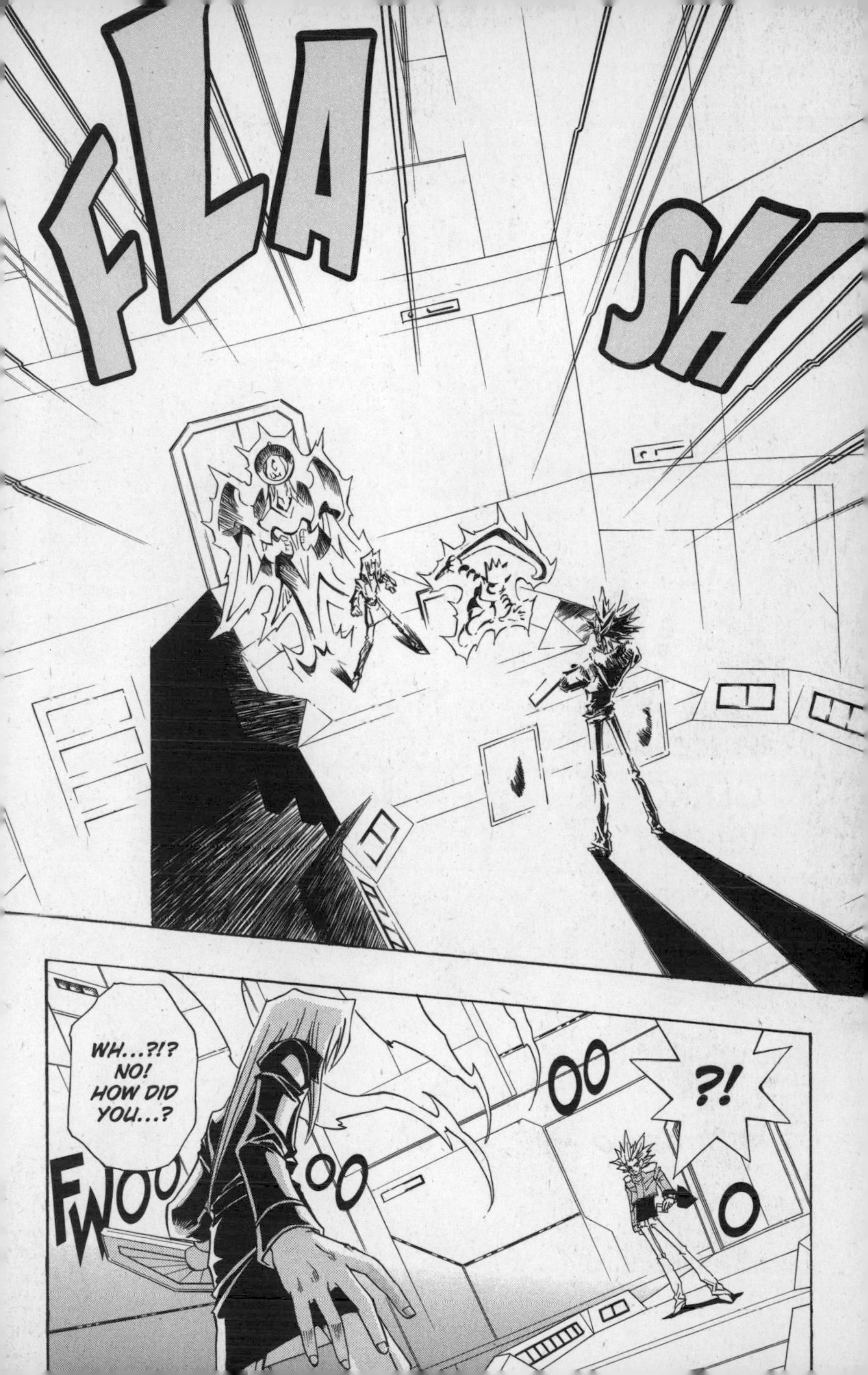
FLASH
?!
WH...?!? NO! HOW DID YOU...?
FWOOOOOOO

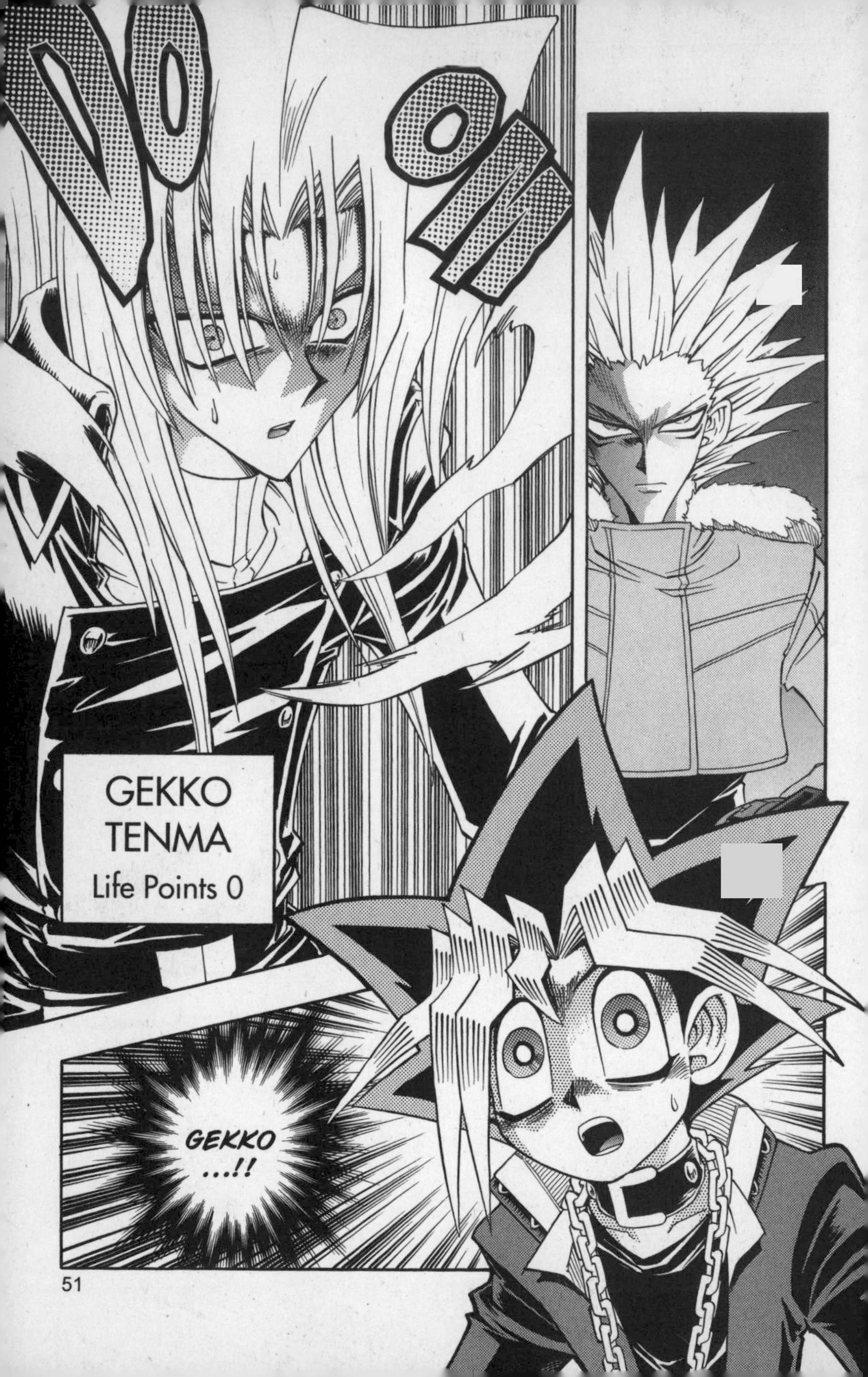
GEKKO
TENMA
Life Points 0
GEKKO
...!!

Duel Round 27:
To Each His Own Battle!!

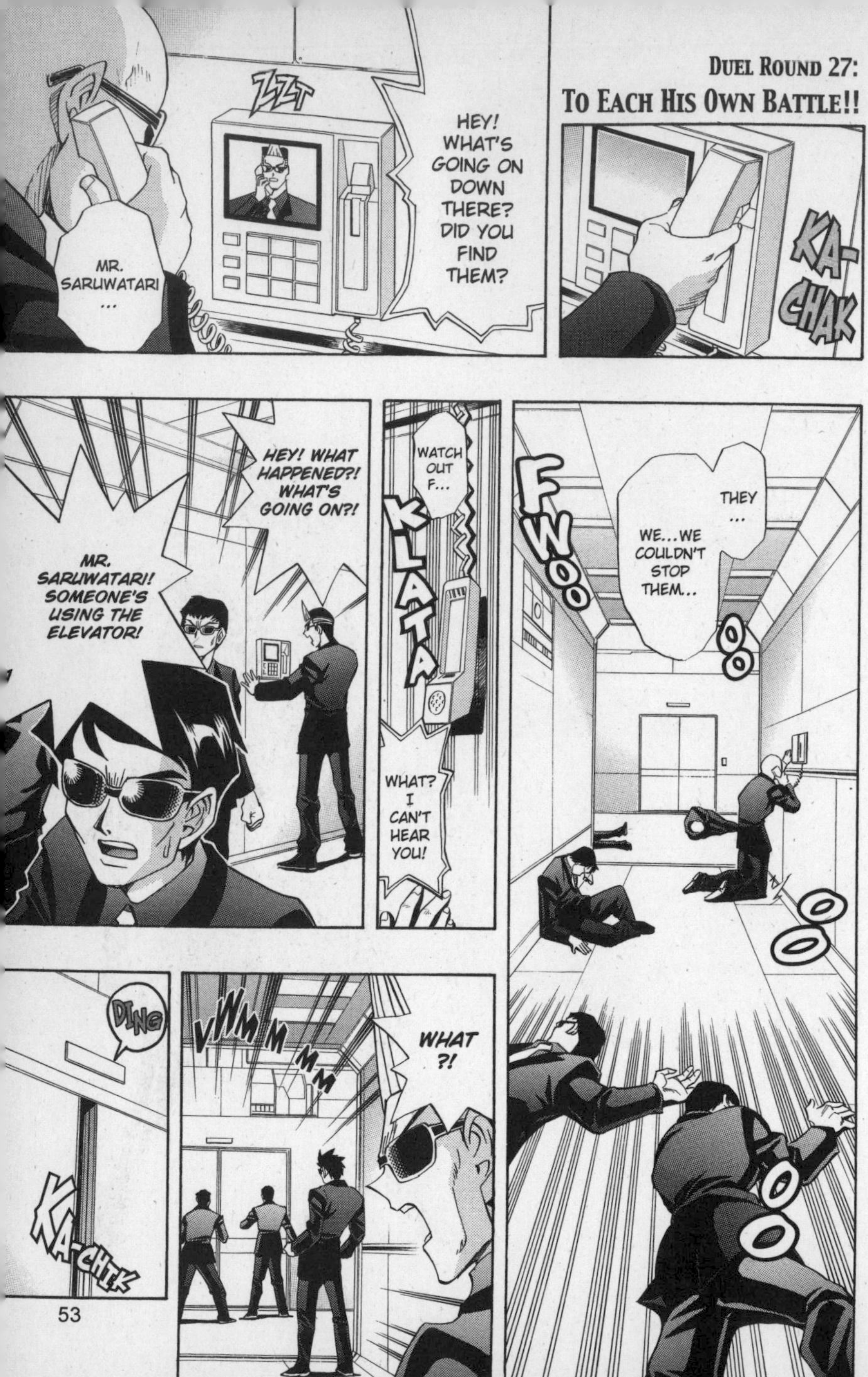
KA-CHAK
ZZZT
HEY! WHAT'S GOING ON DOWN THERE? DID YOU FIND THEM?
MR. SARUWATARI …
FWOO
THEY …
WE…WE COULDN'T STOP THEM…
OOO
OOO
OOO
WATCH OUT F…
KLATA
WHAT? I CAN'T HEAR YOU!
HEY! WHAT HAPPENED?! WHAT'S GOING ON?!
MR. SARUWATARI! SOMEONE'S USING THE ELEVATOR!
WHAT ?!
VWMMMM
DING
KA-CHIK

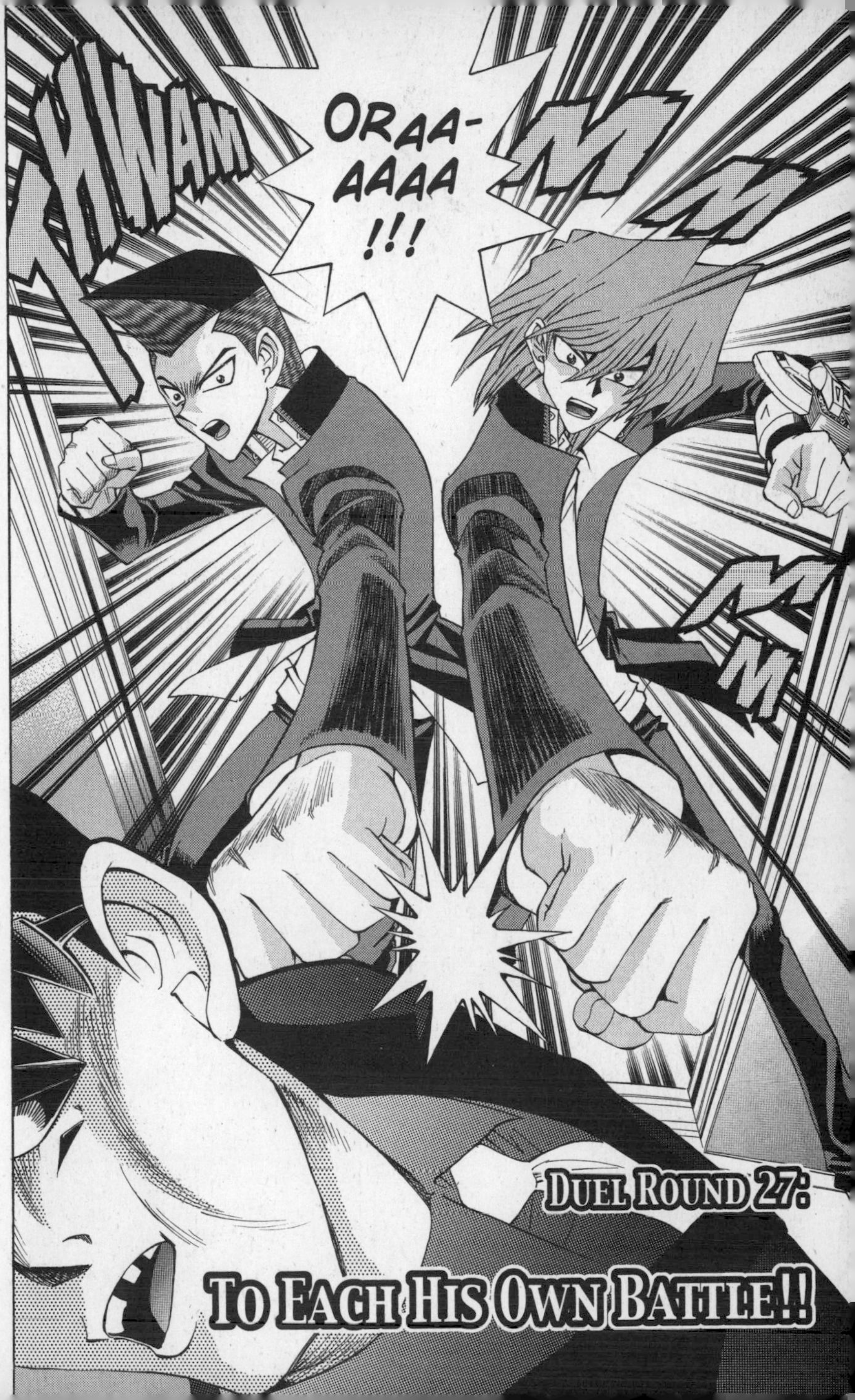
WHAM
ORAA-AAAA!!!

Duel Round 27: To Each His Own Battle!!

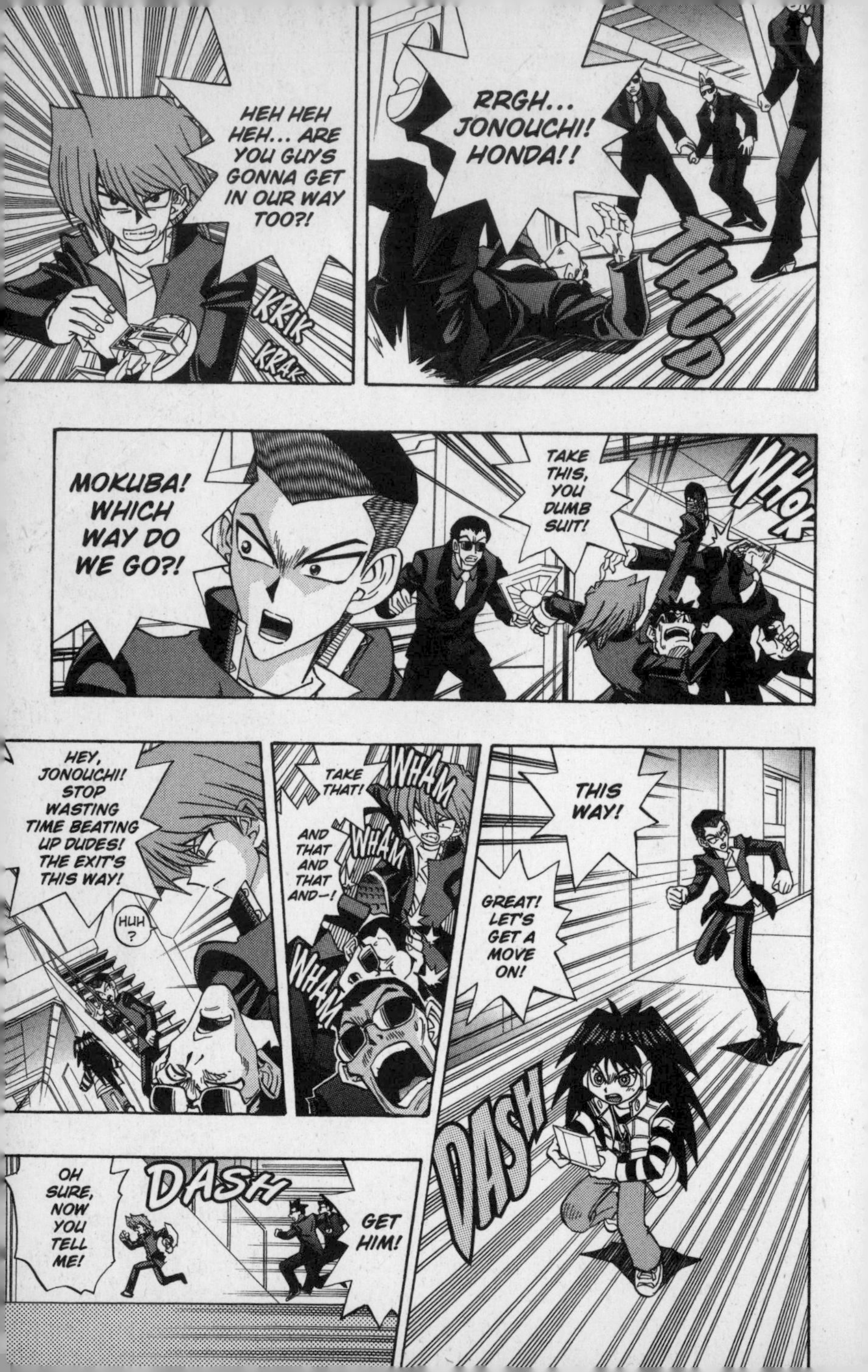
RRGH... JONOUCHI! HONDA!!
THUD
HEH HEH HEH... ARE YOU GUYS GONNA GET IN OUR WAY TOO?!
KRIK
KRAK
WHOK
TAKE THIS, YOU DUMB SUIT!
MOKUBA! WHICH WAY DO WE GO?!
THIS WAY!
GREAT! LET'S GET A MOVE ON!
DASH
TAKE THAT!
WHAM
AND THAT AND THAT AND—!
WHAM
WHAM
HEY, JONOUCHI! STOP WASTING TIME BEATING UP DUDES! THE EXIT'S THIS WAY!
HUH?
GET HIM!
DASH
OH SURE, NOW YOU TELL ME!

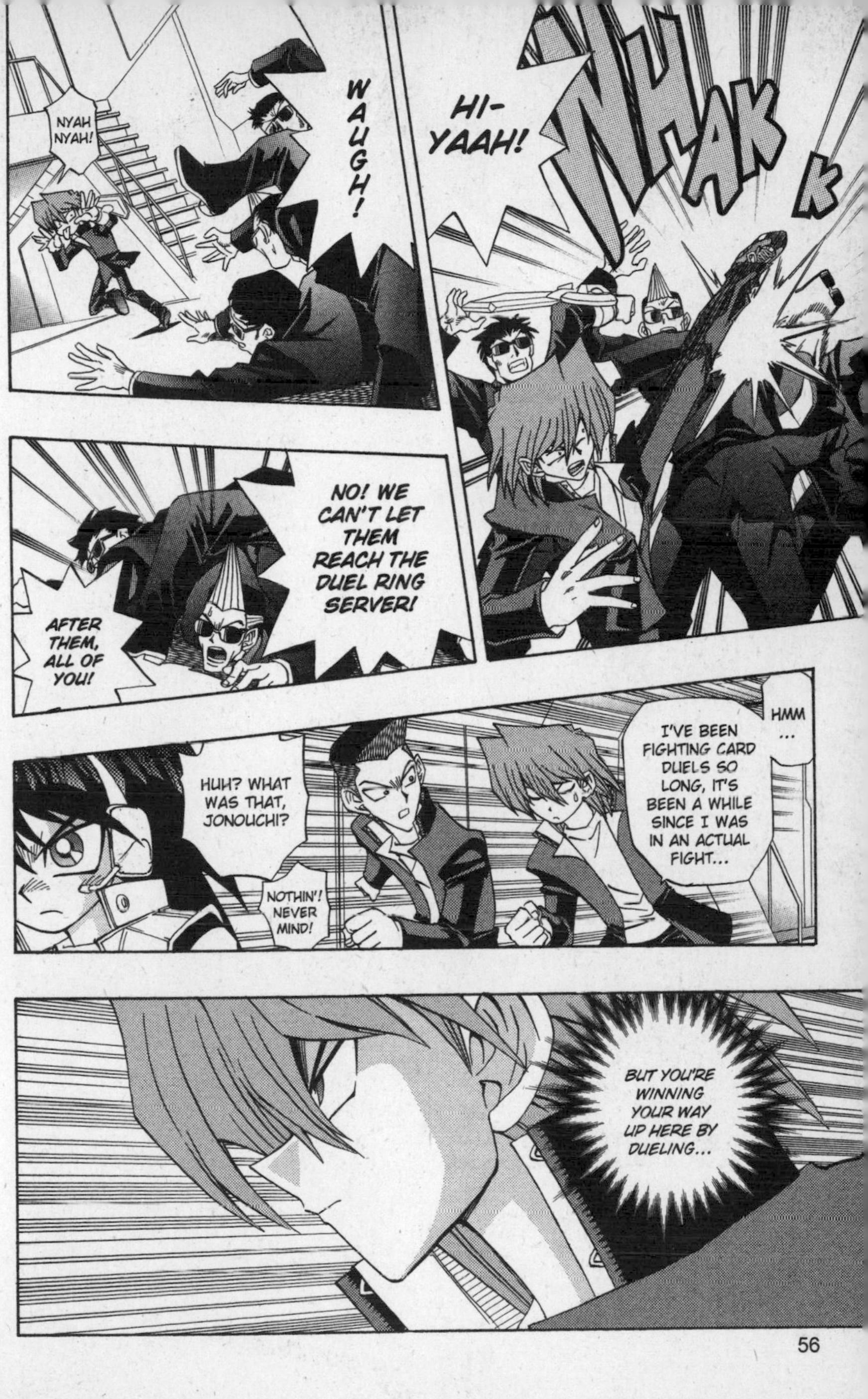
HI-YAAH!
WHAK
k
WAUGH!
NYAH NYAH!
NO! WE CAN'T LET THEM REACH THE DUEL RING SERVER!
AFTER THEM, ALL OF YOU!
HMM...
I'VE BEEN FIGHTING CARD DUELS SO LONG, IT'S BEEN A WHILE SINCE I WAS IN AN ACTUAL FIGHT...
HUH? WHAT WAS THAT, JONOUCHI?
NOTHIN'! NEVER MIND!
BUT YOU'RE WINNING YOUR WAY UP HERE BY DUELING...

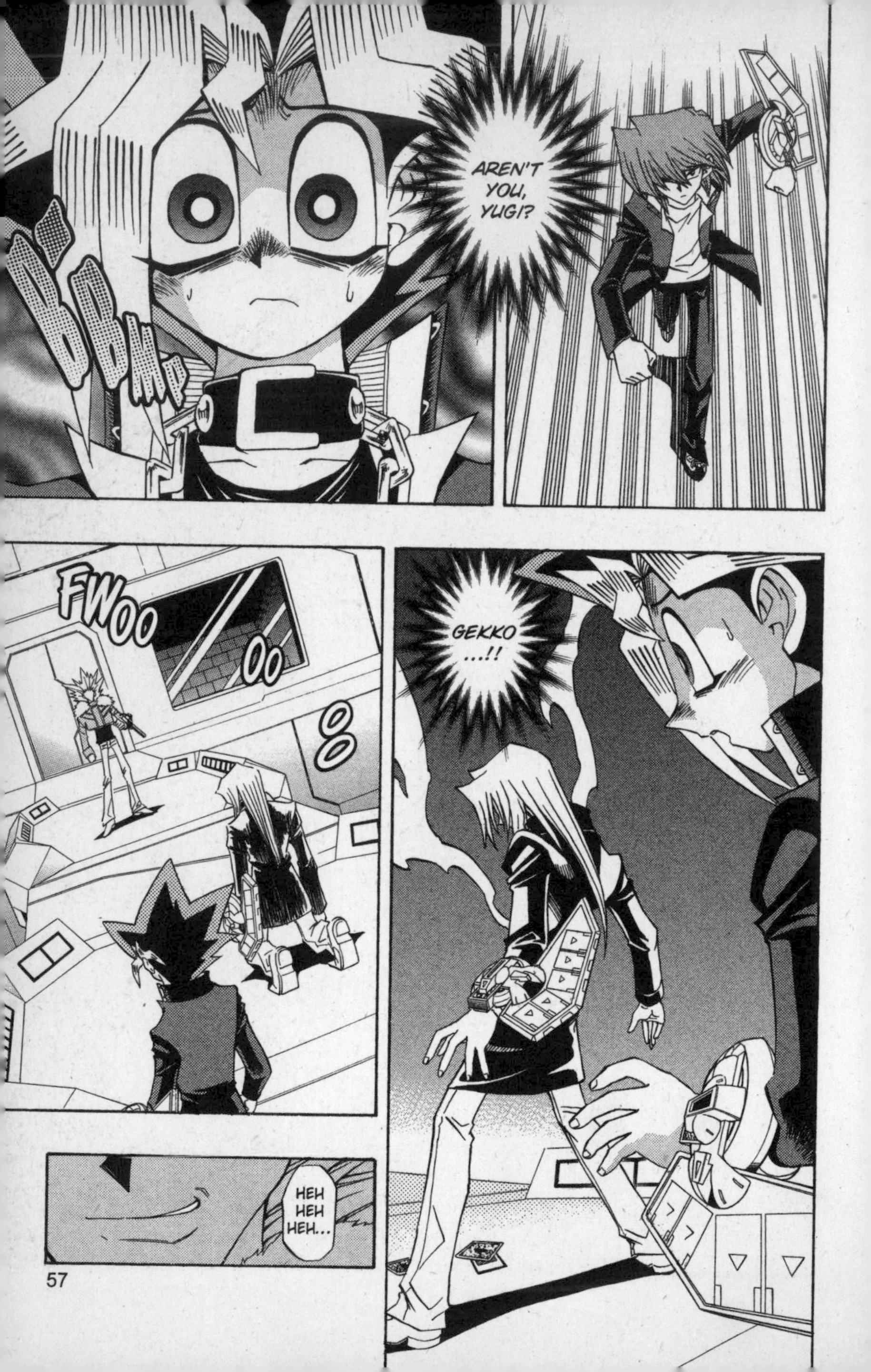
AREN'T YOU, YUGI?
GEKKO ...!!
FWOOOOOO
HEH HEH HEH...

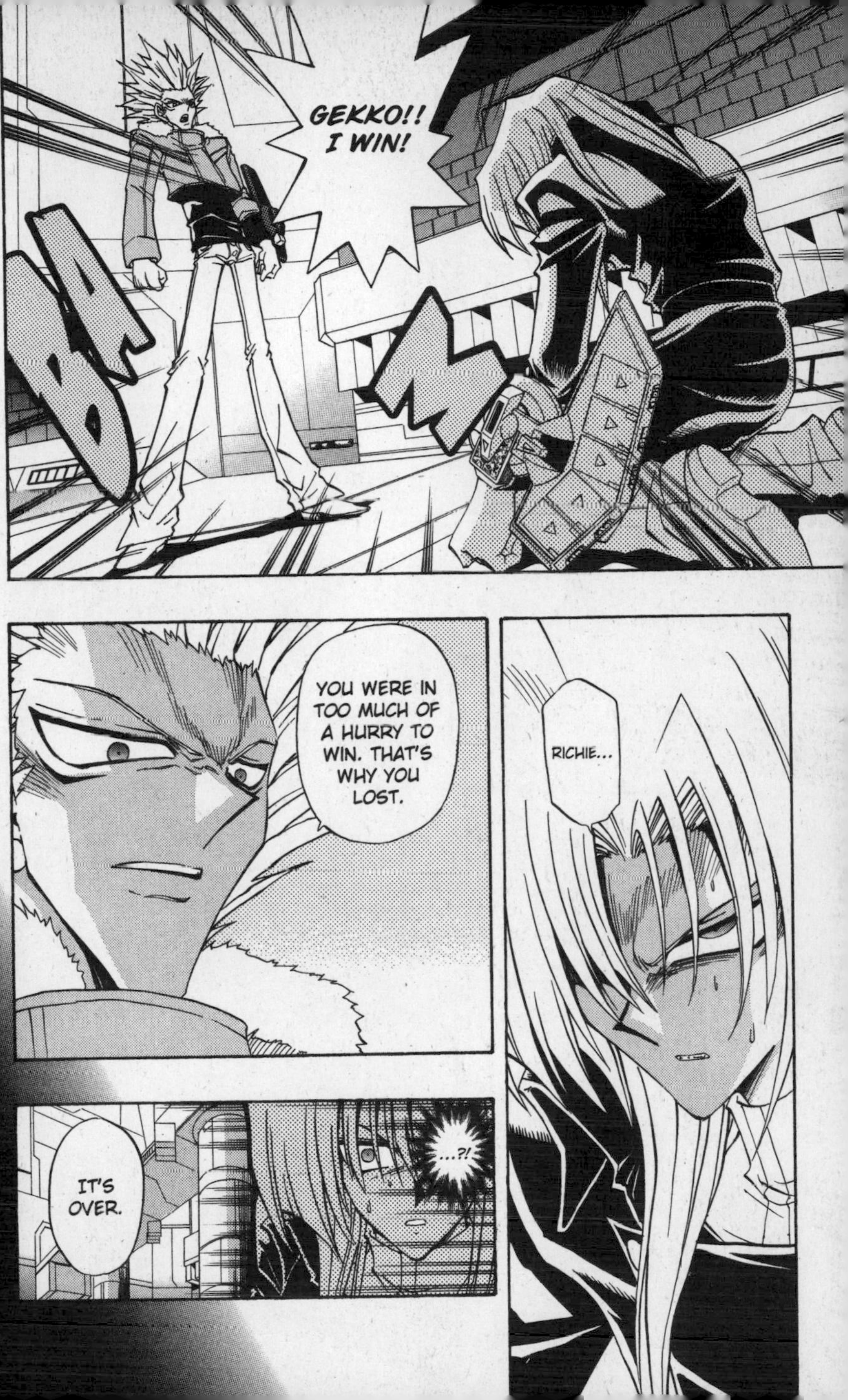
GEKKO!! I WIN!
RICHIE...
YOU WERE IN TOO MUCH OF A HURRY TO WIN. THAT'S WHY YOU LOST.
...?!
IT'S OVER.

READ THIS WAY

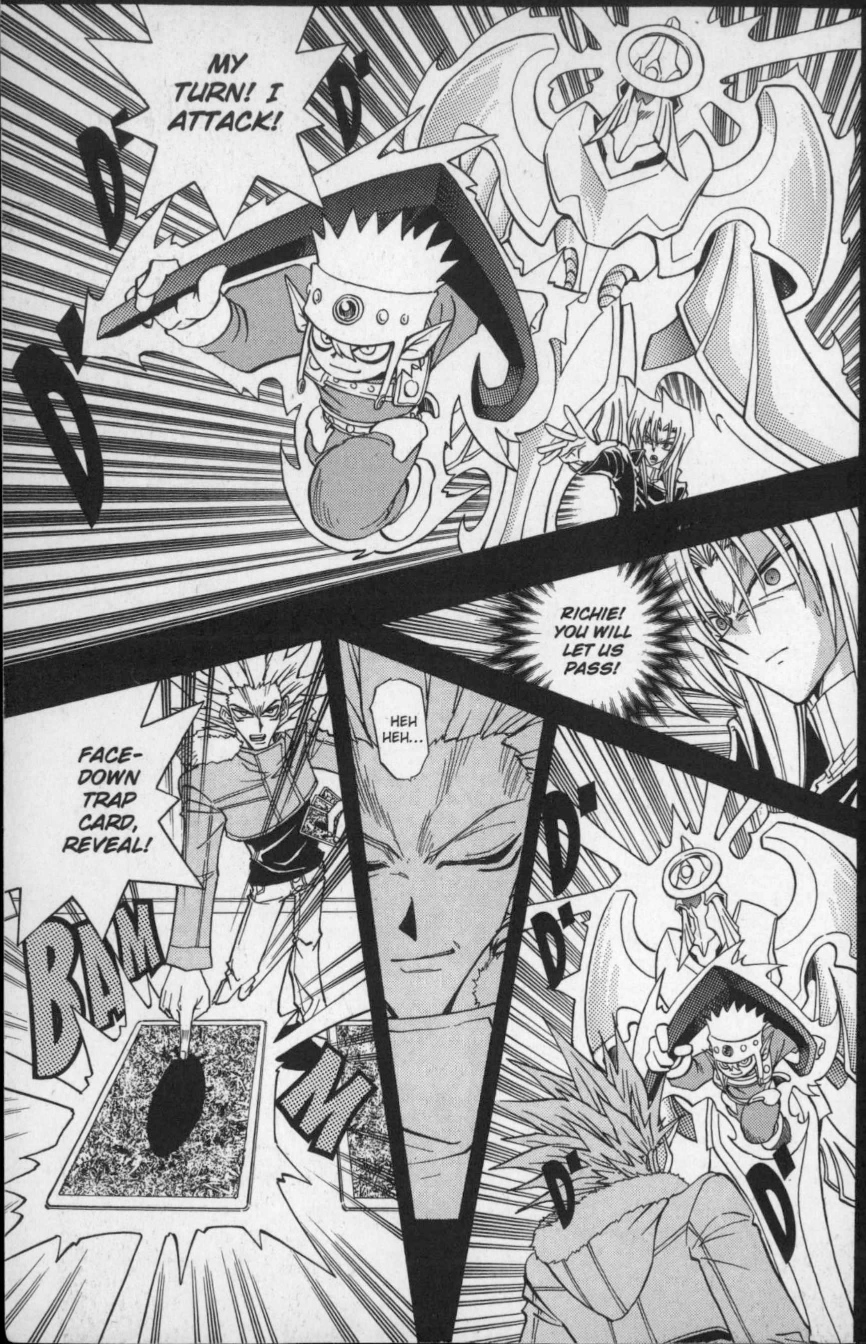
MY TURN! I ATTACK!
RICHIE! YOU WILL LET US PASS!
HEH HEH...
FACE-DOWN TRAP CARD, REVEAL!
BAM
M

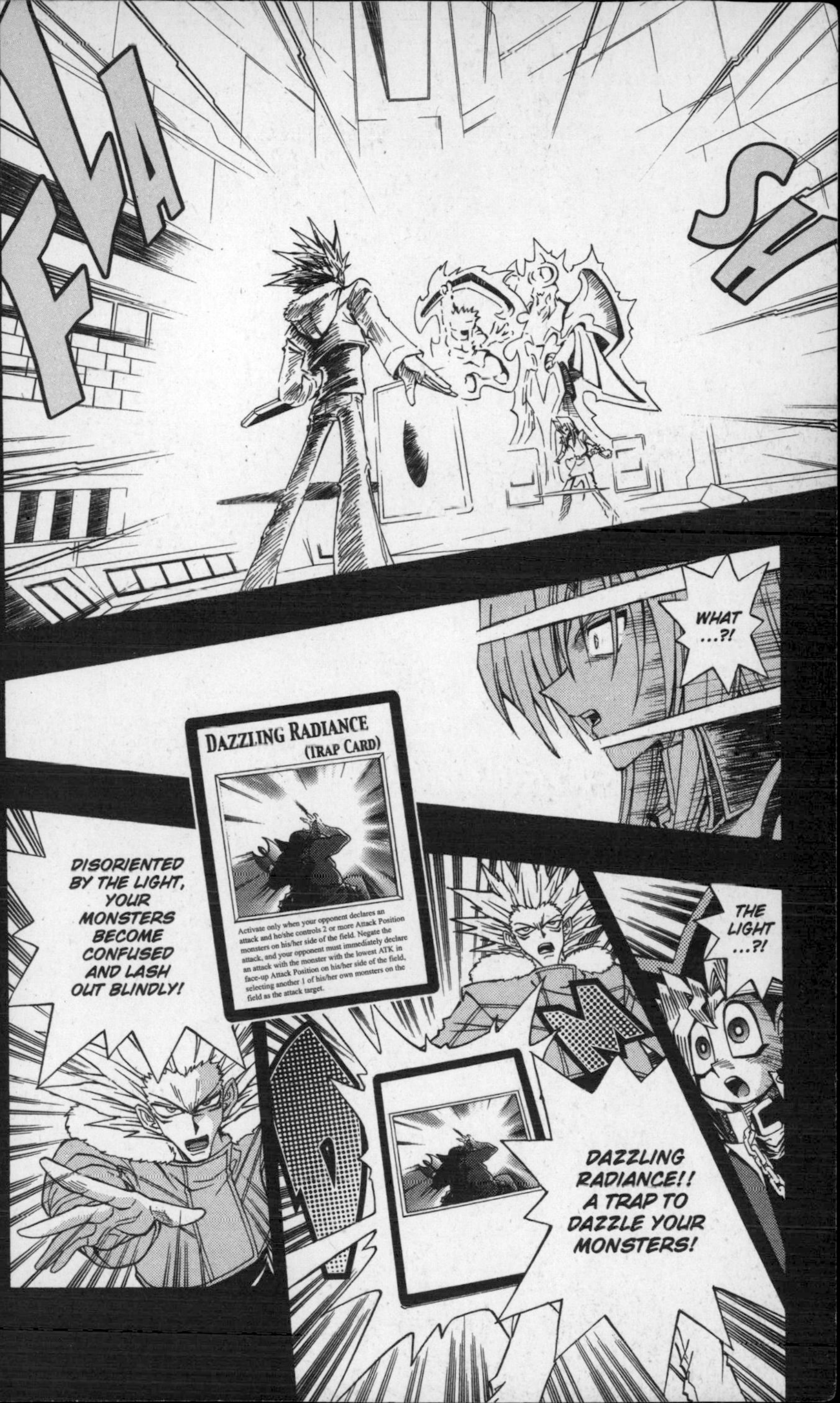
SH
FLA
WHAT ...?!
DAZZLING RADIANCE
(TRAP CARD)
Activate only when your opponent declares an attack and he/she controls 2 or more Attack Position monsters on his/her side of the field. Negate the attack, and your opponent must immediately declare an attack with the monster with the lowest ATK in face-up Attack Position on his/her side of the field, selecting another 1 of his/her own monsters on the field as the attack target.
THE LIGHT ...?!
DISORIENTED BY THE LIGHT, YOUR MONSTERS BECOME CONFUSED AND LASH OUT BLINDLY!
DAZZLING RADIANCE!! A TRAP TO DAZZLE YOUR MONSTERS!

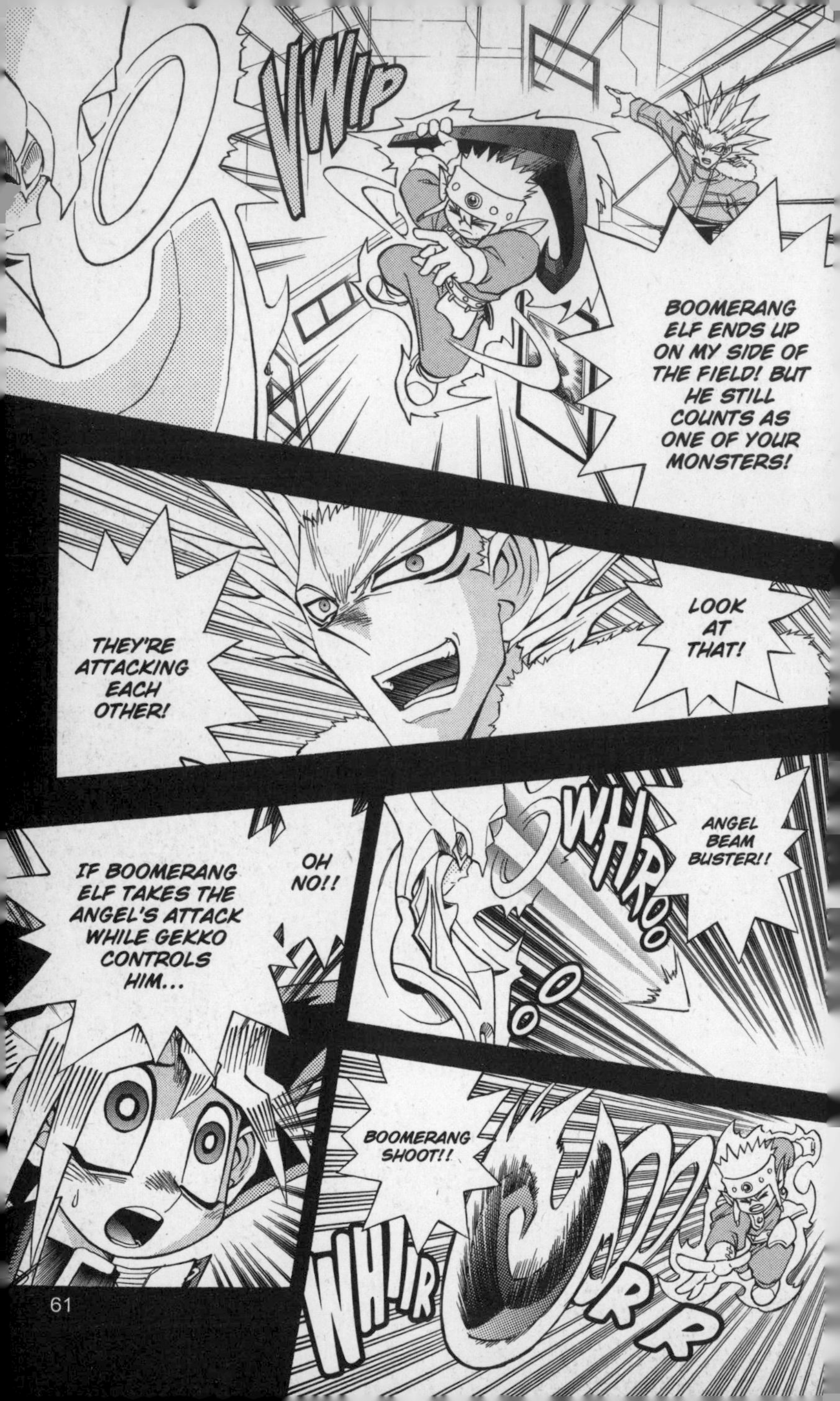
VWHIP
BOOMERANG ELF ENDS UP ON MY SIDE OF THE FIELD! BUT HE STILL COUNTS AS ONE OF YOUR MONSTERS!
LOOK AT THAT!
THEY'RE ATTACKING EACH OTHER!
ANGEL BEAM BUSTER!!
WHROOO
BOOMERANG SHOOT!!
WHIRRRR
OH NO!!
IF BOOMERANG ELF TAKES THE ANGEL'S ATTACK WHILE GEKKO CONTROLS HIM...

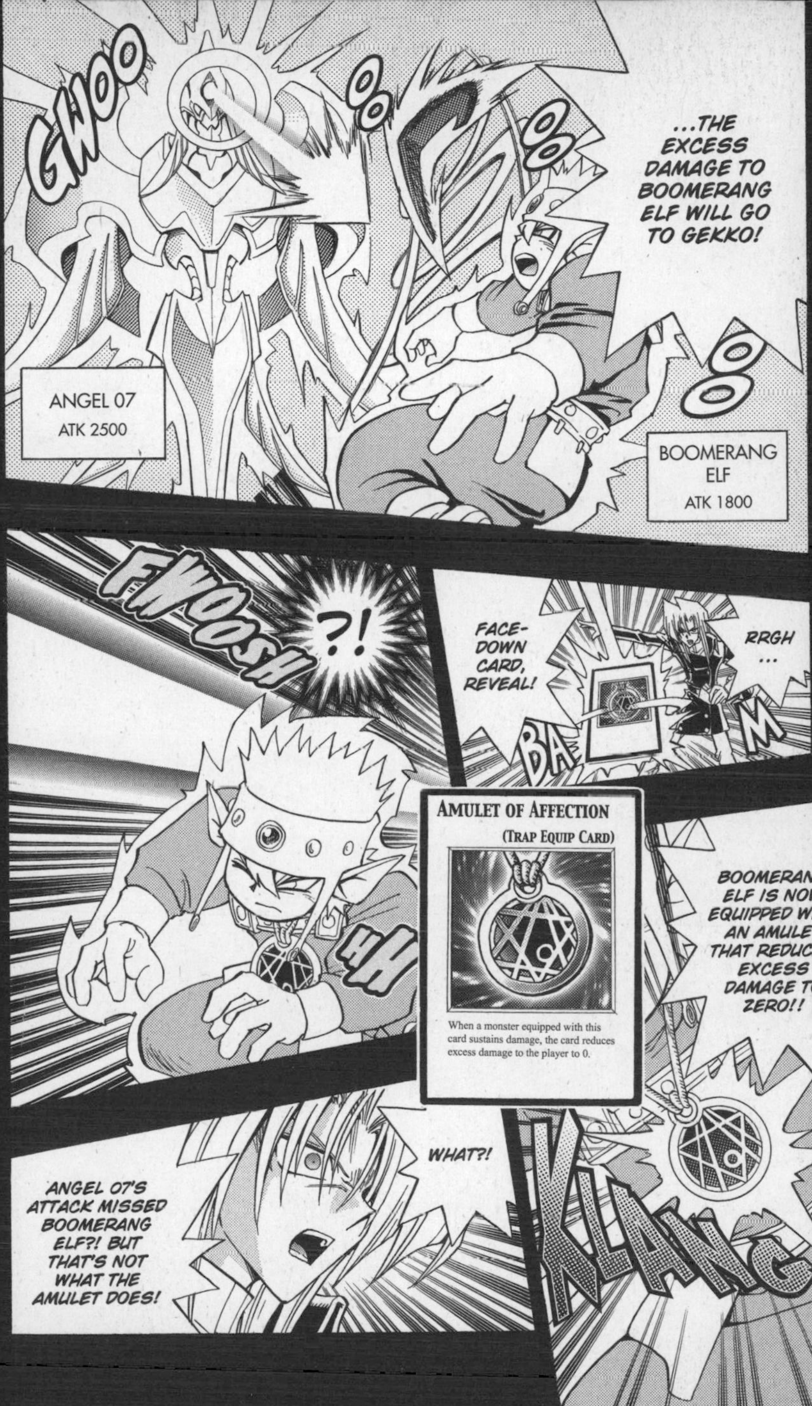
...THE EXCESS DAMAGE TO BOOMERANG ELF WILL GO TO GEKKO!
GWOO
BOOMERANG ELF
ATK 1800
ANGEL 07
ATK 2500
RRGH ...
FACE-DOWN CARD, REVEAL!
BAM
FWOOSH
?!
BOOMERANG ELF IS NOW EQUIPPED WITH AN AMULET THAT REDUCES EXCESS DAMAGE TO ZERO!!
AMULET OF AFFECTION
(TRAP EQUIP CARD)
When a monster equipped with this card sustains damage, the card reduces excess damage to the player to 0.
KLANG
WHAT?!
ANGEL 07'S ATTACK MISSED BOOMERANG ELF?! BUT THAT'S NOT WHAT THE AMULET DOES!

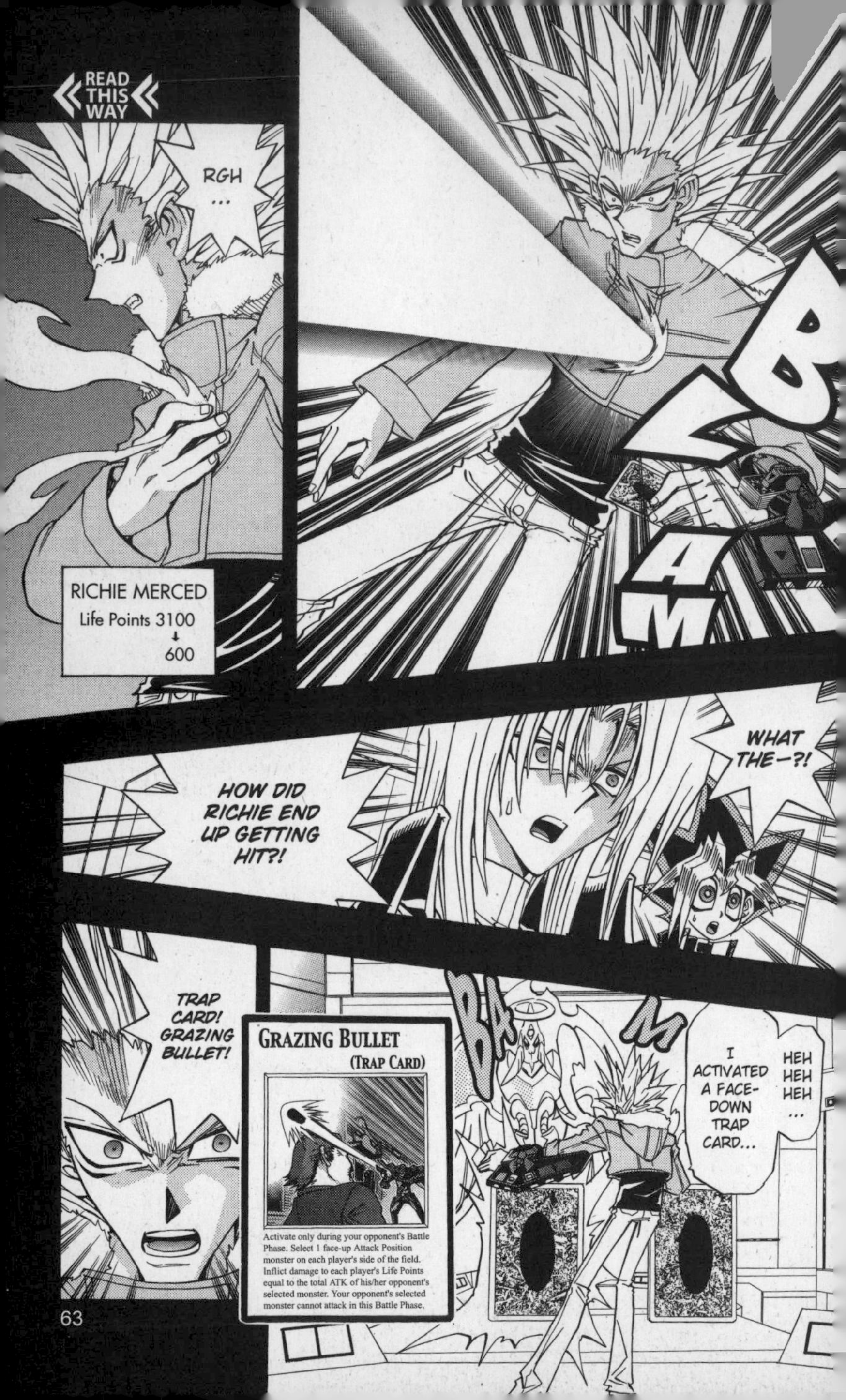
READ THIS WAY
BAM
RGH ...
RICHIE MERCED
Life Points 3100 ↓ 600
WHAT THE—?!
HOW DID RICHIE END UP GETTING HIT?!
BAM
HEH HEH HEH ...
I ACTIVATED A FACE-DOWN TRAP CARD...
TRAP CARD! GRAZING BULLET!
GRAZING BULLET
(TRAP CARD)
Activate only during your opponent's Battle Phase. Select 1 face-up Attack Position monster on each player's side of the field. Inflict damage to each player's Life Points equal to the total ATK of his/her opponent's selected monster. Your opponent's selected monster cannot attack in this Battle Phase.

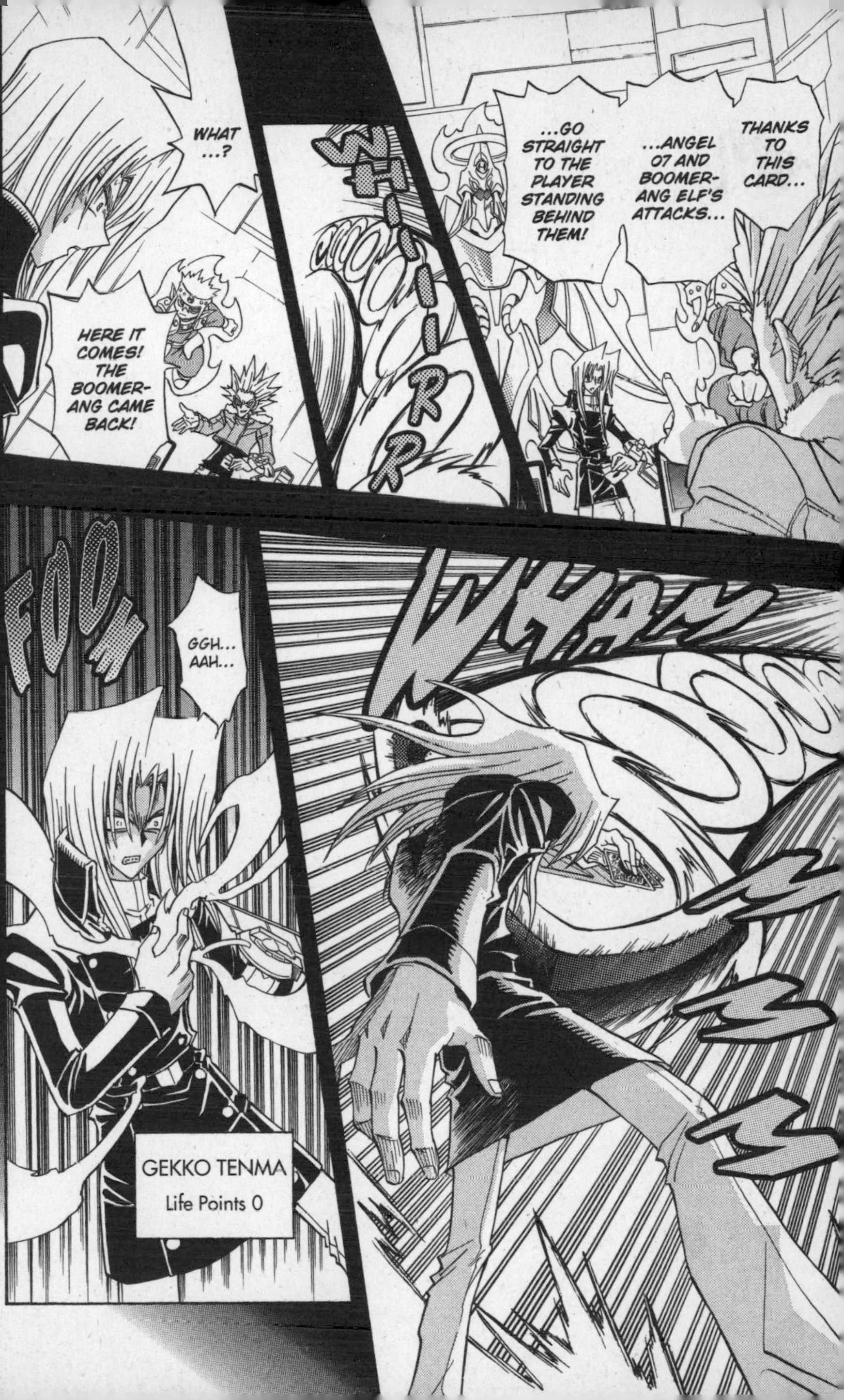
THANKS TO THIS CARD...
...ANGEL 07 AND BOOMER-ANG ELF'S ATTACKS...
...GO STRAIGHT TO THE PLAYER STANDING BEHIND THEM!
WHIRR
WHAT ...?
HERE IT COMES! THE BOOMER-ANG CAME BACK!
WHAM
FOOM
GGH... AAH...
GEKKO TENMA
Life Points 0

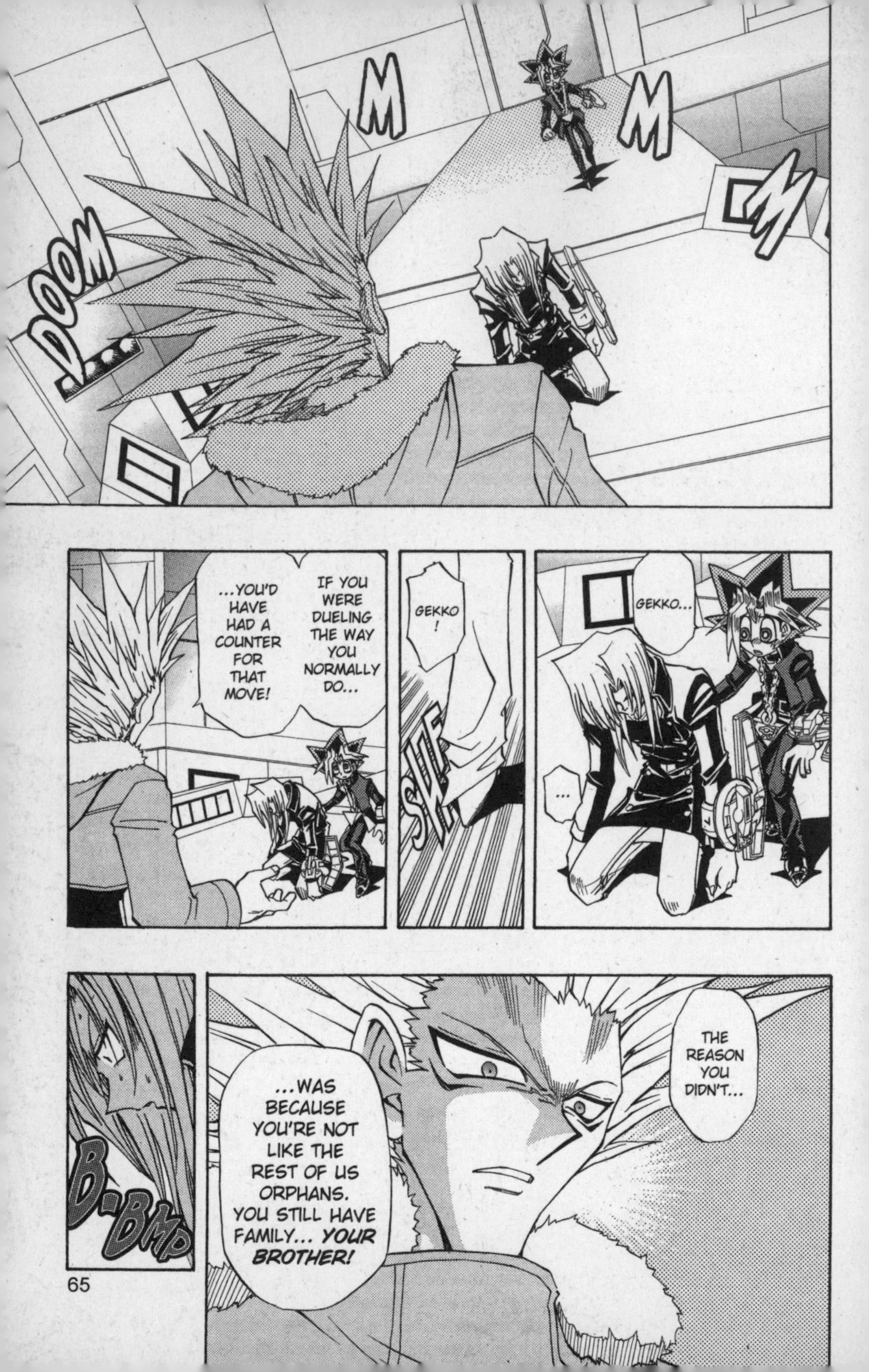
M M M
DOOM...
GEKKO...
...
GEKKO!
IF YOU WERE DUELING THE WAY YOU NORMALLY DO...
...YOU'D HAVE HAD A COUNTER FOR THAT MOVE!
THE REASON YOU DIDN'T...
...WAS BECAUSE YOU'RE NOT LIKE THE REST OF US ORPHANS. YOU STILL HAVE FAMILY... ***YOUR BROTHER!***
B-BMP

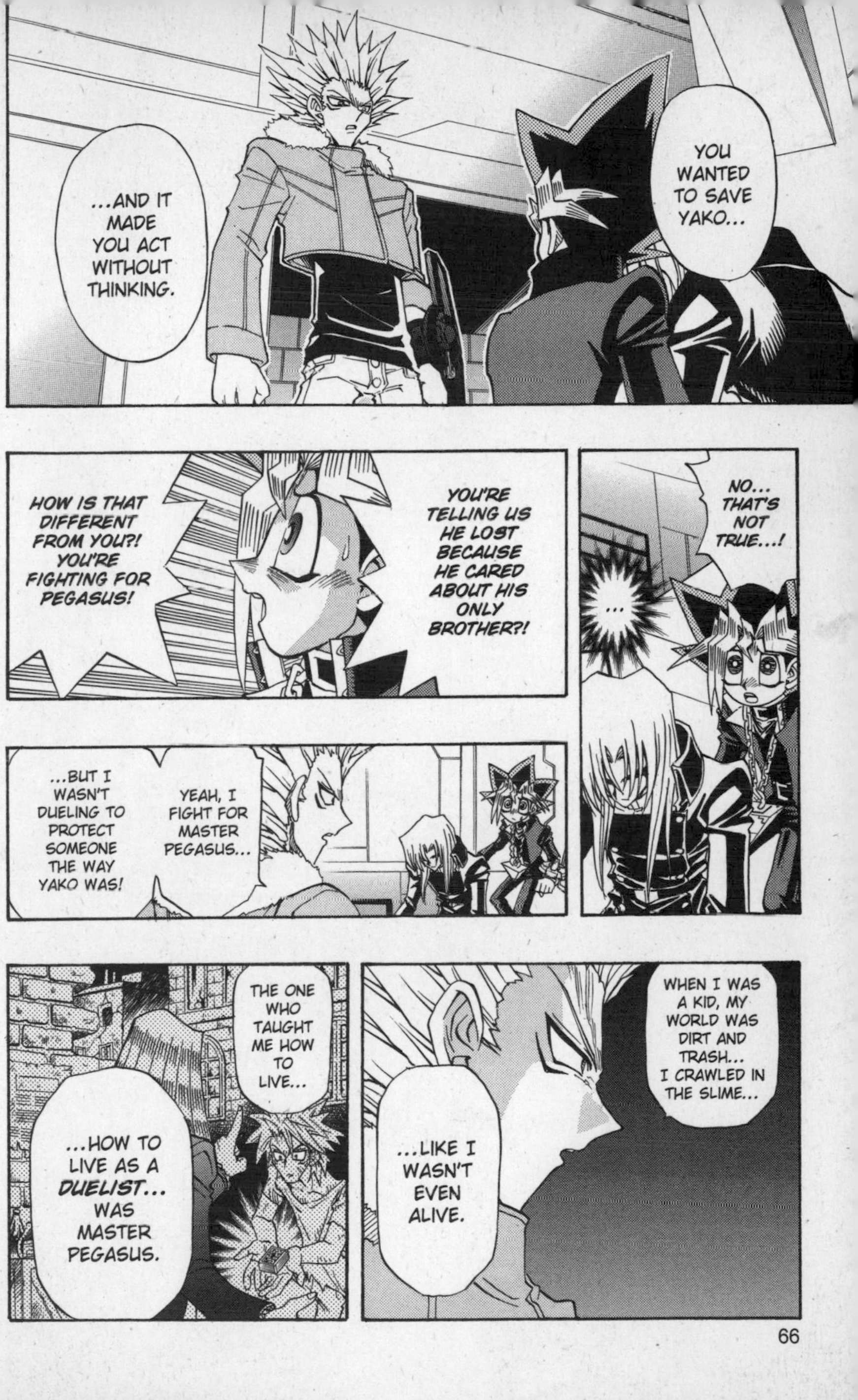
YOU WANTED TO SAVE YAKO...
...AND IT MADE YOU ACT WITHOUT THINKING.
NO... THAT'S NOT TRUE...!
...
YOU'RE TELLING US HE LOST BECAUSE HE CARED ABOUT HIS ONLY BROTHER?!
HOW IS THAT DIFFERENT FROM YOU?! YOU'RE FIGHTING FOR PEGASUS!
YEAH, I FIGHT FOR MASTER PEGASUS...
...BUT I WASN'T DUELING TO PROTECT SOMEONE THE WAY YAKO WAS!
WHEN I WAS A KID, MY WORLD WAS DIRT AND TRASH... I CRAWLED IN THE SLIME...
...LIKE I WASN'T EVEN ALIVE.
THE ONE WHO TAUGHT ME HOW TO LIVE...
...HOW TO LIVE AS A DUELIST... WAS MASTER PEGASUS.

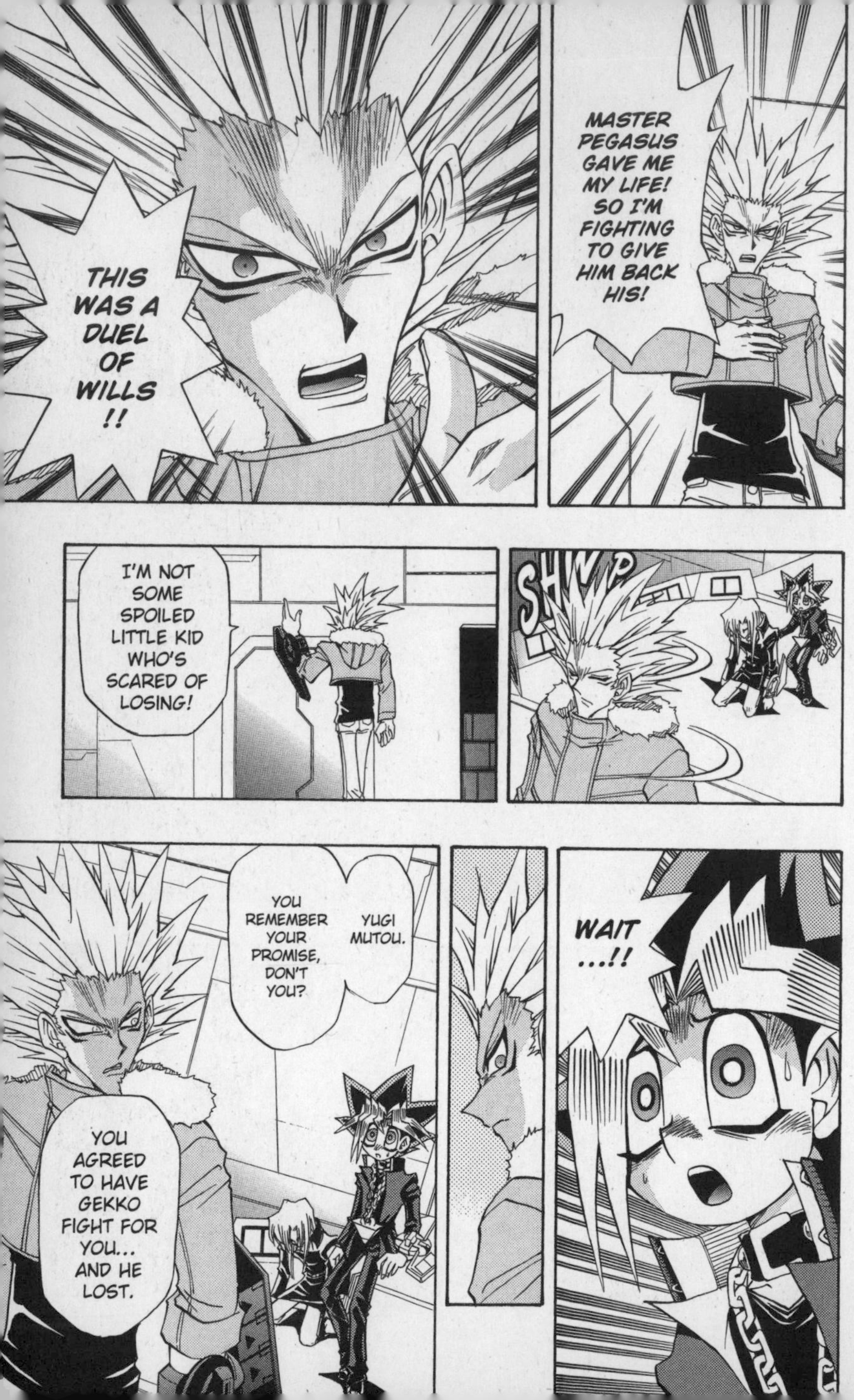
MASTER PEGASUS GAVE ME MY LIFE! SO I'M FIGHTING TO GIVE HIM BACK HIS!
THIS WAS A DUEL OF WILLS !!
I'M NOT SOME SPOILED LITTLE KID WHO'S SCARED OF LOSING!
WAIT ...!!
YUGI MUTOU.
YOU REMEMBER YOUR PROMISE, DON'T YOU?
YOU AGREED TO HAVE GEKKO FIGHT FOR YOU... AND HE LOST.

THIS IS AS FAR AS YOU GO.

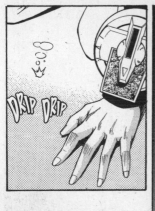

DRIP DRIP

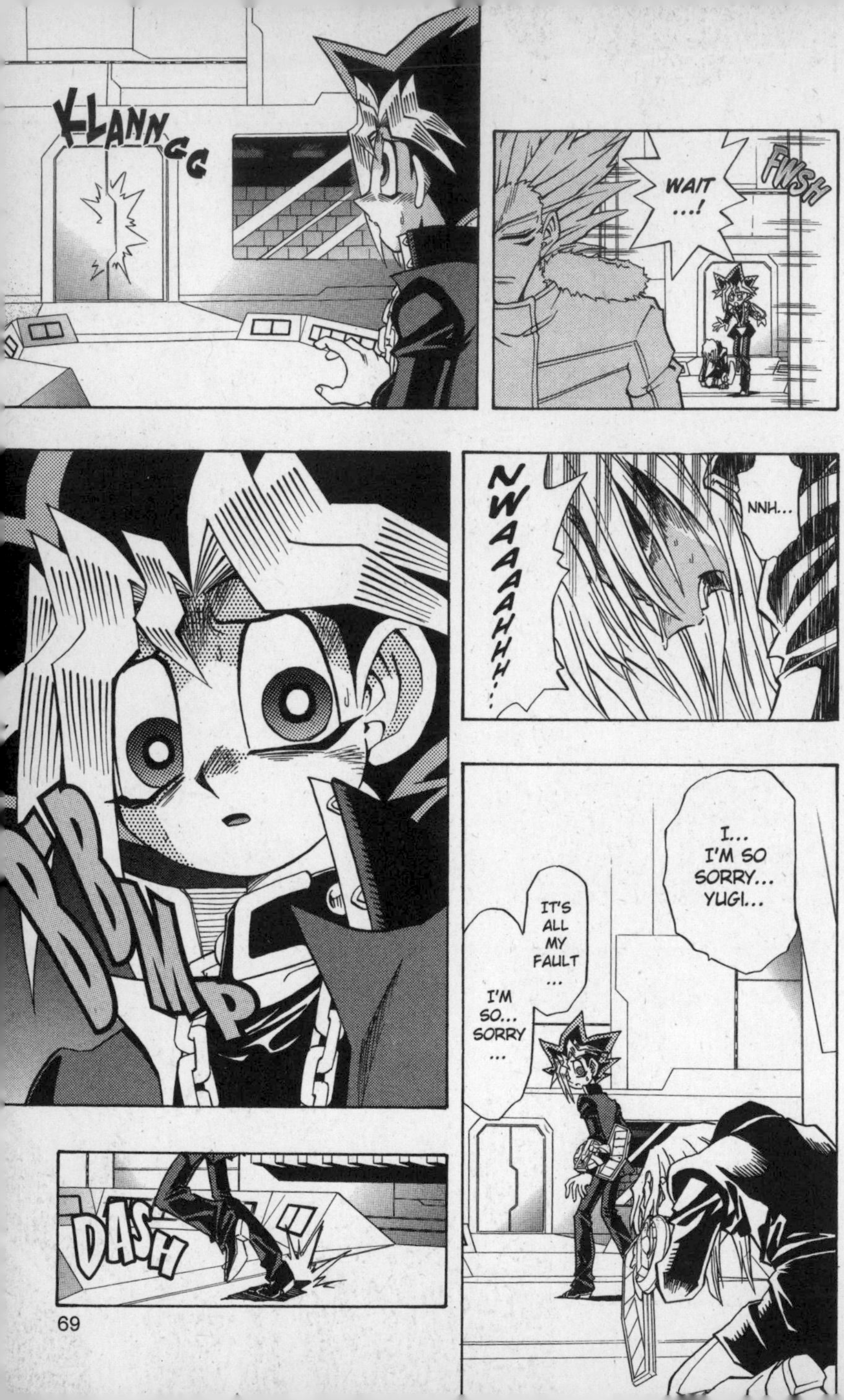
WAIT ...!
FWSH
KLANNGG
NWAAAAHHH..
NNH...
I... I'M SO SORRY... YUGI...
IT'S ALL MY FAULT ...
I'M SO... SORRY ...
BBUMP
DASH

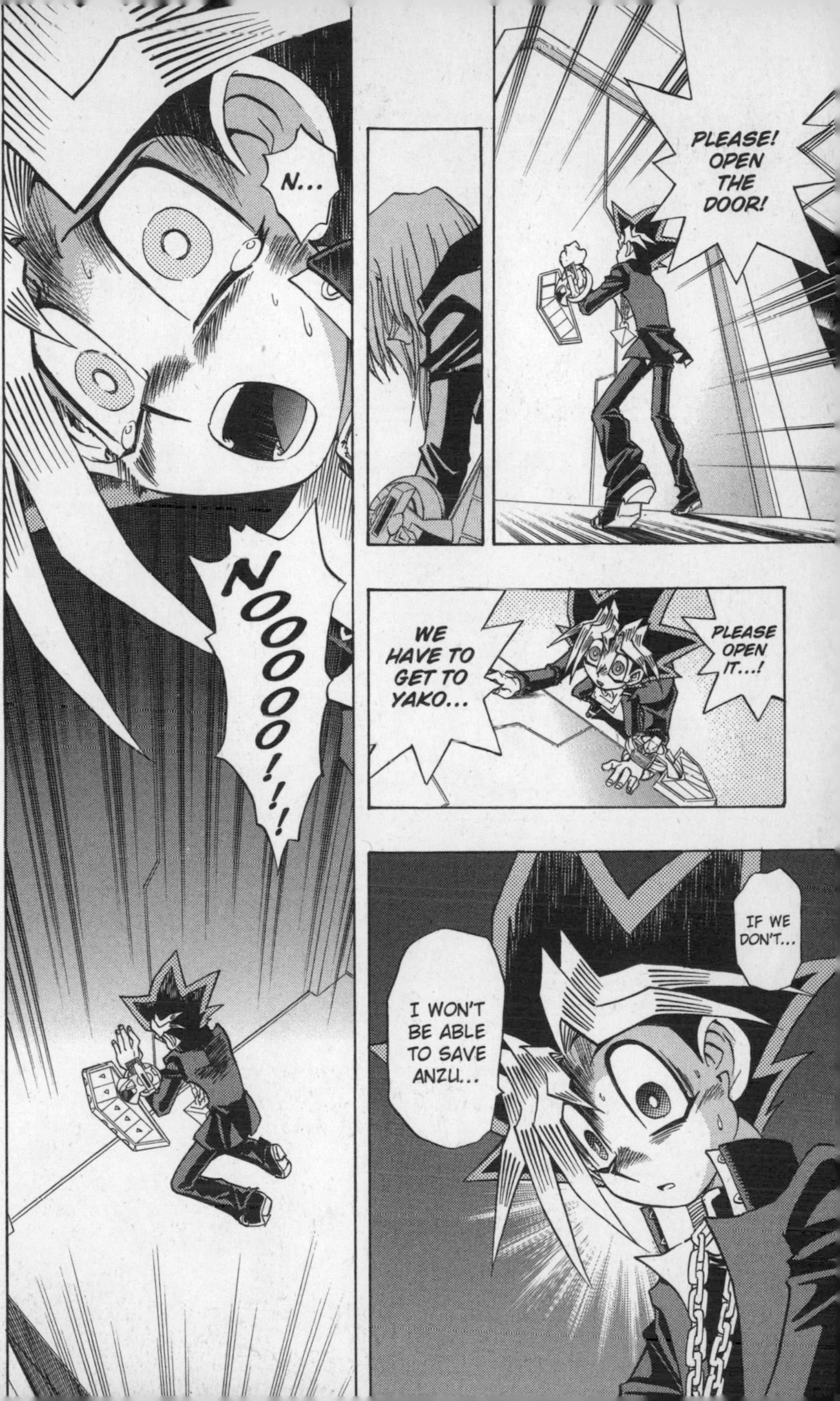
PLEASE! OPEN THE DOOR!
PLEASE OPEN IT...!
WE HAVE TO GET TO YAKO...
IF WE DON'T...
I WON'T BE ABLE TO SAVE ANZU...
N...
NOOOOOO!!!

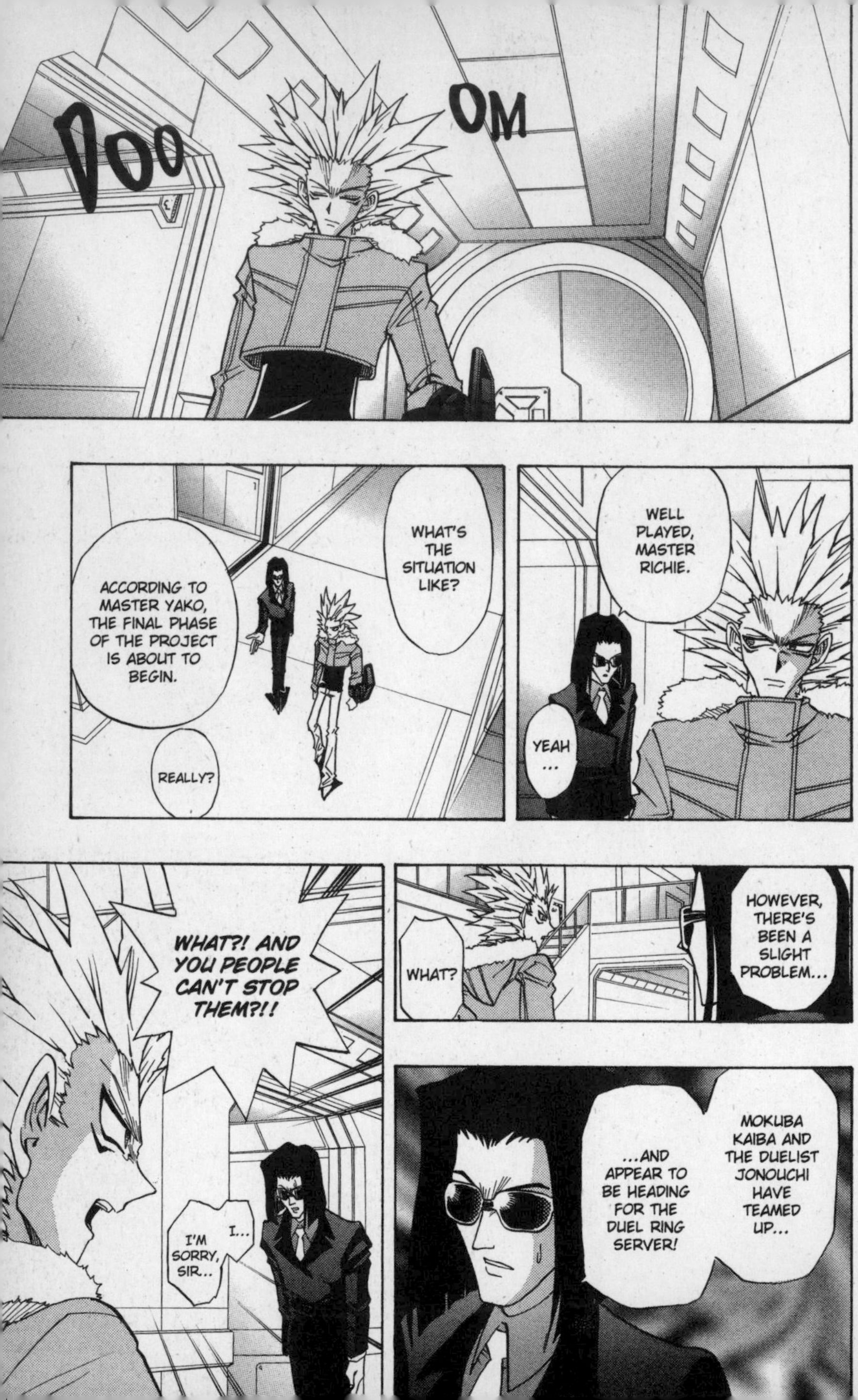
DOOOM
WELL PLAYED, MASTER RICHIE.
YEAH...
WHAT'S THE SITUATION LIKE?
ACCORDING TO MASTER YAKO, THE FINAL PHASE OF THE PROJECT IS ABOUT TO BEGIN.
REALLY?
HOWEVER, THERE'S BEEN A SLIGHT PROBLEM...
WHAT?
MOKUBA KAIBA AND THE DUELIST JONOUCHI HAVE TEAMED UP...
...AND APPEAR TO BE HEADING FOR THE DUEL RING SERVER!
WHAT?! AND YOU PEOPLE CAN'T STOP THEM?!!
I...
I'M SORRY, SIR...

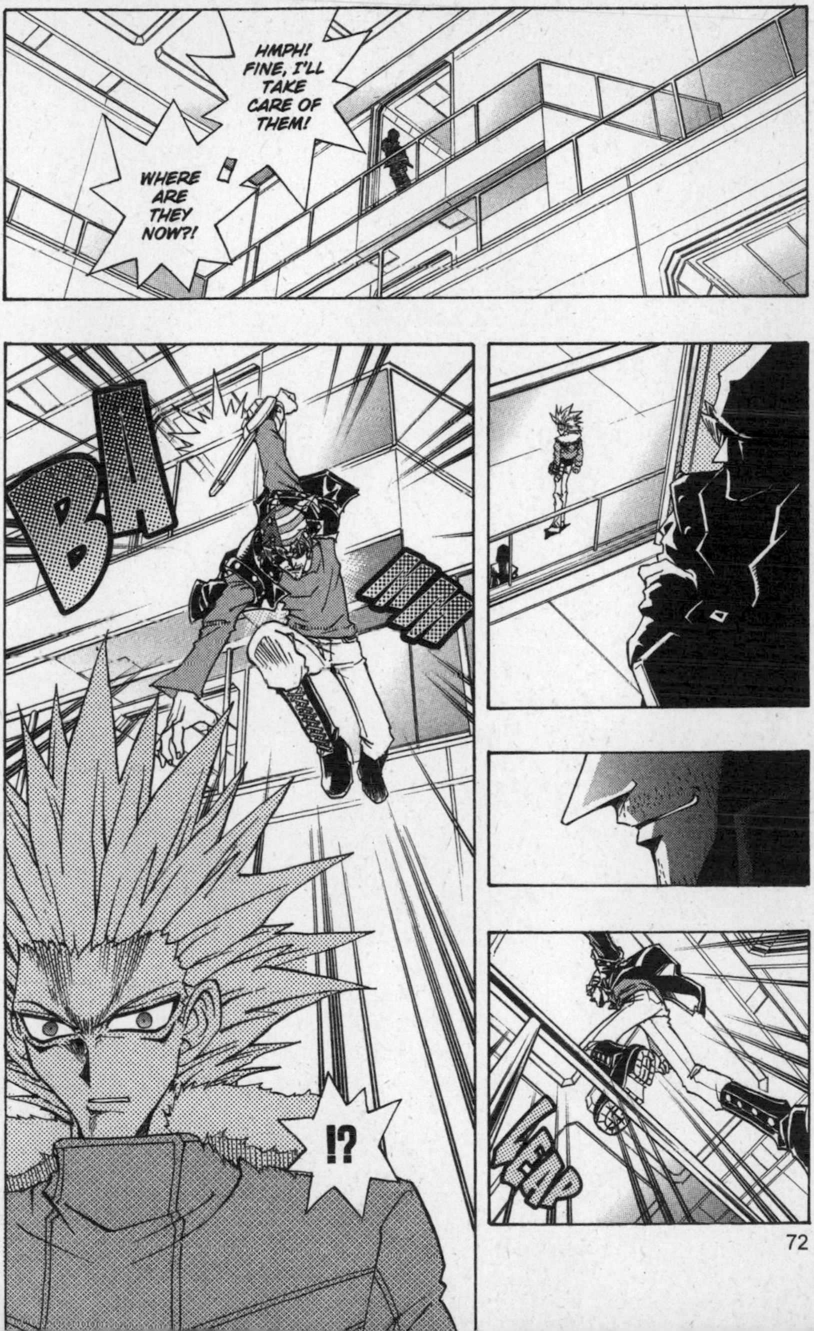
HMPH! FINE, I'LL TAKE CARE OF THEM!
WHERE ARE THEY NOW?!
LEAP
BA
!?

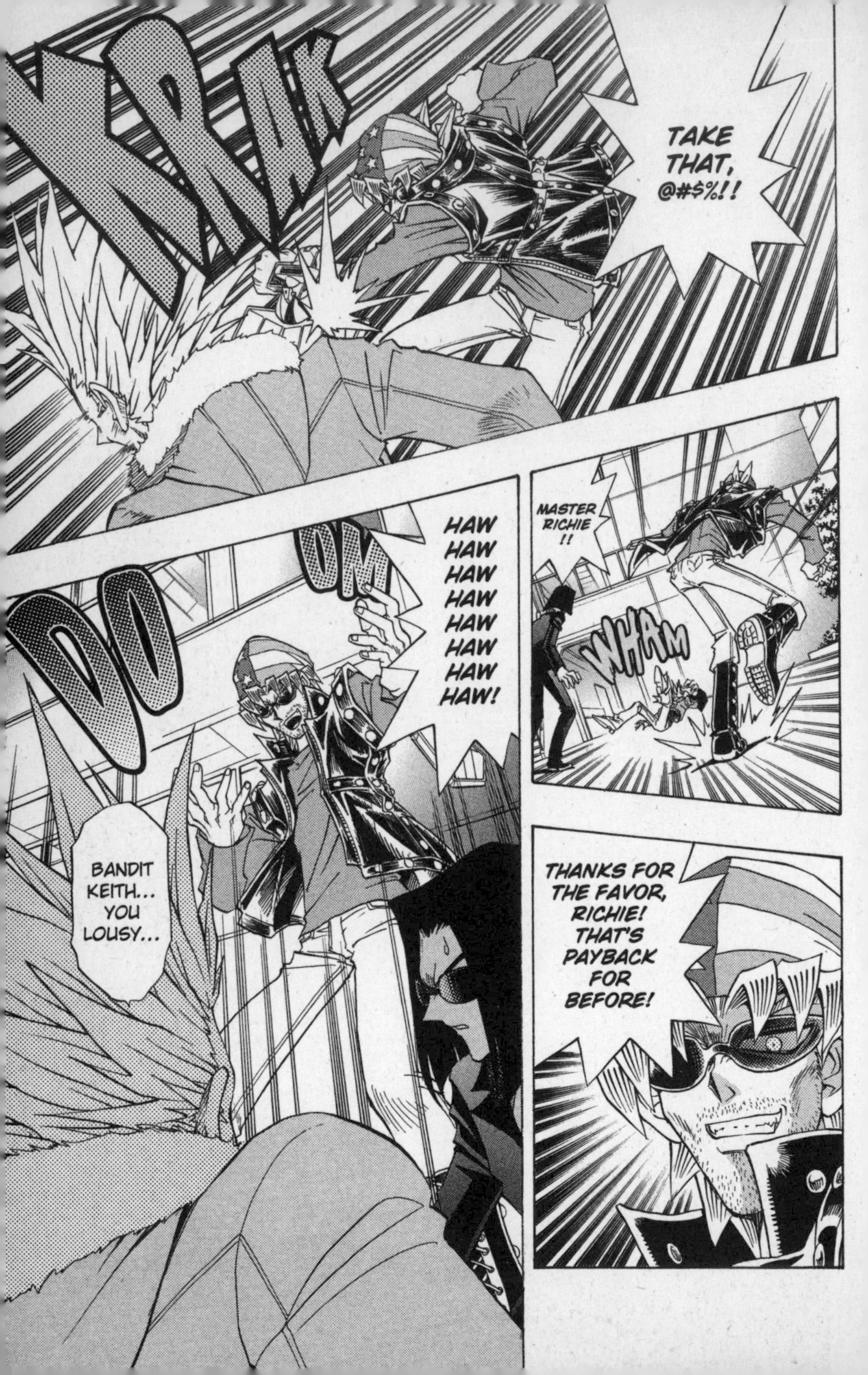
KRAK
TAKE THAT, @#$%!!
MASTER RICHIE!!
WHAM
THANKS FOR THE FAVOR, RICHIE! THAT'S PAYBACK FOR BEFORE!
DOOM
HAW HAW HAW HAW HAW HAW HAW HAW!
BANDIT KEITH... YOU LOUSY...

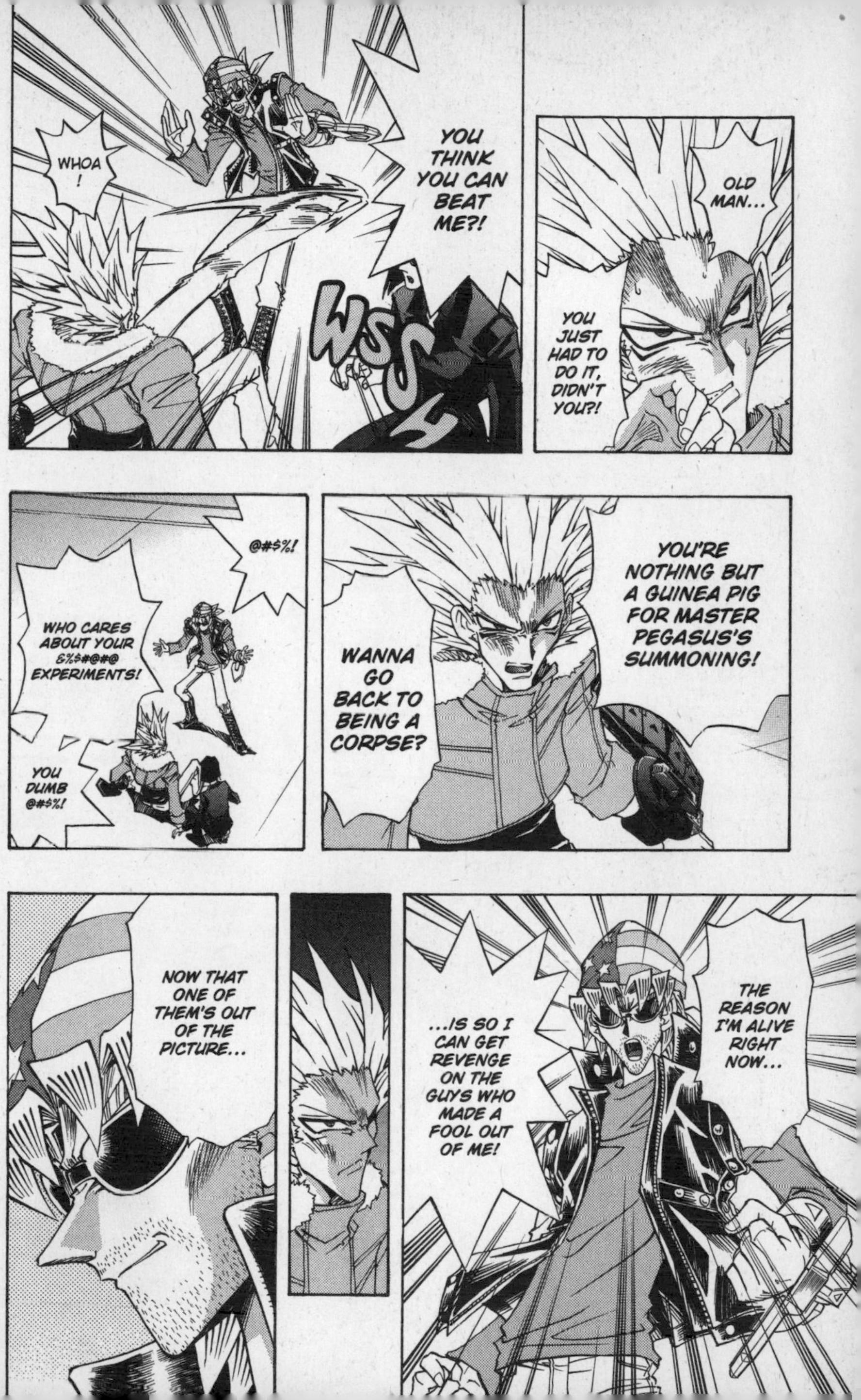
OLD MAN...
YOU JUST HAD TO DO IT, DIDN'T YOU?!
YOU THINK YOU CAN BEAT ME?!
WSSH
WHOA!
YOU'RE NOTHING BUT A GUINEA PIG FOR MASTER PEGASUS'S SUMMONING!
WANNA GO BACK TO BEING A CORPSE?
@#$%!
WHO CARES ABOUT YOUR &%$#@#@ EXPERIMENTS!
YOU DUMB @#$%!
THE REASON I'M ALIVE RIGHT NOW...
...IS SO I CAN GET REVENGE ON THE GUYS WHO MADE A FOOL OUT OF ME!
NOW THAT ONE OF THEM'S OUT OF THE PICTURE...

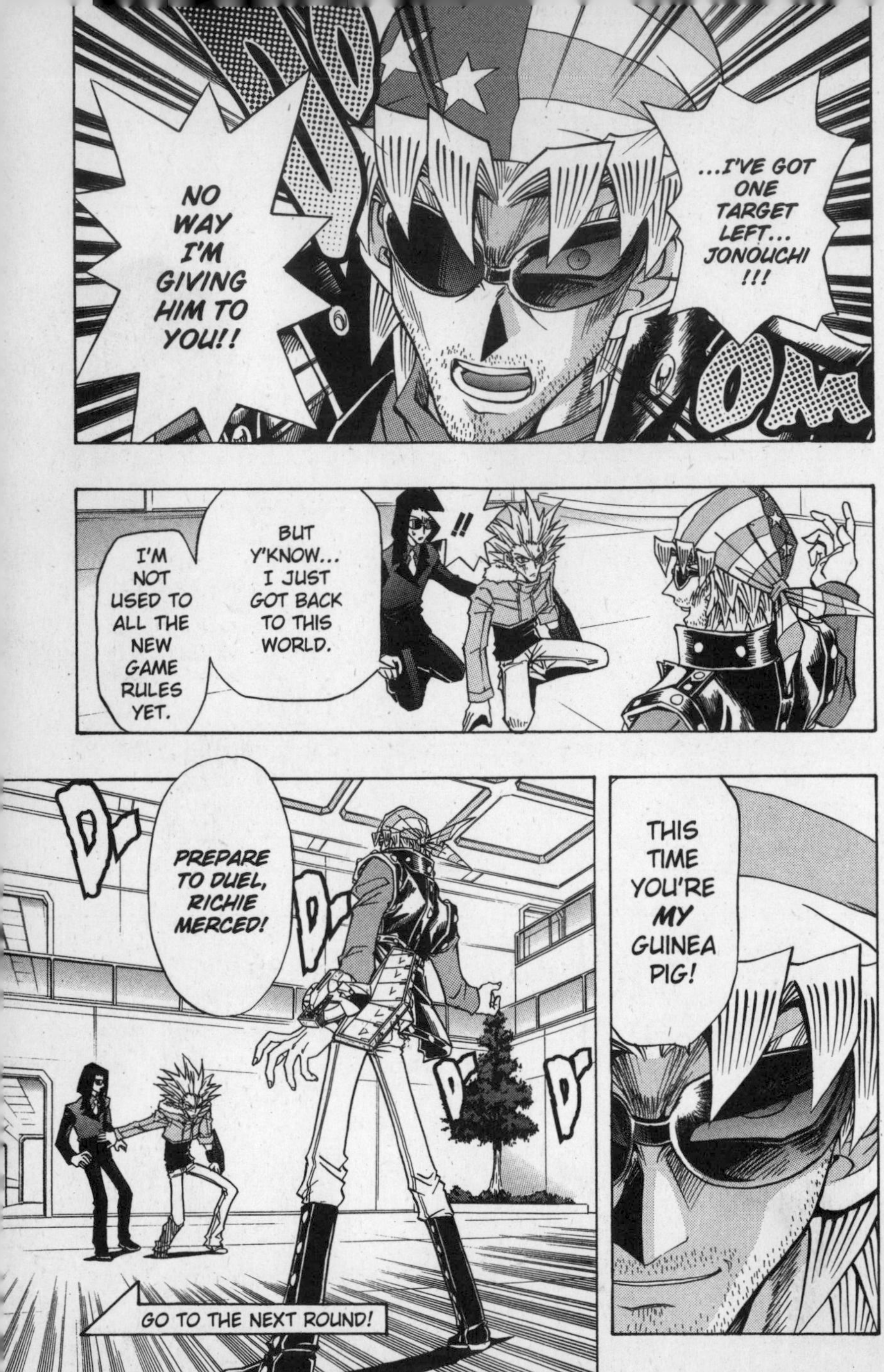
...I'VE GOT ONE TARGET LEFT... JONOUCHI!!!
NO WAY I'M GIVING HIM TO YOU!!
!!
BUT Y'KNOW... I JUST GOT BACK TO THIS WORLD.
I'M NOT USED TO ALL THE NEW GAME RULES YET.
THIS TIME YOU'RE *MY* GUINEA PIG!
PREPARE TO DUEL, RICHIE MERCED!
GO TO THE NEXT ROUND!

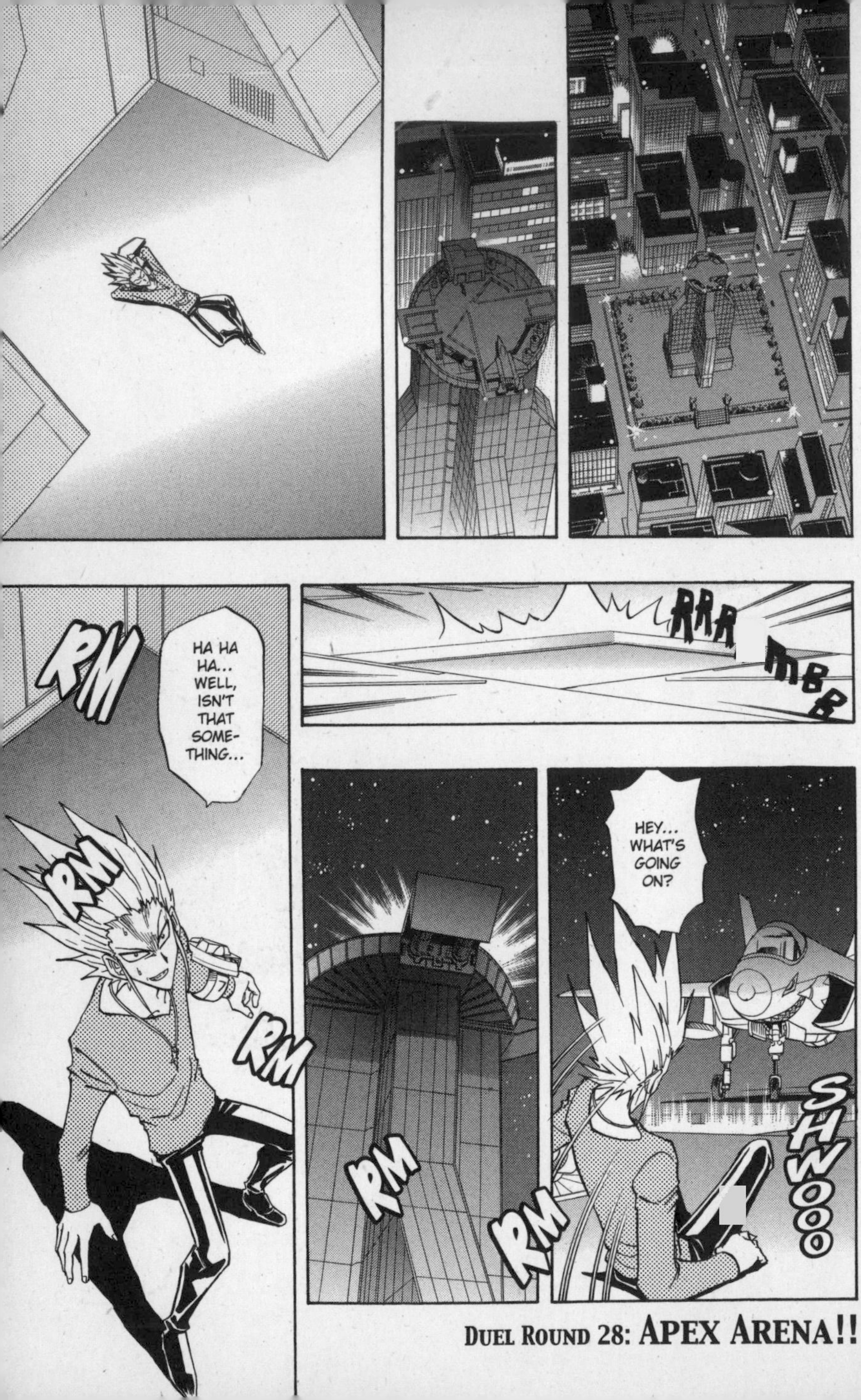
RRR
MBB
HEY... WHAT'S GOING ON?
SHWOOO
RM
RM
RM
HA HA HA... WELL, ISN'T THAT SOME-THING...
RM
RM

Duel Round 28: Apex Arena!!

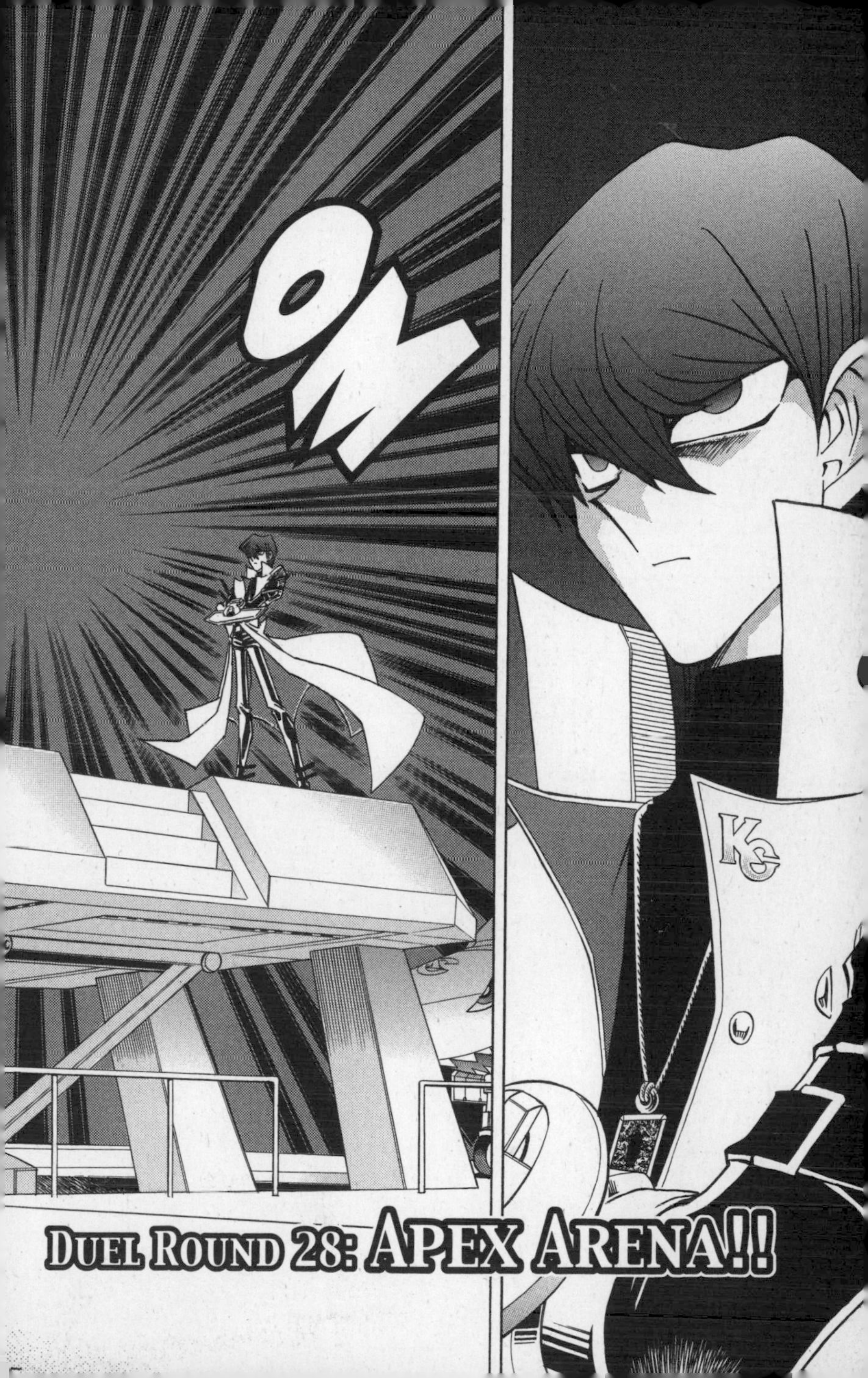
DUEL ROUND 28: APEX ARENA!!

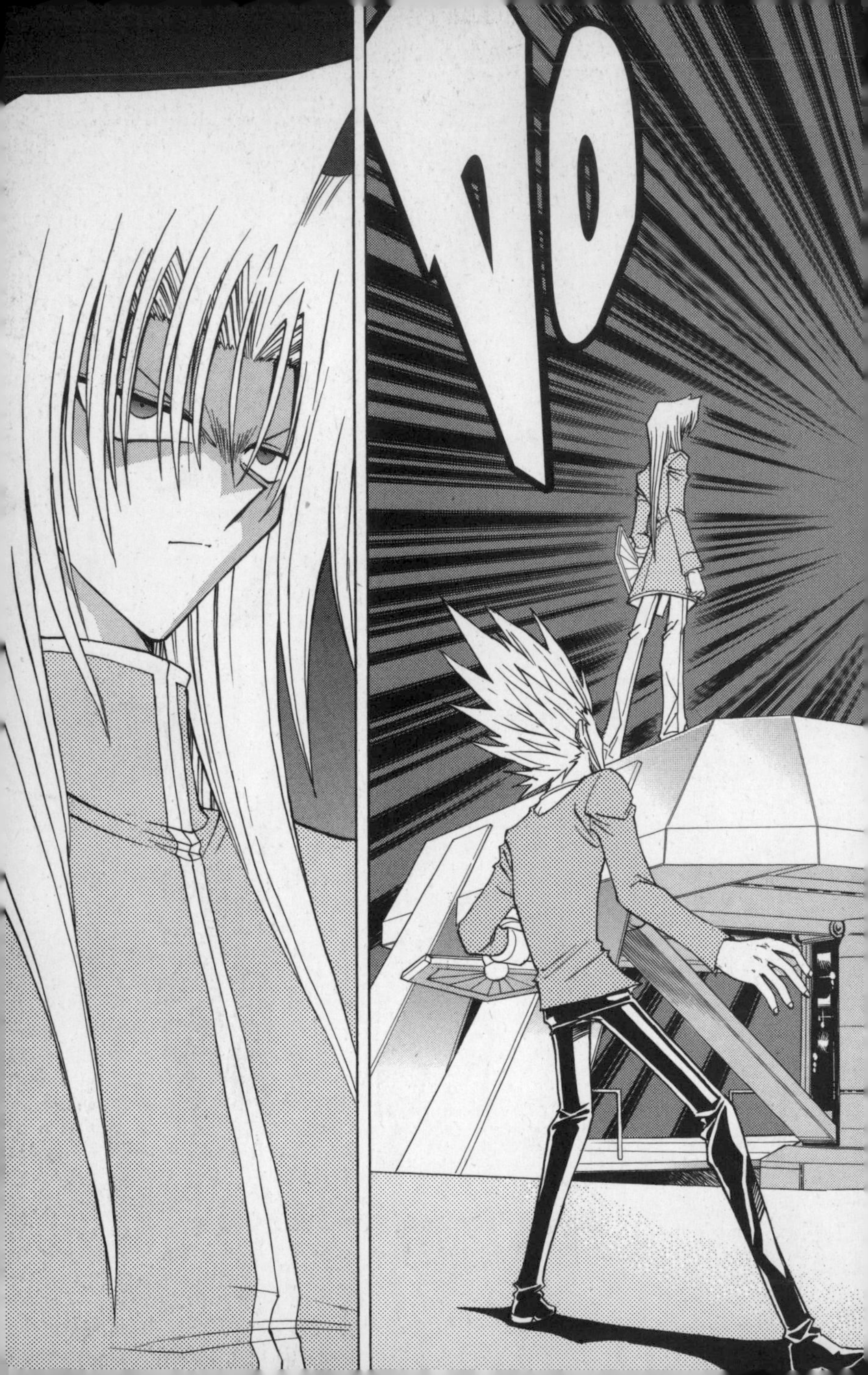

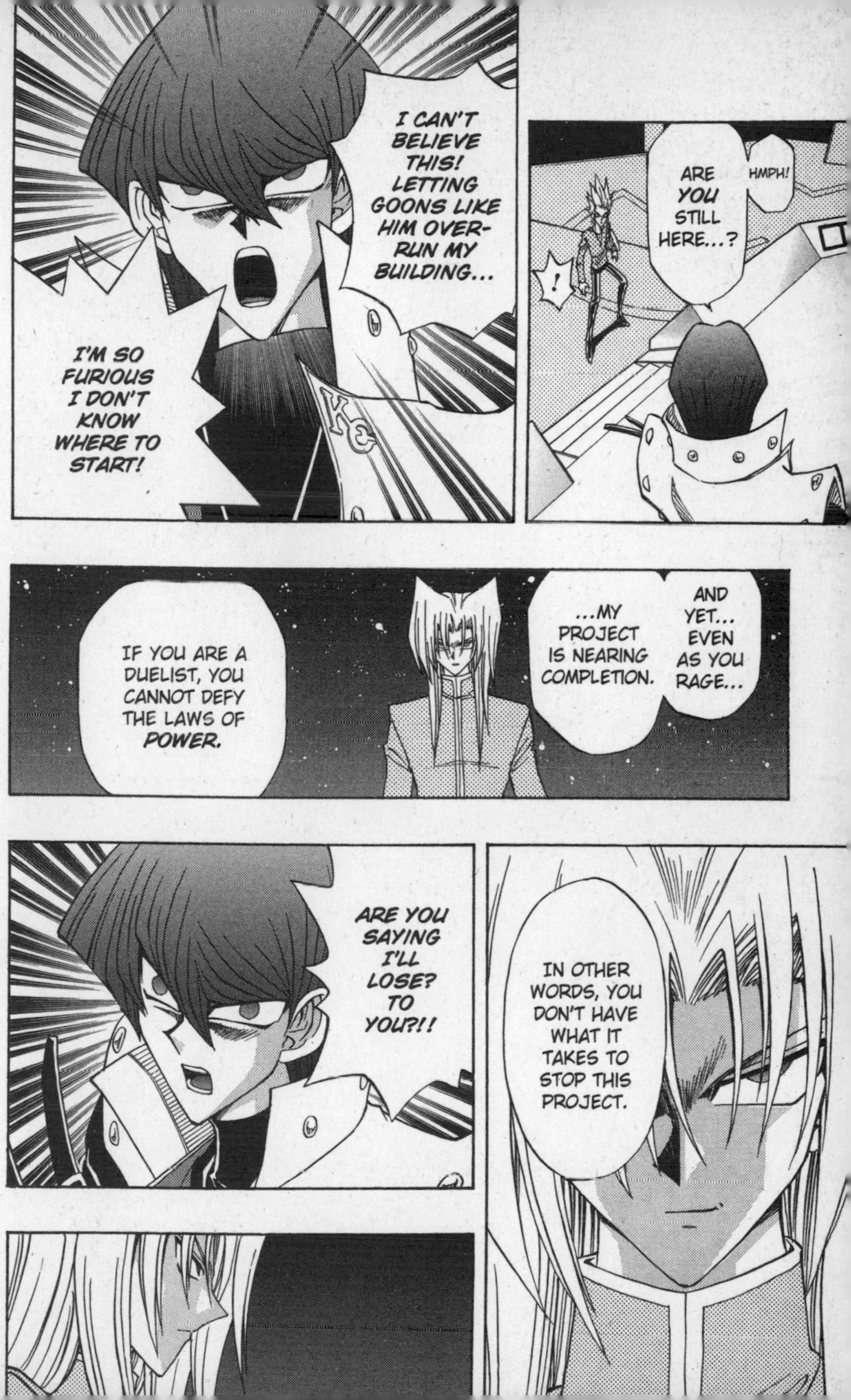
HMPH!
ARE YOU STILL HERE...?
!
I CAN'T BELIEVE THIS! LETTING GOONS LIKE HIM OVER-RUN MY BUILDING...
I'M SO FURIOUS I DON'T KNOW WHERE TO START!
AND YET... EVEN AS YOU RAGE...
...MY PROJECT IS NEARING COMPLETION.
IF YOU ARE A DUELIST, YOU CANNOT DEFY THE LAWS OF POWER.
IN OTHER WORDS, YOU DON'T HAVE WHAT IT TAKES TO STOP THIS PROJECT.
ARE YOU SAYING I'LL LOSE? TO YOU?!!

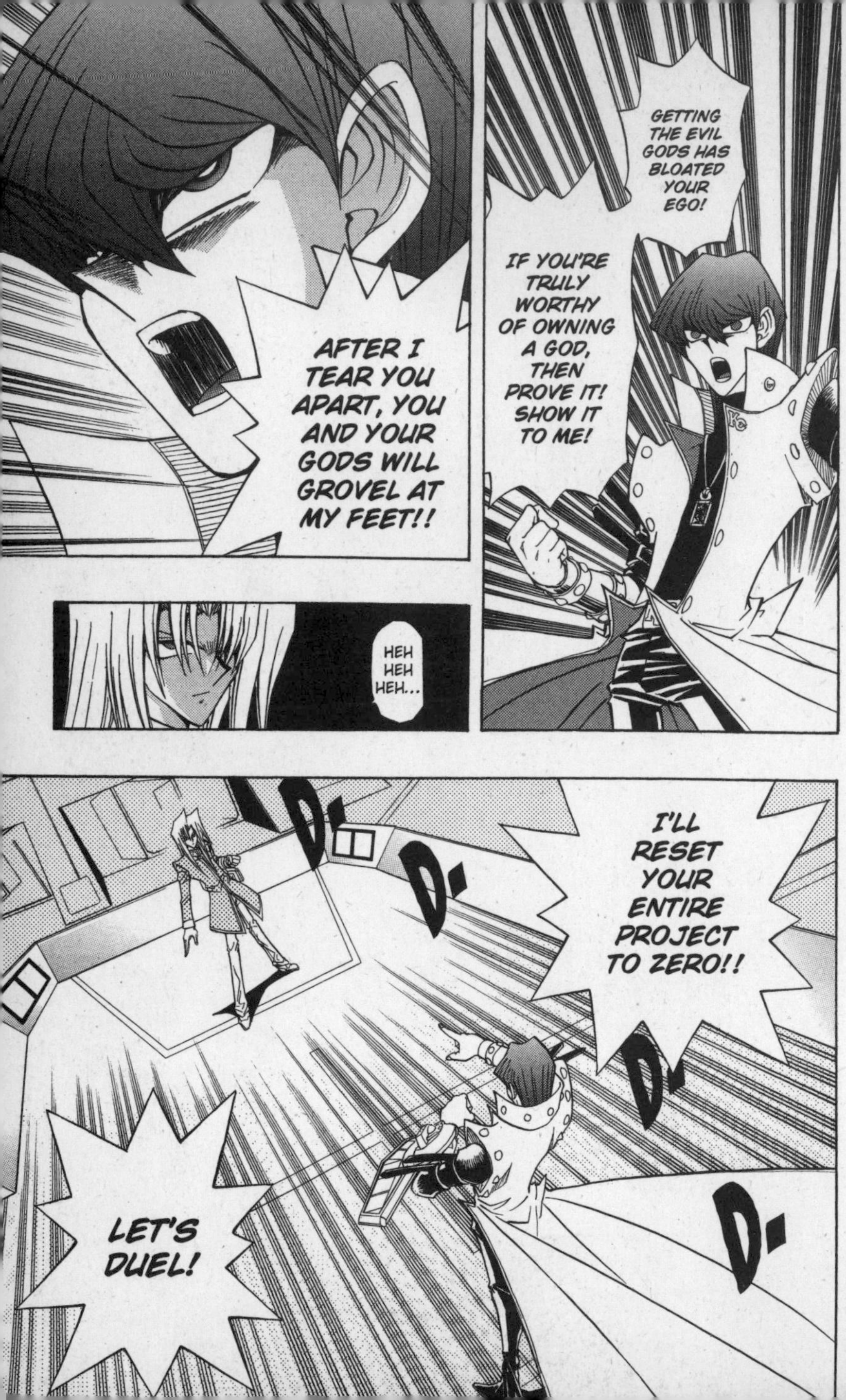
GETTING THE EVIL GODS HAS BLOATED YOUR EGO!
IF YOU'RE TRULY WORTHY OF OWNING A GOD, THEN PROVE IT! SHOW IT TO ME!
AFTER I TEAR YOU APART, YOU AND YOUR GODS WILL GROVEL AT MY FEET!!
HEH HEH HEH...
I'LL RESET YOUR ENTIRE PROJECT TO ZERO!!
LET'S DUEL!

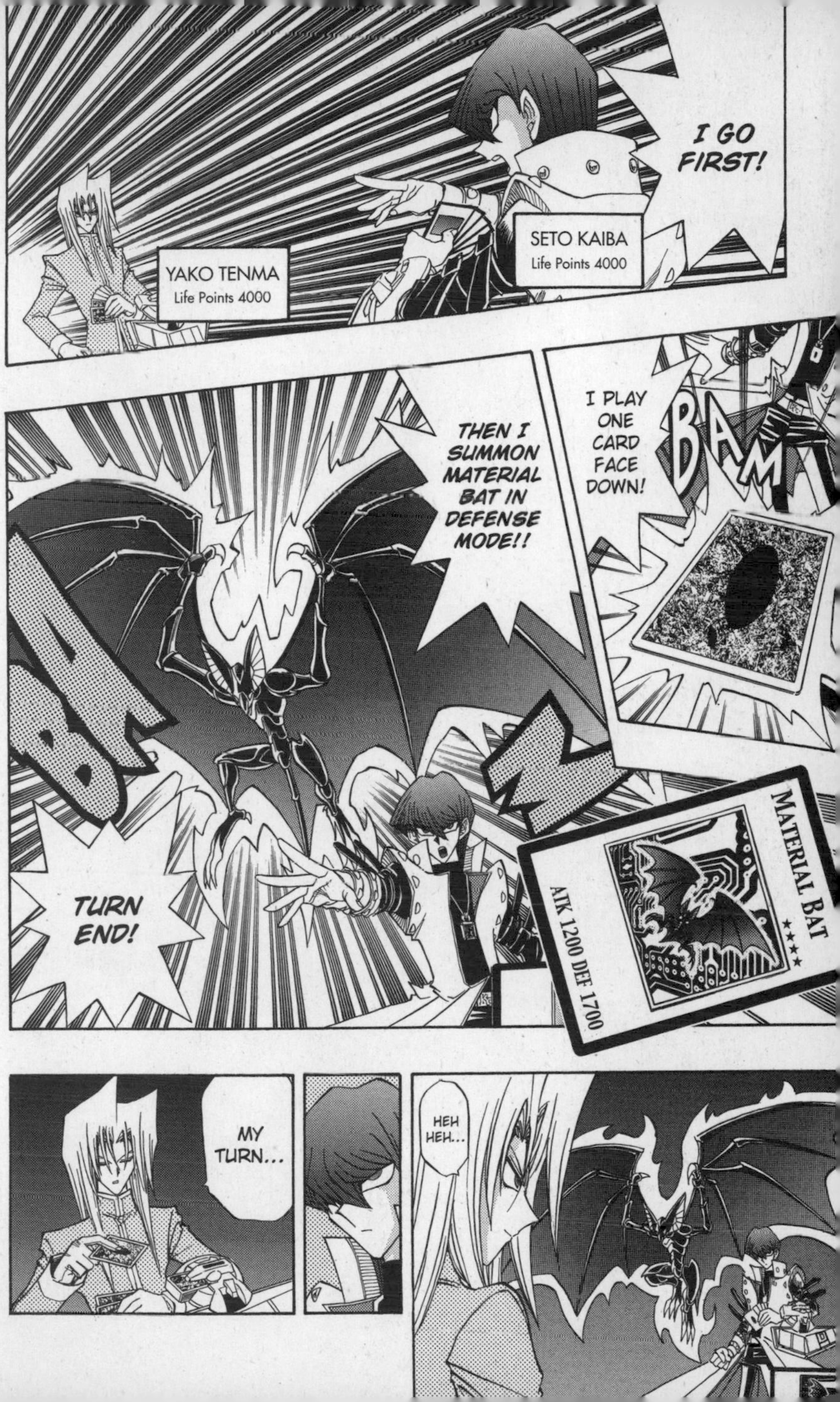
I GO FIRST!
SETO KAIBA
Life Points 4000
YAKO TENMA
Life Points 4000
I PLAY ONE CARD FACE DOWN!
BAM
THEN I SUMMON MATERIAL BAT IN DEFENSE MODE!!
MATERIAL BAT
ATK 1200 DEF 1700
TURN END!
HEH HEH...
MY TURN...

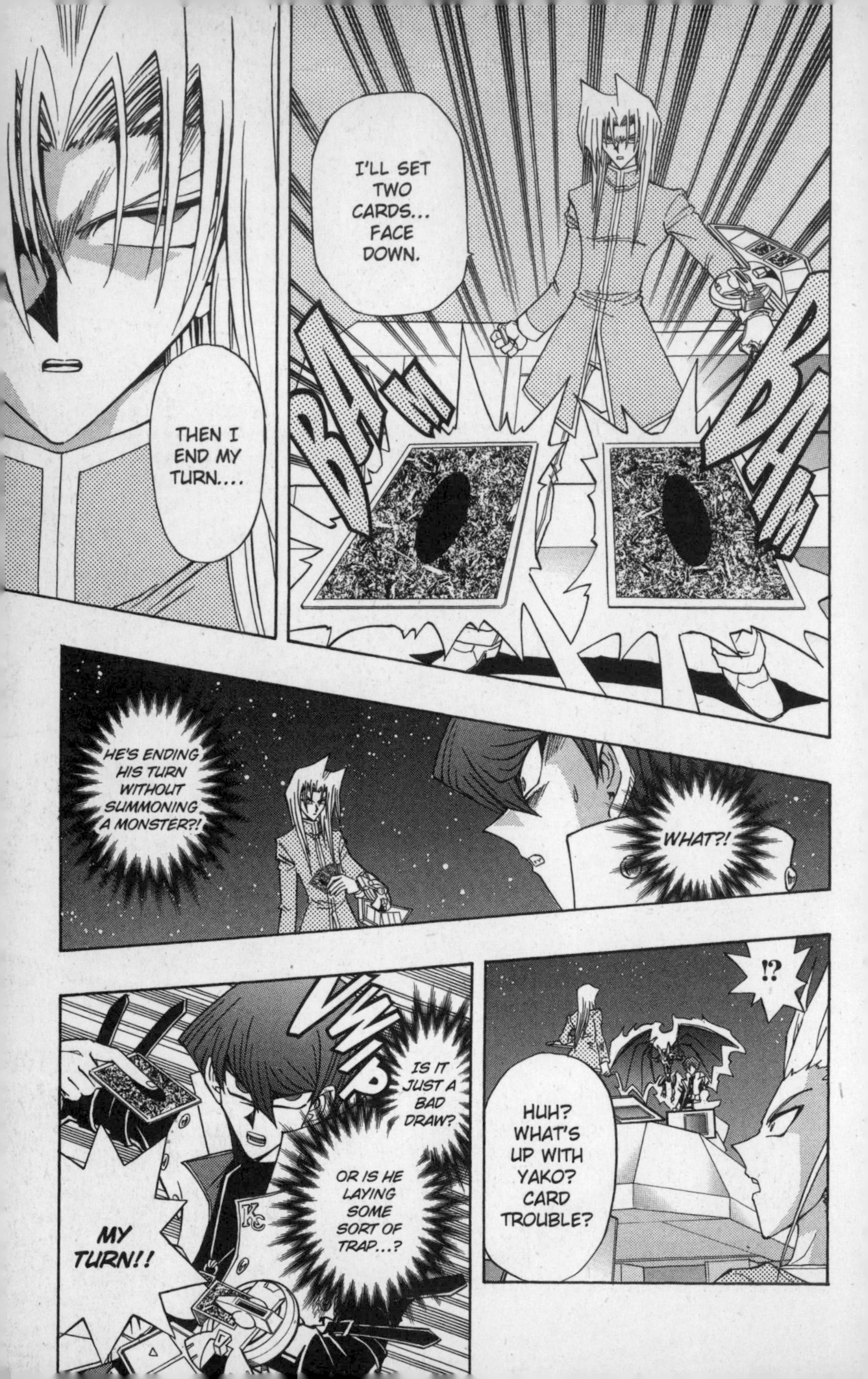

I'LL SET TWO CARDS... FACE DOWN.
BAM
BAM
THEN I END MY TURN....
WHAT?!
HE'S ENDING HIS TURN WITHOUT SUMMONING A MONSTER?!
!?
HUH? WHAT'S UP WITH YAKO? CARD TROUBLE?
VWIP
IS IT JUST A BAD DRAW?
OR IS HE LAYING SOME SORT OF TRAP...?
MY TURN!!

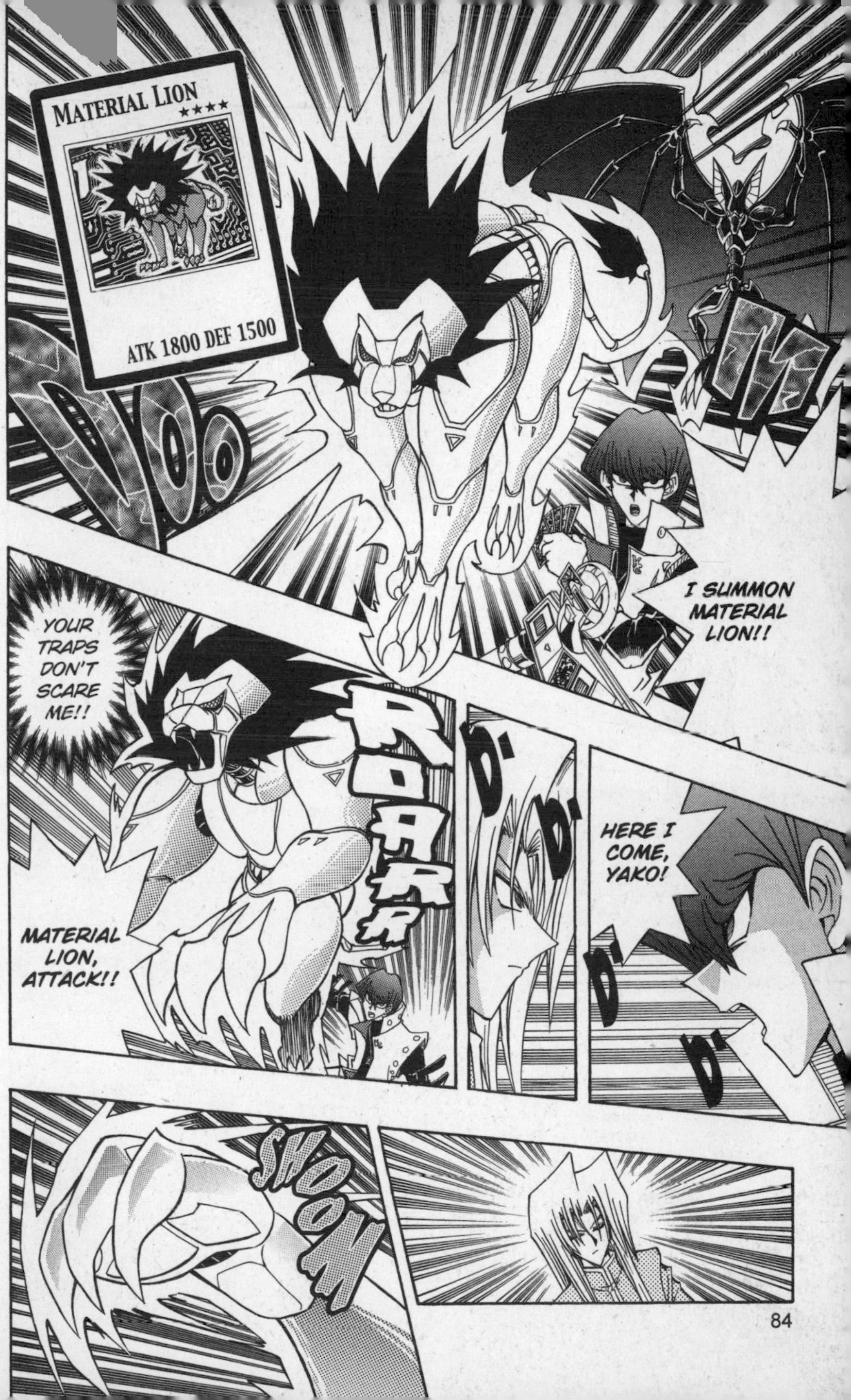
MATERIAL LION ★★★★
ATK 1800 DEF 1500
VOOM
I SUMMON MATERIAL LION!!
HERE I COME, YAKO!
YOUR TRAPS DON'T SCARE ME!!
ROARR
MATERIAL LION, ATTACK!!
SHOOM

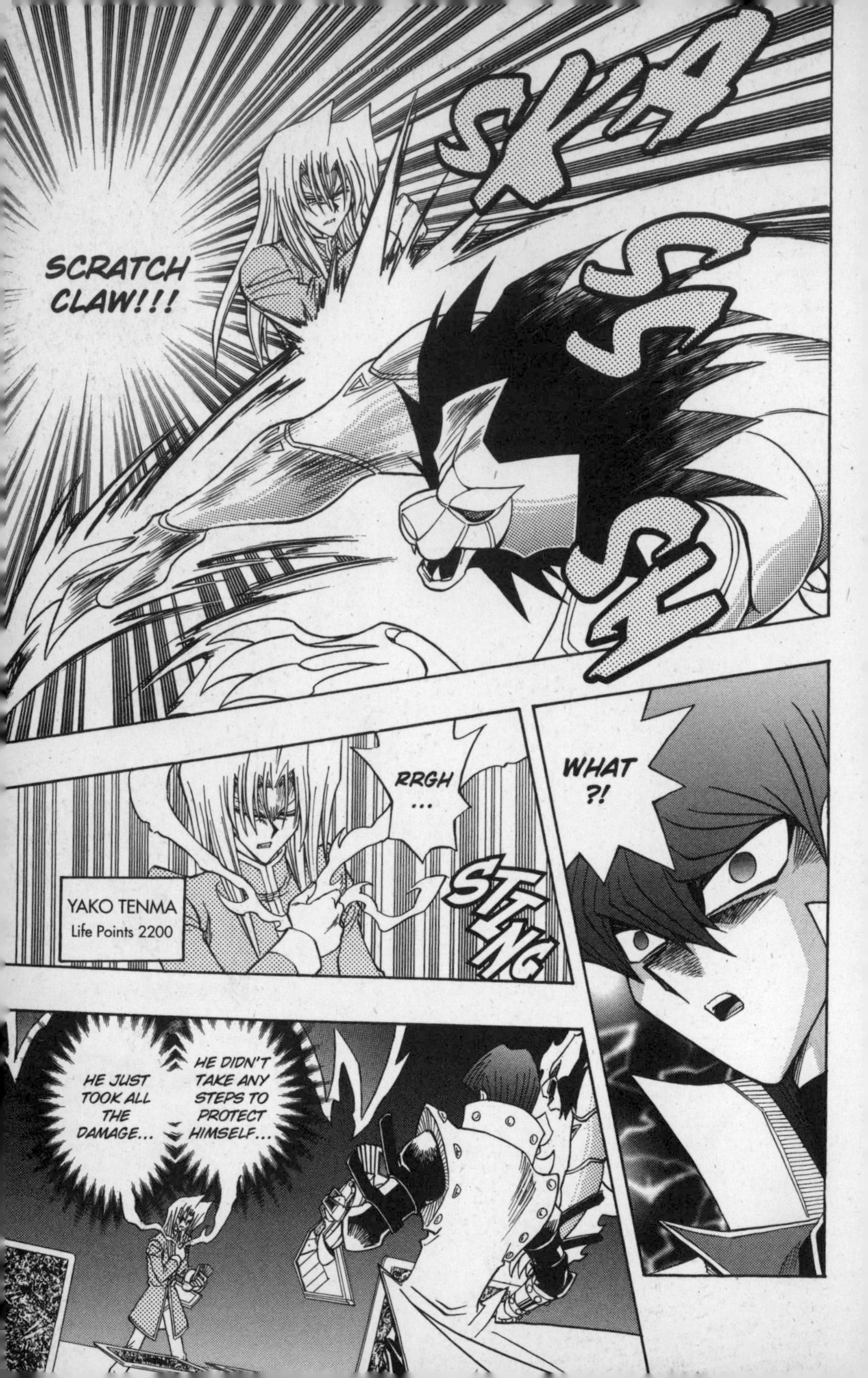
SKA
SCRATCH CLAW!!!
WHAT ?!
RRGH ...
STING
YAKO TENMA Life Points 2200
HE DIDN'T TAKE ANY STEPS TO PROTECT HIMSELF...
HE JUST TOOK ALL THE DAMAGE...

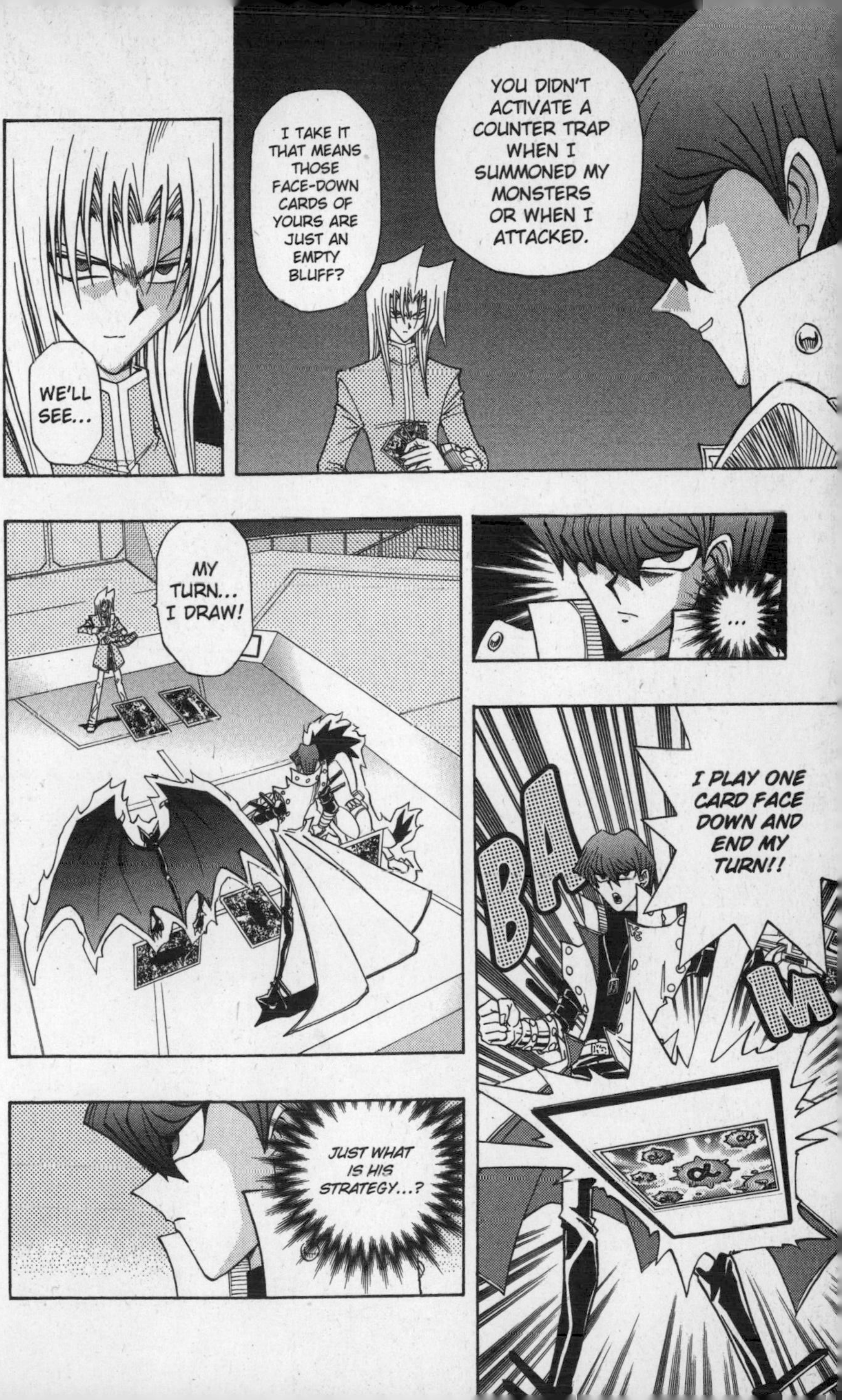
YOU DIDN'T ACTIVATE A COUNTER TRAP WHEN I SUMMONED MY MONSTERS OR WHEN I ATTACKED.
I TAKE IT THAT MEANS THOSE FACE-DOWN CARDS OF YOURS ARE JUST AN EMPTY BLUFF?
WE'LL SEE...
...
MY TURN... I DRAW!
BA
I PLAY ONE CARD FACE DOWN AND END MY TURN!!
JUST WHAT IS HIS STRATEGY...?

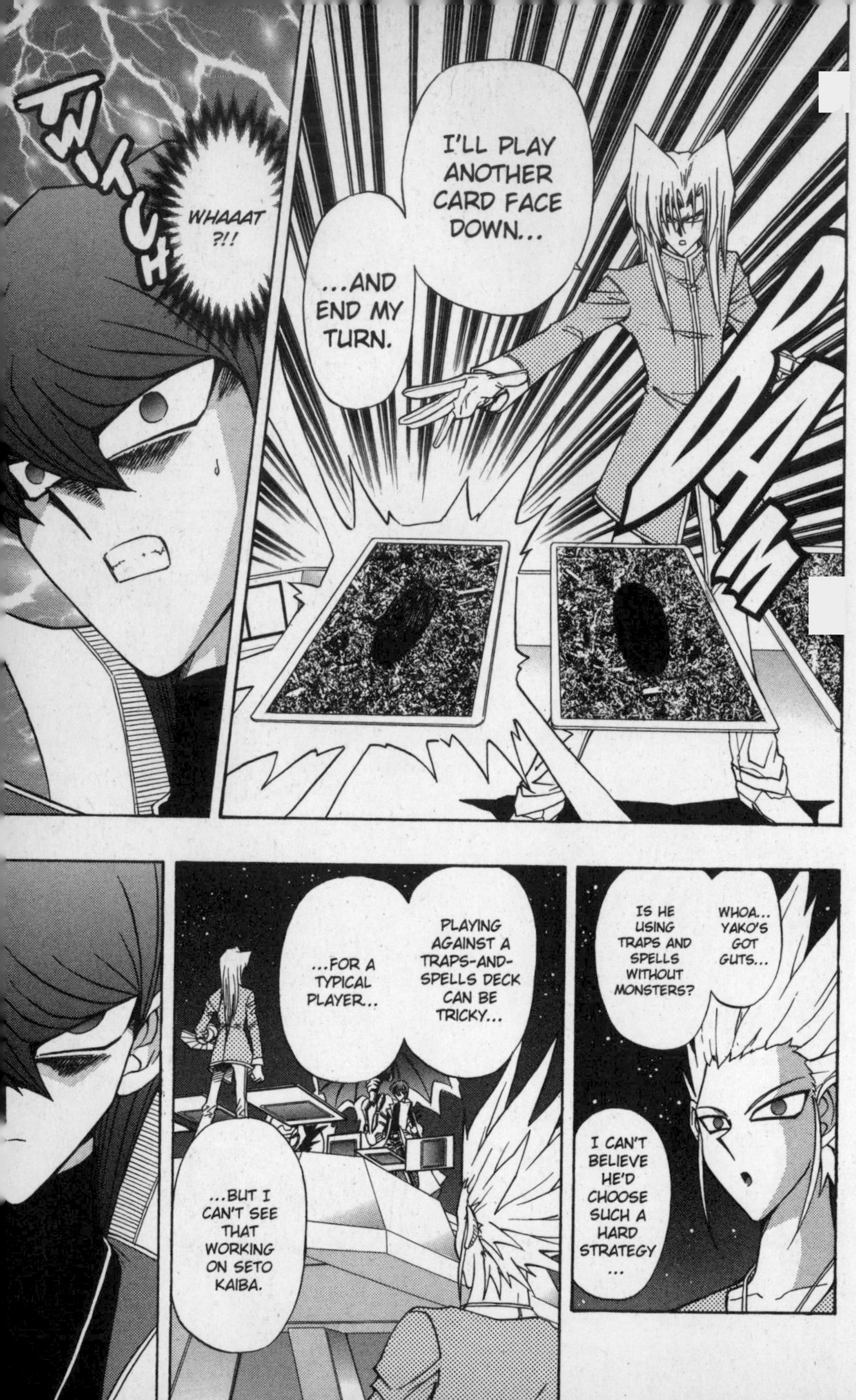
I'LL PLAY ANOTHER CARD FACE DOWN...
...AND END MY TURN.
TWITCH
WHAAAT ?!!
WHOA... YAKO'S GOT GUTS...
IS HE USING TRAPS AND SPELLS WITHOUT MONSTERS?
I CAN'T BELIEVE HE'D CHOOSE SUCH A HARD STRATEGY ...
PLAYING AGAINST A TRAPS-AND-SPELLS DECK CAN BE TRICKY...
...FOR A TYPICAL PLAYER..
...BUT I CAN'T SEE THAT WORKING ON SETO KAIBA.

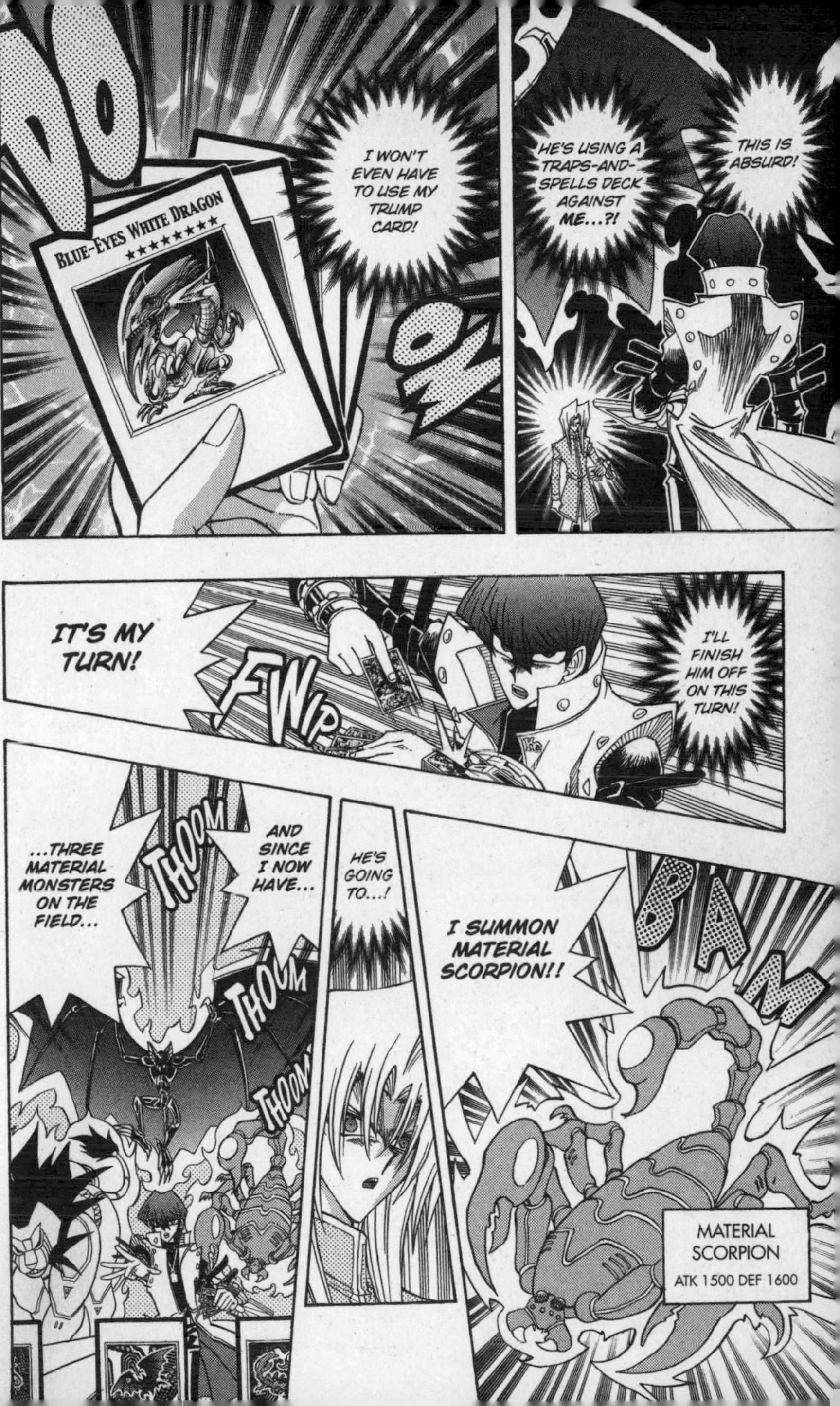
THIS IS ABSURD!
HE'S USING A TRAPS-AND-SPELLS DECK AGAINST ME...?!
I WON'T EVEN HAVE TO USE MY TRUMP CARD!
DO
OM
BLUE-EYES WHITE DRAGON
I'LL FINISH HIM OFF ON THIS TURN!
FWIP
IT'S MY TURN!
BAM
I SUMMON MATERIAL SCORPION!!
MATERIAL SCORPION
ATK 1500 DEF 1600
HE'S GOING TO...!
AND SINCE I NOW HAVE...
THOOM
...THREE MATERIAL MONSTERS ON THE FIELD...
THOOM
THOOM

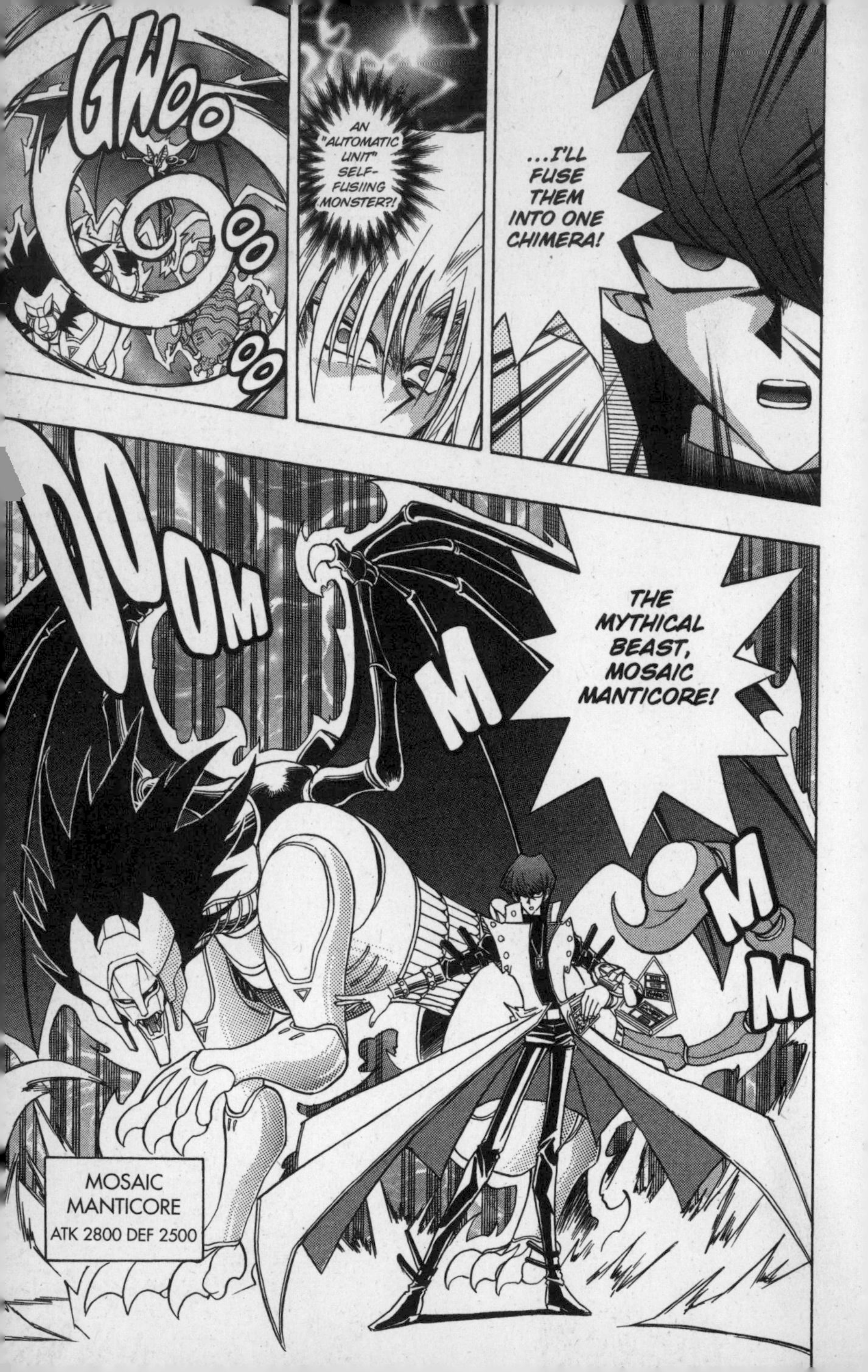
...I'LL FUSE THEM INTO ONE CHIMERA!
AN "AUTOMATIC UNIT" SELF-FUSIING MONSTER?!
GWOOOOOO
THE MYTHICAL BEAST, MOSAIC MANTICORE!
DOOOMMMM
MOSAIC MANTICORE
ATK 2800 DEF 2500

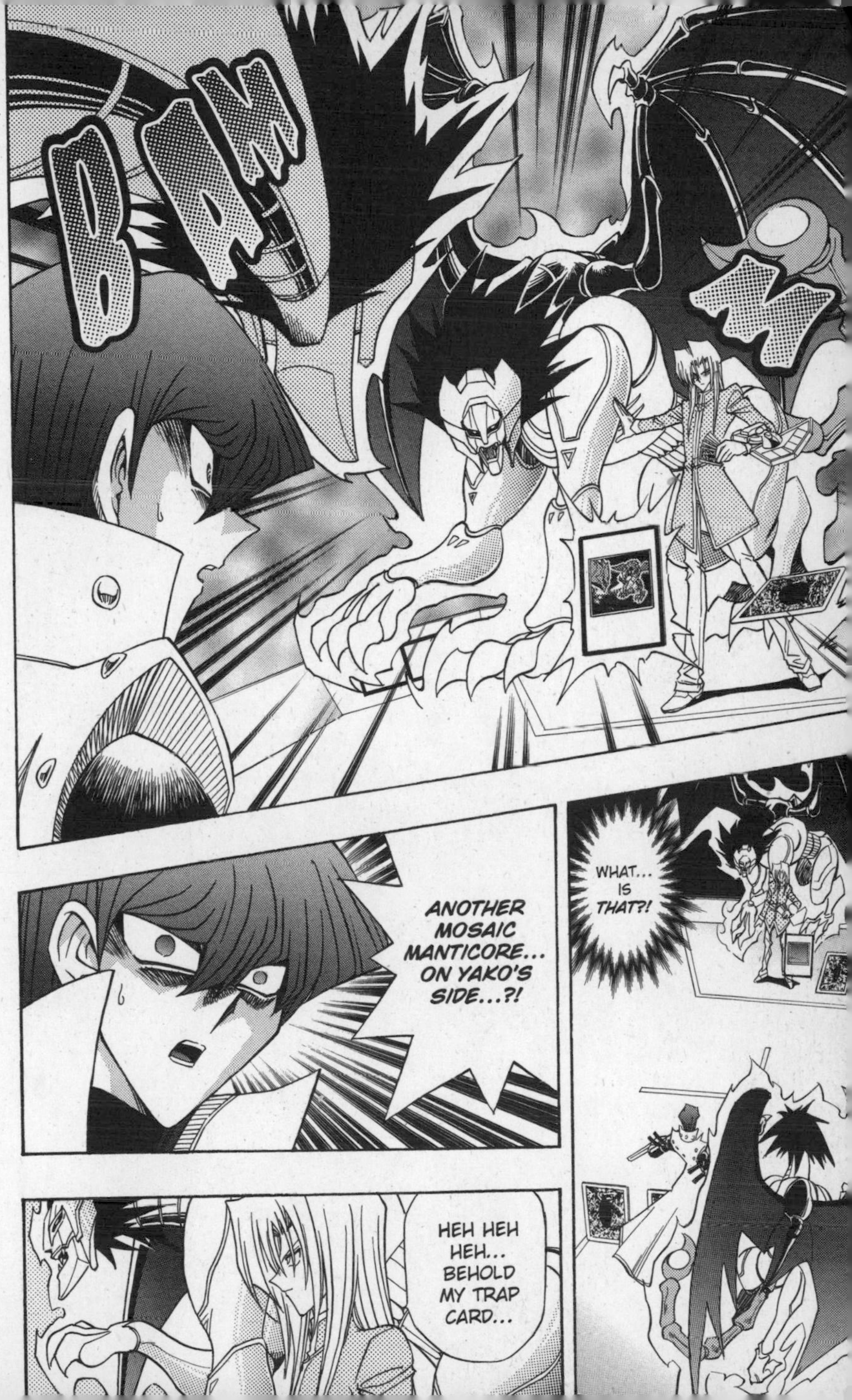
BAM
M
WHAT... IS THAT?!
ANOTHER MOSAIC MANTICORE... ON YAKO'S SIDE...?!
HEH HEH HEH... BEHOLD MY TRAP CARD...

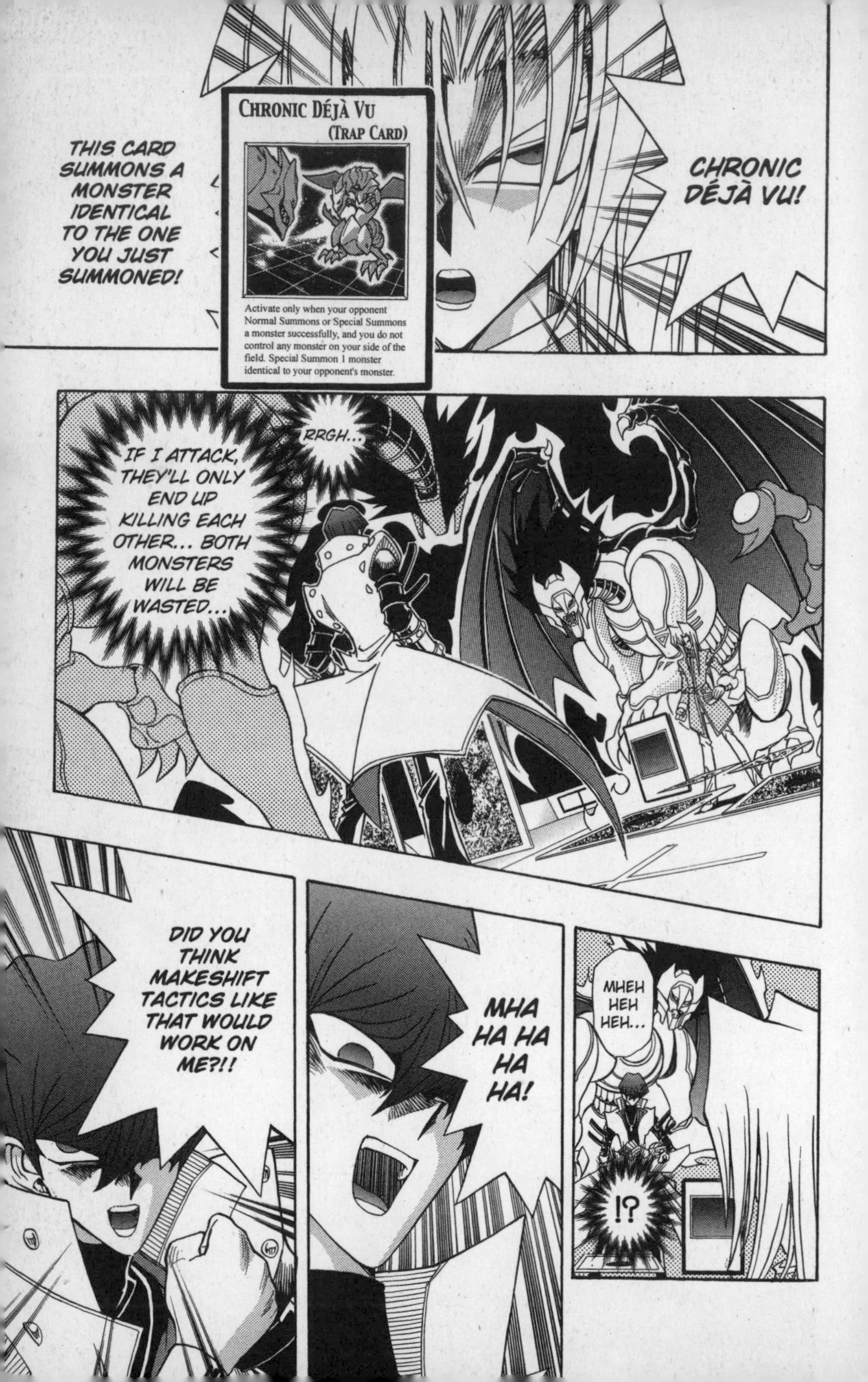
CHRONIC DÉJÀ VU!
CHRONIC DÉJÀ VU
(TRAP CARD)
Activate only when your opponent Normal Summons or Special Summons a monster successfully, and you do not control any monster on your side of the field. Special Summon 1 monster identical to your opponent's monster.
THIS CARD SUMMONS A MONSTER IDENTICAL TO THE ONE YOU JUST SUMMONED!
RRGH...
IF I ATTACK, THEY'LL ONLY END UP KILLING EACH OTHER... BOTH MONSTERS WILL BE WASTED...
MHEH HEH HEH...
!?
MHA HA HA HA HA!
DID YOU THINK MAKESHIFT TACTICS LIKE THAT WOULD WORK ON ME?!!

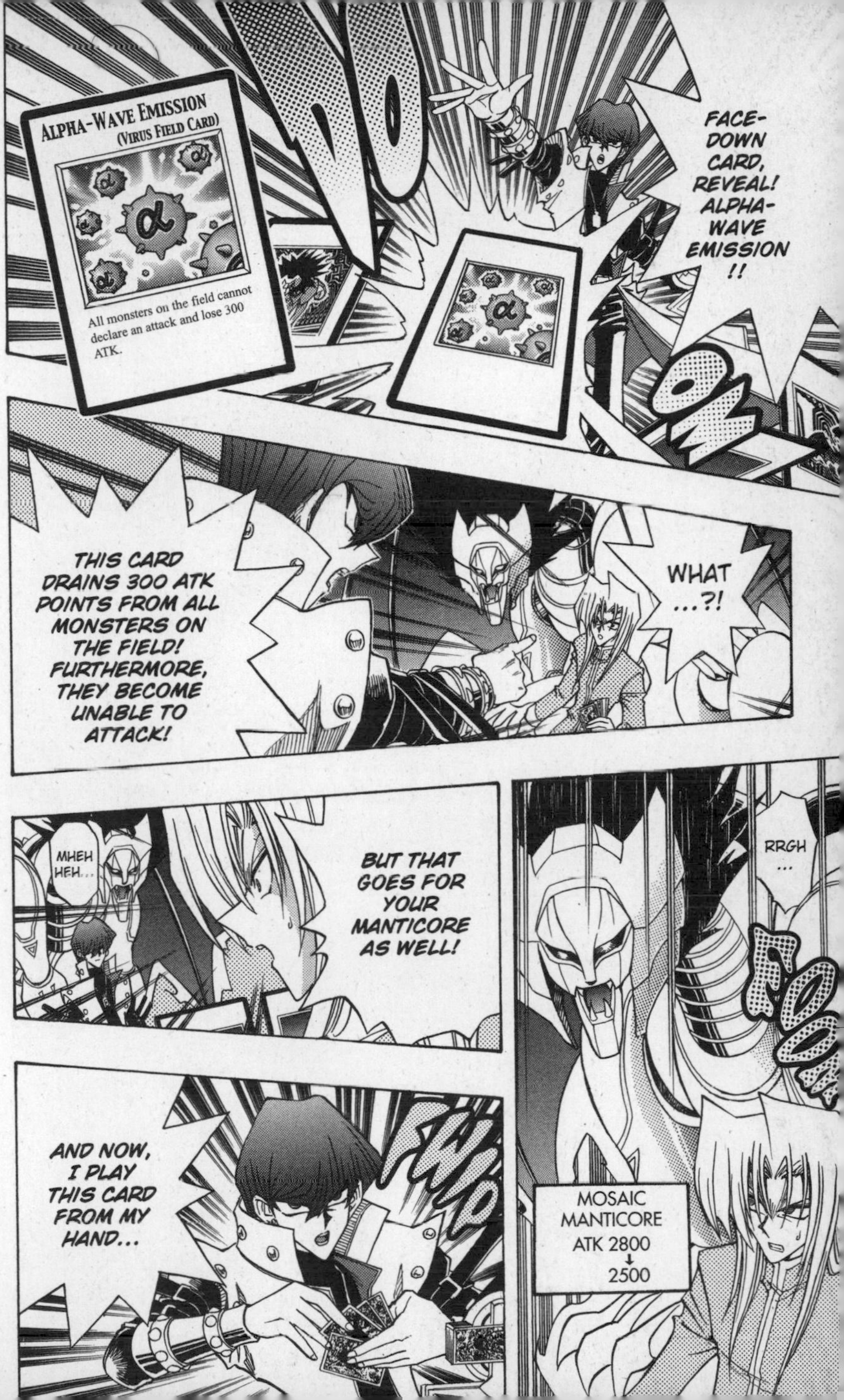
FACE-DOWN CARD, REVEAL! ALPHA-WAVE EMISSION !!
ALPHA-WAVE EMISSION
(VIRUS FIELD CARD)
All monsters on the field cannot declare an attack and lose 300 ATK.
WHAT ...?!
THIS CARD DRAINS 300 ATK POINTS FROM ALL MONSTERS ON THE FIELD! FURTHERMORE, THEY BECOME UNABLE TO ATTACK!
RRGH ...
MOSAIC MANTICORE ATK 2800 ↓ 2500
BUT THAT GOES FOR YOUR MANTICORE AS WELL!
MHEH HEH...
AND NOW, I PLAY THIS CARD FROM MY HAND...

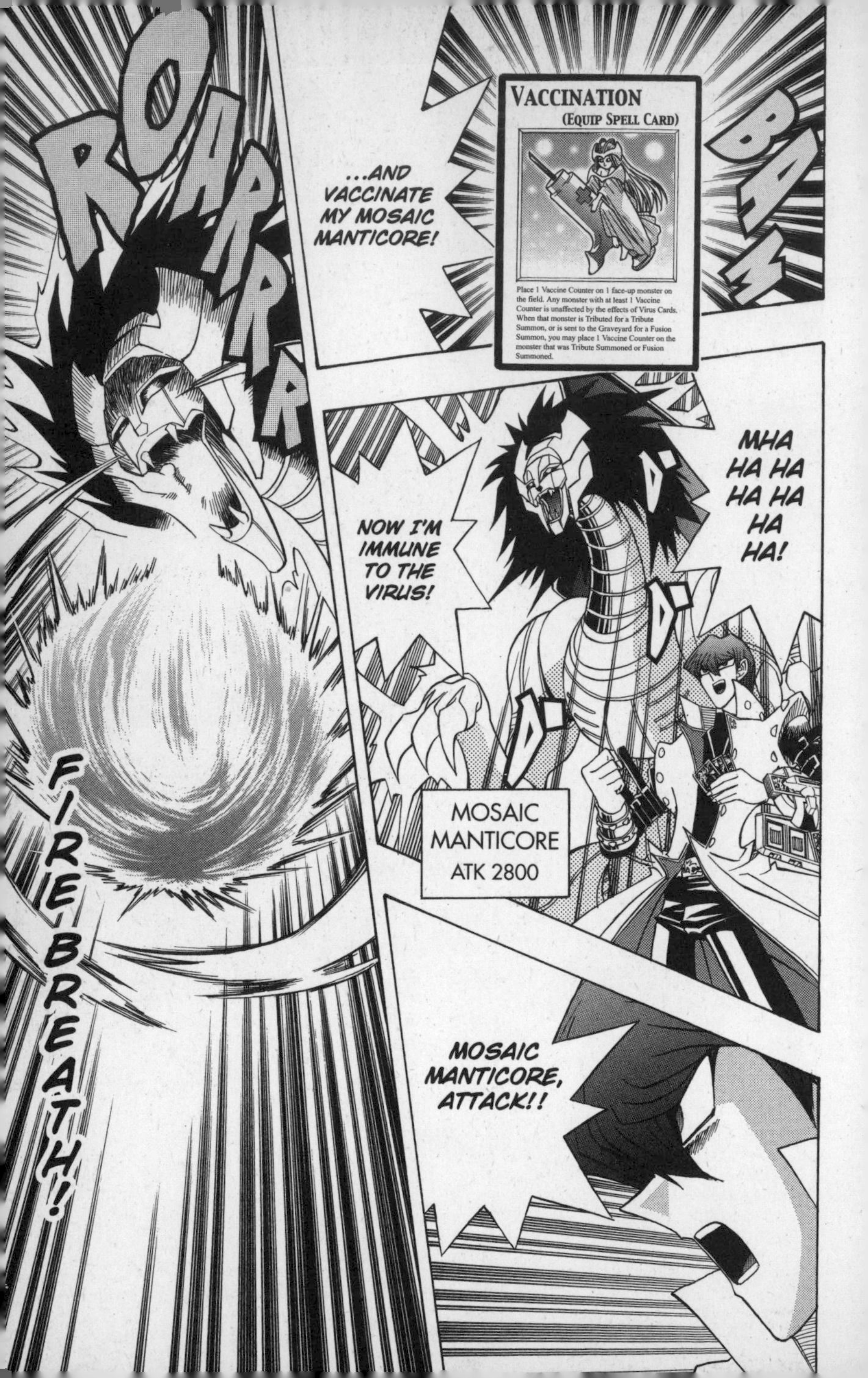
BAM
VACCINATION
(EQUIP SPELL CARD)
Place 1 Vaccine Counter on 1 face-up monster on the field. Any monster with at least 1 Vaccine Counter is unaffected by the effects of Virus Cards. When that monster is Tributed for a Tribute Summon, or is sent to the Graveyard for a Fusion Summon, you may place 1 Vaccine Counter on the monster that was Tribute Summoned or Fusion Summoned.
...AND VACCINATE MY MOSAIC MANTICORE!
MHA HA HA HA HA HA HA HA!
NOW I'M IMMUNE TO THE VIRUS!
MOSAIC MANTICORE ATK 2800
MOSAIC MANTICORE, ATTACK!!
ROAAR
FIRE BREATH!

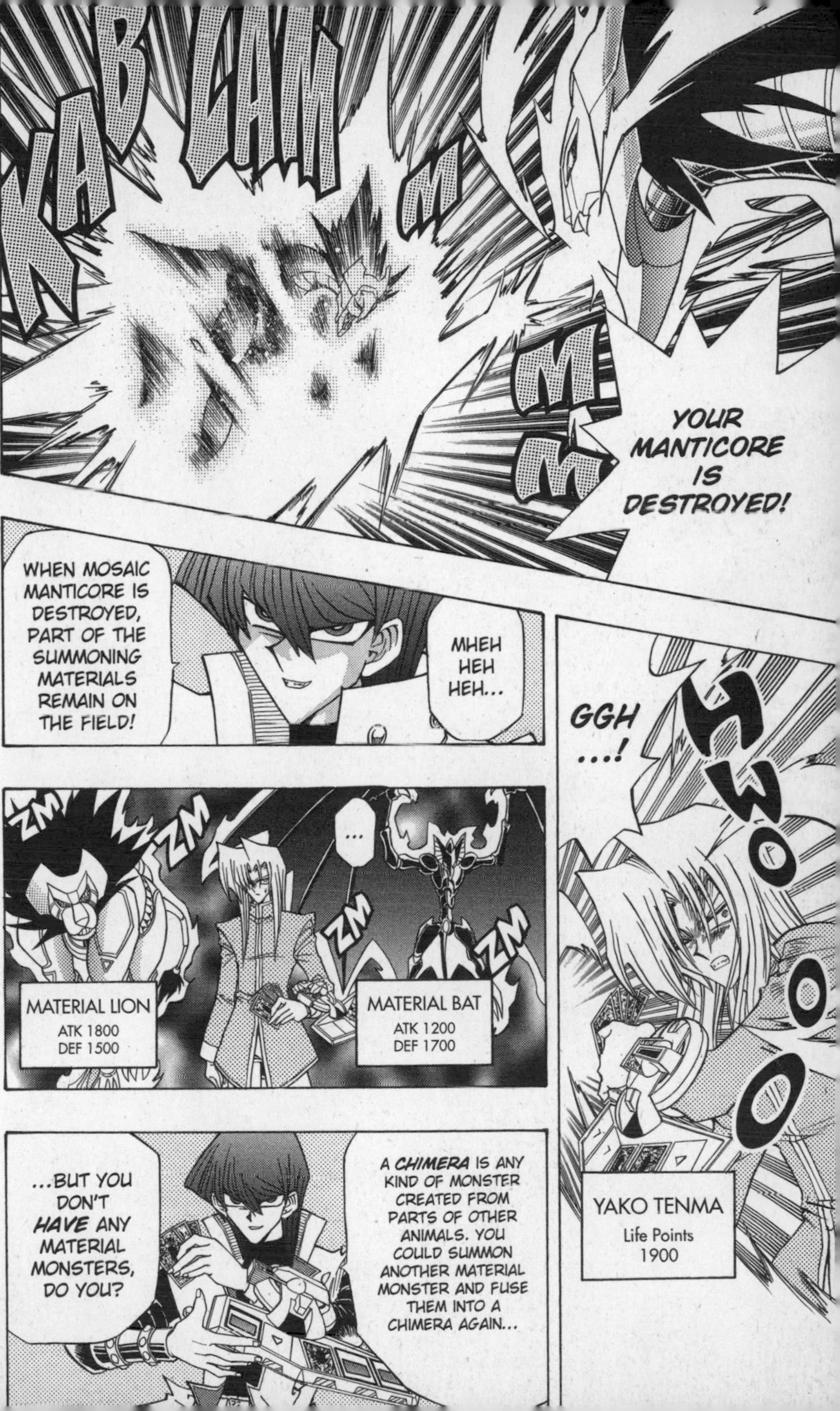
KA BLAM
M
M
M
YOUR MANTICORE IS DESTROYED!
GGH ...!
HWOOOO
YAKO TENMA
Life Points
1900
MHEH HEH HEH...
WHEN MOSAIC MANTICORE IS DESTROYED, PART OF THE SUMMONING MATERIALS REMAIN ON THE FIELD!
ZM
ZM
...
ZM
ZM
MATERIAL BAT
ATK 1200
DEF 1700
MATERIAL LION
ATK 1800
DEF 1500
A *CHIMERA* IS ANY KIND OF MONSTER CREATED FROM PARTS OF OTHER ANIMALS. YOU COULD SUMMON ANOTHER MATERIAL MONSTER AND FUSE THEM INTO A CHIMERA AGAIN...
...BUT YOU DON'T *HAVE* ANY MATERIAL MONSTERS, DO YOU?

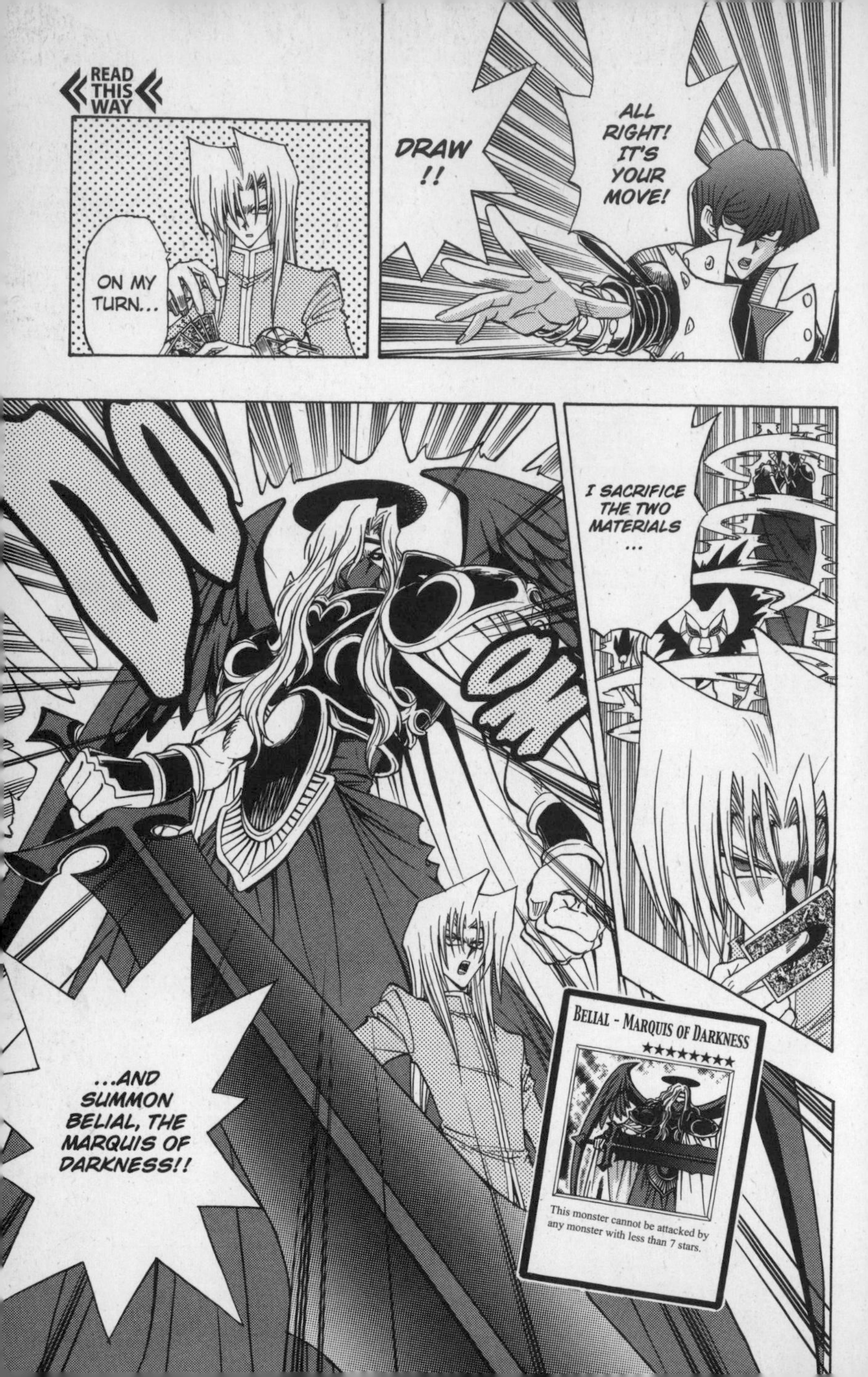
READ THIS WAY
ALL RIGHT! IT'S YOUR MOVE!
DRAW!!
ON MY TURN...
I SACRIFICE THE TWO MATERIALS ...
...AND SUMMON BELIAL, THE MARQUIS OF DARKNESS!!
BELIAL - MARQUIS OF DARKNESS
This monster cannot be attacked by any monster with less than 7 stars.

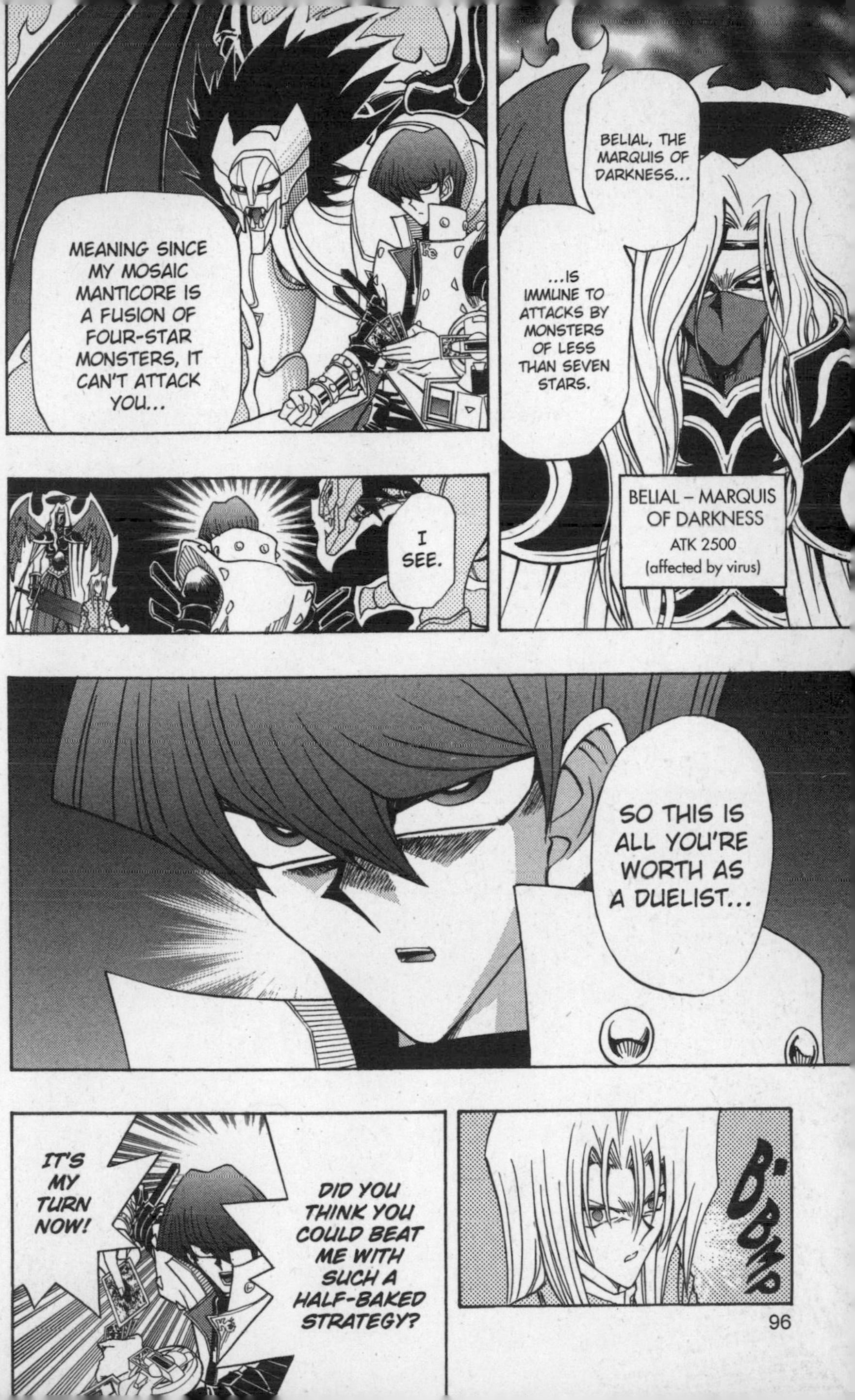
BELIAL, THE MARQUIS OF DARKNESS...
...IS IMMUNE TO ATTACKS BY MONSTERS OF LESS THAN SEVEN STARS.
BELIAL – MARQUIS OF DARKNESS
ATK 2500
(affected by virus)
MEANING SINCE MY MOSAIC MANTICORE IS A FUSION OF FOUR-STAR MONSTERS, IT CAN'T ATTACK YOU...
I SEE.
SO THIS IS ALL YOU'RE WORTH AS A DUELIST...
B'DMP
DID YOU THINK YOU COULD BEAT ME WITH SUCH A HALF-BAKED STRATEGY?
IT'S MY TURN NOW!

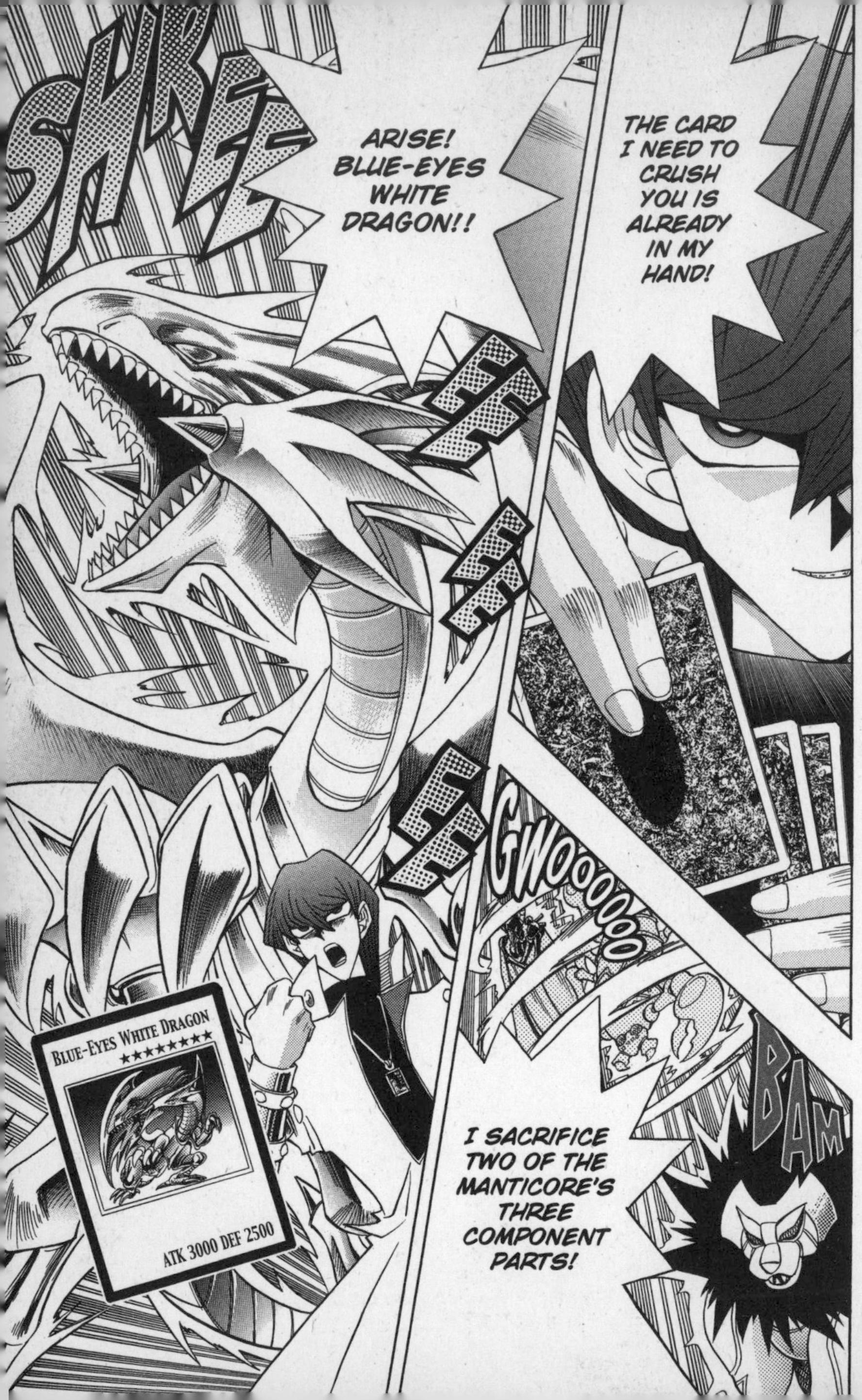
THE CARD I NEED TO CRUSH YOU IS ALREADY IN MY HAND!
GWOOOOOOO
I SACRIFICE TWO OF THE MANTICORE'S THREE COMPONENT PARTS!
BAM
SHKEEE
EEEEEE
ARISE! BLUE-EYES WHITE DRAGON!!
BLUE-EYES WHITE DRAGON
ATK 3000 DEF 2500

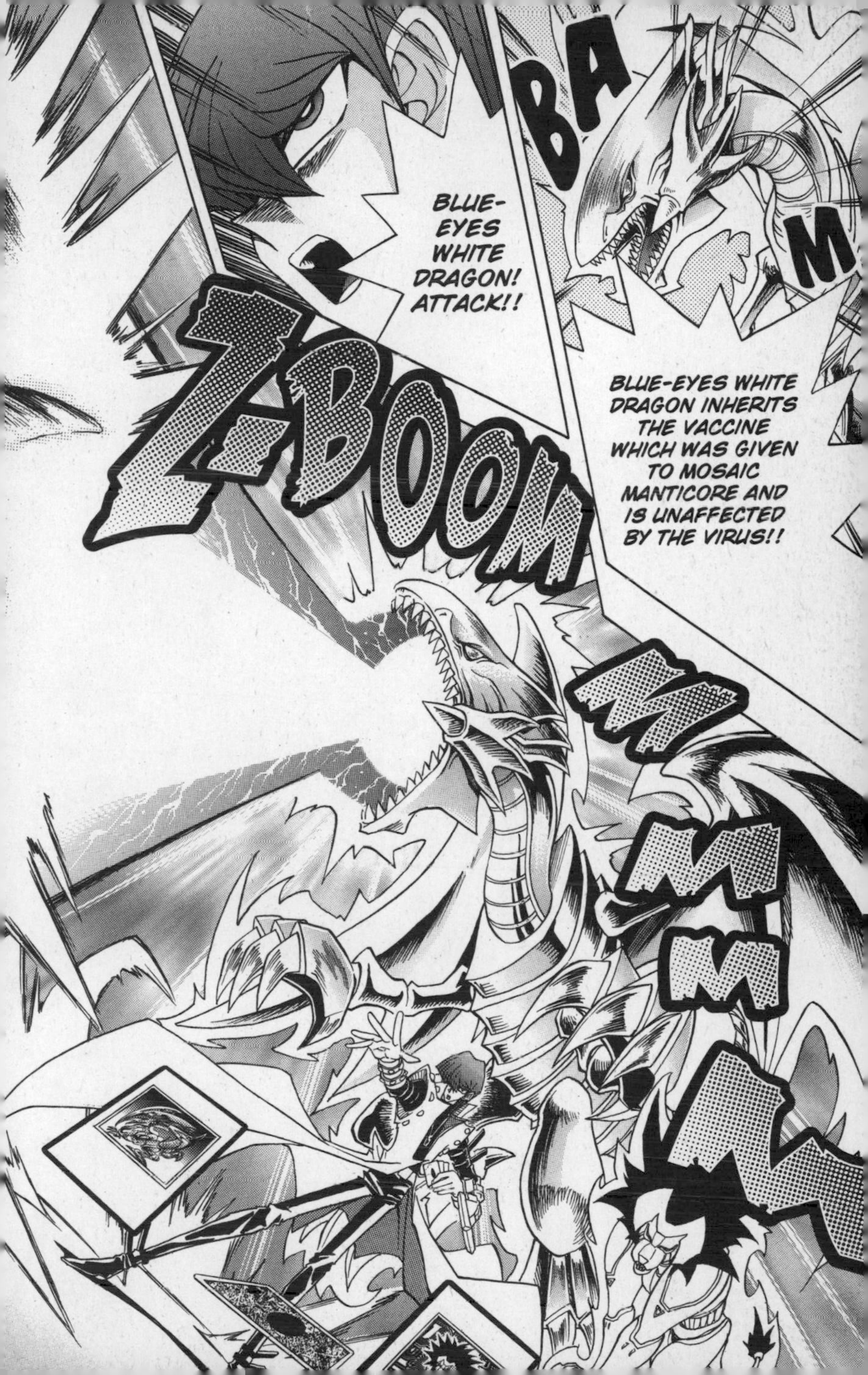
BAM
BLUE-EYES WHITE DRAGON! ATTACK!!
Z-BOOM
BLUE-EYES WHITE DRAGON INHERITS THE VACCINE WHICH WAS GIVEN TO MOSAIC MANTICORE AND IS UNAFFECTED BY THE VIRUS!!
MMMM

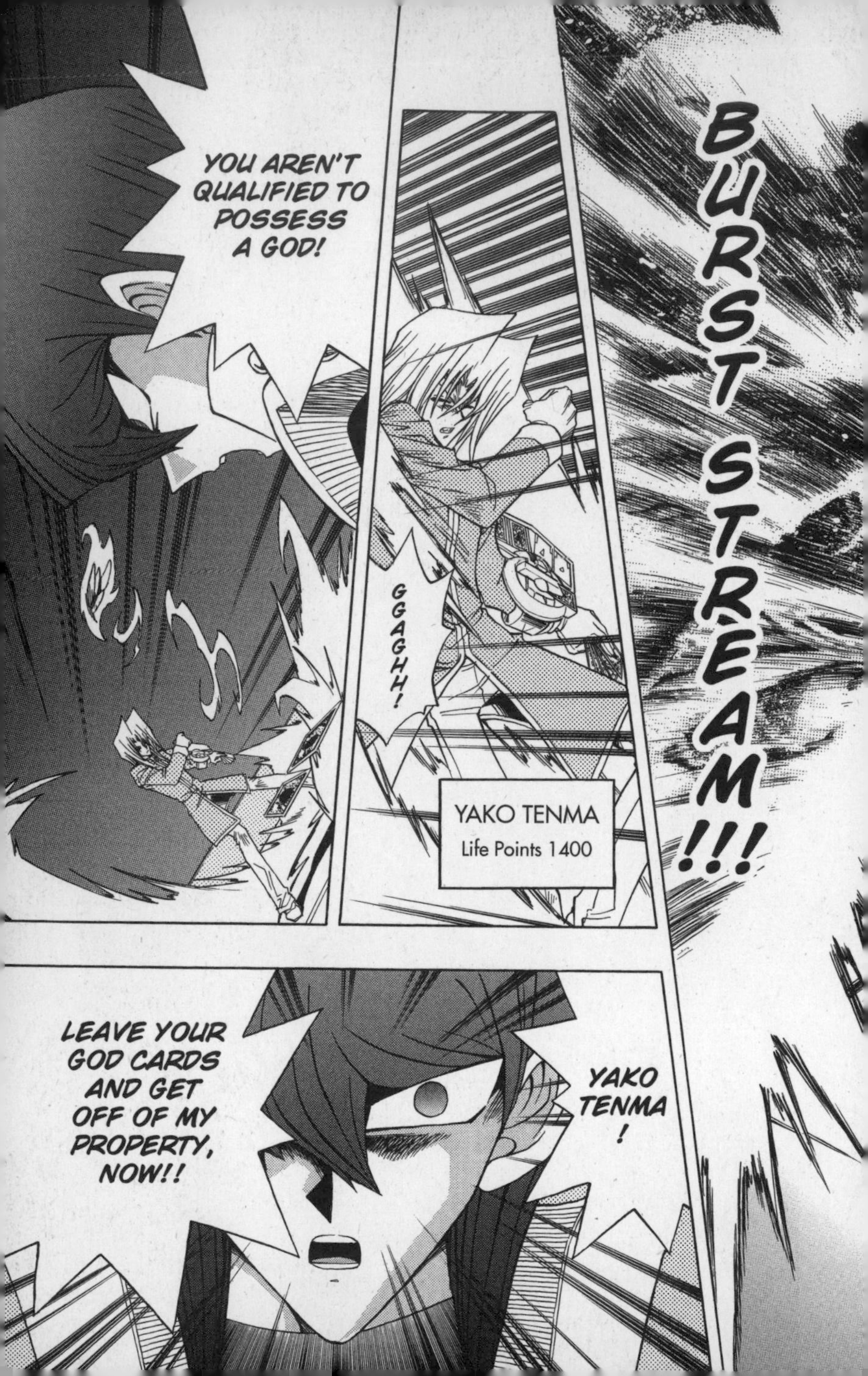
BURST STREAM!!!
GGAGHH!
YAKO TENMA
Life Points 1400
YOU AREN'T QUALIFIED TO POSSESS A GOD!
YAKO TENMA!
LEAVE YOUR GOD CARDS AND GET OFF OF MY PROPERTY, NOW!!

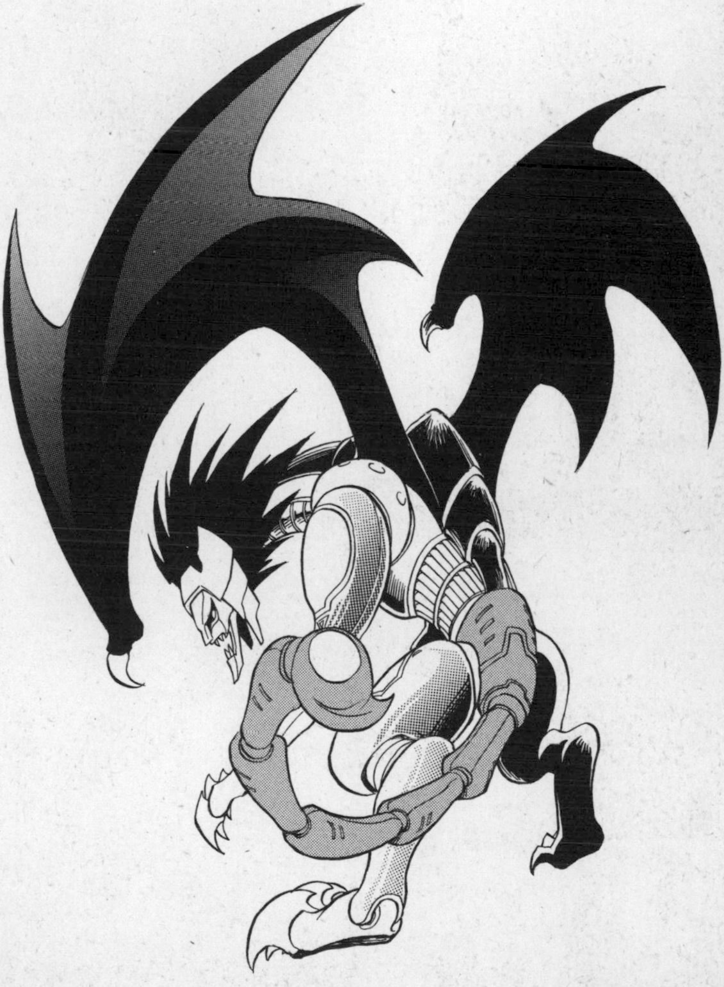

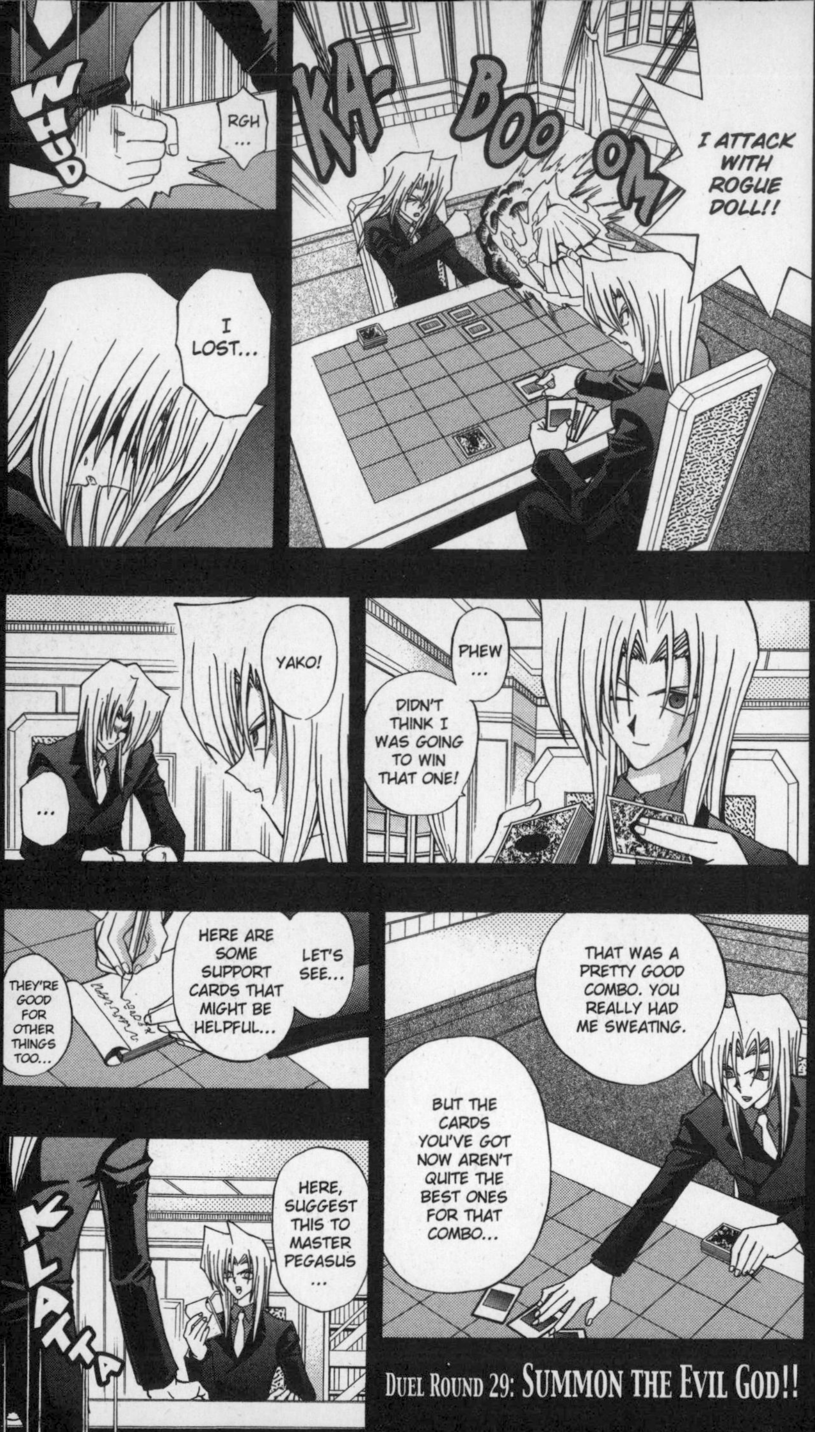
KA-BOOOM
I ATTACK WITH ROGUE DOLL!!
WHUD
RGH ...
I LOST...
PHEW ...
DIDN'T THINK I WAS GOING TO WIN THAT ONE!
YAKO!
...
THAT WAS A PRETTY GOOD COMBO. YOU REALLY HAD ME SWEATING.
BUT THE CARDS YOU'VE GOT NOW AREN'T QUITE THE BEST ONES FOR THAT COMBO...
LET'S SEE...
HERE ARE SOME SUPPORT CARDS THAT MIGHT BE HELPFUL...
THEY'RE GOOD FOR OTHER THINGS TOO...
KLATTA
HERE, SUGGEST THIS TO MASTER PEGASUS ...

Duel Round 29: Summon the Evil God!!

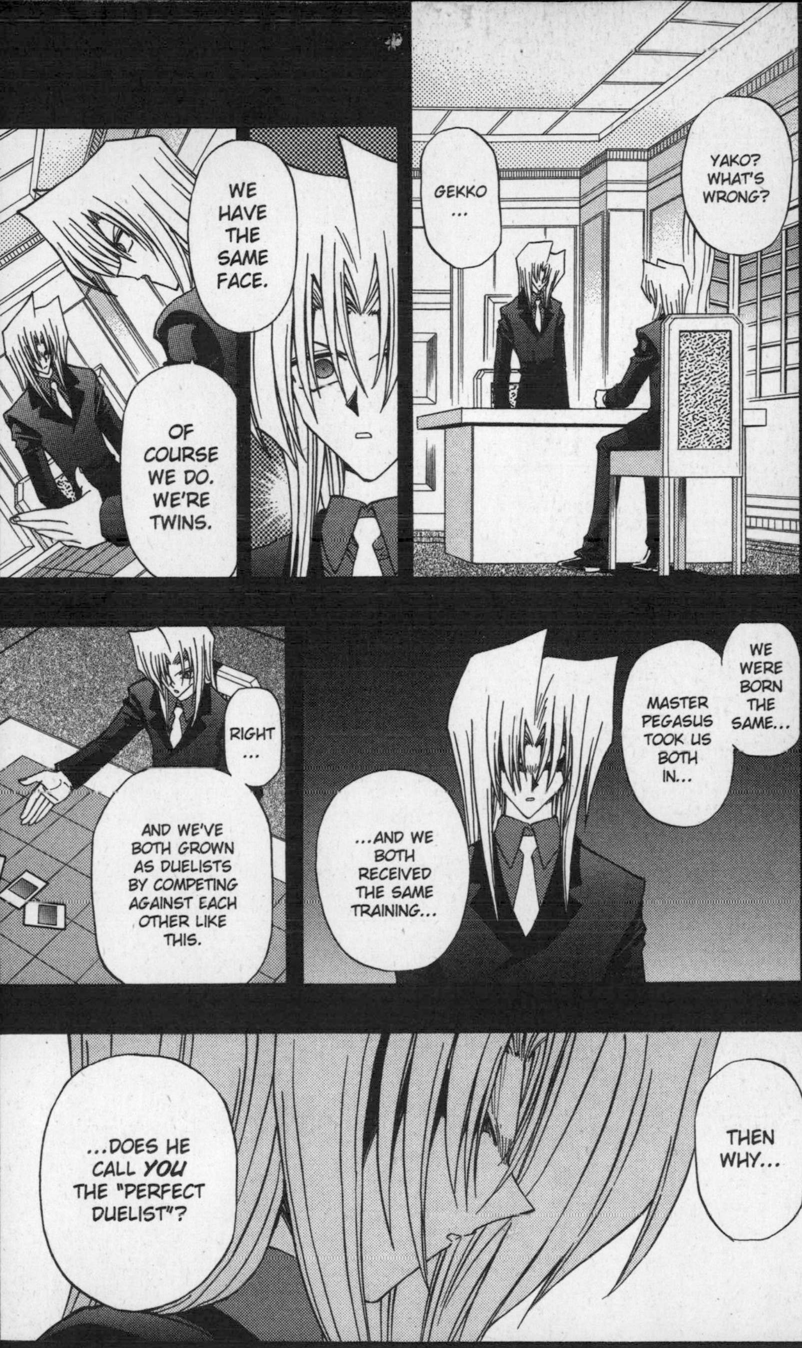
YAKO? WHAT'S WRONG?
GEKKO...
WE HAVE THE SAME FACE.
OF COURSE WE DO. WE'RE TWINS.
WE WERE BORN THE SAME...
MASTER PEGASUS TOOK US BOTH IN...
...AND WE BOTH RECEIVED THE SAME TRAINING...
RIGHT...
AND WE'VE BOTH GROWN AS DUELISTS BY COMPETING AGAINST EACH OTHER LIKE THIS.
THEN WHY...
...DOES HE CALL *YOU* THE "PERFECT DUELIST"?

READ THIS WAY

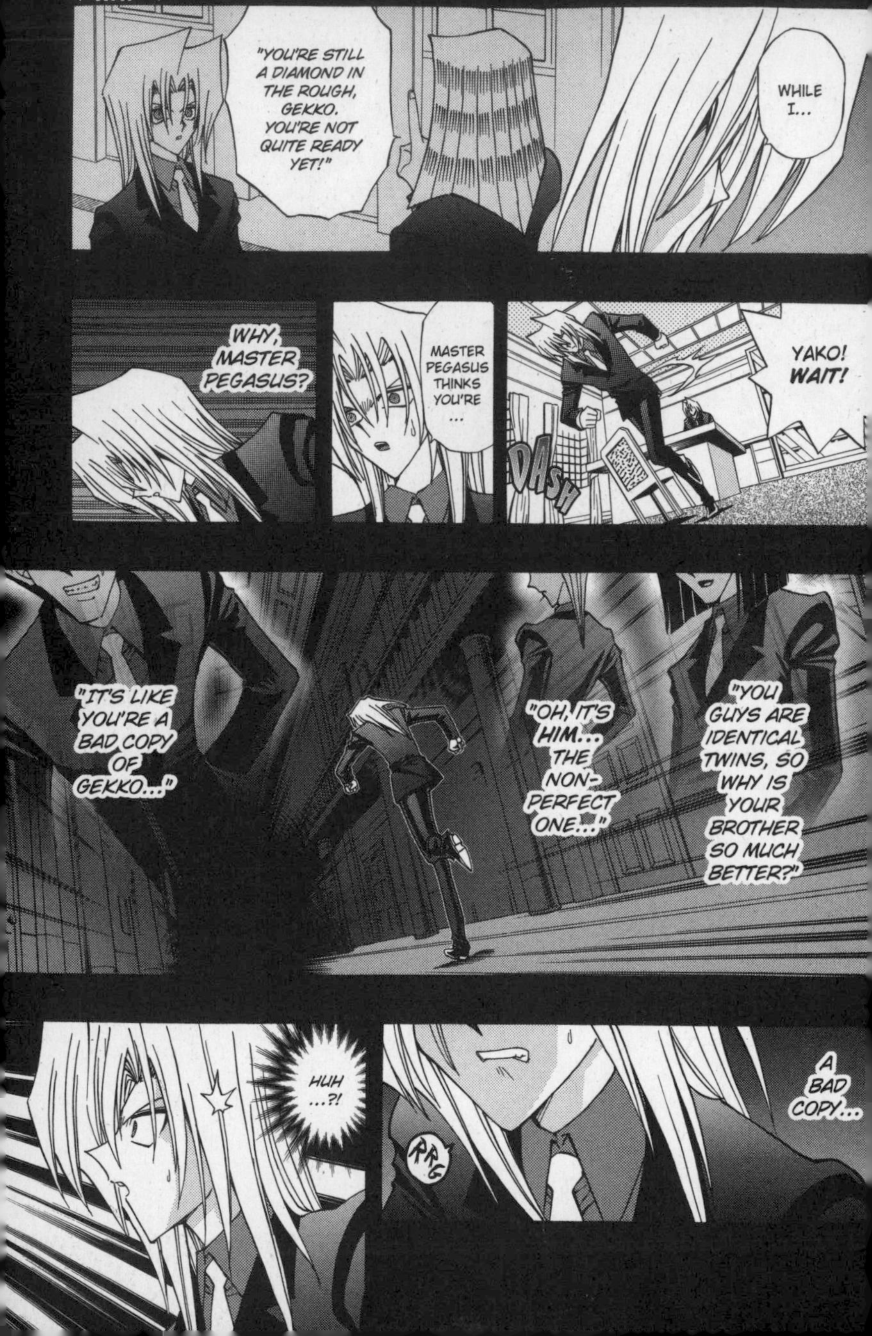
WHILE I...
"YOU'RE STILL A DIAMOND IN THE ROUGH, GEKKO. YOU'RE NOT QUITE READY YET!"
YAKO! WAIT!
DASH
MASTER PEGASUS THINKS YOU'RE ...
WHY, MASTER PEGASUS?
"YOU GUYS ARE IDENTICAL TWINS, SO WHY IS YOUR BROTHER SO MUCH BETTER?"
"OH, IT'S HIM... THE NON-PERFECT ONE..."
"IT'S LIKE YOU'RE A BAD COPY OF GEKKO..."
A BAD COPY...
RRG
HUH ...?!

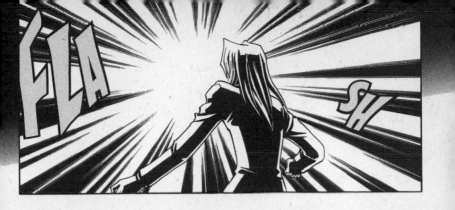

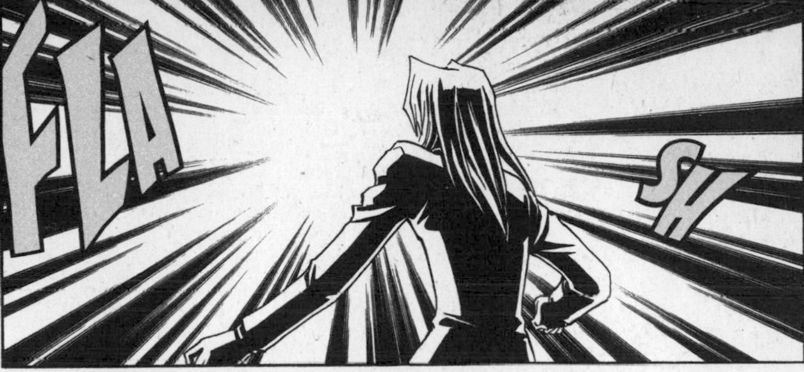
FLA
SH

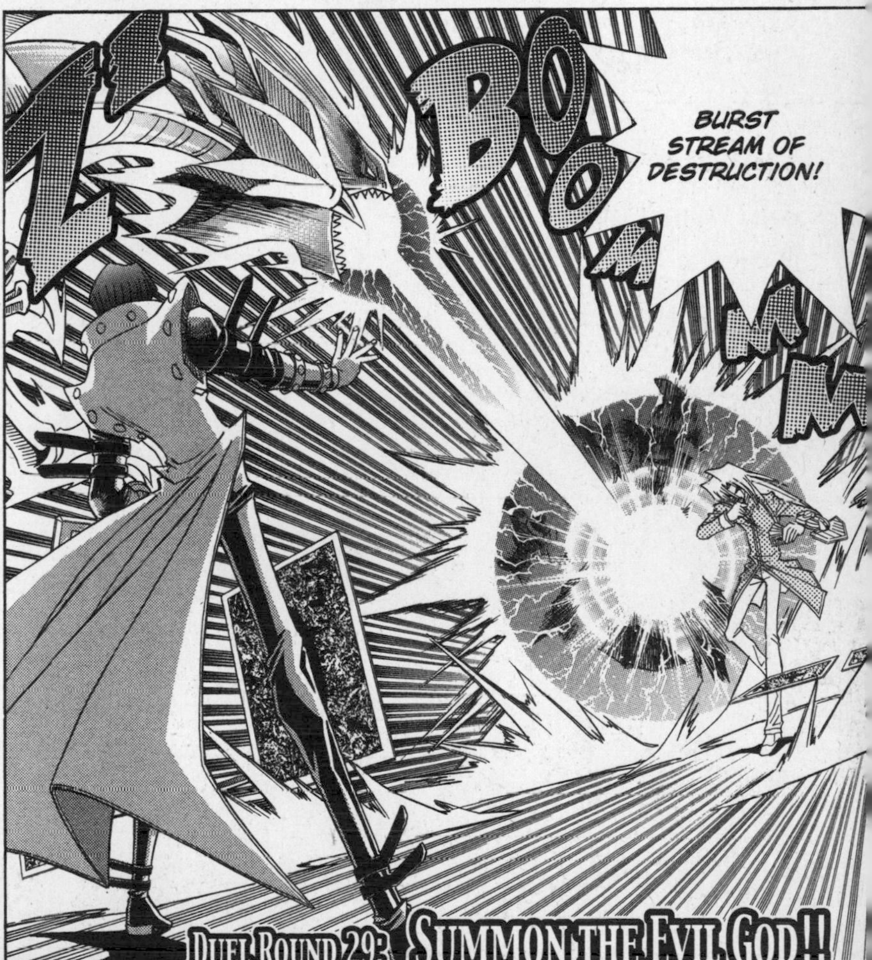
BOOOMMM
BURST STREAM OF DESTRUCTION!

DUEL ROUND 29: SUMMON THE EVIL GOD!!

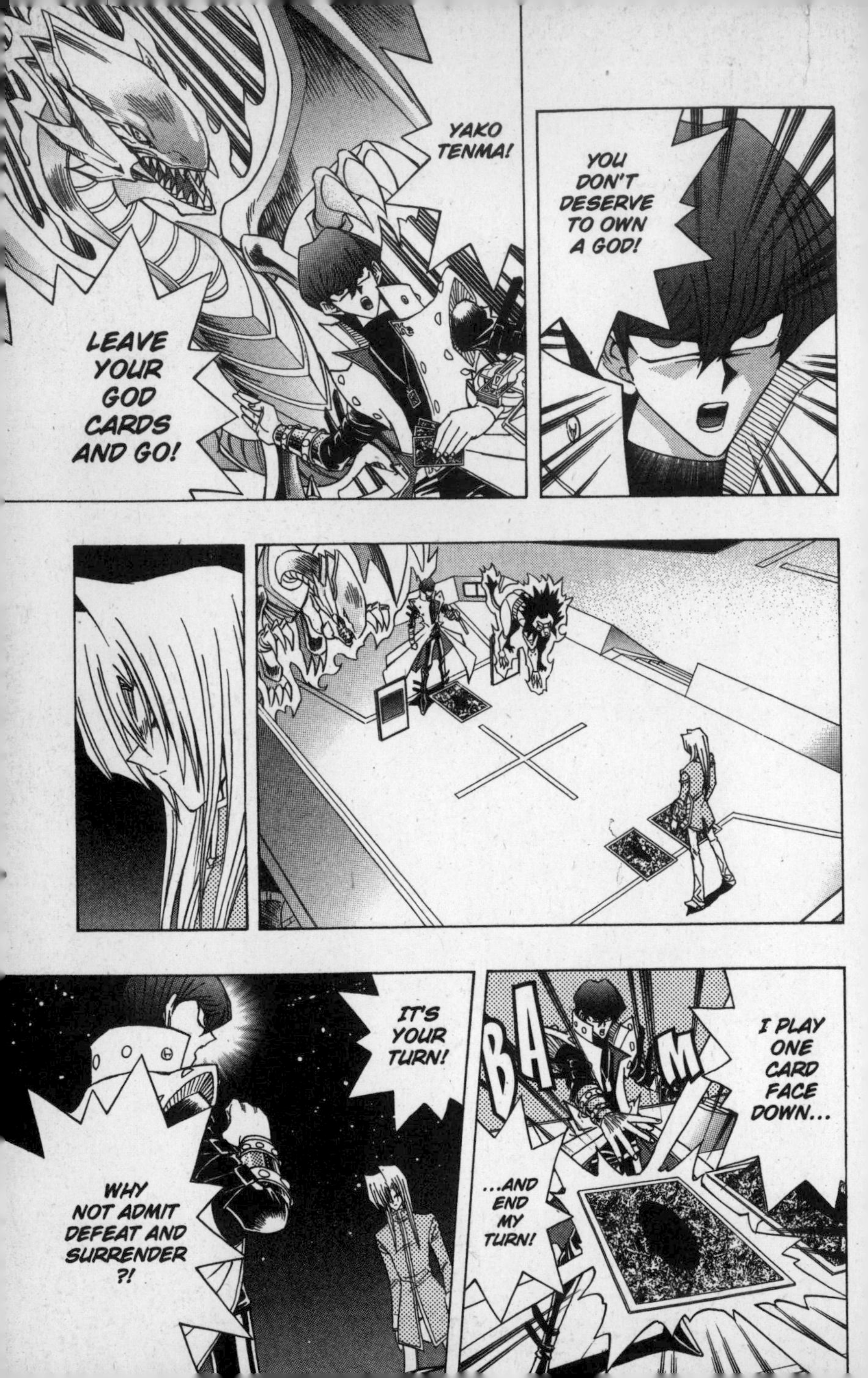
YOU DON'T DESERVE TO OWN A GOD!
YAKO TENMA!
LEAVE YOUR GOD CARDS AND GO!
BAM
I PLAY ONE CARD FACE DOWN...
...AND END MY TURN!
IT'S YOUR TURN!
WHY NOT ADMIT DEFEAT AND SURRENDER ?!

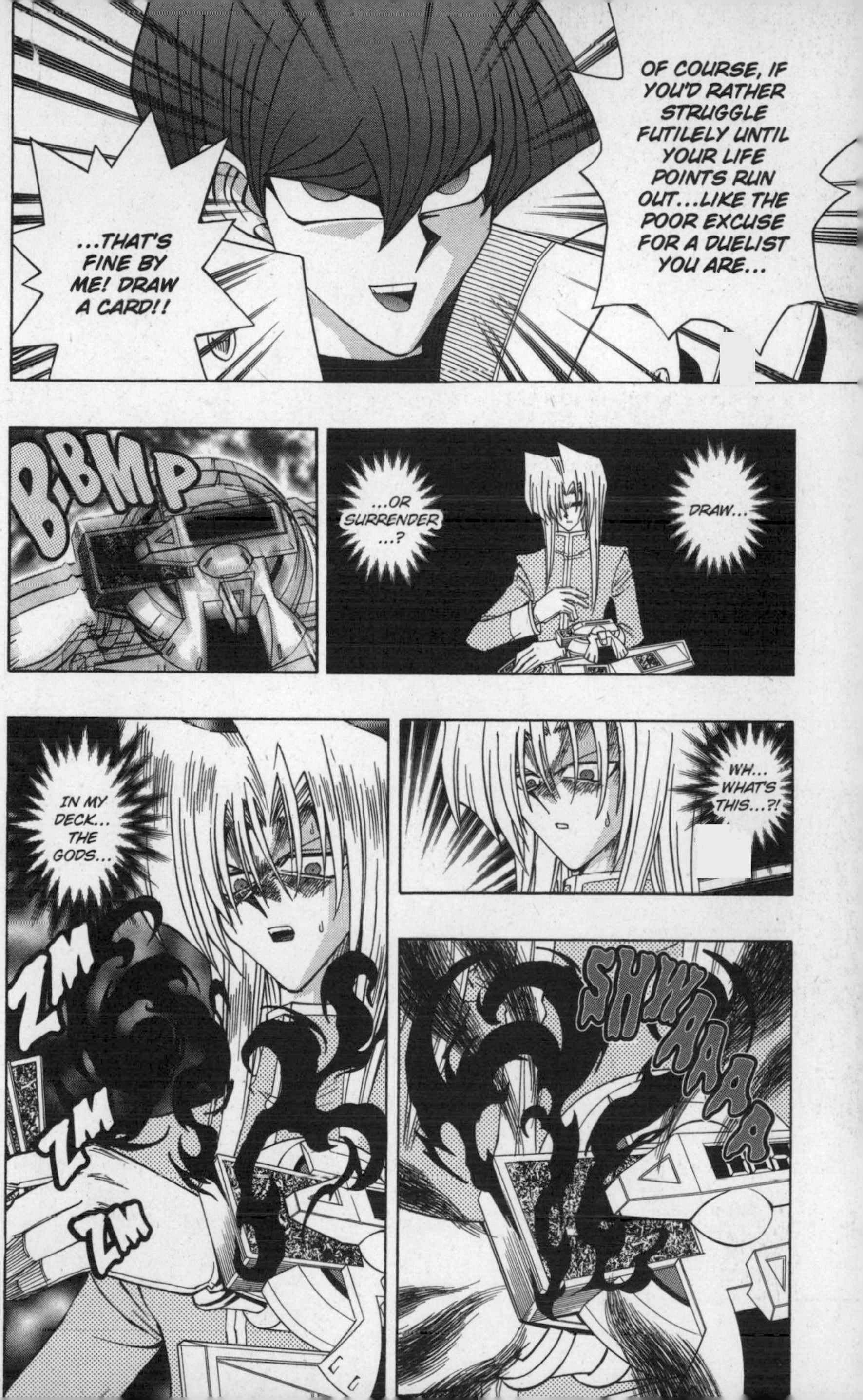
OF COURSE, IF YOU'D RATHER STRUGGLE FUTILELY UNTIL YOUR LIFE POINTS RUN OUT...LIKE THE POOR EXCUSE FOR A DUELIST YOU ARE...
...THAT'S FINE BY ME! DRAW A CARD!!
DRAW...
...OR SURRENDER ...?
BBMP
WH... WHAT'S THIS...?!
SHWAAAAA
IN MY DECK... THE GODS...
ZM
ZM
ZM

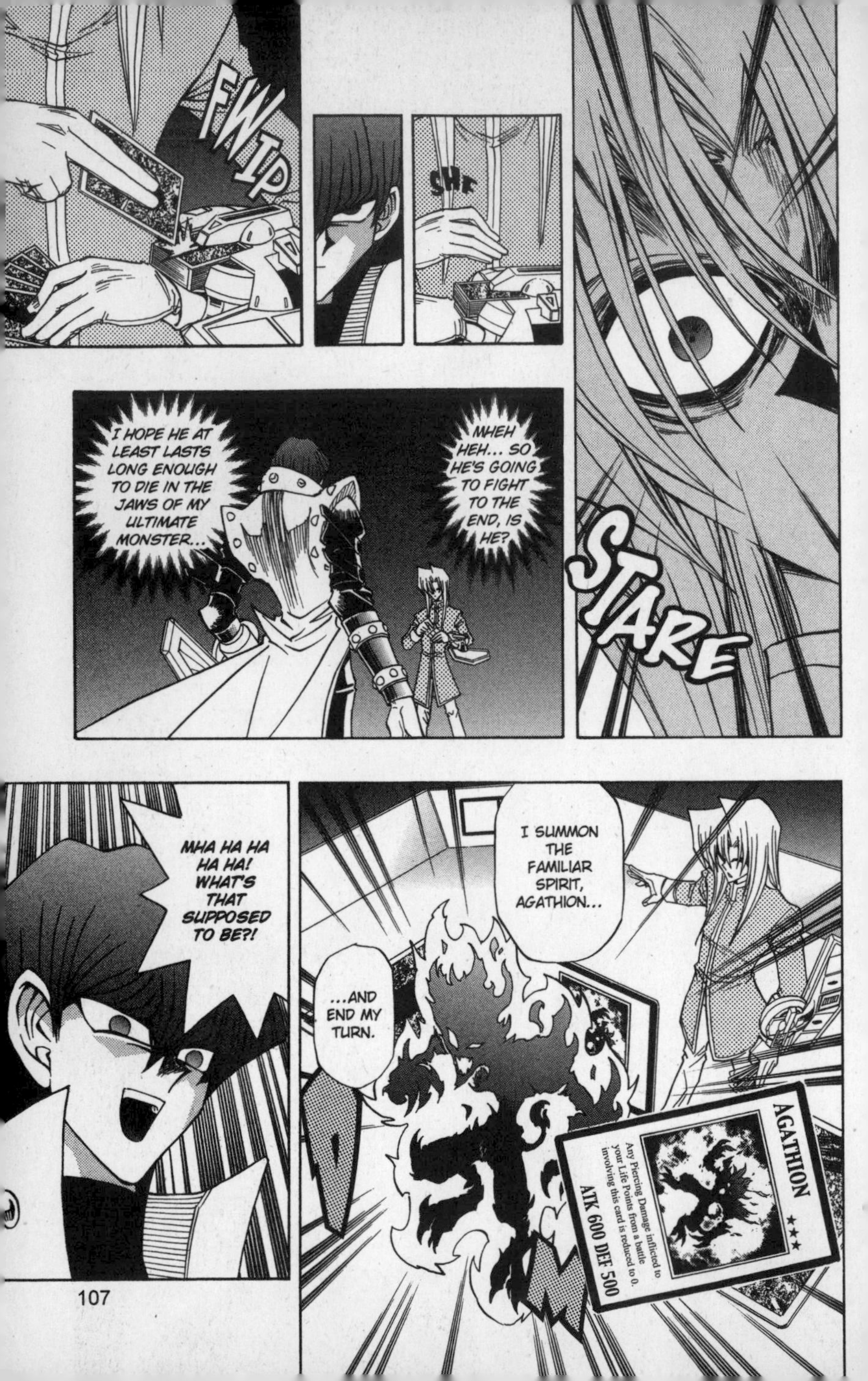
STARE
SHF
FWIP
MHEH HEH... SO HE'S GOING TO FIGHT TO THE END, IS HE?
I HOPE HE AT LEAST LASTS LONG ENOUGH TO DIE IN THE JAWS OF MY ULTIMATE MONSTER...
I SUMMON THE FAMILIAR SPIRIT, AGATHION...
...AND END MY TURN.
AGATHION
Any Piercing Damage inflicted to your Life Points from a battle involving this card is reduced to 0.
ATK 600 DEF 500
MHA HA HA HA HA! WHAT'S THAT SUPPOSED TO BE?!

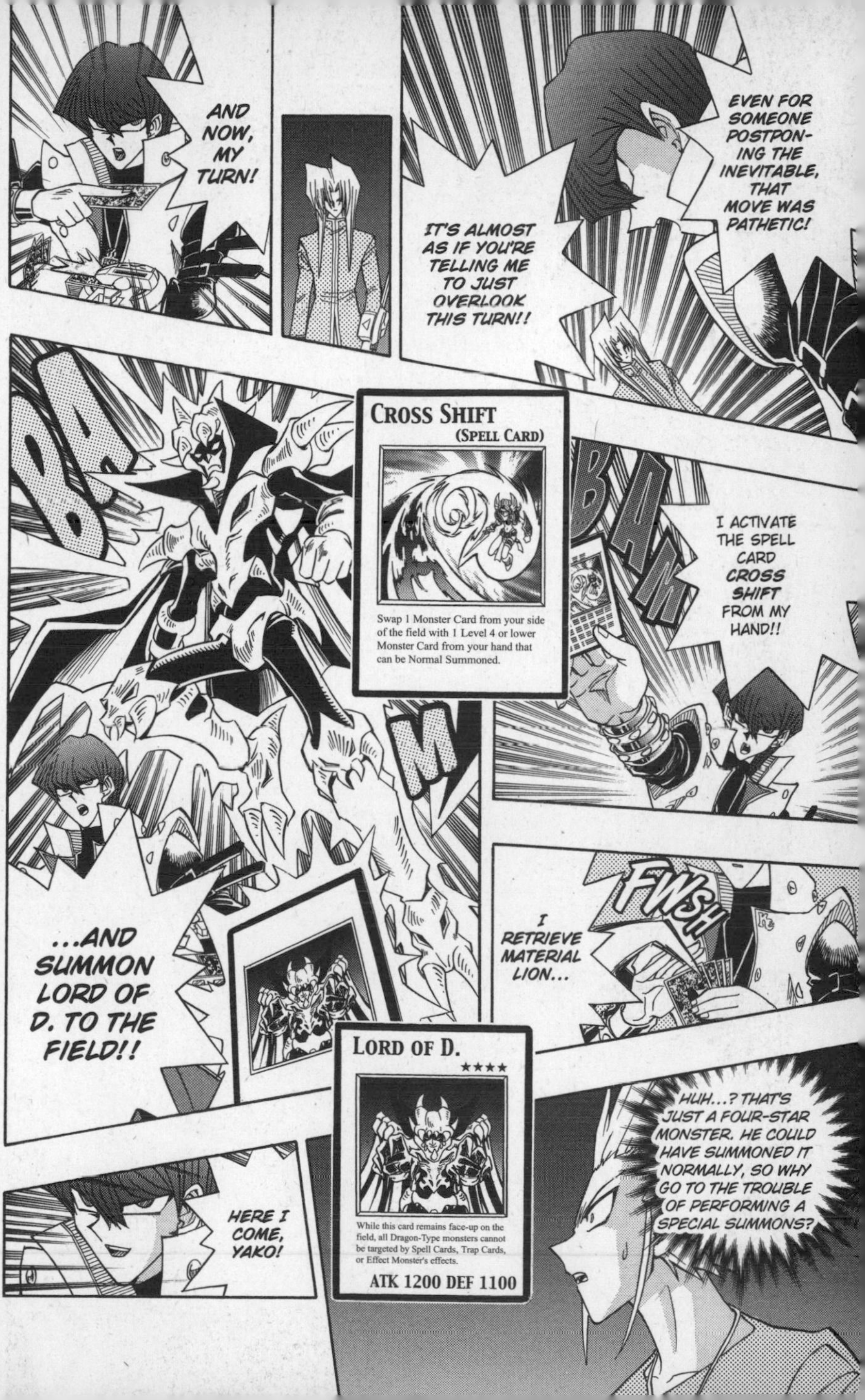
EVEN FOR SOMEONE POSTPONING THE INEVITABLE, THAT MOVE WAS PATHETIC!
IT'S ALMOST AS IF YOU'RE TELLING ME TO JUST OVERLOOK THIS TURN!!
AND NOW, MY TURN!
BAM
I ACTIVATE THE SPELL CARD CROSS SHIFT FROM MY HAND!!
CROSS SHIFT
(SPELL CARD)
Swap 1 Monster Card from your side of the field with 1 Level 4 or lower Monster Card from your hand that can be Normal Summoned.
FWSH
I RETRIEVE MATERIAL LION...
BAM
...AND SUMMON LORD OF D. TO THE FIELD!!
LORD OF D.
★★★★
While this card remains face-up on the field, all Dragon-Type monsters cannot be targeted by Spell Cards, Trap Cards, or Effect Monster's effects.
ATK 1200 DEF 1100
HUH...? THAT'S JUST A FOUR-STAR MONSTER. HE COULD HAVE SUMMONED IT NORMALLY, SO WHY GO TO THE TROUBLE OF PERFORMING A SPECIAL SUMMONS?
HERE I COME, YAKO!

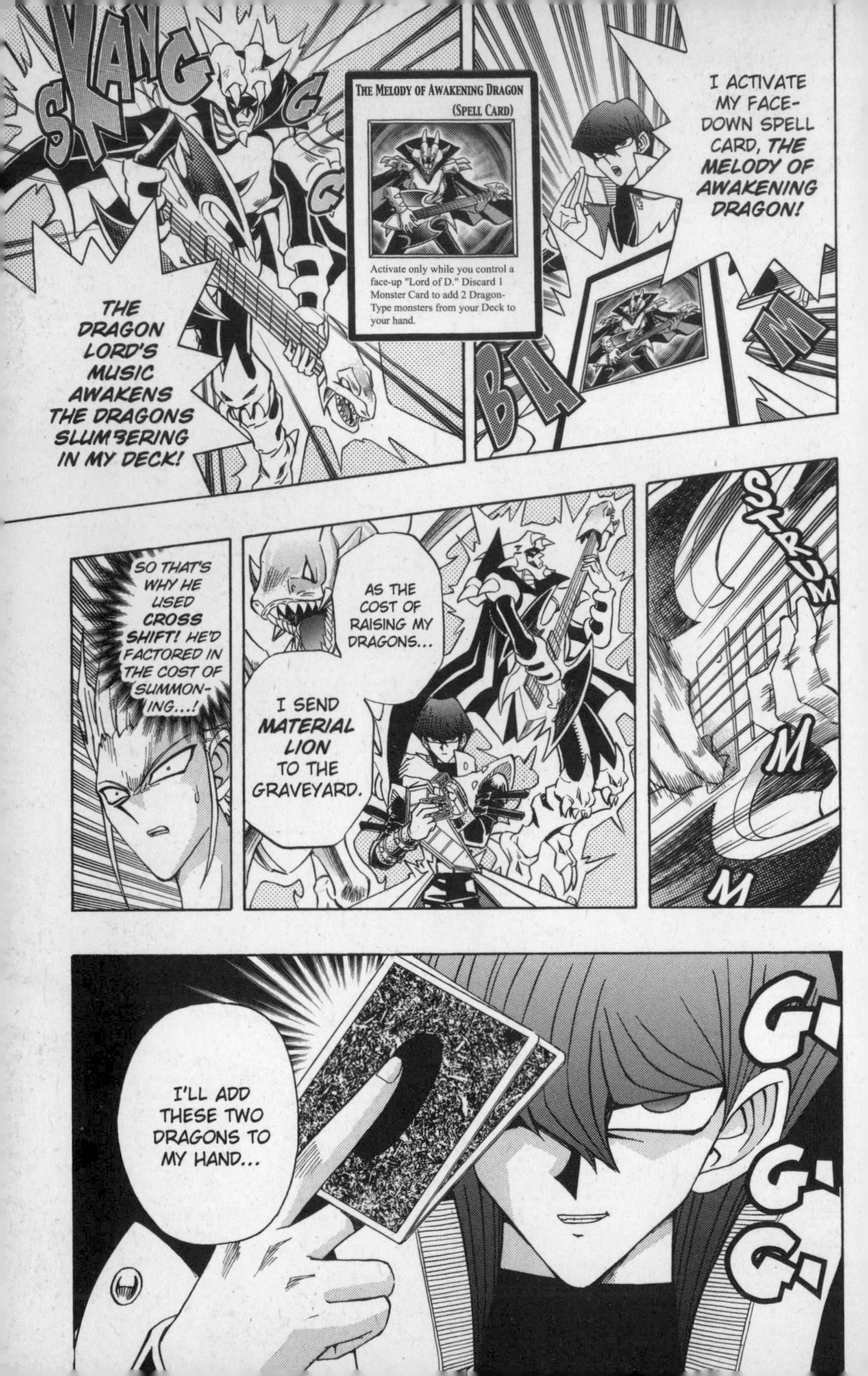
I ACTIVATE MY FACE-DOWN SPELL CARD, THE MELODY OF AWAKENING DRAGON!
BAM
THE MELODY OF AWAKENING DRAGON
(SPELL CARD)
Activate only while you control a face-up "Lord of D." Discard 1 Monster Card to add 2 Dragon-Type monsters from your Deck to your hand.
SKYANG
THE DRAGON LORD'S MUSIC AWAKENS THE DRAGONS SLUMBERING IN MY DECK!
SKRUM
MM
AS THE COST OF RAISING MY DRAGONS...
I SEND MATERIAL LION TO THE GRAVEYARD.
SO THAT'S WHY HE USED CROSS SHIFT! HE'D FACTORED IN THE COST OF SUMMONING...!
GGG
I'LL ADD THESE TWO DRAGONS TO MY HAND...

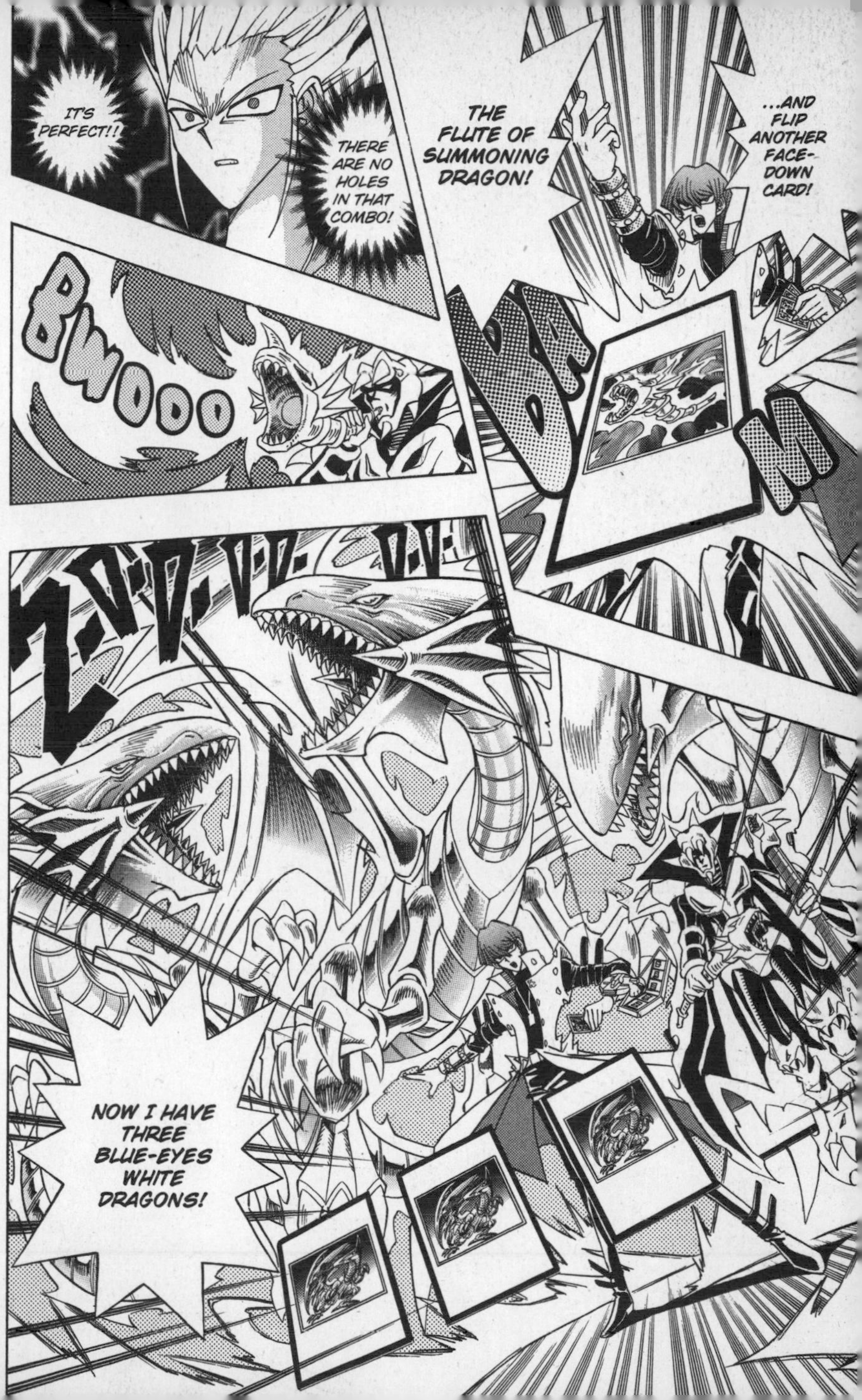

...AND FLIP ANOTHER FACE-DOWN CARD!
THE FLUTE OF SUMMONING DRAGON!
IT'S PERFECT!!
THERE ARE NO HOLES IN THAT COMBO!
BWOOO
NOW I HAVE THREE BLUE-EYES WHITE DRAGONS!

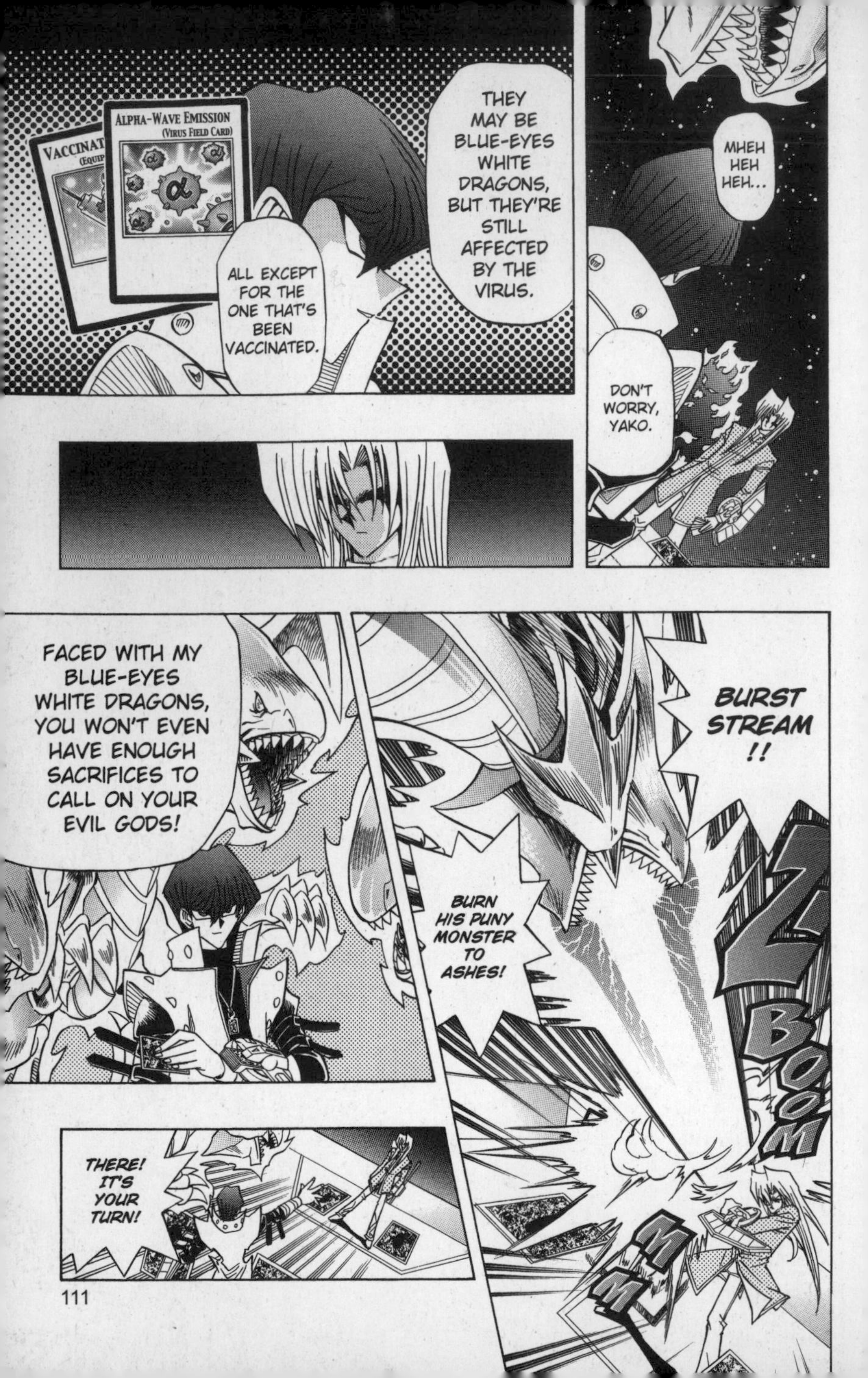
MHEH HEH HEH...
DON'T WORRY, YAKO.
THEY MAY BE BLUE-EYES WHITE DRAGONS, BUT THEY'RE STILL AFFECTED BY THE VIRUS.
ALL EXCEPT FOR THE ONE THAT'S BEEN VACCINATED.
ALPHA-WAVE EMISSION
(VIRUS FIELD CARD)
BURST STREAM!!
BURN HIS PUNY MONSTER TO ASHES!
ZBOOOOM
MMM
FACED WITH MY BLUE-EYES WHITE DRAGONS, YOU WON'T EVEN HAVE ENOUGH SACRIFICES TO CALL ON YOUR EVIL GODS!
THERE! IT'S YOUR TURN!

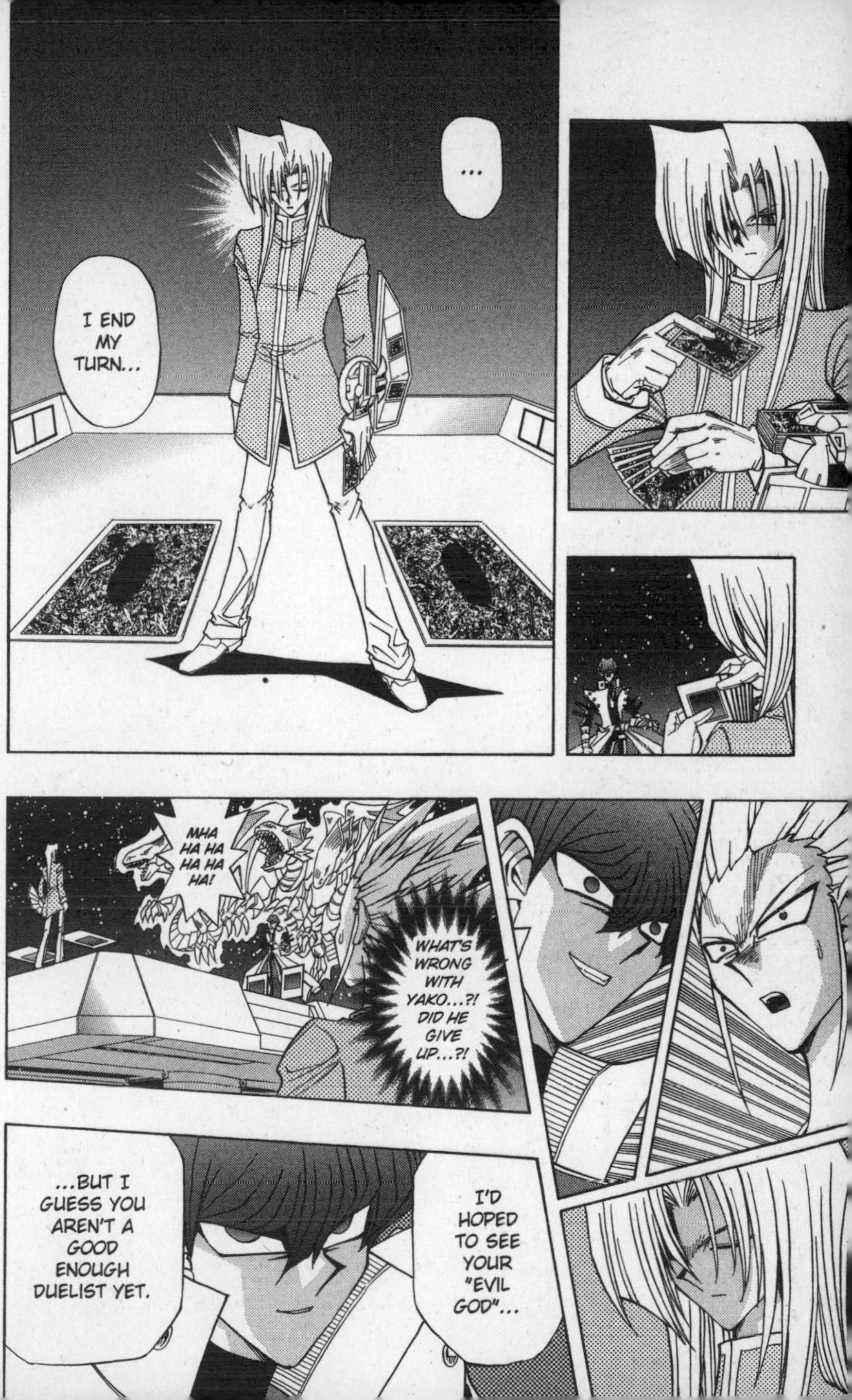
...
I END MY TURN...
MHA HA HA HA HA HA HA!
WHAT'S WRONG WITH YAKO...?! DID HE GIVE UP...?!
I'D HOPED TO SEE YOUR "EVIL GOD"...
...BUT I GUESS YOU AREN'T A GOOD ENOUGH DUELIST YET.

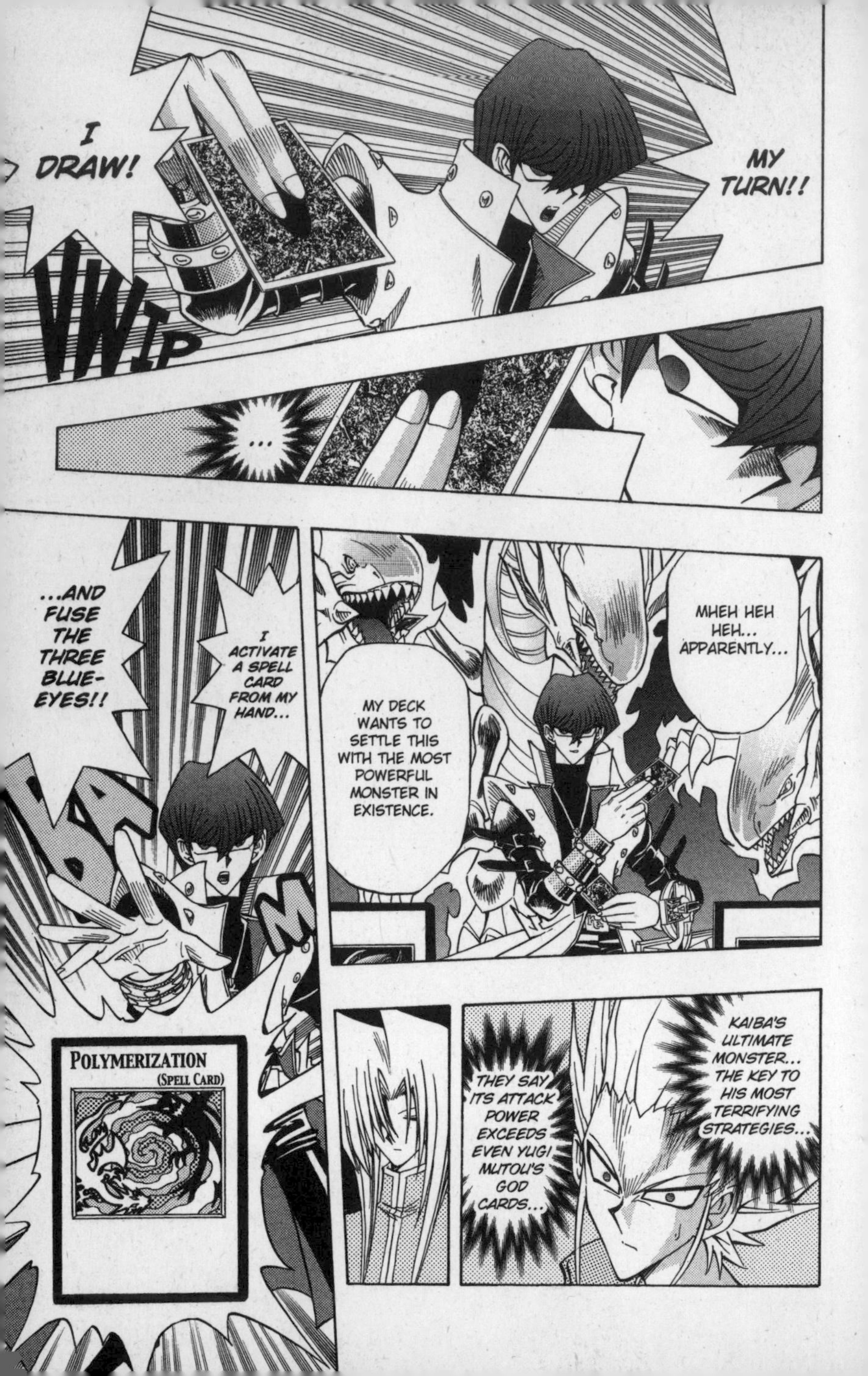
MY TURN!!
I DRAW!
VWIP
...
MHEH HEH HEH... APPARENTLY...
MY DECK WANTS TO SETTLE THIS WITH THE MOST POWERFUL MONSTER IN EXISTENCE.
I ACTIVATE A SPELL CARD FROM MY HAND...
...AND FUSE THE THREE BLUE-EYES!!
BAM
KAIBA'S ULTIMATE MONSTER... THE KEY TO HIS MOST TERRIFYING STRATEGIES...
THEY SAY ITS ATTACK POWER EXCEEDS EVEN YUGI MUTOU'S GOD CARDS...
POLYMERIZATION
(SPELL CARD)

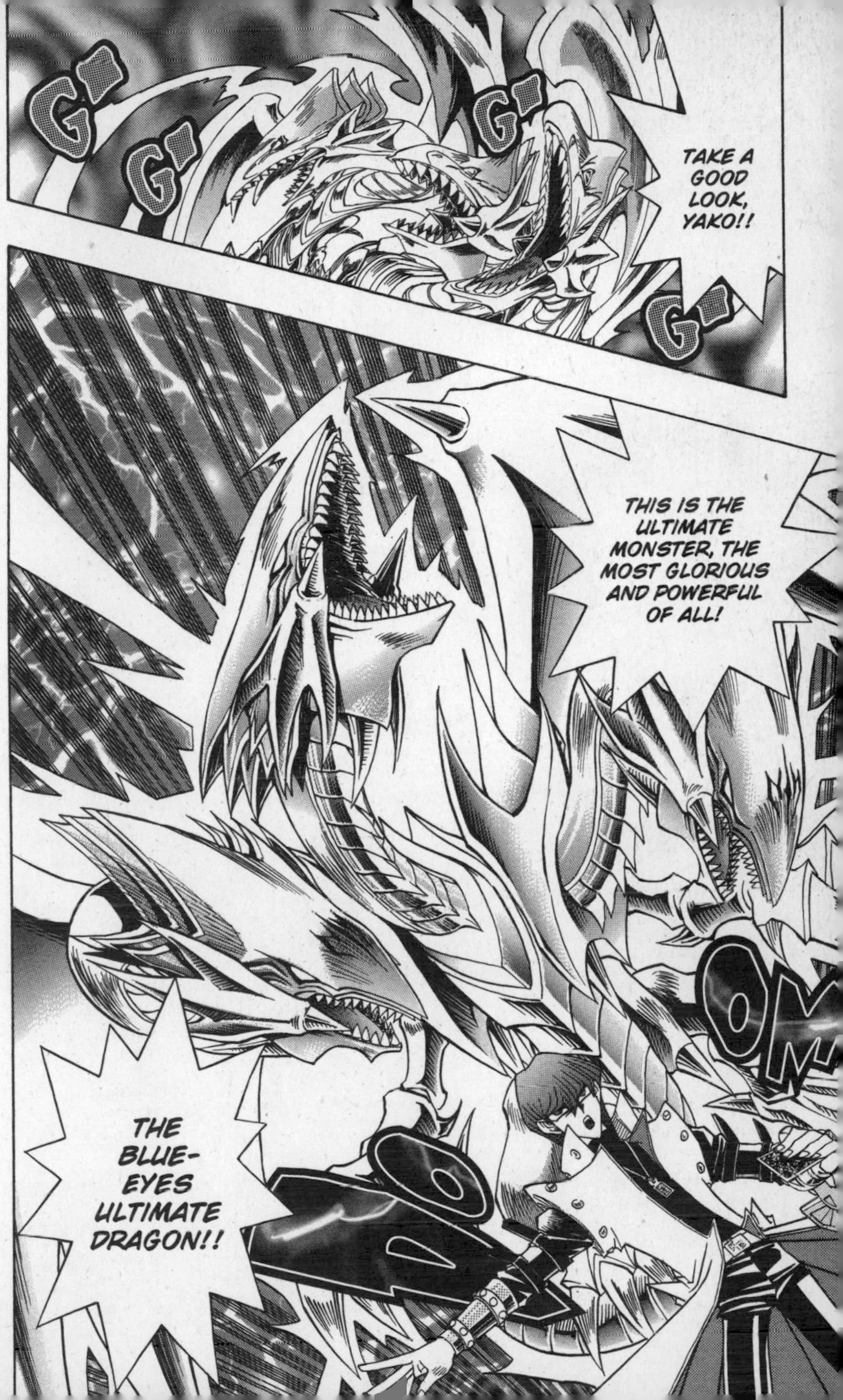
G'
G'
G'
G'
TAKE A GOOD LOOK, YAKO!!
THIS IS THE ULTIMATE MONSTER, THE MOST GLORIOUS AND POWERFUL OF ALL!
OM
THE BLUE-EYES ULTIMATE DRAGON!!

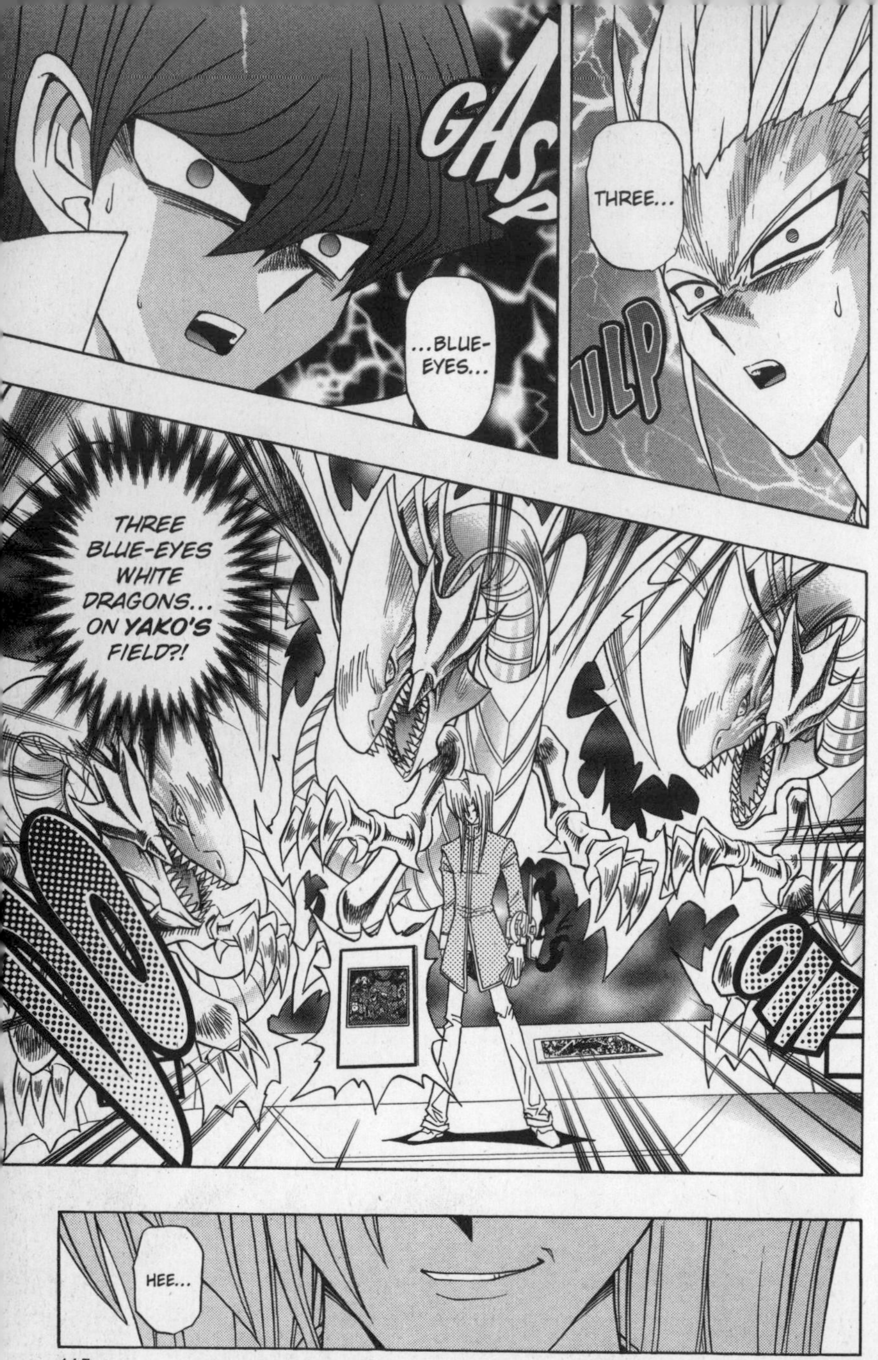
THREE...
ULP
GASP
...BLUE-EYES...
THREE BLUE-EYES WHITE DRAGONS... ON YAKO'S FIELD?!
HEE...

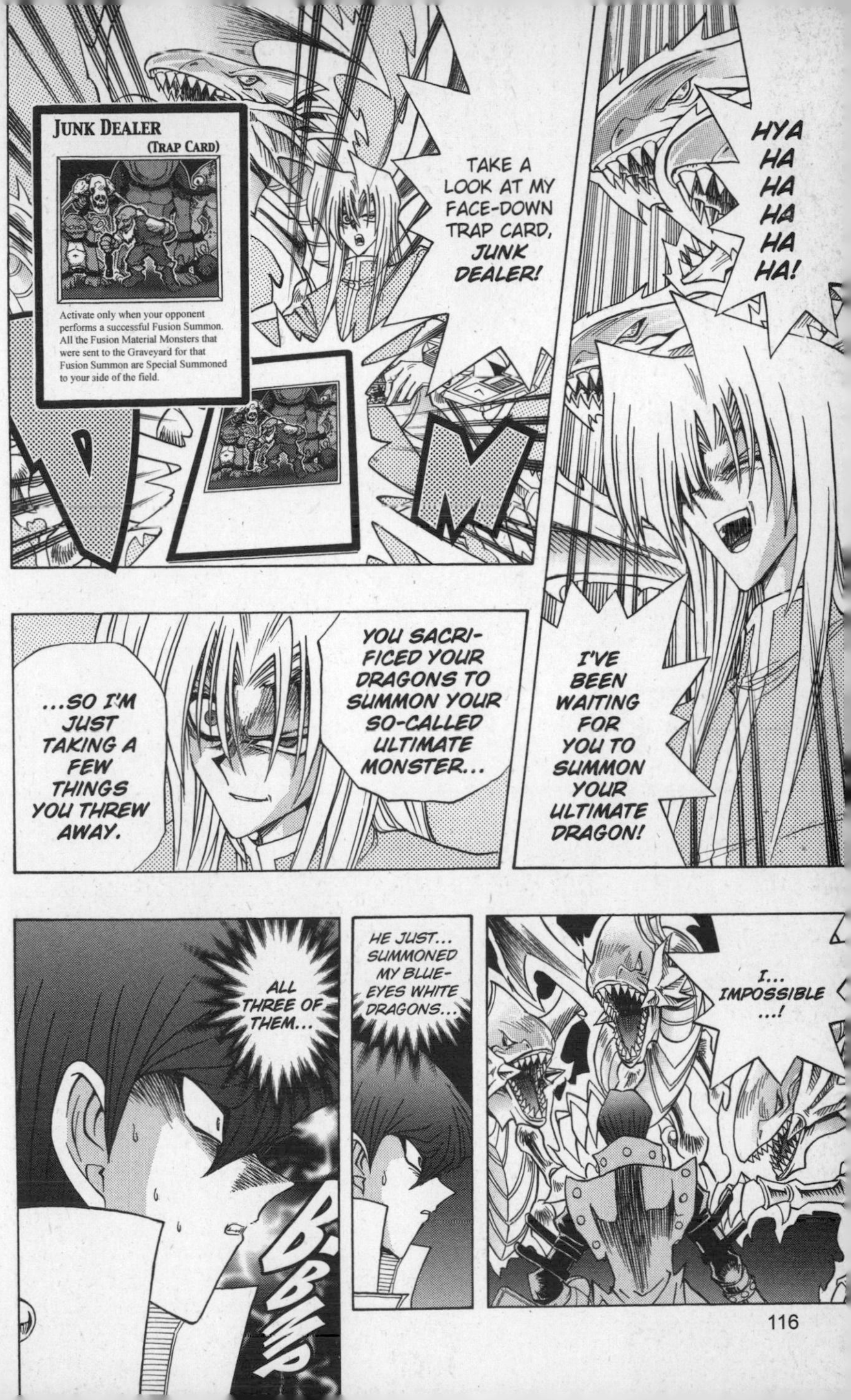
HYA HA HA HA HA HA!
I'VE BEEN WAITING FOR YOU TO SUMMON YOUR ULTIMATE DRAGON!
TAKE A LOOK AT MY FACE-DOWN TRAP CARD, JUNK DEALER!
JUNK DEALER
(TRAP CARD)
Activate only when your opponent performs a successful Fusion Summon. All the Fusion Material Monsters that were sent to the Graveyard for that Fusion Summon are Special Summoned to your side of the field.
YOU SACRIFICED YOUR DRAGONS TO SUMMON YOUR SO-CALLED ULTIMATE MONSTER...
...SO I'M JUST TAKING A FEW THINGS YOU THREW AWAY.
I... IMPOSSIBLE ...!
HE JUST... SUMMONED MY BLUE-EYES WHITE DRAGONS...
ALL THREE OF THEM...

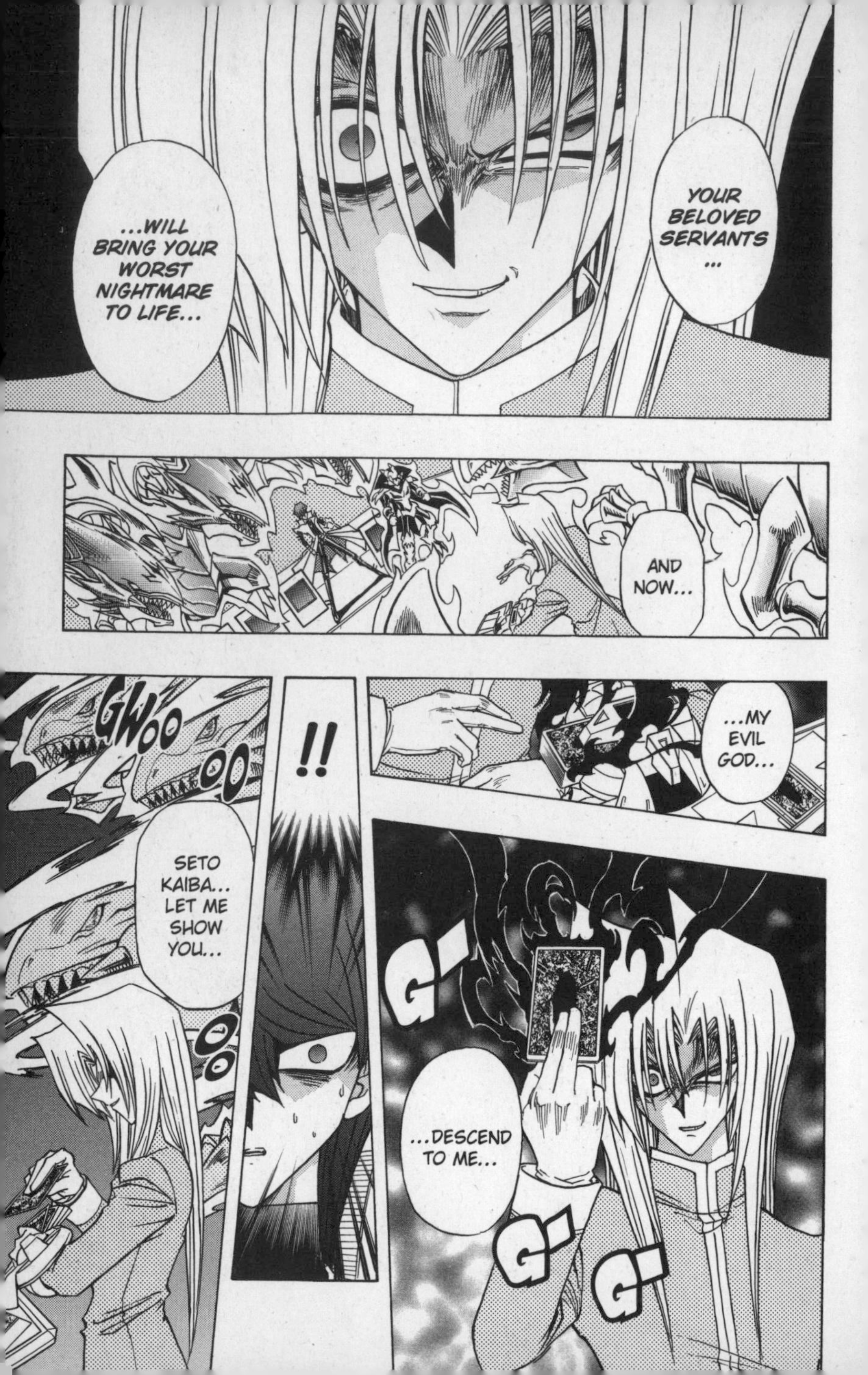
YOUR BELOVED SERVANTS ...
...WILL BRING YOUR WORST NIGHTMARE TO LIFE...
AND NOW...
...MY EVIL GOD...
G
...DESCEND TO ME...
G
G
!!
GWOOOO
SETO KAIBA... LET ME SHOW YOU...
OOO

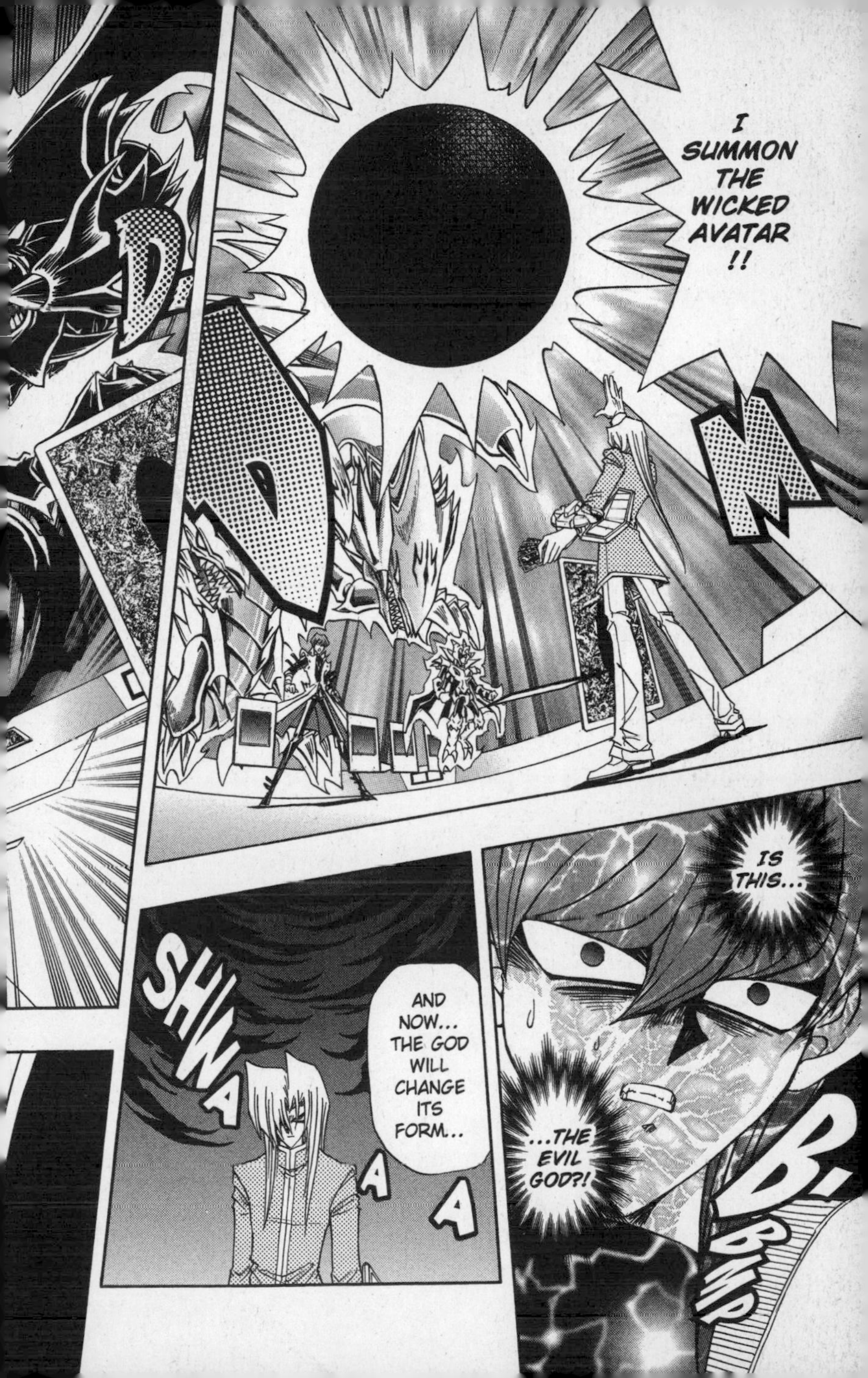
I SUMMON THE WICKED AVATAR!!
IS THIS...
...THE EVIL GOD?!
AND NOW... THE GOD WILL CHANGE ITS FORM..
SHWAAAA

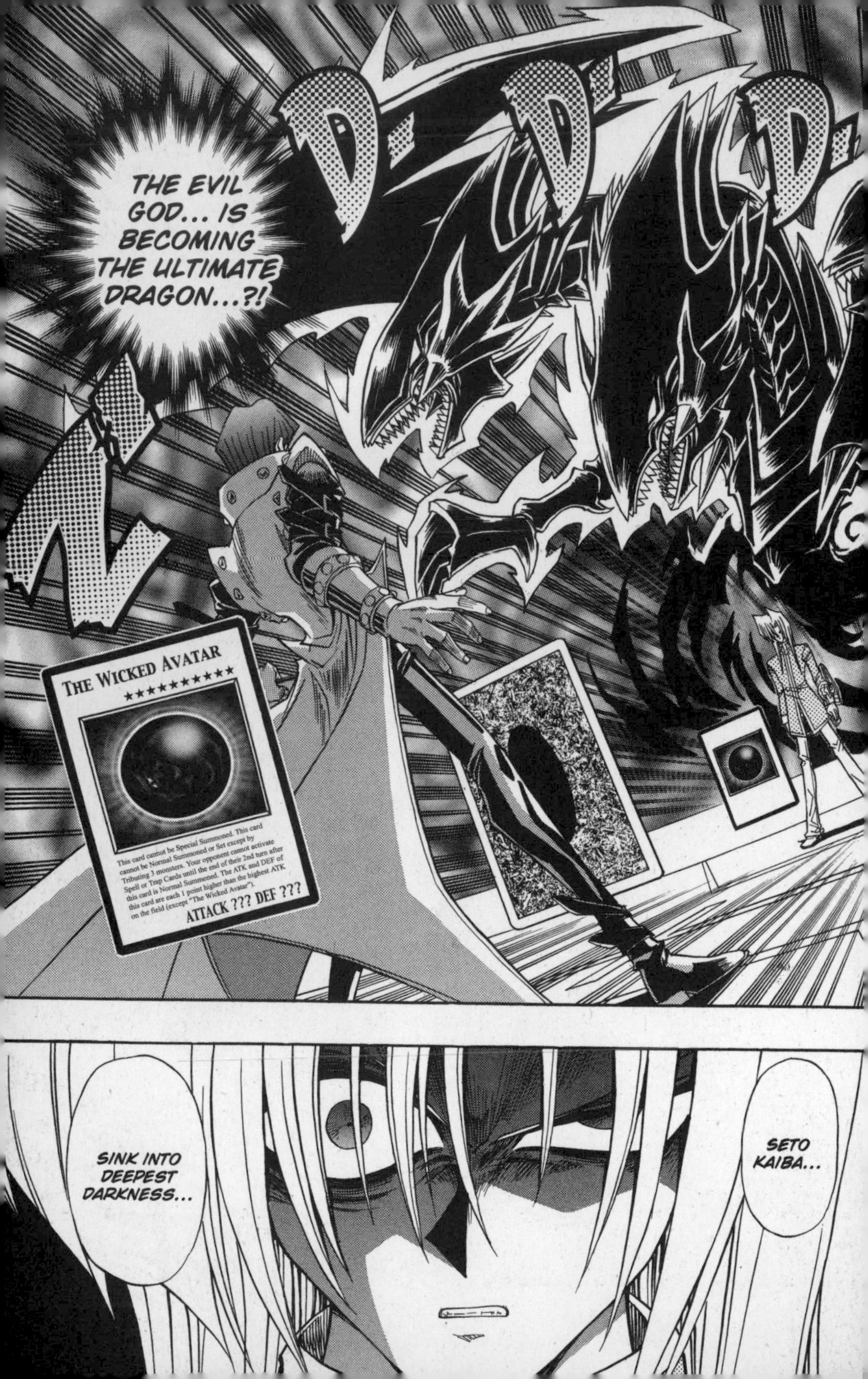
THE EVIL GOD... IS BECOMING THE ULTIMATE DRAGON...?!
THE WICKED AVATAR
This card cannot be Special Summoned. This card cannot be Normal Summoned or Set except by Tributing 3 monsters. Your opponent cannot activate Spell or Trap Cards until the end of their 2nd turn after this card is Normal Summoned. The ATK and DEF of this card are each 1 point higher than the highest ATK on the field (except "The Wicked Avatar").
ATTACK ??? DEF ???
SETO KAIBA...
SINK INTO DEEPEST DARKNESS...

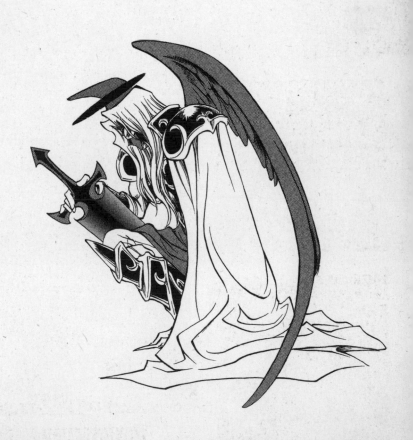

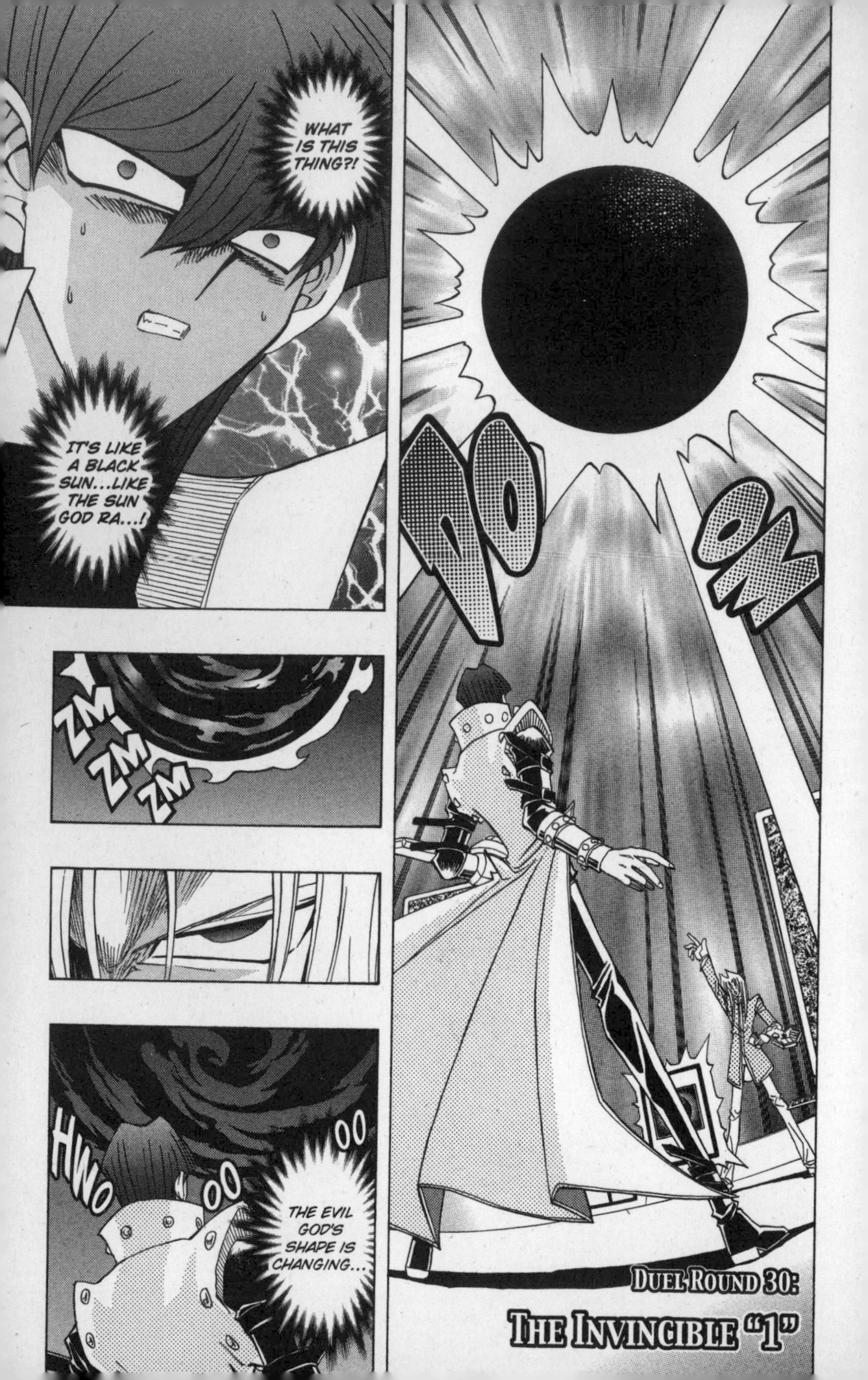
DOOOM
DUEL ROUND 30:
THE INVINCIBLE "1"
WHAT IS THIS THING?!
IT'S LIKE A BLACK SUN...LIKE THE SUN GOD RA...!
ZM ZM ZM
HWOOOOO
THE EVIL GOD'S SHAPE IS CHANGING...

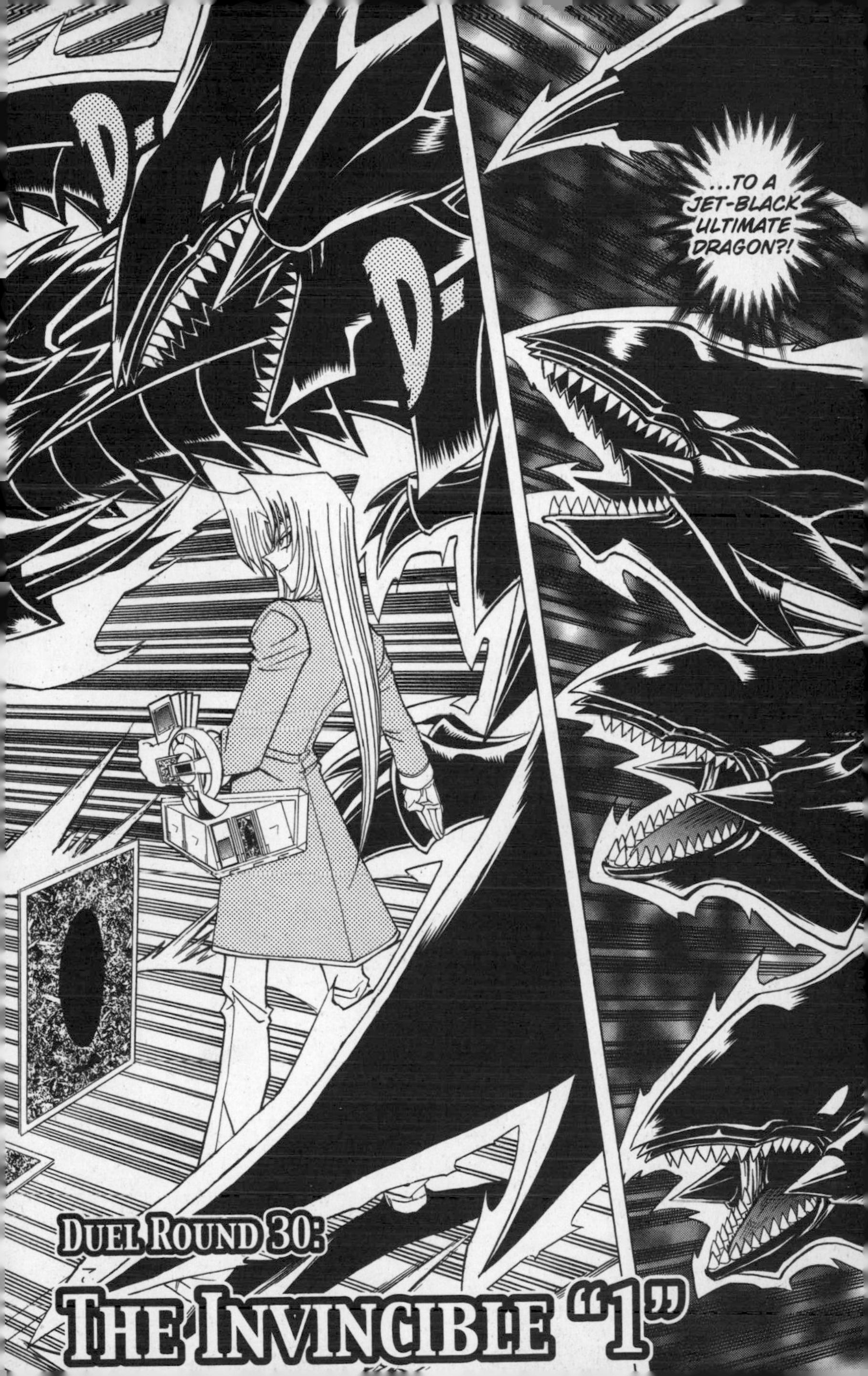

...TO A JET-BLACK ULTIMATE DRAGON?!

Duel Round 30: The Invincible "1"

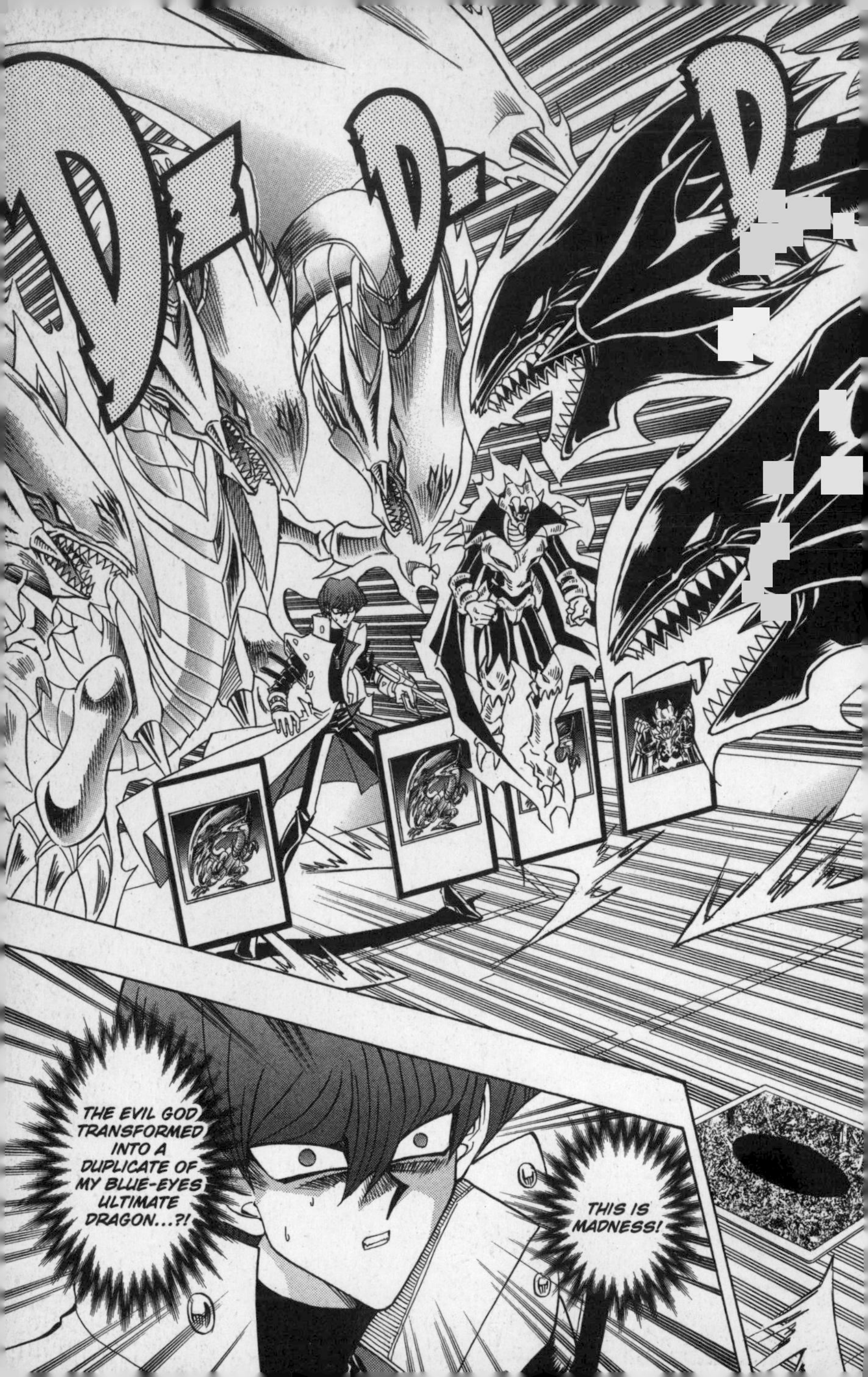
THIS IS MADNESS!
THE EVIL GOD TRANSFORMED INTO A DUPLICATE OF MY BLUE-EYES ULTIMATE DRAGON...?!

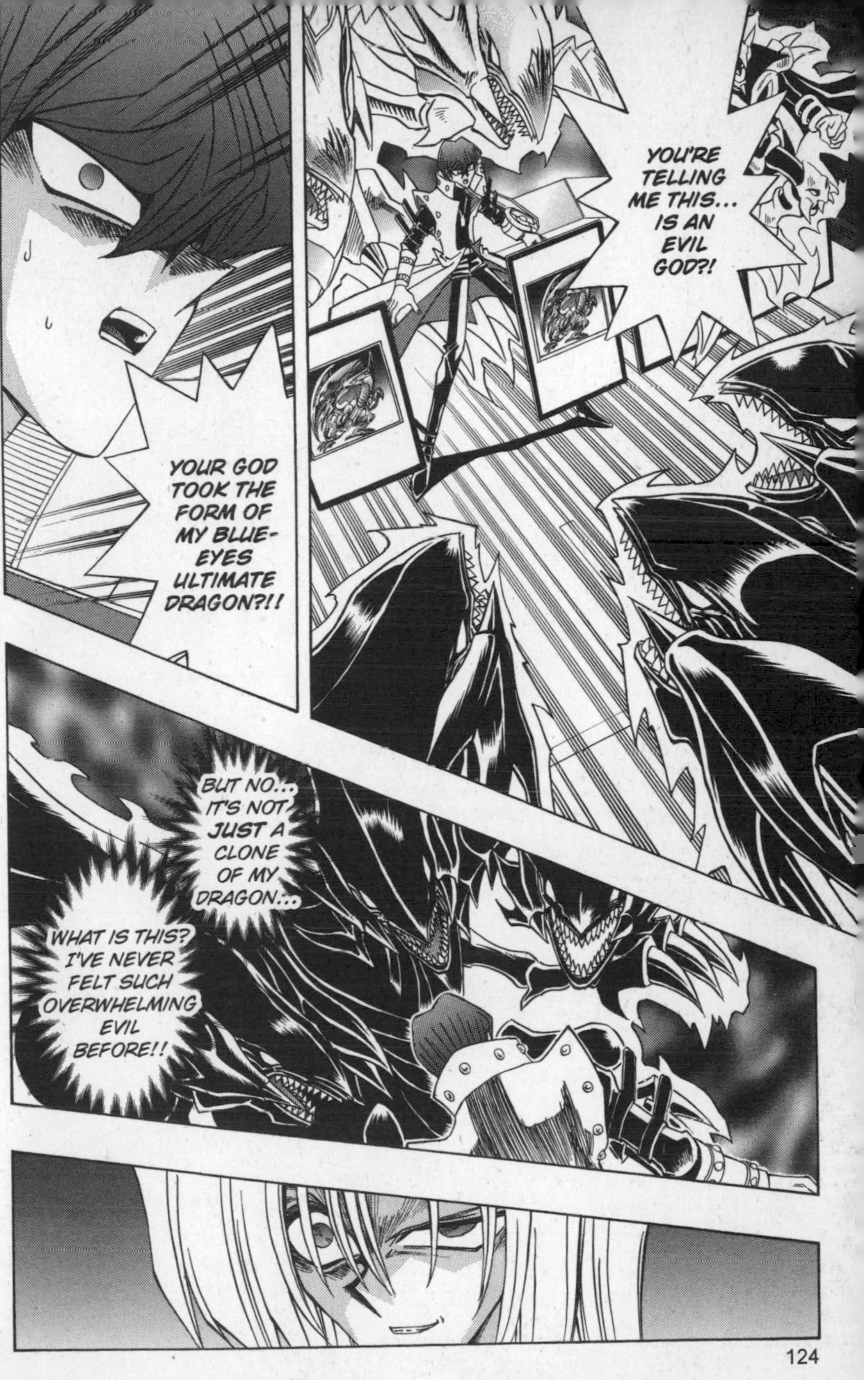
YOU'RE TELLING ME THIS... IS AN EVIL GOD?!
YOUR GOD TOOK THE FORM OF MY BLUE-EYES ULTIMATE DRAGON?!!
BUT NO... IT'S NOT JUST A CLONE OF MY DRAGON...
WHAT IS THIS? I'VE NEVER FELT SUCH OVERWHELMING EVIL BEFORE!!

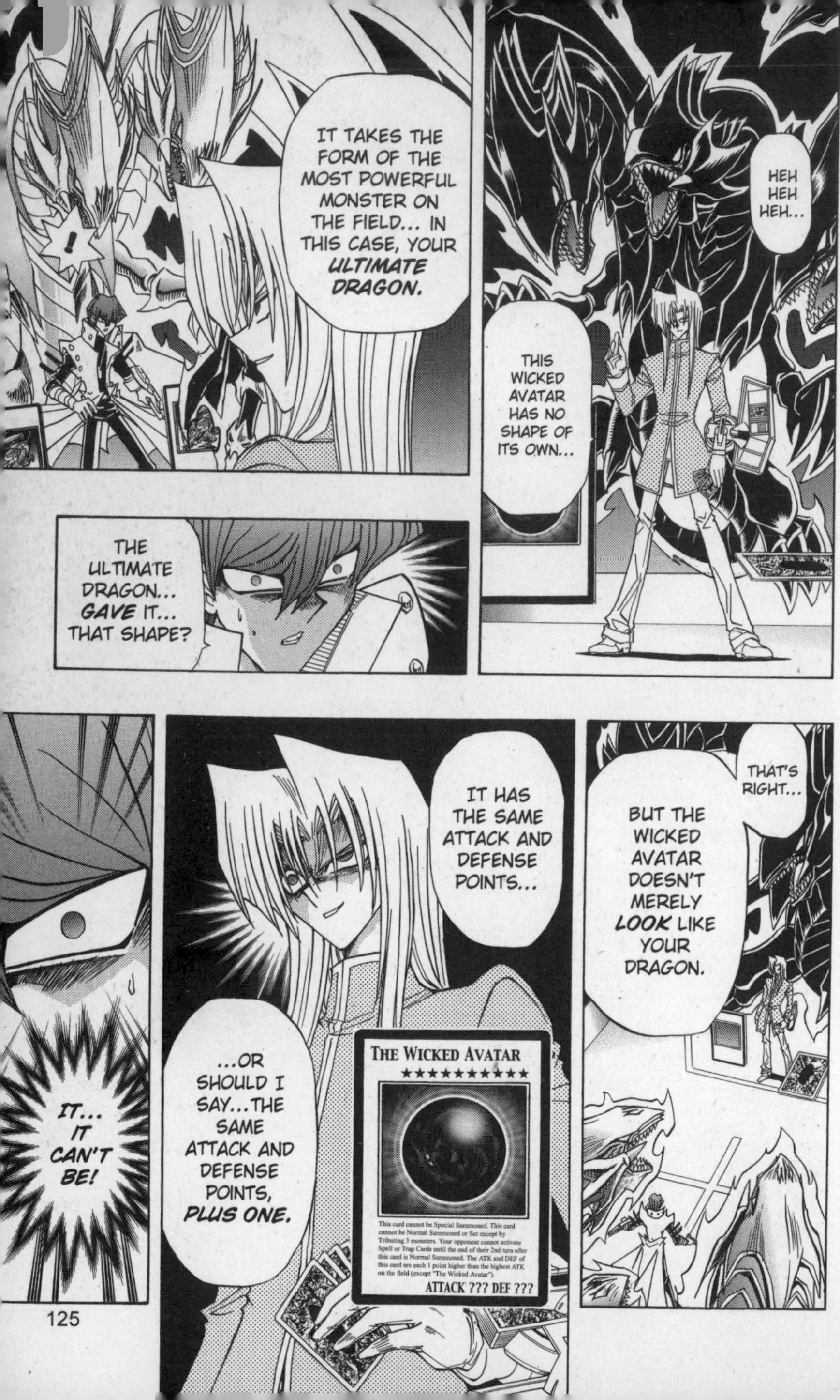
HEH HEH HEH...
THIS WICKED AVATAR HAS NO SHAPE OF ITS OWN...
!
IT TAKES THE FORM OF THE MOST POWERFUL MONSTER ON THE FIELD... IN THIS CASE, YOUR ***ULTIMATE DRAGON.***
THE ULTIMATE DRAGON... ***GAVE*** IT... THAT SHAPE?
THAT'S RIGHT...
BUT THE WICKED AVATAR DOESN'T MERELY ***LOOK*** LIKE YOUR DRAGON.
IT HAS THE SAME ATTACK AND DEFENSE POINTS...
...OR SHOULD I SAY...THE SAME ATTACK AND DEFENSE POINTS, ***PLUS ONE.***
THE WICKED AVATAR
★★★★★★★★★★
This card cannot be Special Summoned. This card cannot be Normal Summoned or Set except by Tributing 3 monsters. Your opponent cannot activate Spell or Trap Cards until the end of their 2nd turn after this card is Normal Summoned. The ATK and DEF of this card are each 1 point higher than the highest ATK on the field (except "The Wicked Avatar").
ATTACK ??? DEF ???
IT... IT CAN'T BE!

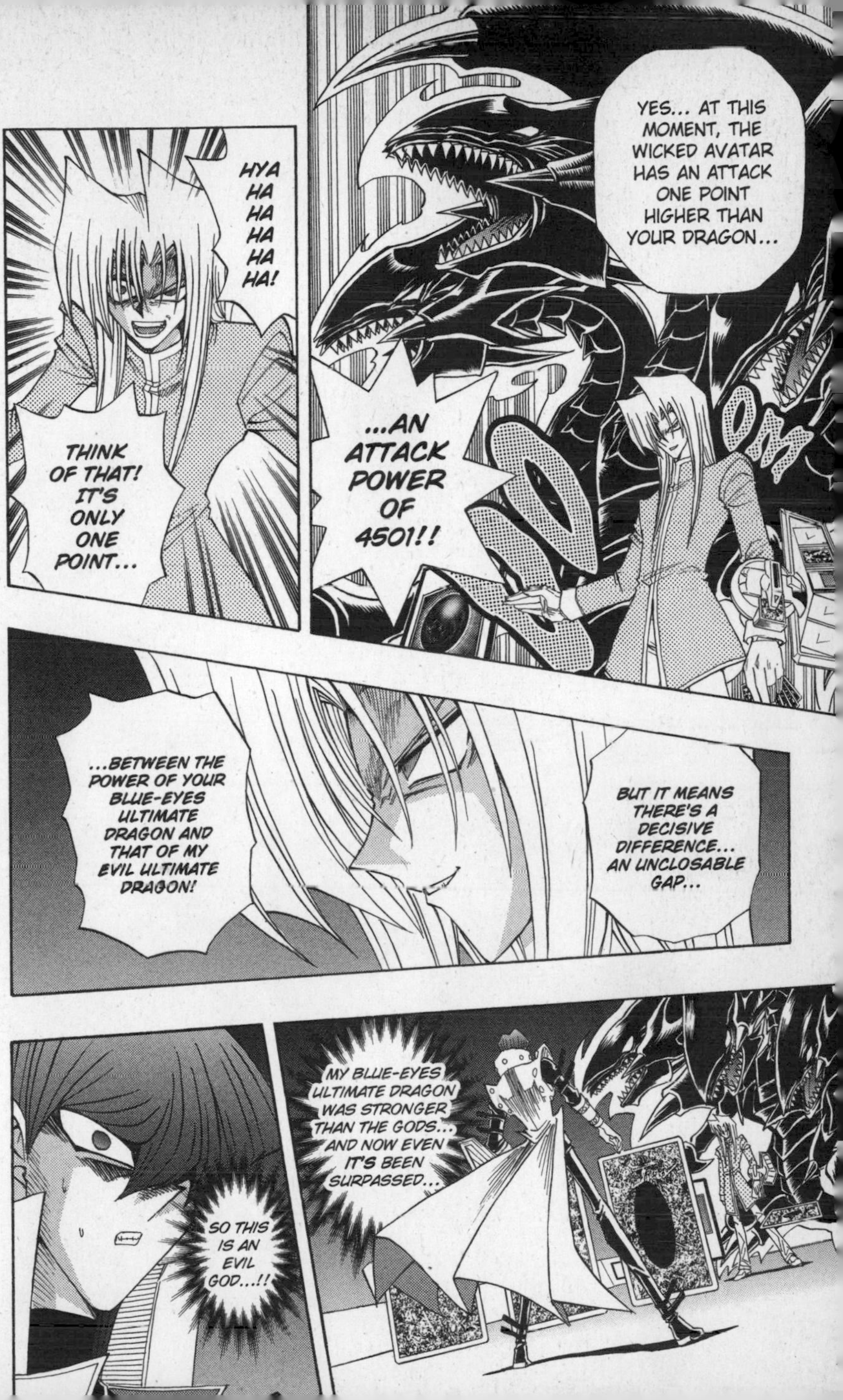
YES... AT THIS MOMENT, THE WICKED AVATAR HAS AN ATTACK ONE POINT HIGHER THAN YOUR DRAGON...
...AN ATTACK POWER OF 4501!!
HYA HA HA HA HA HA!
THINK OF THAT! IT'S ONLY ONE POINT...
BUT IT MEANS THERE'S A DECISIVE DIFFERENCE... AN UNCLOSABLE GAP...
...BETWEEN THE POWER OF YOUR BLUE-EYES ULTIMATE DRAGON AND THAT OF MY EVIL ULTIMATE DRAGON!
MY BLUE-EYES ULTIMATE DRAGON WAS STRONGER THAN THE GODS... AND NOW EVEN IT'S BEEN SURPASSED...
SO THIS IS AN EVIL GOD...!!

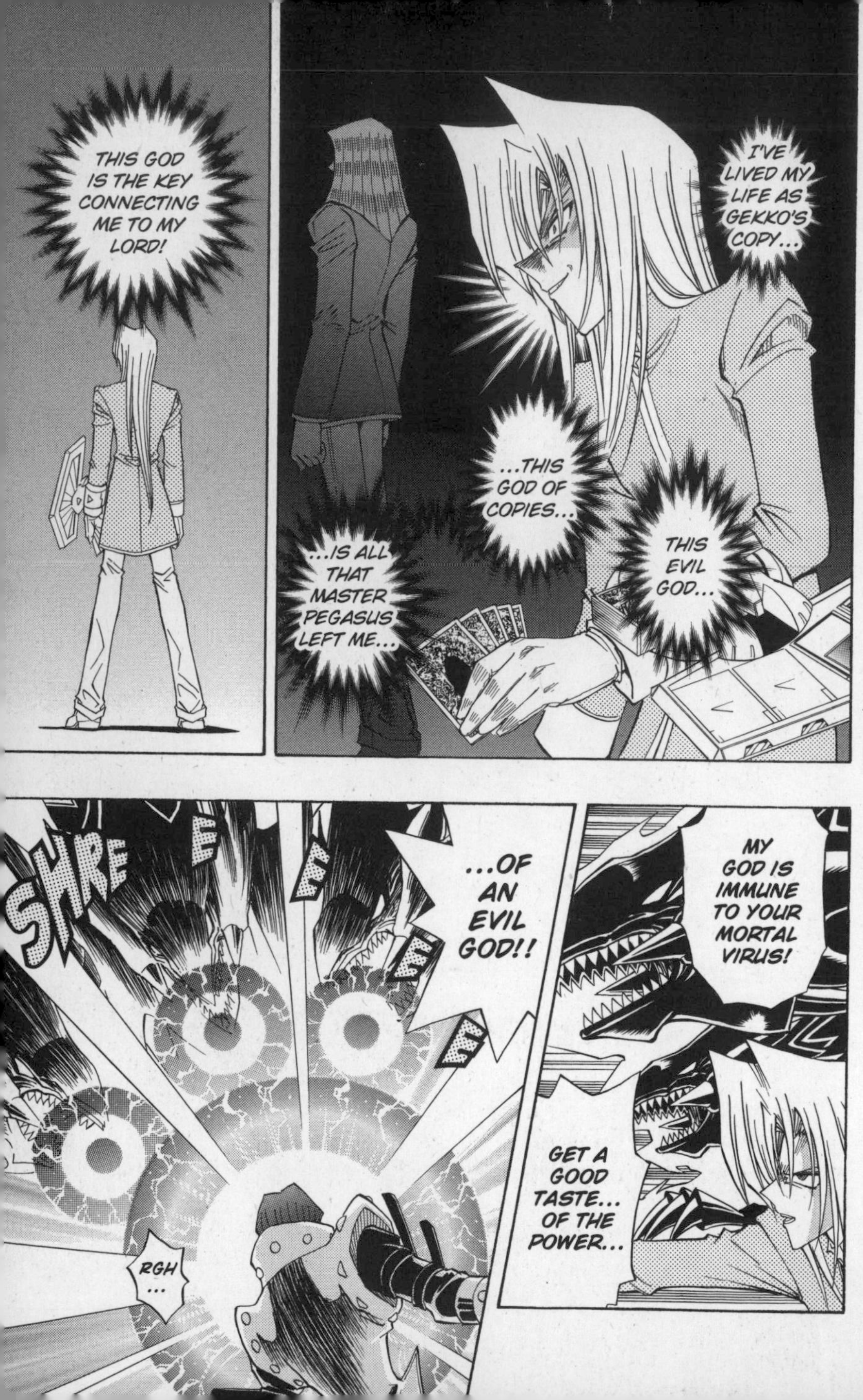
I'VE LIVED MY LIFE AS GEKKO'S COPY...
...THIS GOD OF COPIES...
THIS EVIL GOD...
...IS ALL THAT MASTER PEGASUS LEFT ME...
THIS GOD IS THE KEY CONNECTING ME TO MY LORD!
MY GOD IS IMMUNE TO YOUR MORTAL VIRUS!
GET A GOOD TASTE... OF THE POWER...
...OF AN EVIL GOD!!
SHREEEEE
RGH ...

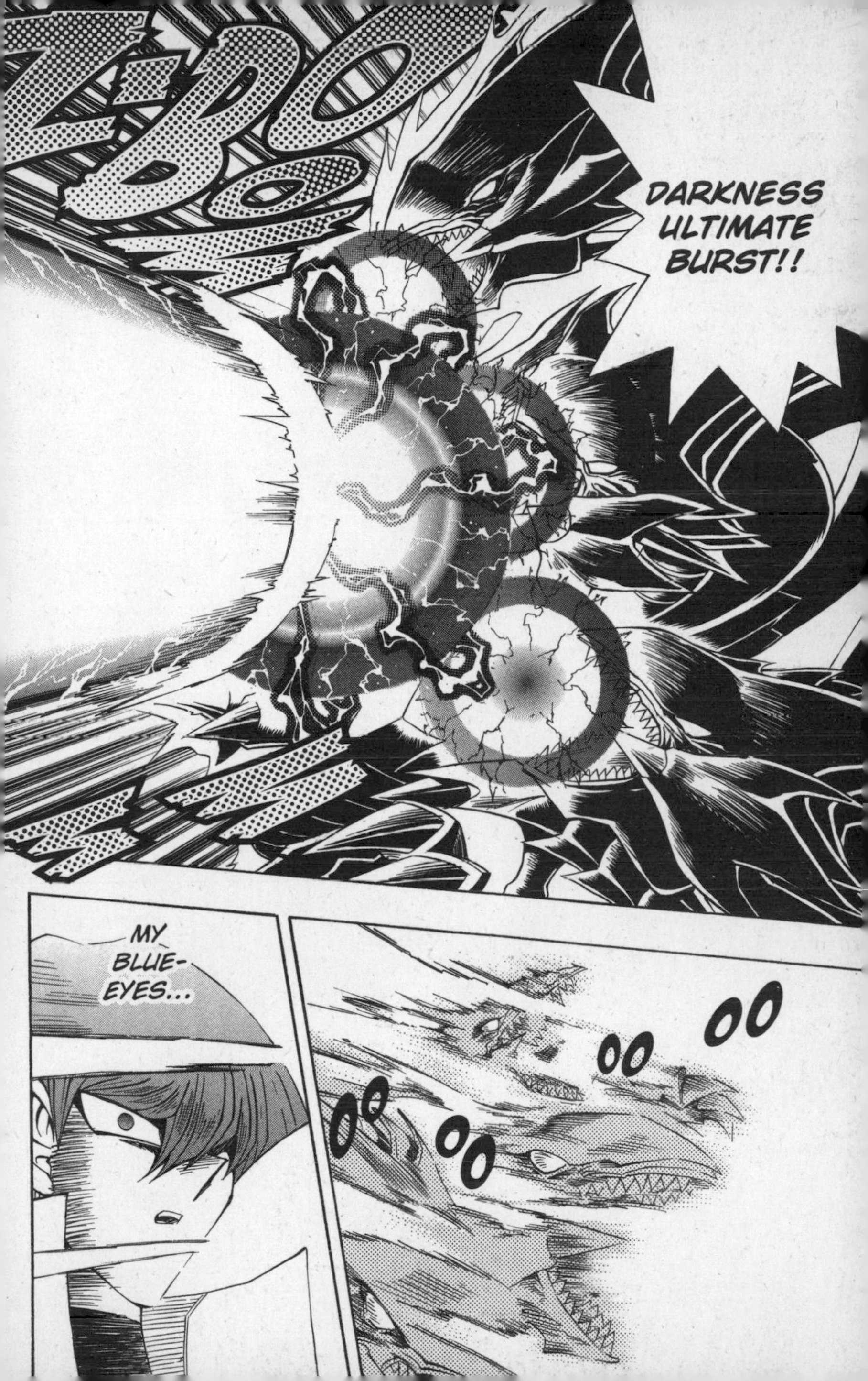
DARKNESS ULTIMATE BURST!!
MY BLUE-EYES...

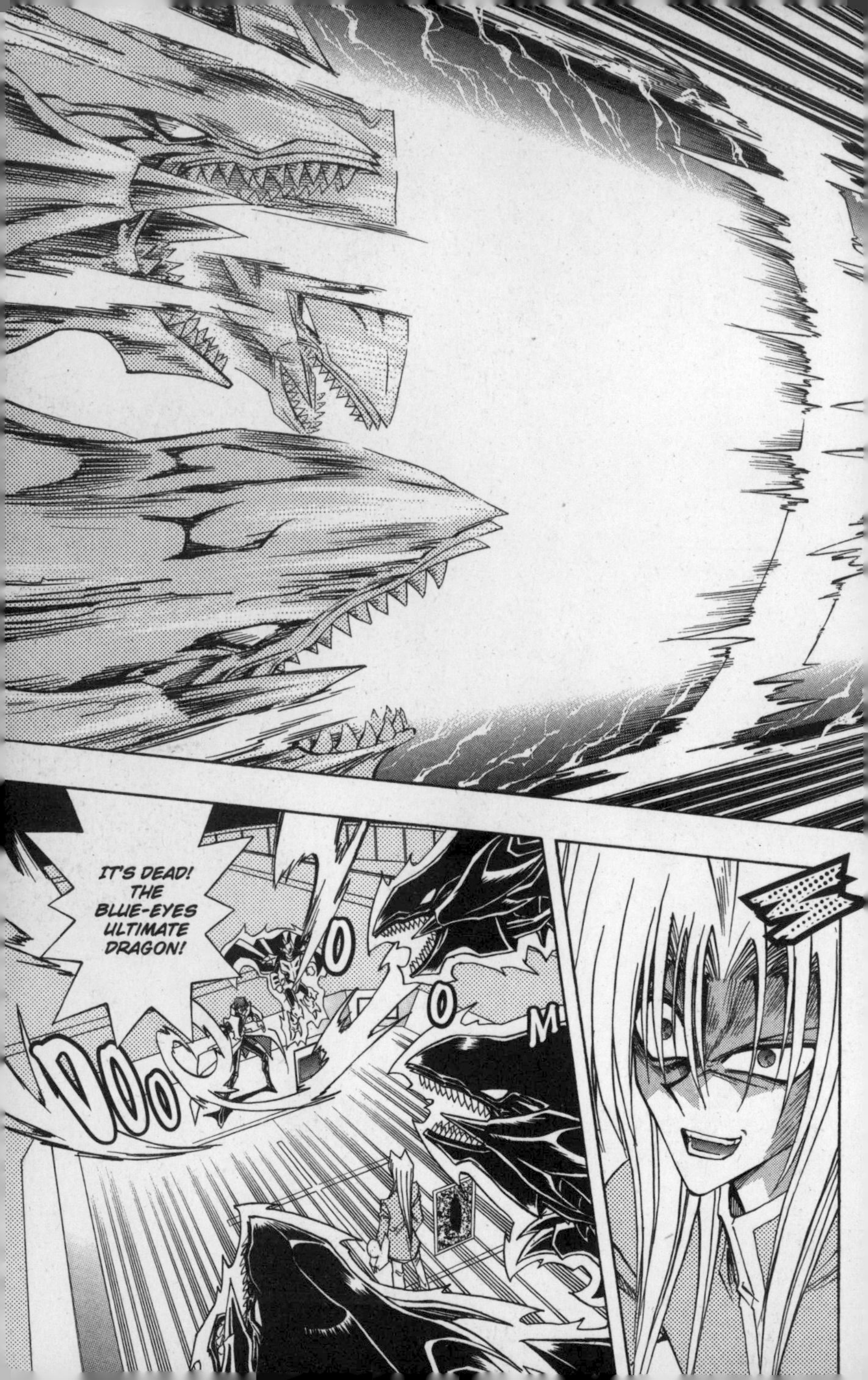
IT'S DEAD! THE BLUE-EYES ULTIMATE DRAGON!

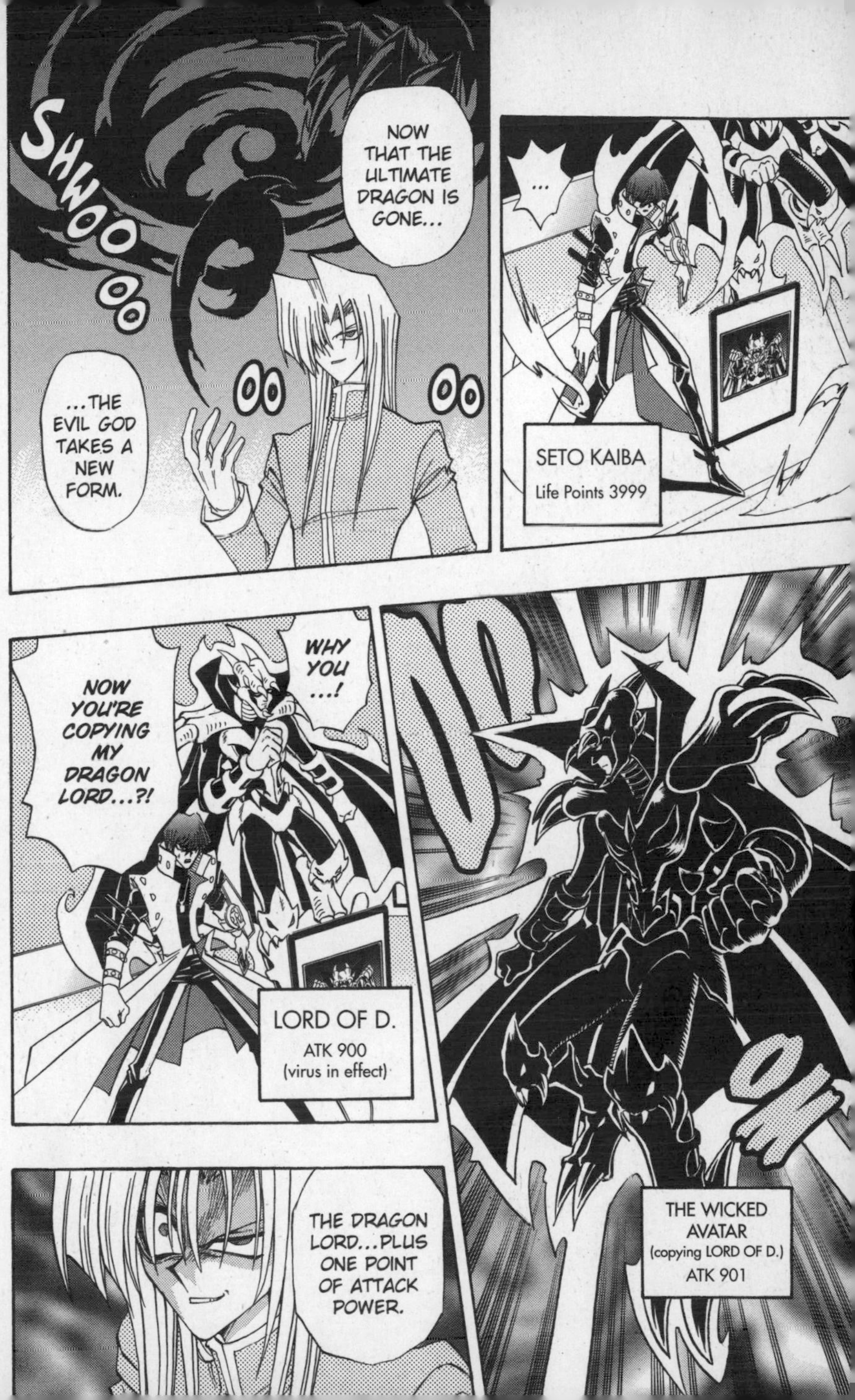
...
SETO KAIBA
Life Points 3999
NOW THAT THE ULTIMATE DRAGON IS GONE...
SHWOOOOOOO
...THE EVIL GOD TAKES A NEW FORM.
THE WICKED AVATAR
(copying LORD OF D.)
ATK 901
WHY YOU ...!
NOW YOU'RE COPYING MY DRAGON LORD...?!
LORD OF D.
ATK 900
(virus in effect)
THE DRAGON LORD...PLUS ONE POINT OF ATTACK POWER.

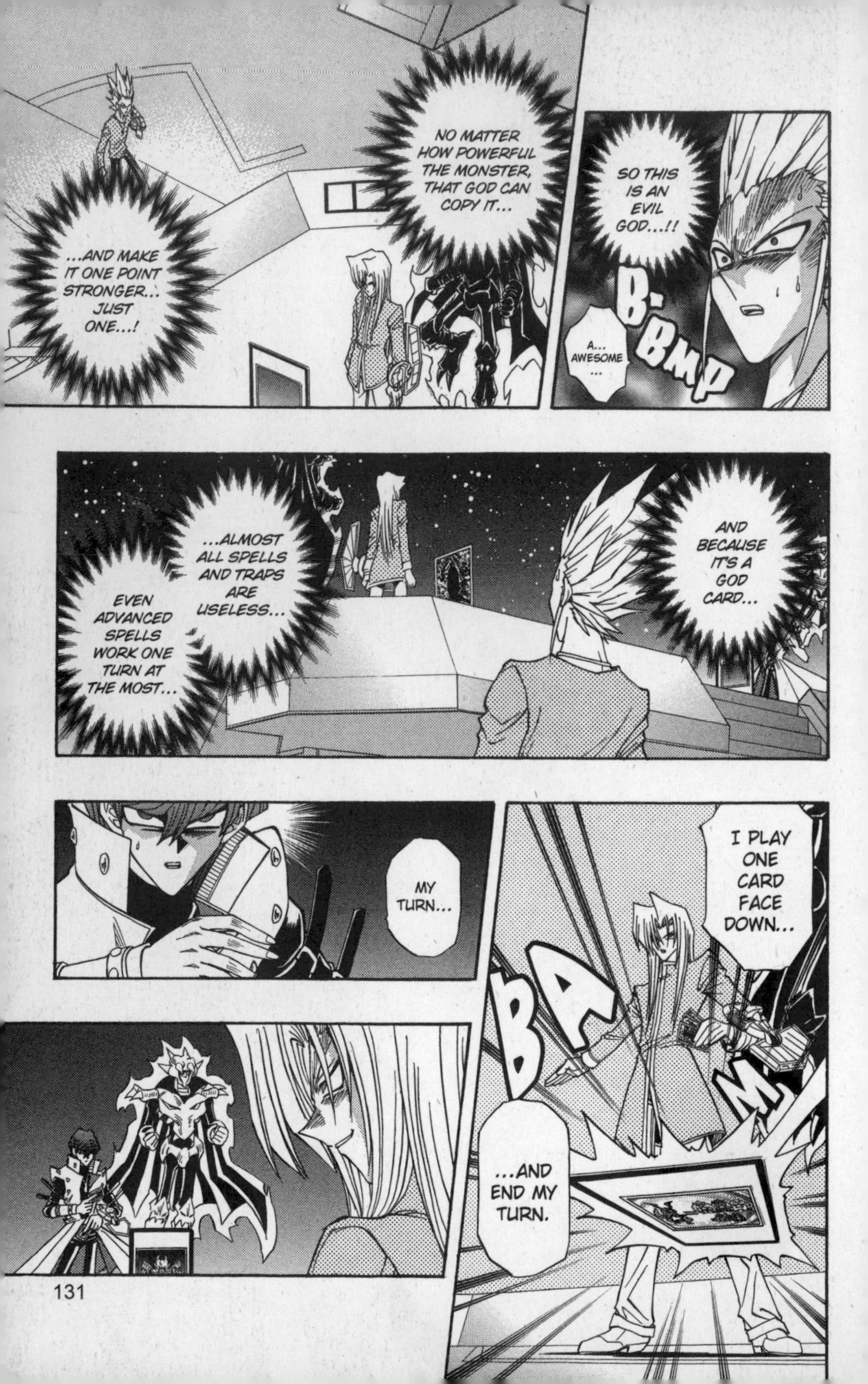
SO THIS IS AN EVIL GOD...!!
B-BMP
A... AWESOME...
NO MATTER HOW POWERFUL THE MONSTER, THAT GOD CAN COPY IT...
...AND MAKE IT ONE POINT STRONGER... JUST ONE...!
AND BECAUSE IT'S A GOD CARD...
...ALMOST ALL SPELLS AND TRAPS ARE USELESS...
EVEN ADVANCED SPELLS WORK ONE TURN AT THE MOST...
I PLAY ONE CARD FACE DOWN...
BAM
...AND END MY TURN.
MY TURN...

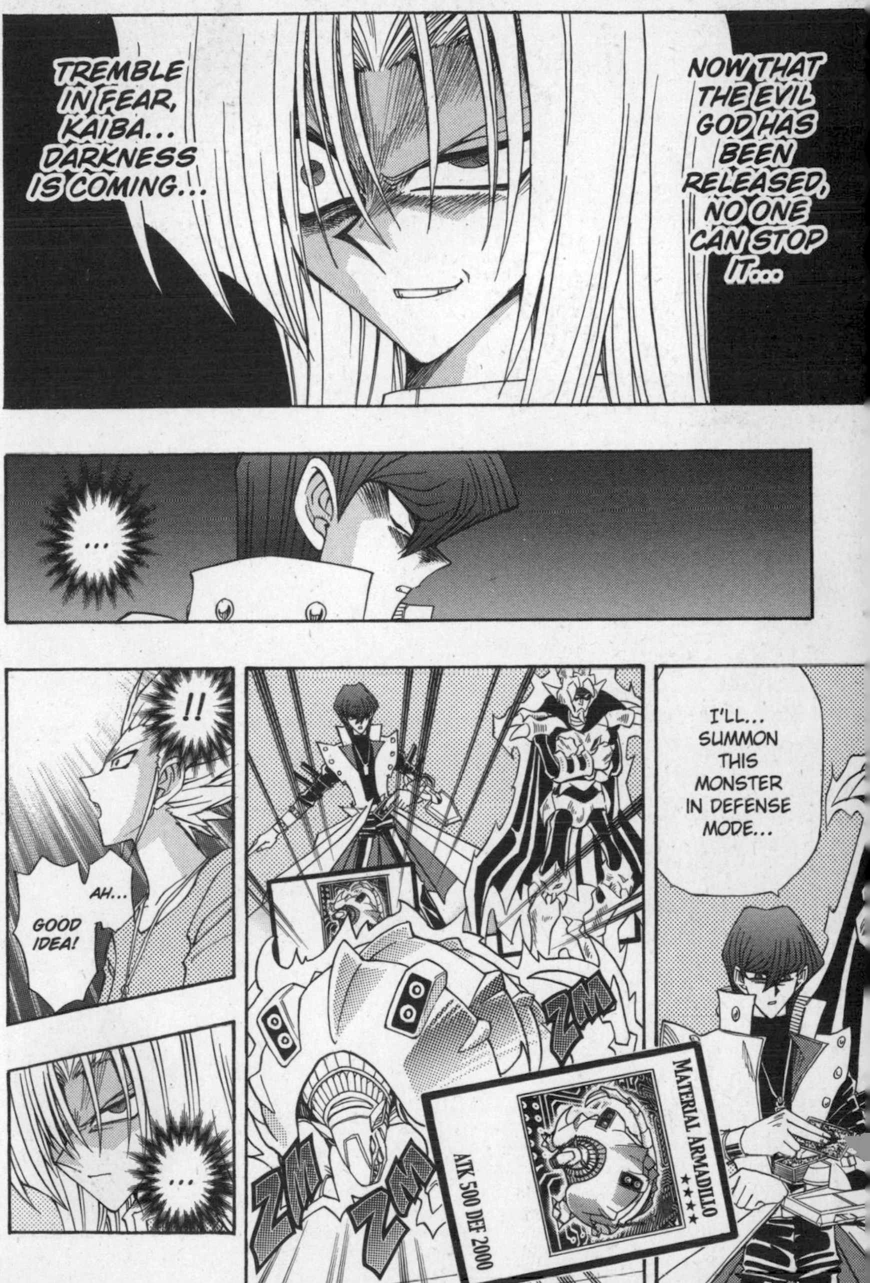
NOW THAT THE EVIL GOD HAS BEEN RELEASED, NO ONE CAN STOP IT...
TREMBLE IN FEAR, KAIBA... DARKNESS IS COMING...
...
I'LL... SUMMON THIS MONSTER IN DEFENSE MODE...
ZM
MATERIAL ARMADILLO
ATK 500 DEF 2000
ZM
ZM
!!
AH... GOOD IDEA!
...

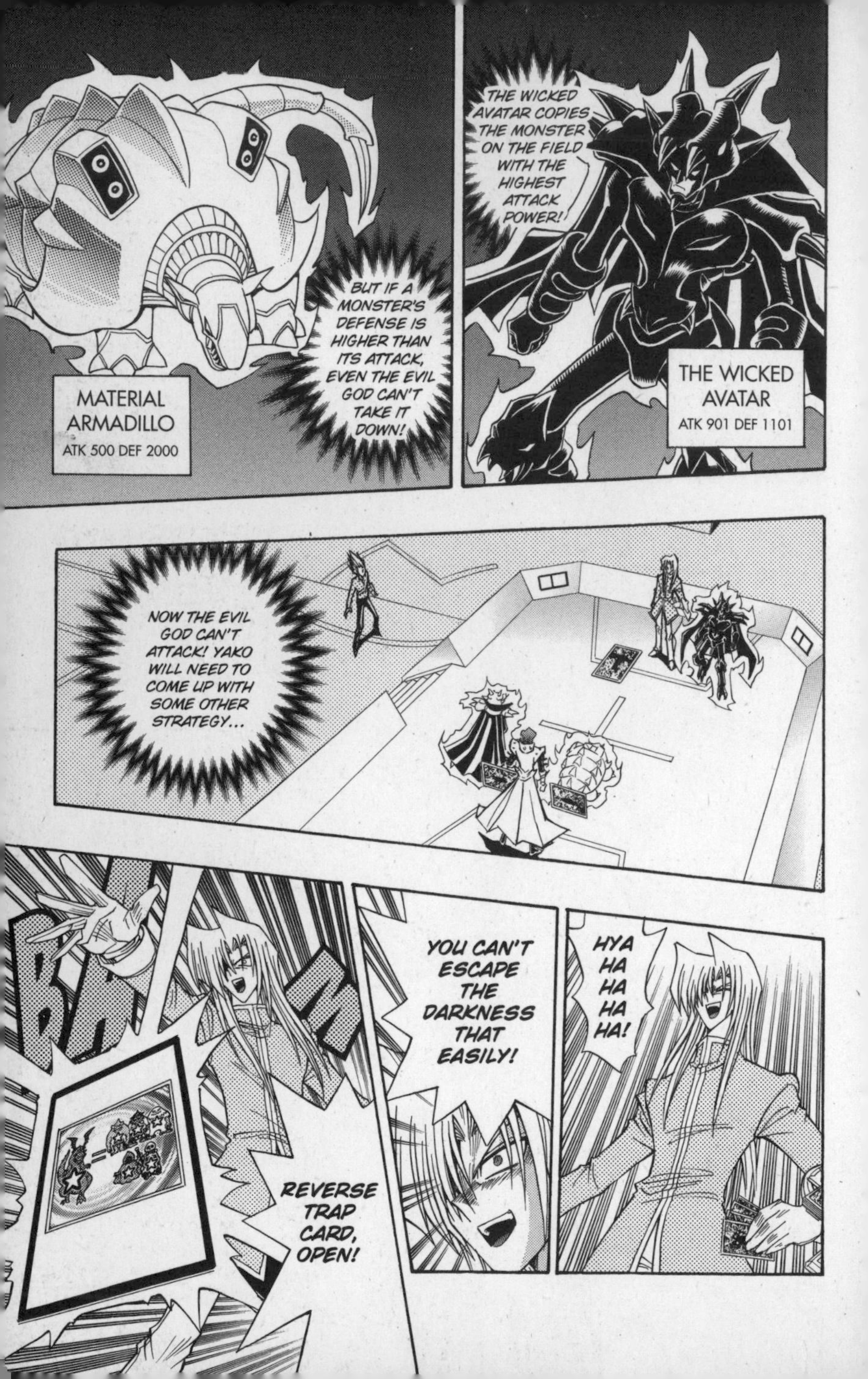
THE WICKED AVATAR COPIES THE MONSTER ON THE FIELD WITH THE HIGHEST ATTACK POWER!
THE WICKED AVATAR
ATK 901 DEF 1101
BUT IF A MONSTER'S DEFENSE IS HIGHER THAN ITS ATTACK, EVEN THE EVIL GOD CAN'T TAKE IT DOWN!
MATERIAL ARMADILLO
ATK 500 DEF 2000
NOW THE EVIL GOD CAN'T ATTACK! YAKO WILL NEED TO COME UP WITH SOME OTHER STRATEGY...
HYA HA HA HA HA!
YOU CAN'T ESCAPE THE DARKNESS THAT EASILY!
REVERSE TRAP CARD, OPEN!

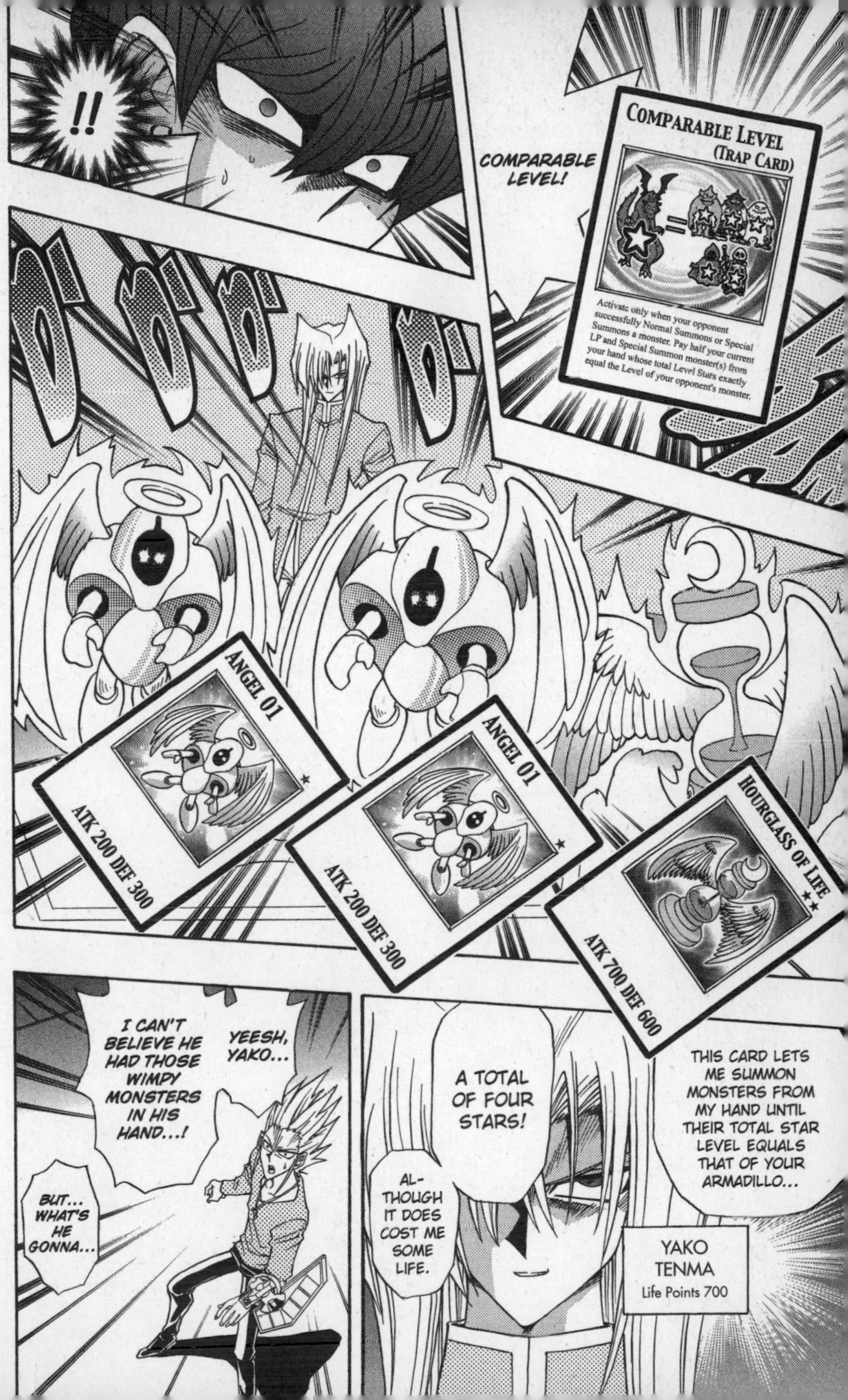
COMPARABLE LEVEL!
Comparable Level
(Trap Card)
Activate only when your opponent successfully Normal Summons or Special Summons a monster. Pay half your current LP and Special Summon monster(s) from your hand whose total Level Stars exactly equal the Level of your opponent's monster.
!!
Angel 01
ATK 200 DEF 300
Angel 01
ATK 200 DEF 300
Hourglass of Life
ATK 700 DEF 600
THIS CARD LETS ME SUMMON MONSTERS FROM MY HAND UNTIL THEIR TOTAL STAR LEVEL EQUALS THAT OF YOUR ARMADILLO...
A TOTAL OF FOUR STARS!
AL-THOUGH IT DOES COST ME SOME LIFE.
YAKO TENMA
Life Points 700
YEESH, YAKO...
I CAN'T BELIEVE HE HAD THOSE WIMPY MONSTERS IN HIS HAND...!
BUT... WHAT'S HE GONNA...

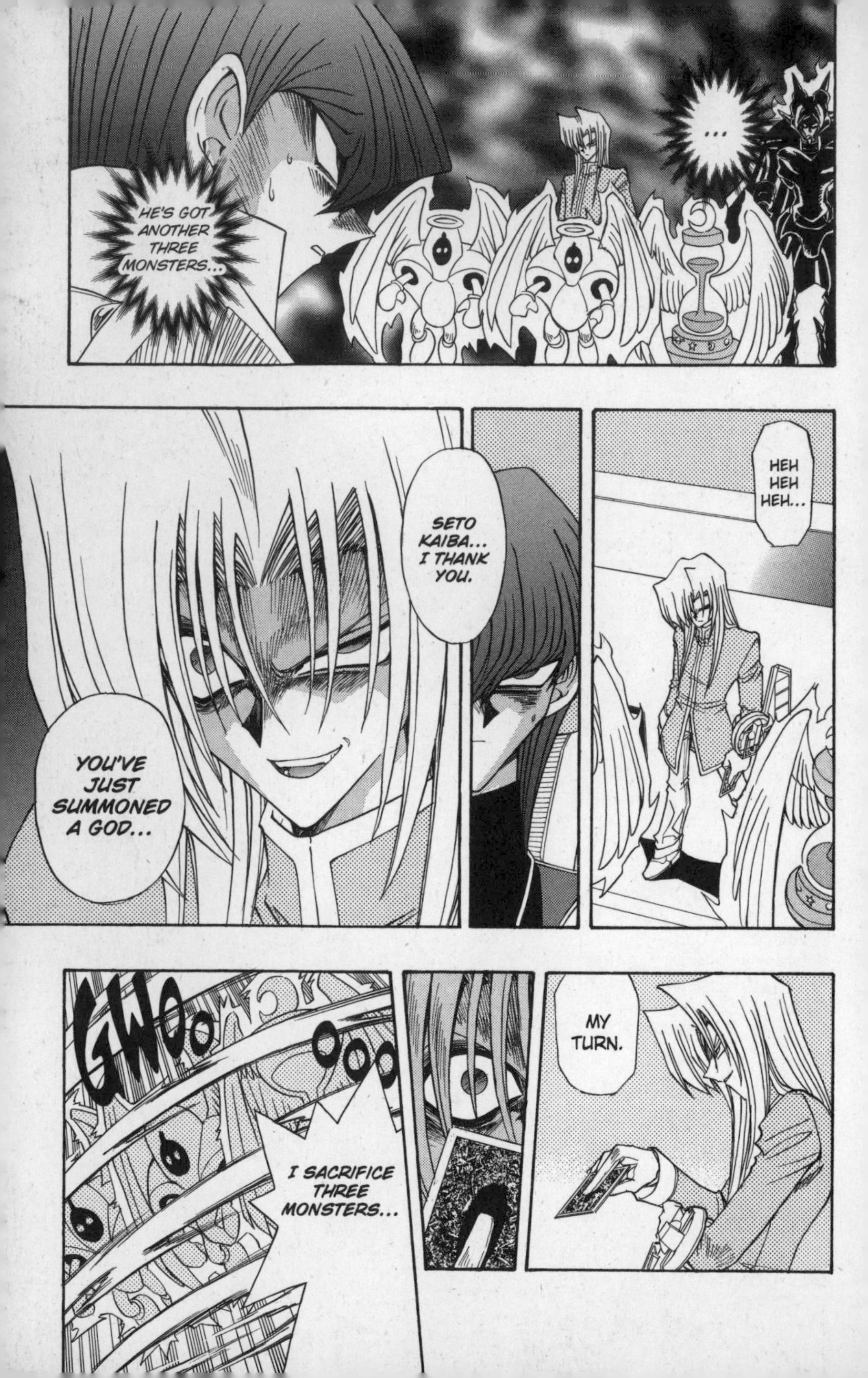
...
HE'S GOT ANOTHER THREE MONSTERS...
HEH HEH HEH...
SETO KAIBA... I THANK YOU.
YOU'VE JUST SUMMONED A GOD...
MY TURN.
GHOOOOOOO
I SACRIFICE THREE MONSTERS...

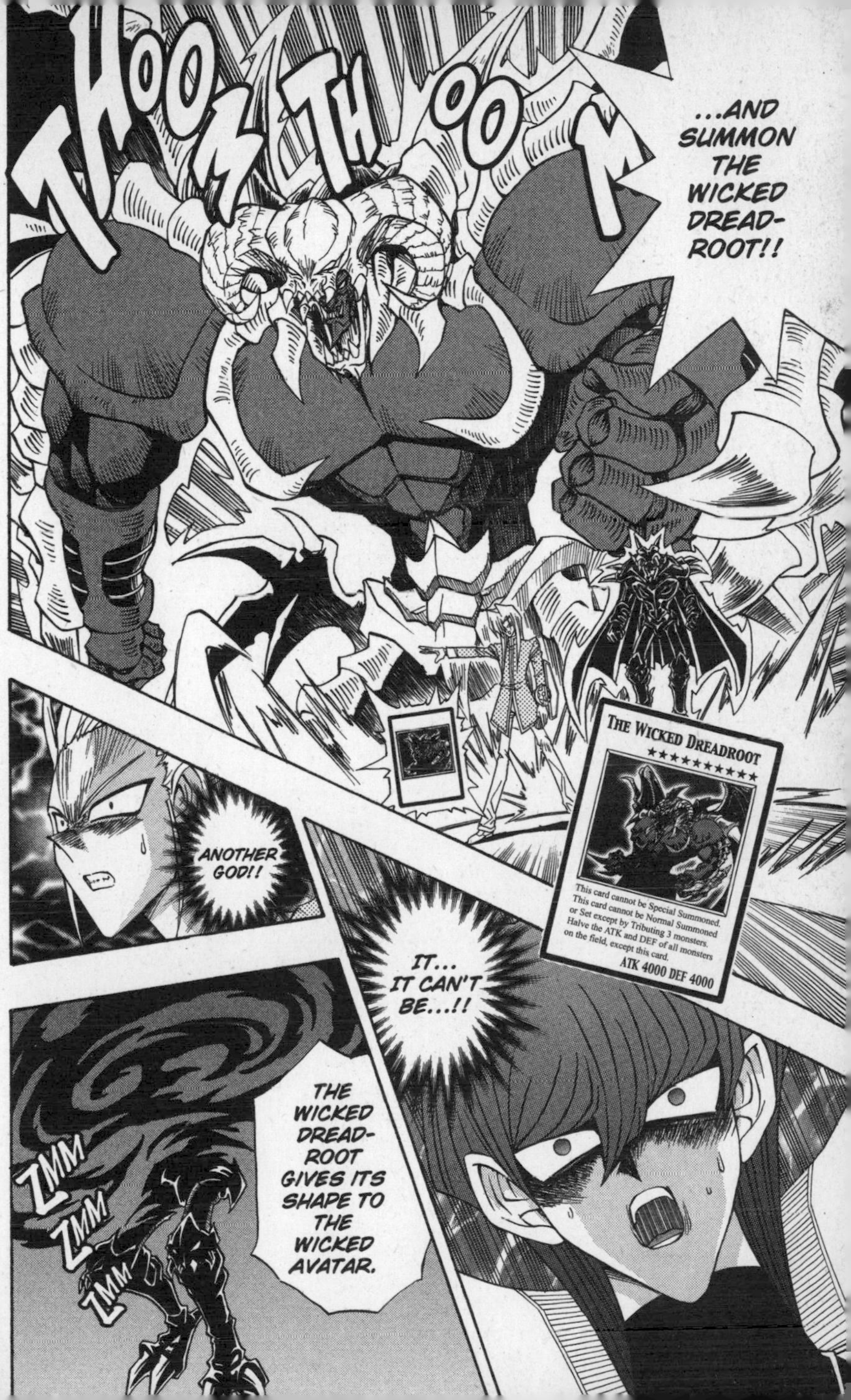
THOOM
THOOM
...AND SUMMON THE WICKED DREAD-ROOT!!
THE WICKED DREADROOT
★★★★★★★★★★
This card cannot be Special Summoned. This card cannot be Normal Summoned or Set except by Tributing 3 monsters. Halve the ATK and DEF of all monsters on the field, except this card.
ATK 4000 DEF 4000
IT... IT CAN'T BE...!!
ANOTHER GOD!!
THE WICKED DREAD-ROOT GIVES ITS SHAPE TO THE WICKED AVATAR.
ZMM
ZMM
ZMM

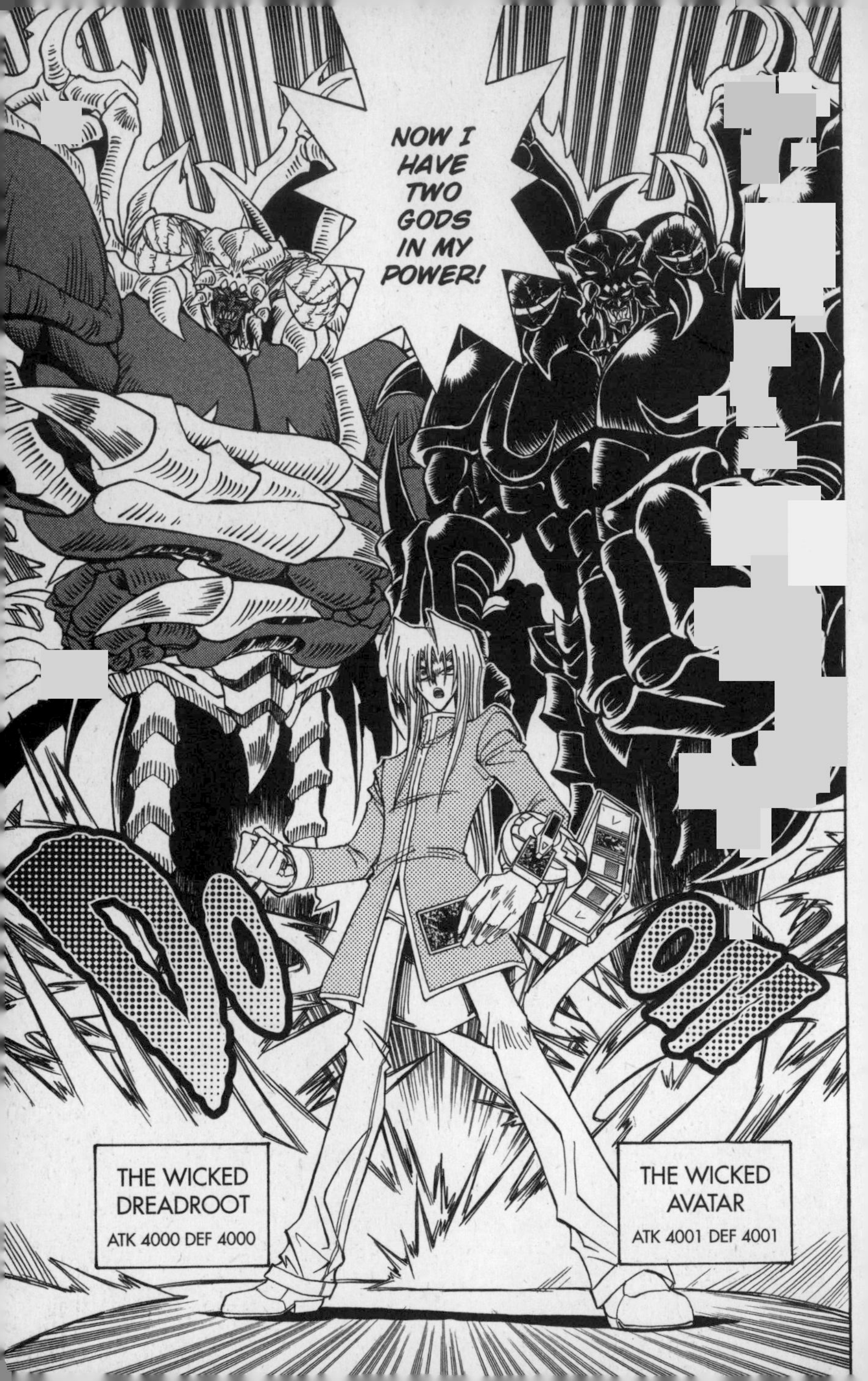
NOW I HAVE TWO GODS IN MY POWER!
THE WICKED AVATAR
ATK 4001 DEF 4001
THE WICKED DREADROOT
ATK 4000 DEF 4000

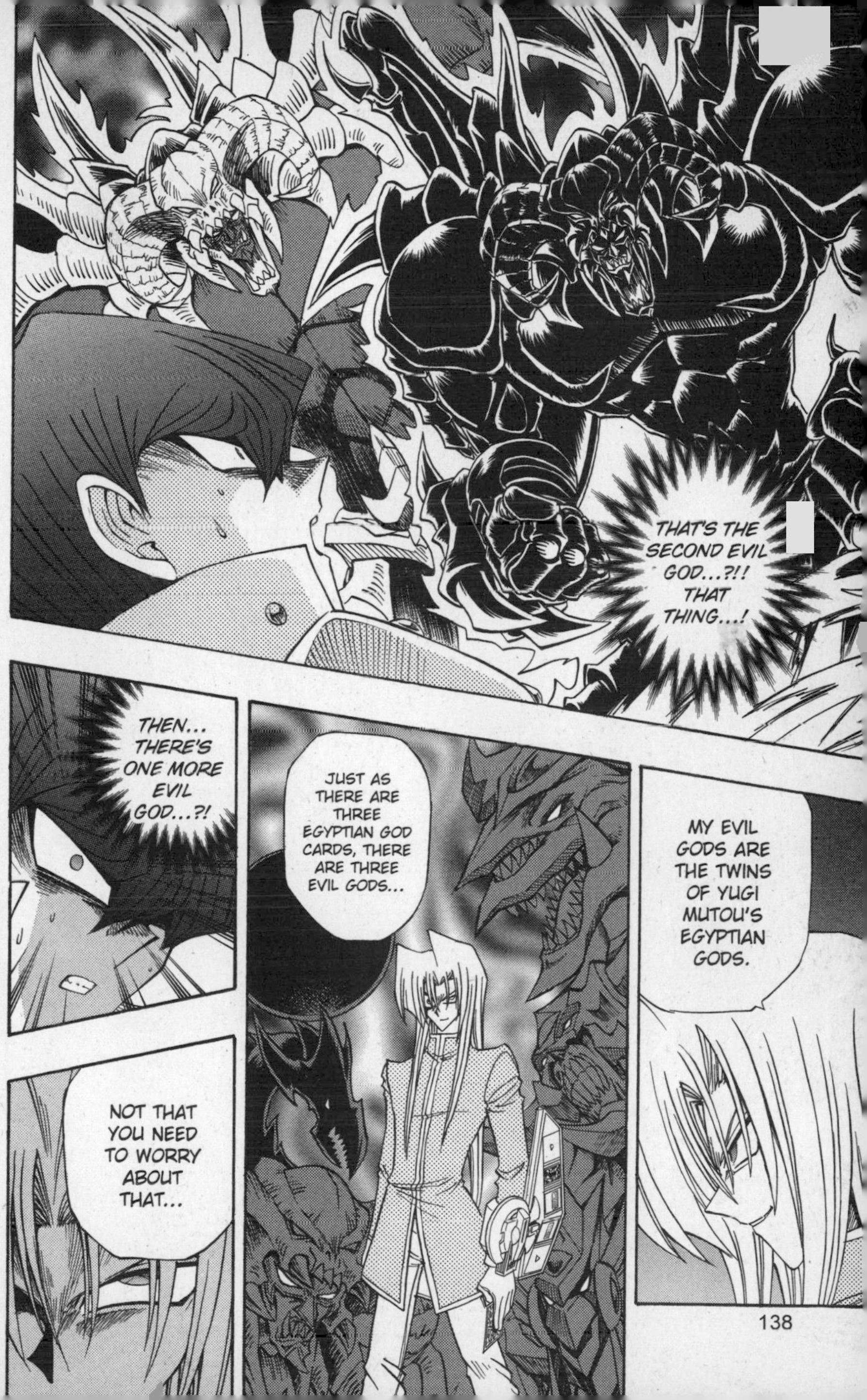
THAT'S THE SECOND EVIL GOD...?!! THAT THING...!
MY EVIL GODS ARE THE TWINS OF YUGI MUTOU'S EGYPTIAN GODS.
JUST AS THERE ARE THREE EGYPTIAN GOD CARDS, THERE ARE THREE EVIL GODS...
THEN... THERE'S ONE MORE EVIL GOD...?!
NOT THAT YOU NEED TO WORRY ABOUT THAT...

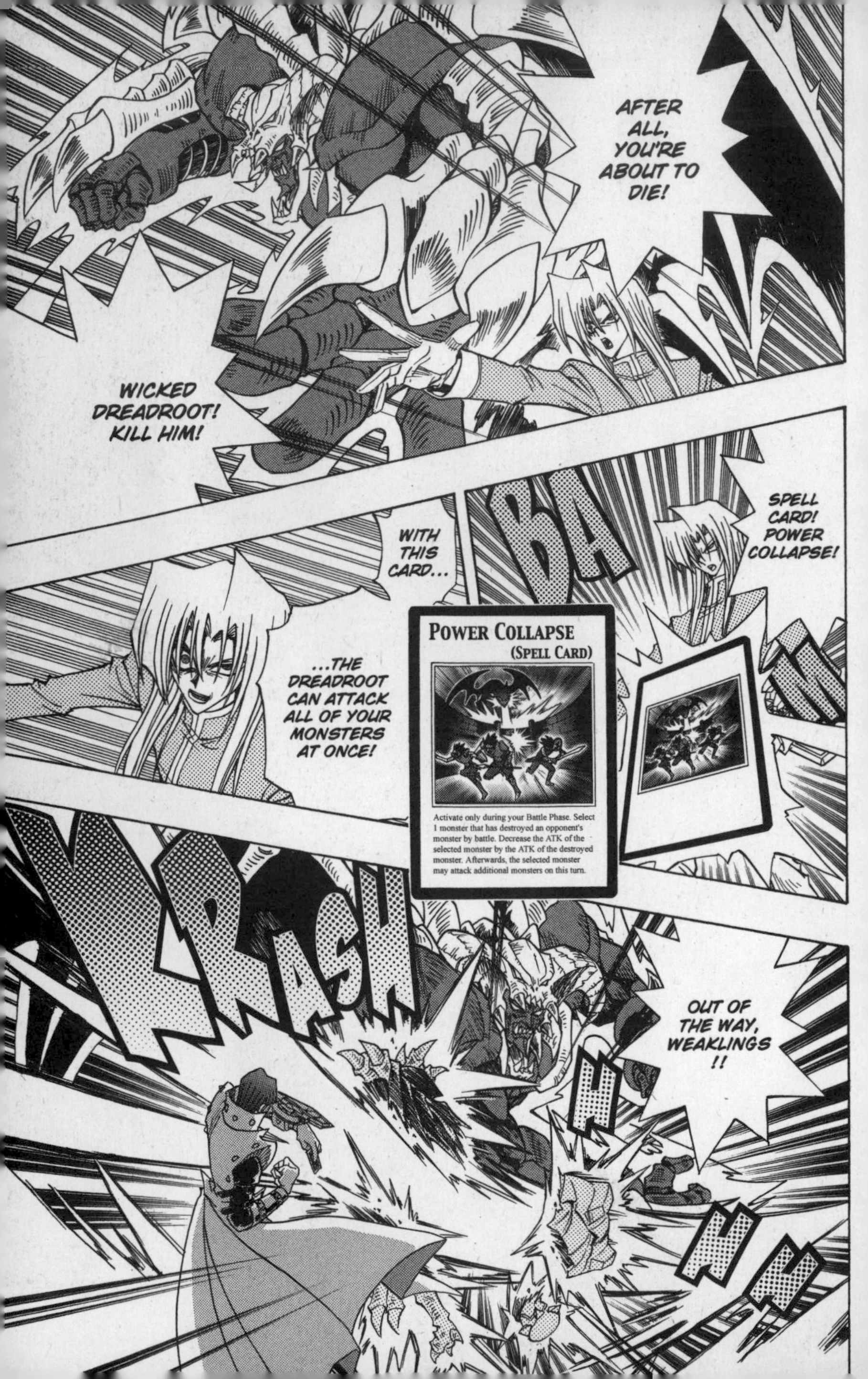
AFTER ALL, YOU'RE ABOUT TO DIE!
WICKED DREADROOT! KILL HIM!
BA
SPELL CARD! POWER COLLAPSE!
POWER COLLAPSE
(SPELL CARD)
Activate only during your Battle Phase. Select 1 monster that has destroyed an opponent's monster by battle. Decrease the ATK of the selected monster by the ATK of the destroyed monster. Afterwards, the selected monster may attack additional monsters on this turn.
WITH THIS CARD...
...THE DREADROOT CAN ATTACK ALL OF YOUR MONSTERS AT ONCE!
OUT OF THE WAY, WEAKLINGS !!

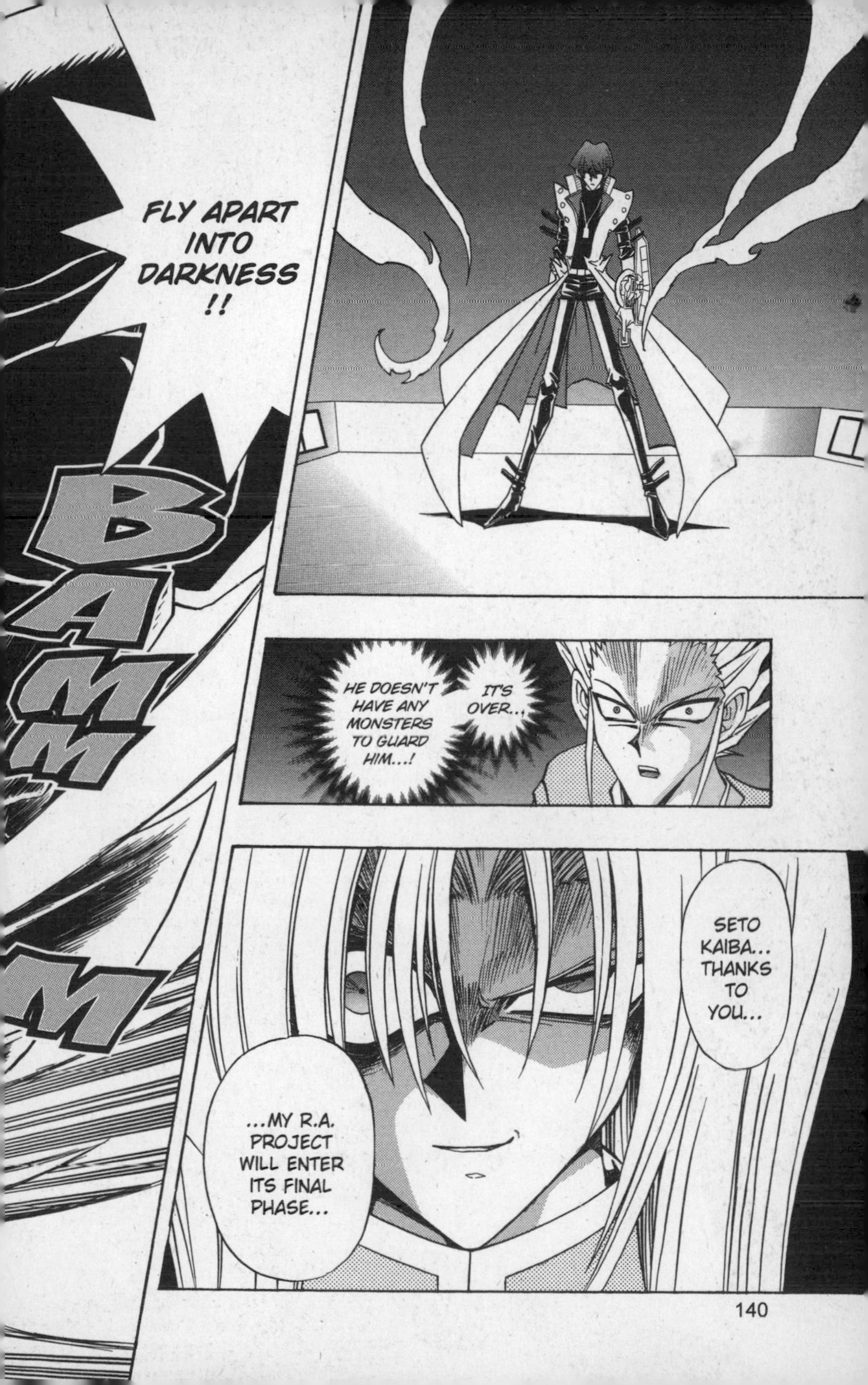
IT'S OVER...
HE DOESN'T HAVE ANY MONSTERS TO GUARD HIM...!
SETO KAIBA... THANKS TO YOU...
...MY R.A. PROJECT WILL ENTER ITS FINAL PHASE...
FLY APART INTO DARKNESS!!
BAMM

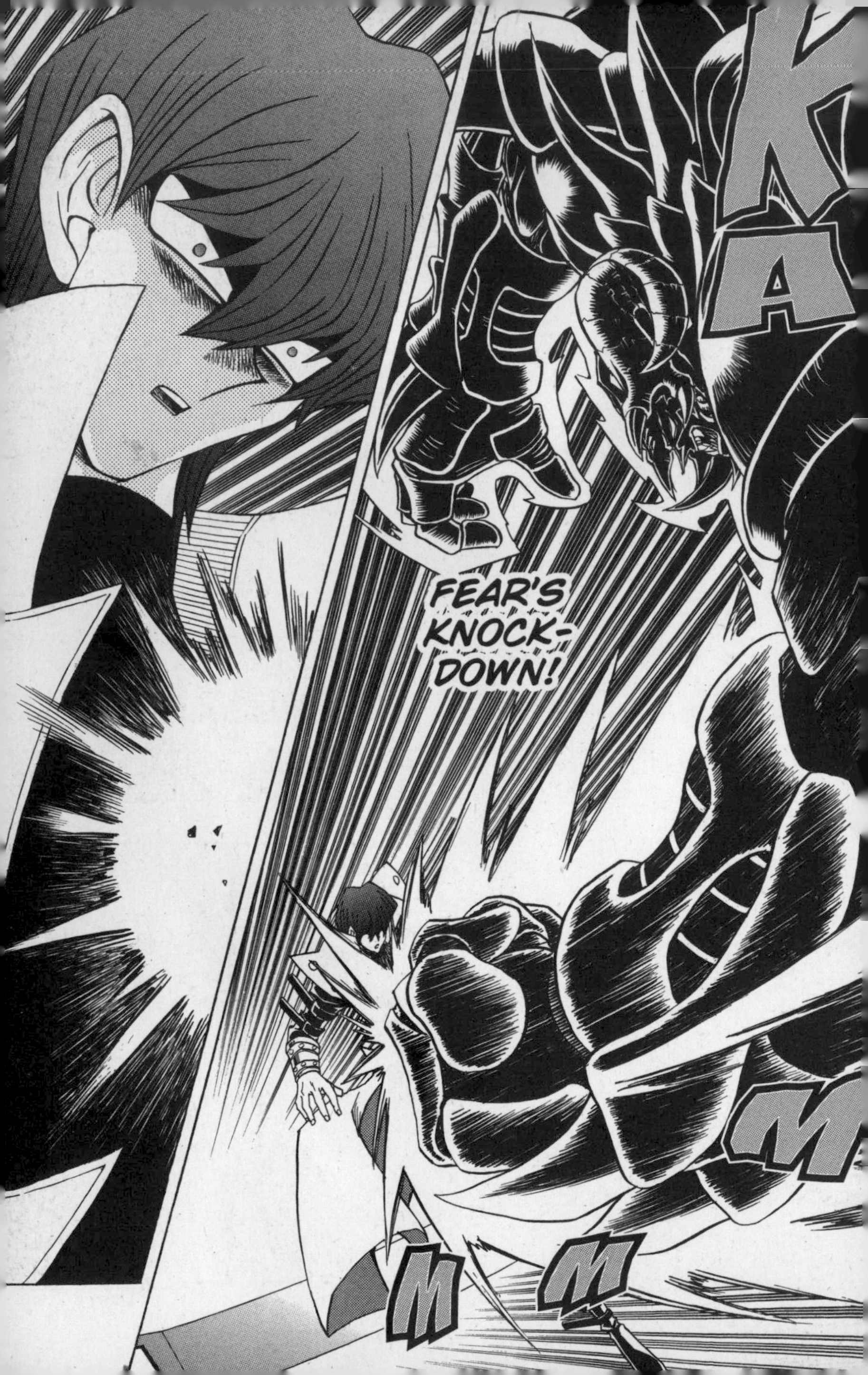
KA
FEAR'S KNOCK-DOWN!
MMM

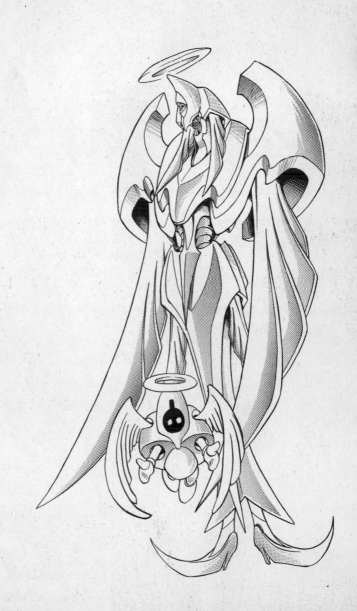

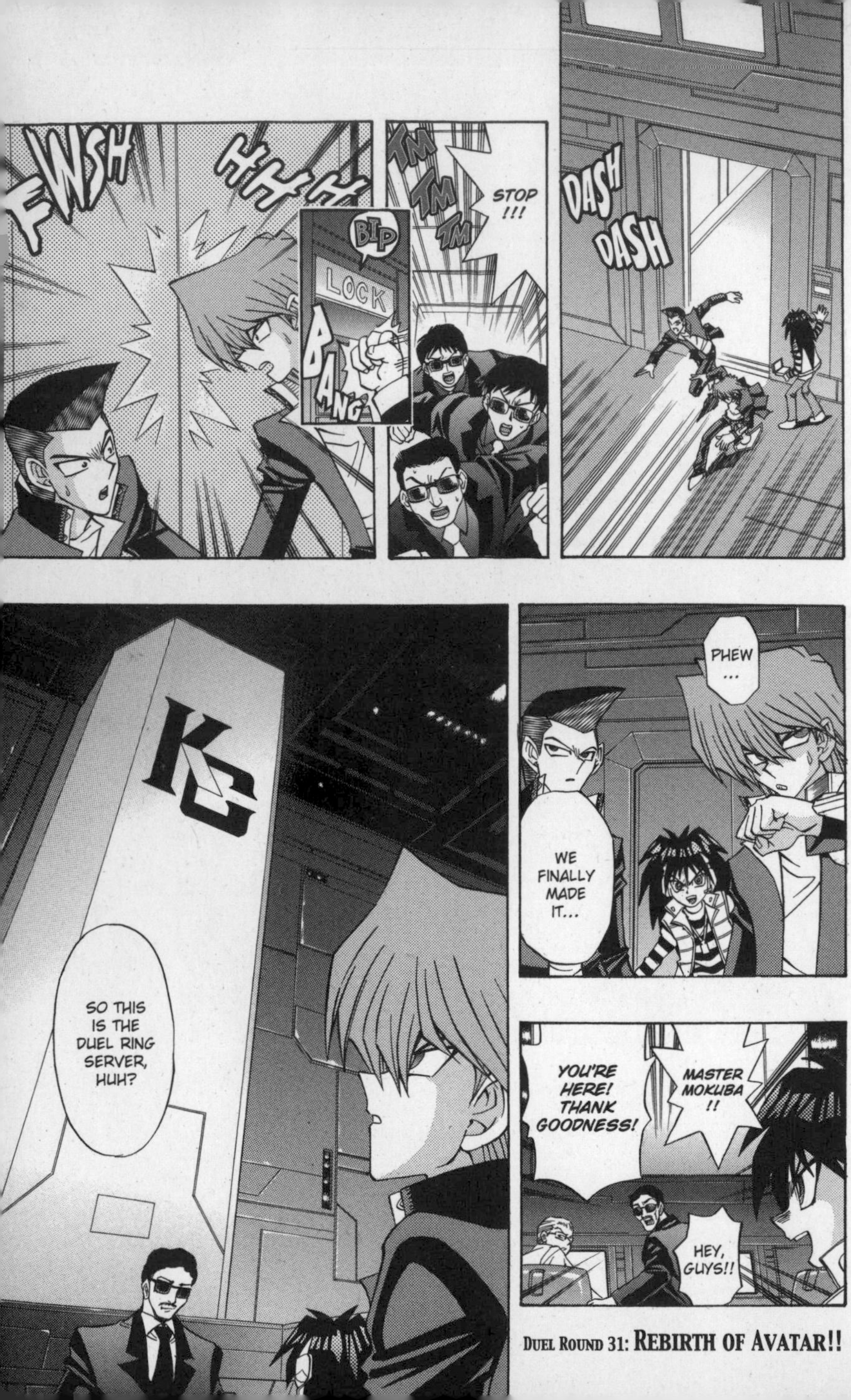
DASH
DASH
STOP!!!
TM TM TM
BIP
LOCK
BANG
HHH
FWSH
PHEW...
WE FINALLY MADE IT...
MASTER MOKUBA!!
YOU'RE HERE! THANK GOODNESS!
HEY, GUYS!!
SO THIS IS THE DUEL RING SERVER, HUH?

Duel Round 31: Rebirth of Avatar!!

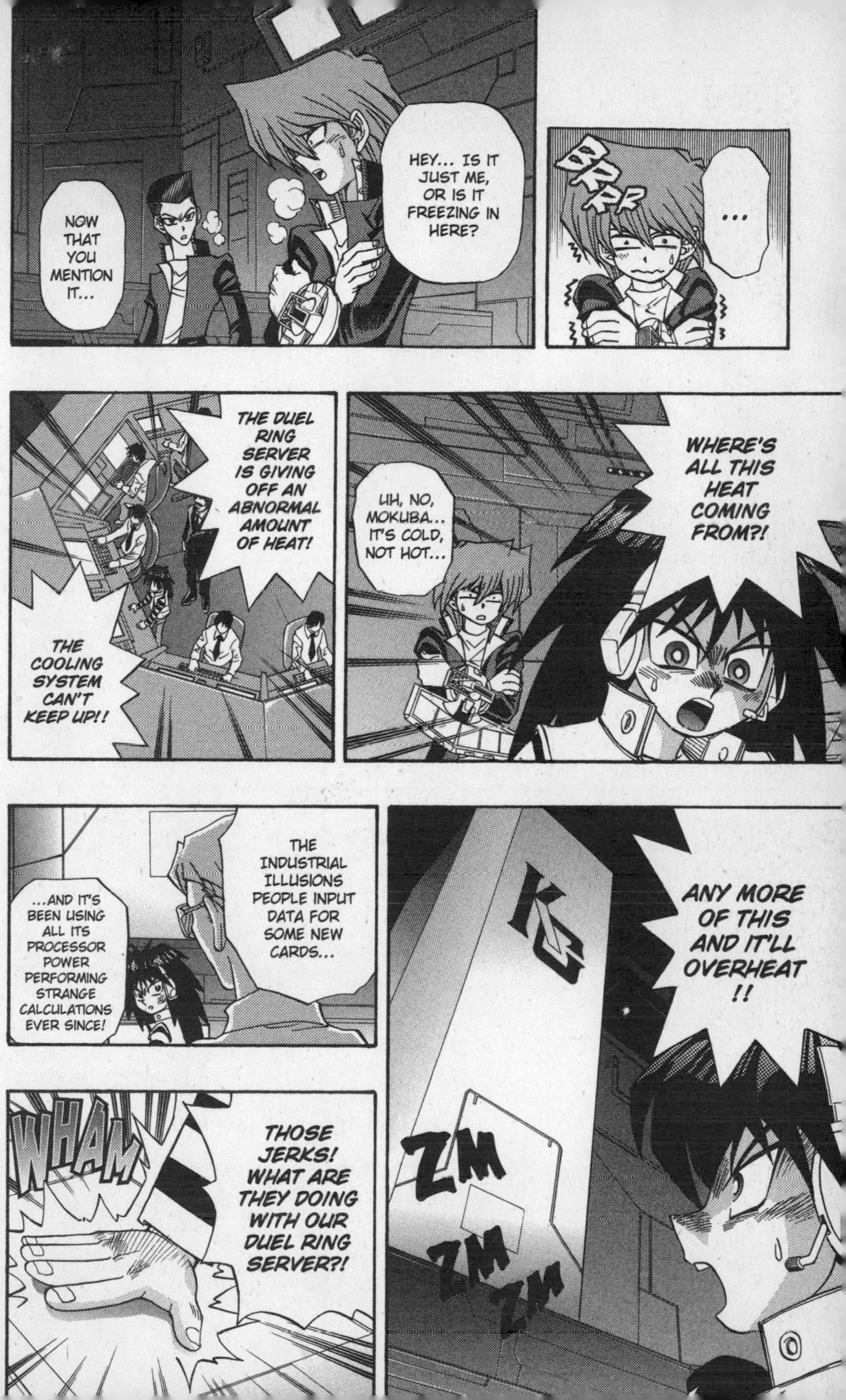
BRRR
...
HEY... IS IT JUST ME, OR IS IT FREEZING IN HERE?
NOW THAT YOU MENTION IT...
WHERE'S ALL THIS HEAT COMING FROM?!
UH, NO, MOKUBA... IT'S COLD, NOT HOT...
THE DUEL RING SERVER IS GIVING OFF AN ABNORMAL AMOUNT OF HEAT!
THE COOLING SYSTEM CAN'T KEEP UP!!
ANY MORE OF THIS AND IT'LL OVERHEAT!!
ZM
ZM
ZM
THE INDUSTRIAL ILLUSIONS PEOPLE INPUT DATA FOR SOME NEW CARDS...
...AND IT'S BEEN USING ALL ITS PROCESSOR POWER PERFORMING STRANGE CALCULATIONS EVER SINCE!
WHAM
THOSE JERKS! WHAT ARE THEY DOING WITH OUR DUEL RING SERVER?!

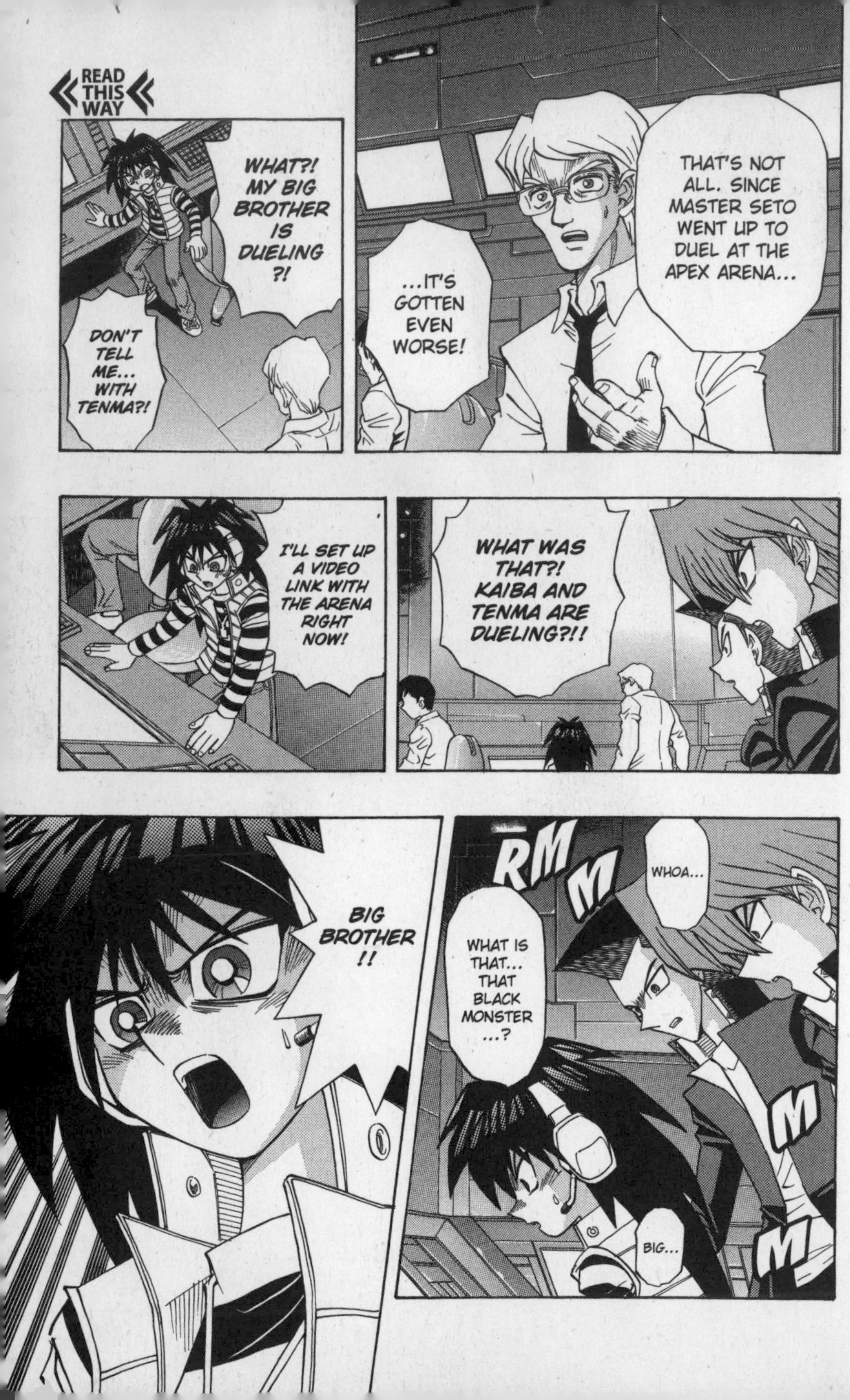
READ THIS WAY
THAT'S NOT ALL. SINCE MASTER SETO WENT UP TO DUEL AT THE APEX ARENA...
...IT'S GOTTEN EVEN WORSE!
WHAT?! MY BIG BROTHER IS DUELING?!
DON'T TELL ME... WITH TENMA?!
WHAT WAS THAT?! KAIBA AND TENMA ARE DUELING?!!
I'LL SET UP A VIDEO LINK WITH THE ARENA RIGHT NOW!
RMMM
WHOA...
WHAT IS THAT... THAT BLACK MONSTER ...?
MM
BIG...
BIG BROTHER !!

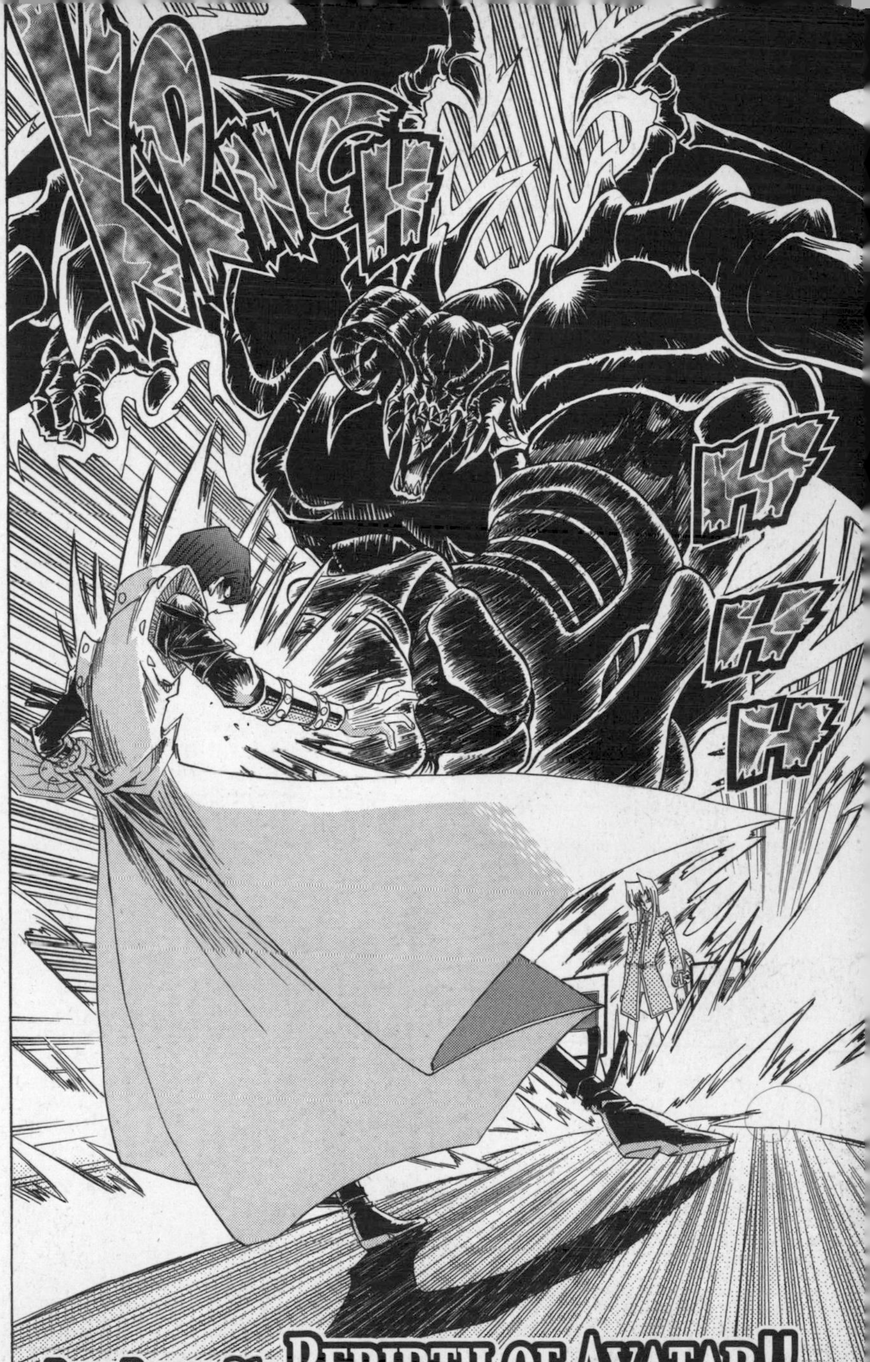

KRUNCH
H
H
H

Duel Round 31: Rebirth of Avatar!!

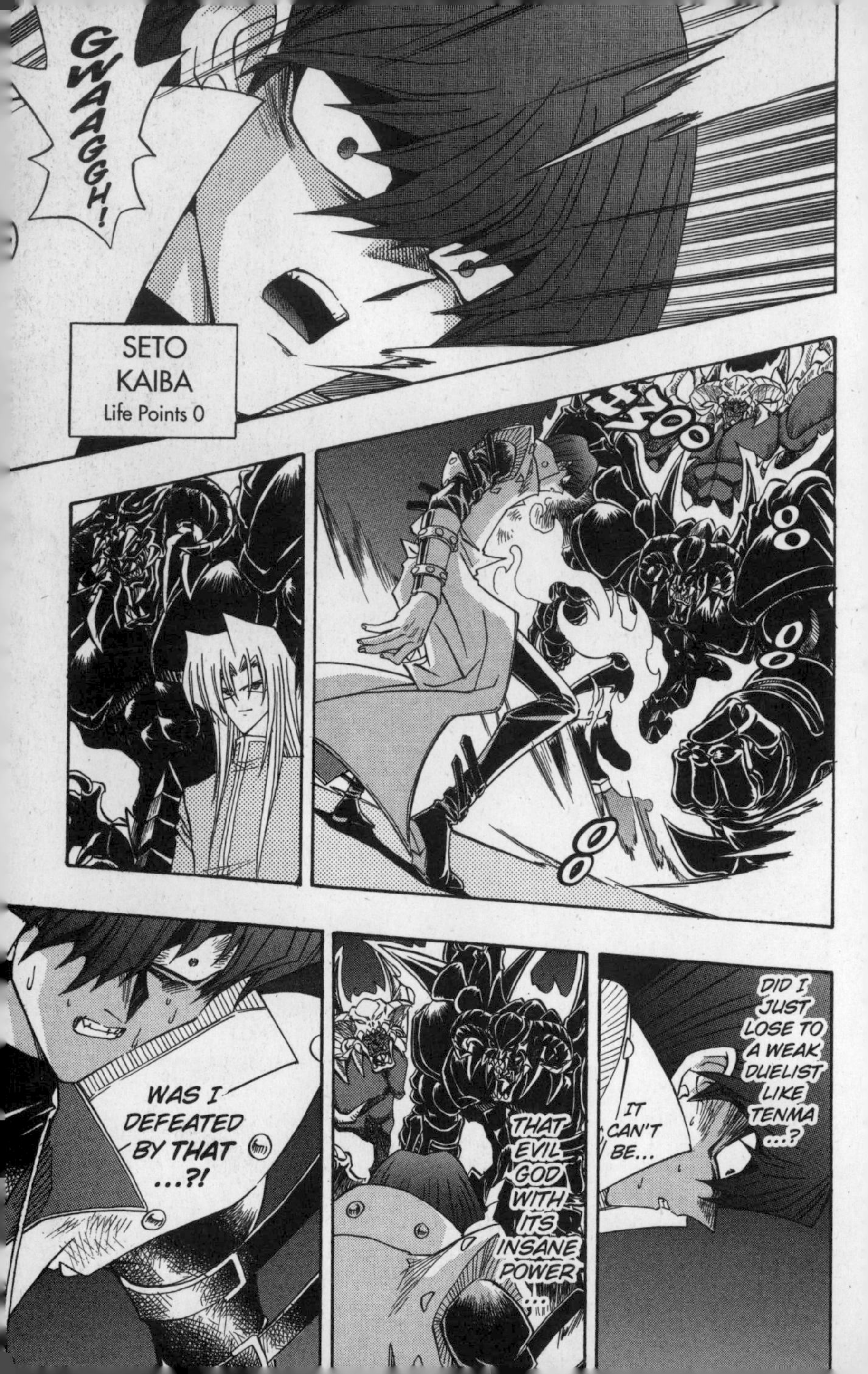
GWAAAGGH!
SETO KAIBA Life Points 0
DID I JUST LOSE TO A WEAK DUELIST LIKE TENMA ...?
IT CAN'T BE...
THAT EVIL GOD WITH ITS INSANE POWER ...
WAS I DEFEATED BY THAT ...?!

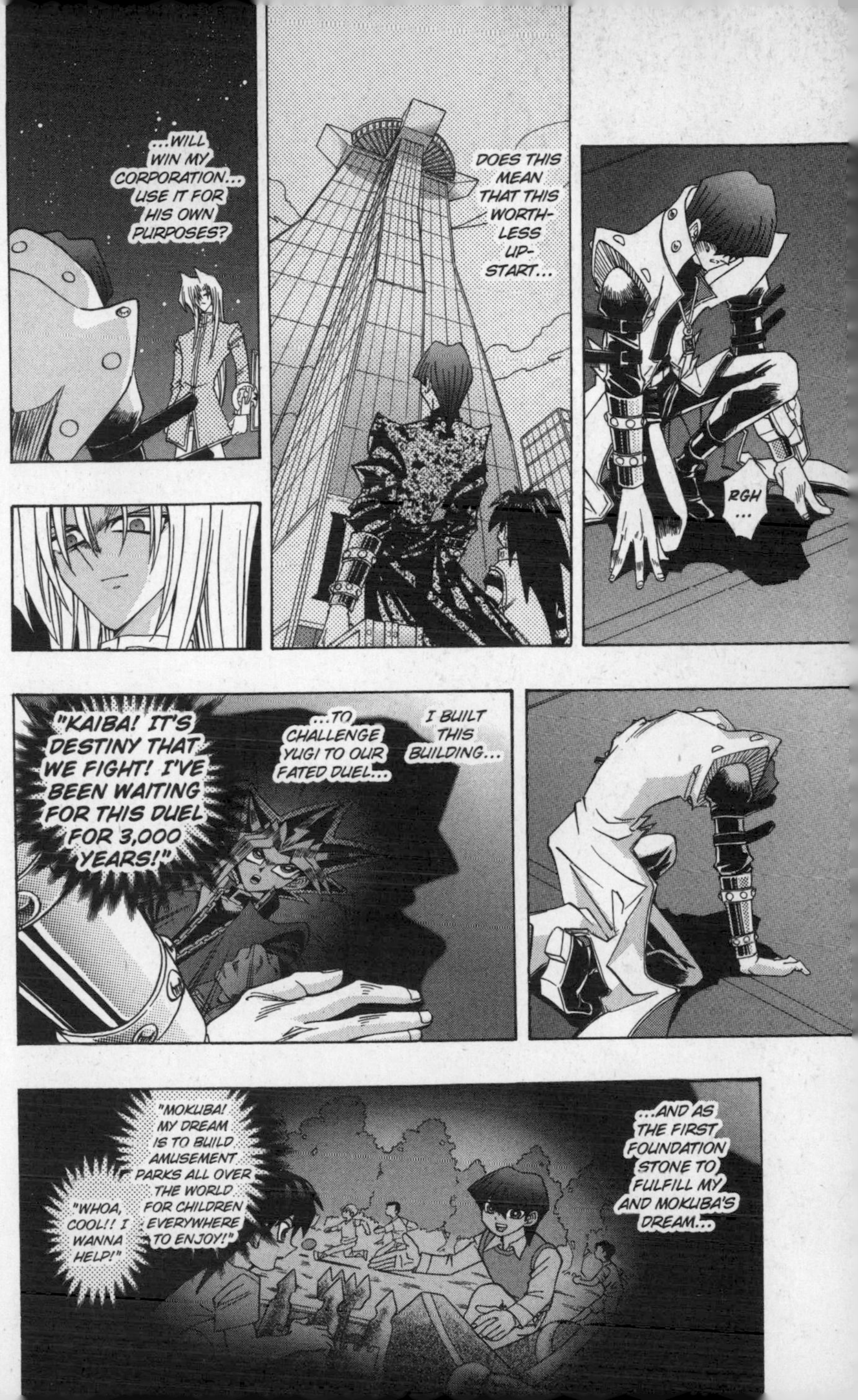
RGH...
DOES THIS MEAN THAT THIS WORTHLESS UPSTART...
...WILL WIN MY CORPORATION... USE IT FOR HIS OWN PURPOSES?
I BUILT THIS BUILDING...
...TO CHALLENGE YUGI TO OUR FATED DUEL...
"KAIBA! IT'S DESTINY THAT WE FIGHT! I'VE BEEN WAITING FOR THIS DUEL FOR 3,000 YEARS!"
...AND AS THE FIRST FOUNDATION STONE TO FULFILL MY AND MOKUBA'S DREAM...
"MOKUBA! MY DREAM IS TO BUILD AMUSEMENT PARKS ALL OVER THE WORLD FOR CHILDREN EVERYWHERE TO ENJOY!"
"WHOA, COOL!! I WANNA HELP!"

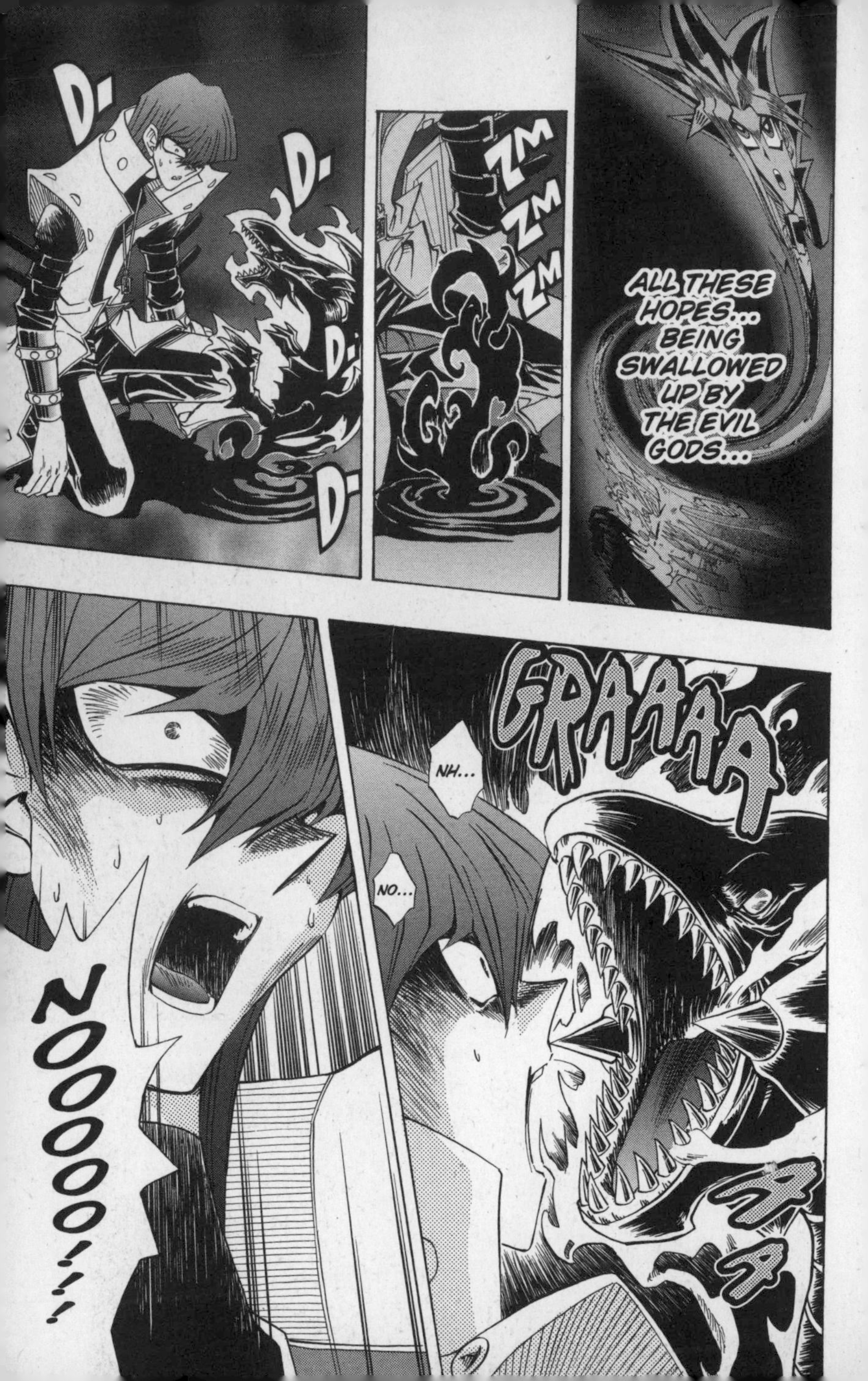
ALL THESE HOPES... BEING SWALLOWED UP BY THE EVIL GODS...
ZM ZM ZM ZM
D- D- D- D-
GRAAAAAA
NH...
NO...
NOOOOO!!!!

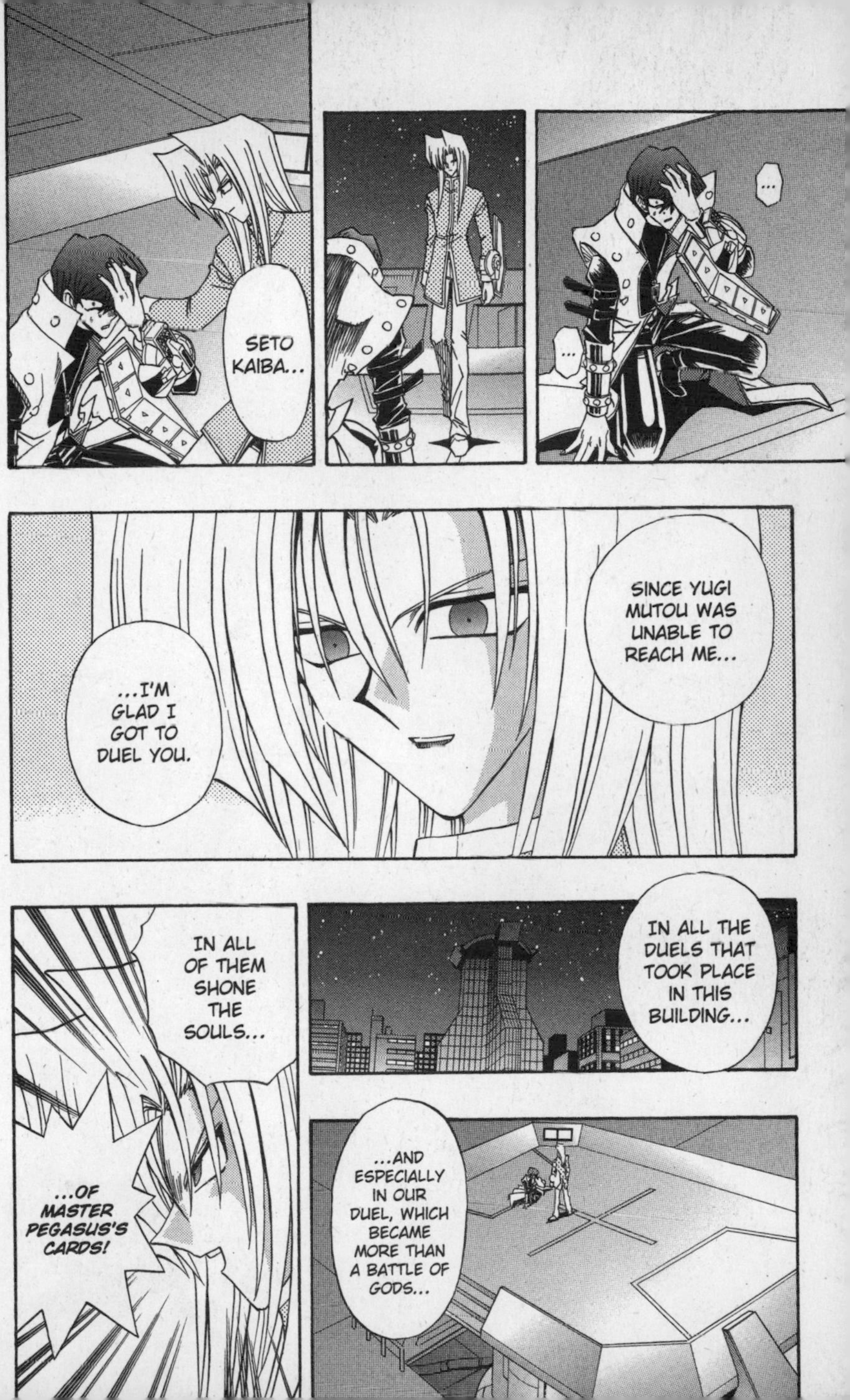
...
...
SETO KAIBA...
SINCE YUGI MUTOU WAS UNABLE TO REACH ME...
...I'M GLAD I GOT TO DUEL YOU.
IN ALL THE DUELS THAT TOOK PLACE IN THIS BUILDING...
...AND ESPECIALLY IN OUR DUEL, WHICH BECAME MORE THAN A BATTLE OF GODS...
IN ALL OF THEM SHONE THE SOULS...
...OF MASTER PEGASUS'S CARDS!

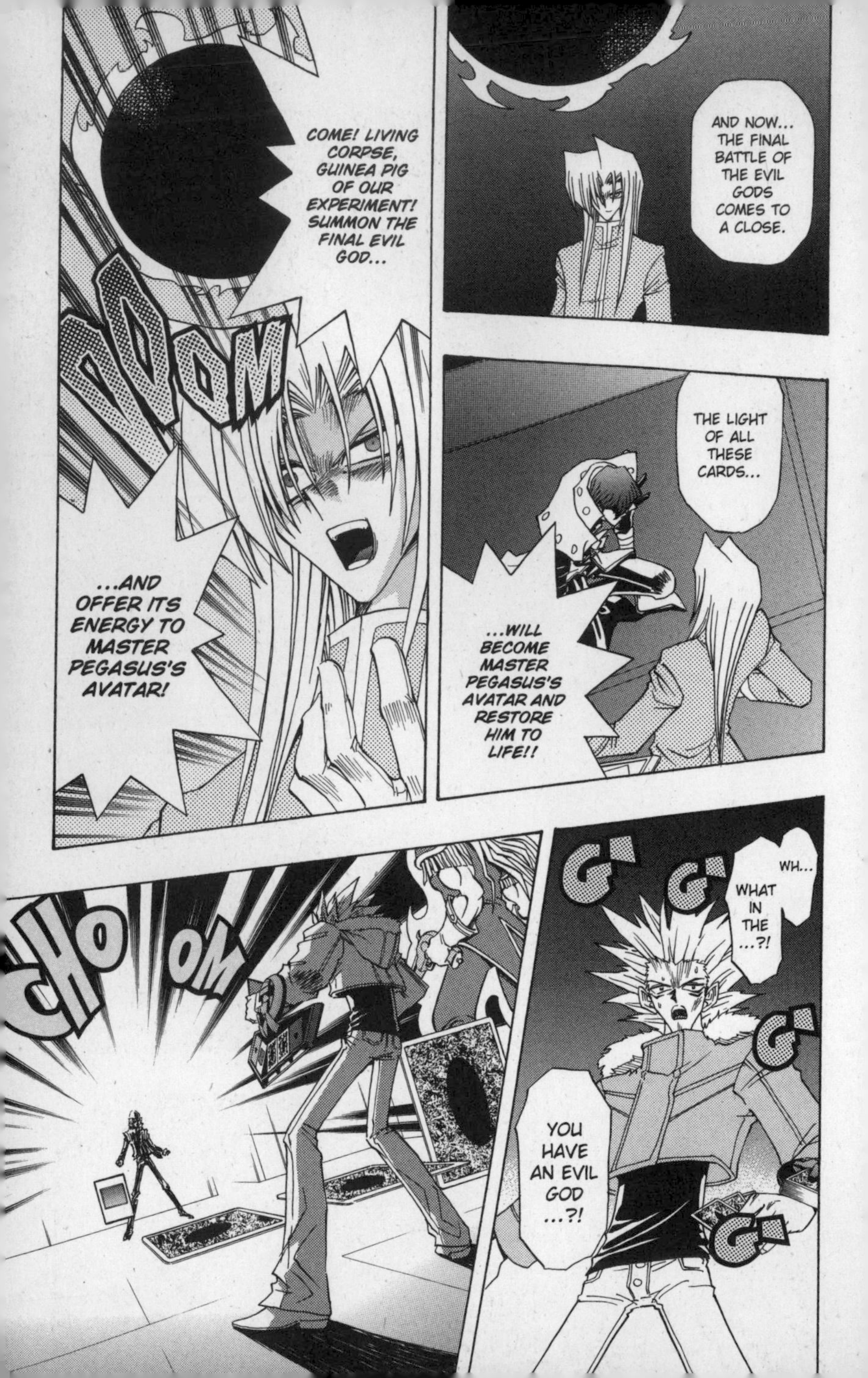
AND NOW... THE FINAL BATTLE OF THE EVIL GODS COMES TO A CLOSE.
THE LIGHT OF ALL THESE CARDS...
...WILL BECOME MASTER PEGASUS'S AVATAR AND RESTORE HIM TO LIFE!!
COME! LIVING CORPSE, GUINEA PIG OF OUR EXPERIMENT! SUMMON THE FINAL EVIL GOD...
DOOM
...AND OFFER ITS ENERGY TO MASTER PEGASUS'S AVATAR!
G' G'
WH... WHAT IN THE ...?!
G'
YOU HAVE AN EVIL GOD ...?!
G'
CHO OM

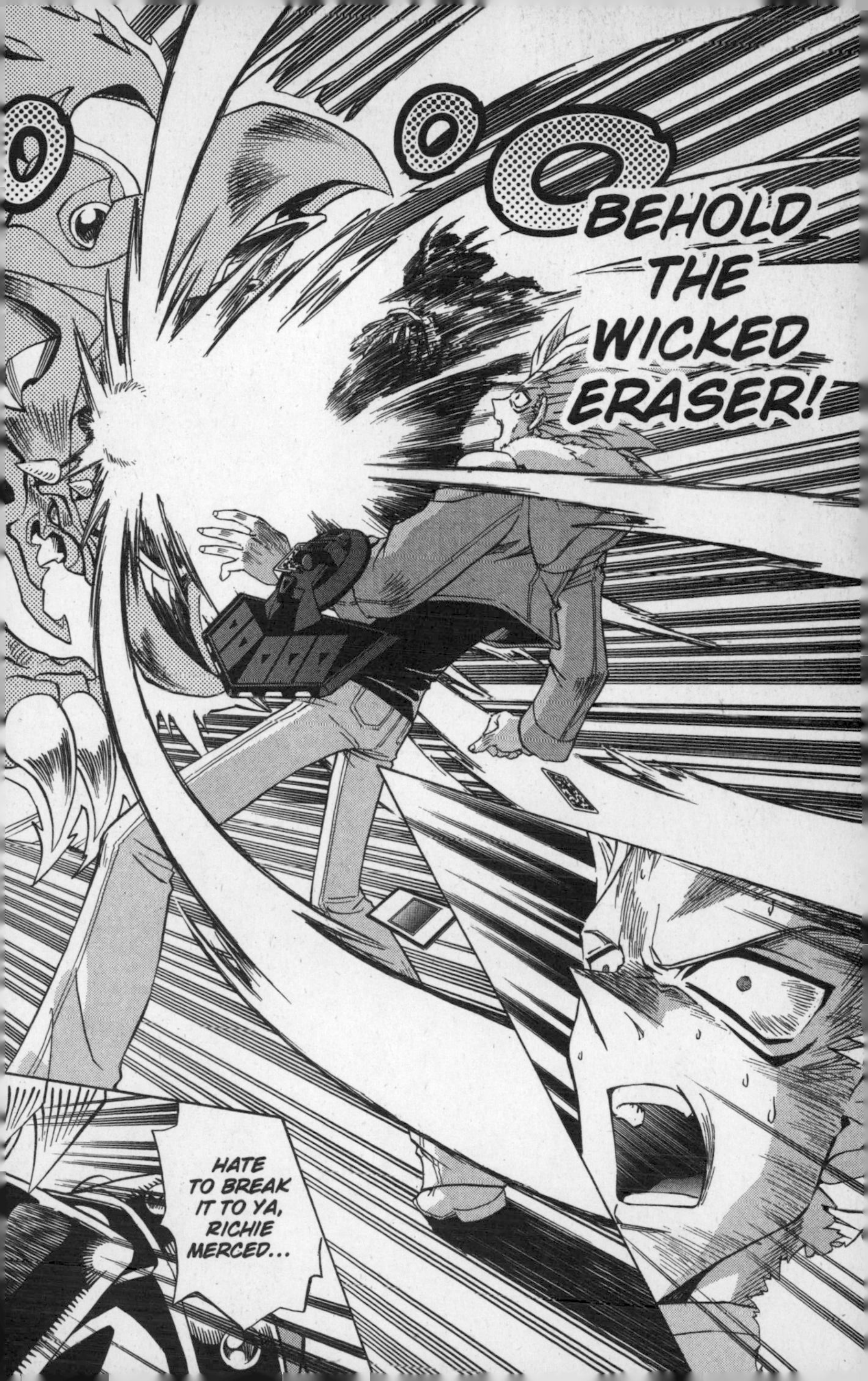
BEHOLD THE WICKED ERASER!
HATE TO BREAK IT TO YA, RICHIE MERCED...

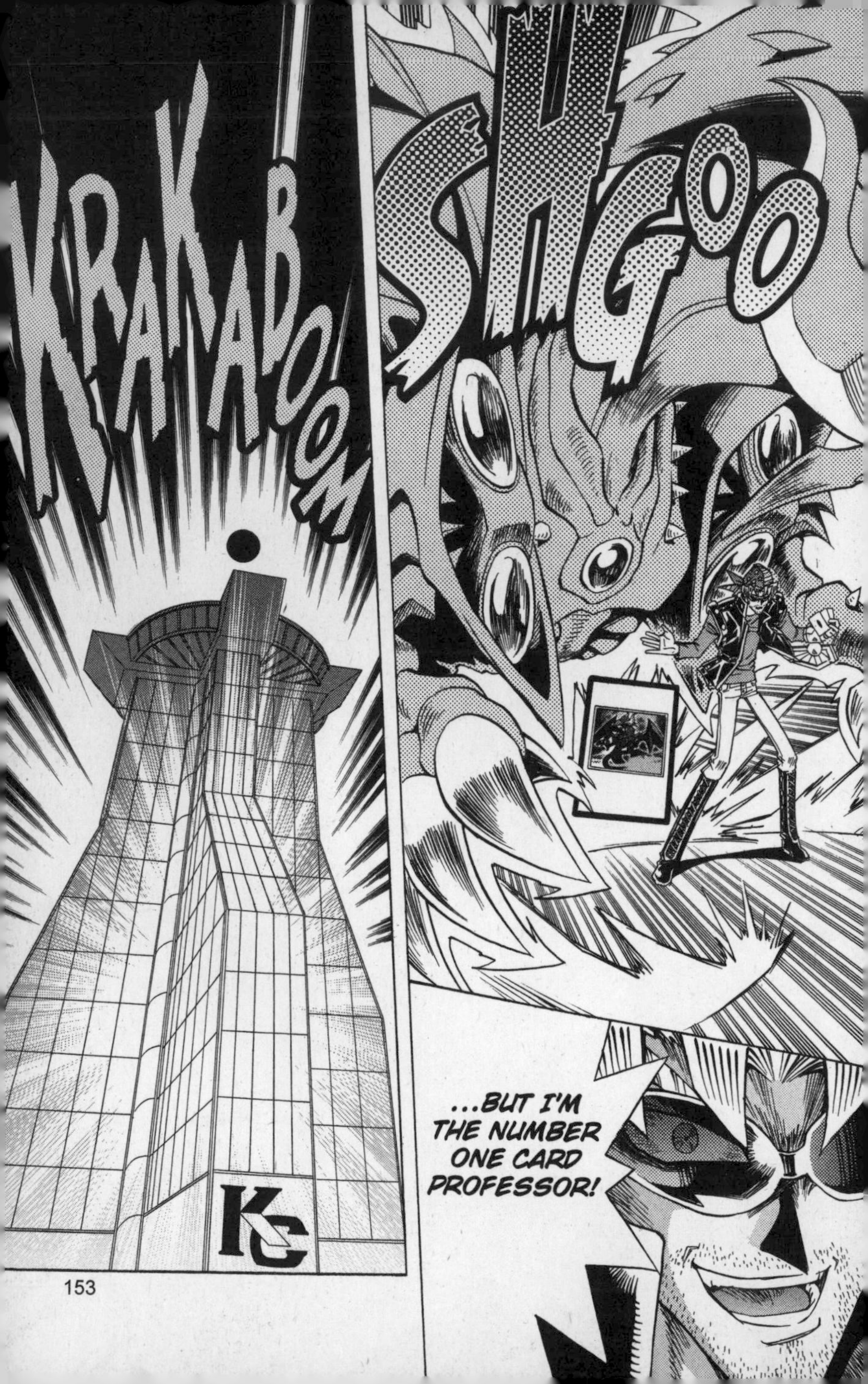
SHGOO
...BUT I'M THE NUMBER ONE CARD PROFESSOR!
KRAKABOOM

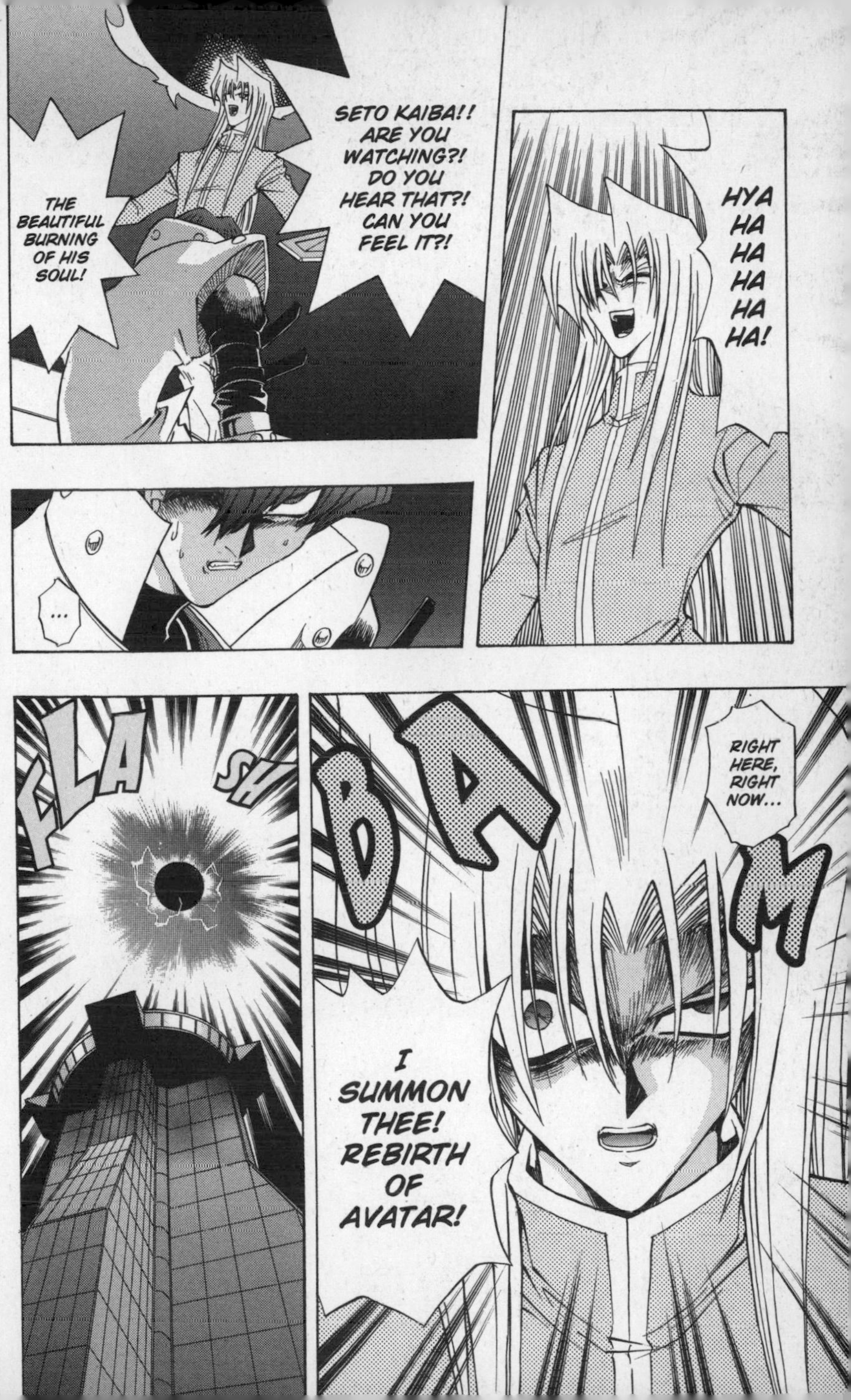
HYA HA HA HA HA HA!
SETO KAIBA!! ARE YOU WATCHING?! DO YOU HEAR THAT?! CAN YOU FEEL IT?!
THE BEAUTIFUL BURNING OF HIS SOUL!
...
RIGHT HERE, RIGHT NOW...
BAM
I SUMMON THEE! REBIRTH OF AVATAR!
FLASH

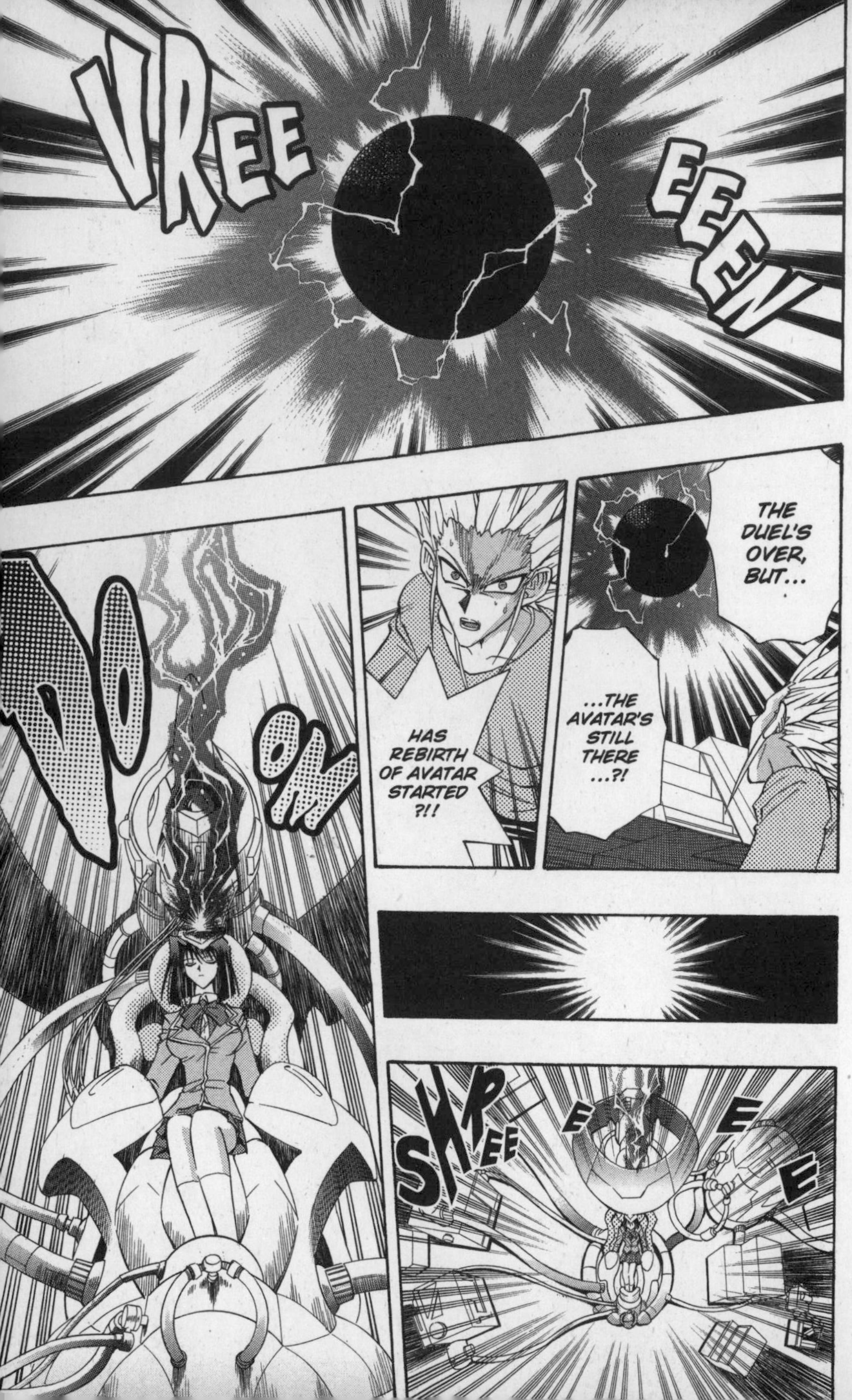
VREE
EEEN
THE DUEL'S OVER, BUT...
...THE AVATAR'S STILL THERE ...?!
HAS REBIRTH OF AVATAR STARTED ?!!
SHREE
E
E
E
DO
OM

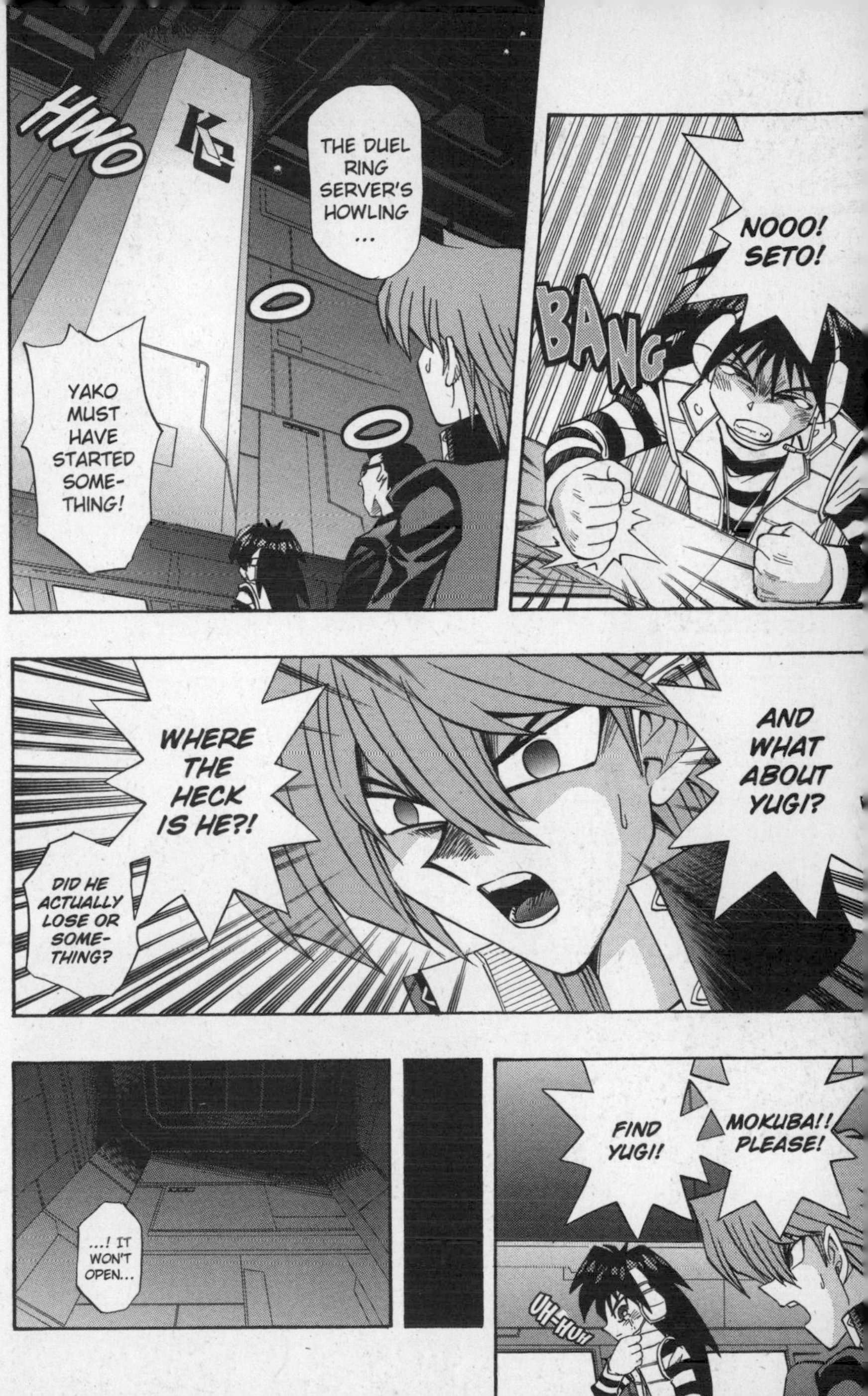
NOOO! SETO!
BANG
THE DUEL RING SERVER'S HOWLING ...
HWO
YAKO MUST HAVE STARTED SOME-THING!
AND WHAT ABOUT YUGI?
WHERE THE HECK IS HE?!
DID HE ACTUALLY LOSE OR SOME-THING?
MOKUBA!! PLEASE!
FIND YUGI!
UH-HUH
...! IT WON'T OPEN...

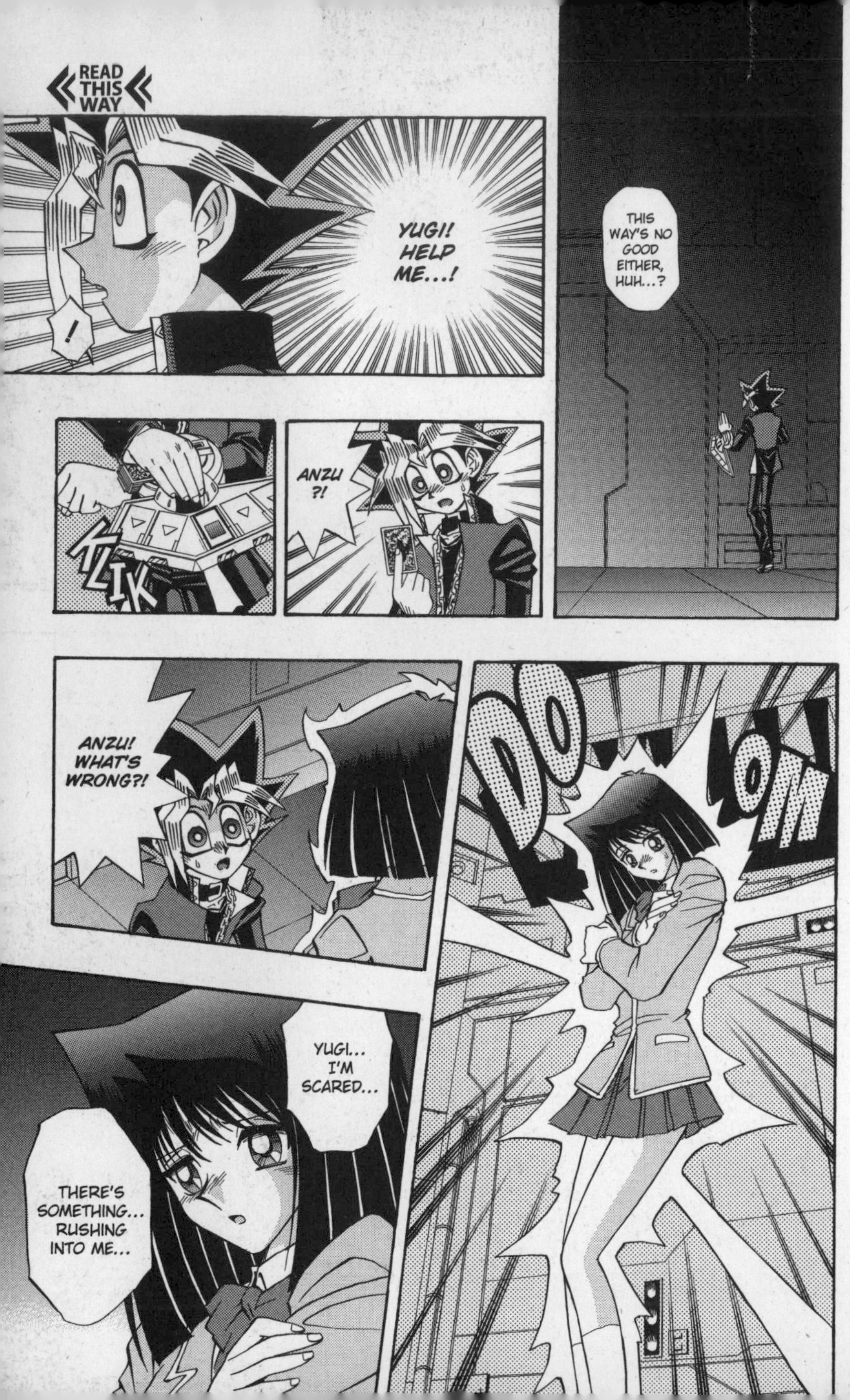
READ THIS WAY
THIS WAY'S NO GOOD EITHER, HUH...?
YUGI! HELP ME...!
!
ANZU ?!
KLIK
DO...OM
ANZU! WHAT'S WRONG?!
YUGI... I'M SCARED...
THERE'S SOMETHING... RUSHING INTO ME...

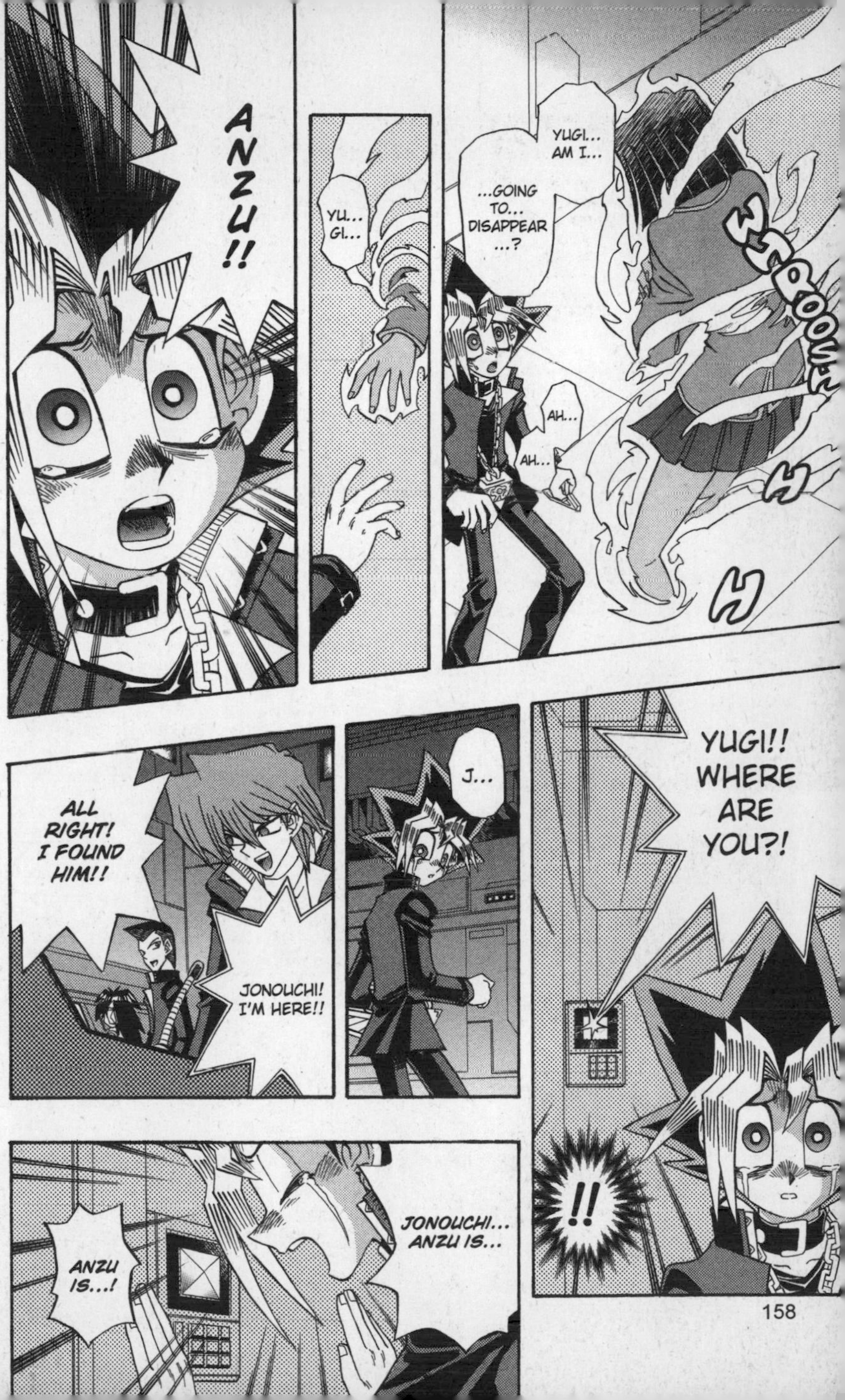
YUGI... AM I...
...GOING TO... DISAPPEAR ...?
AH...
AH...
WHOOOSHH
YU... GI...
ANZU!!
YUGI!! WHERE ARE YOU?!
!!
J...
ALL RIGHT! I FOUND HIM!!
JONOUCHI! I'M HERE!!
JONOUCHI... ANZU IS...
ANZU IS...!

READ THIS WAY

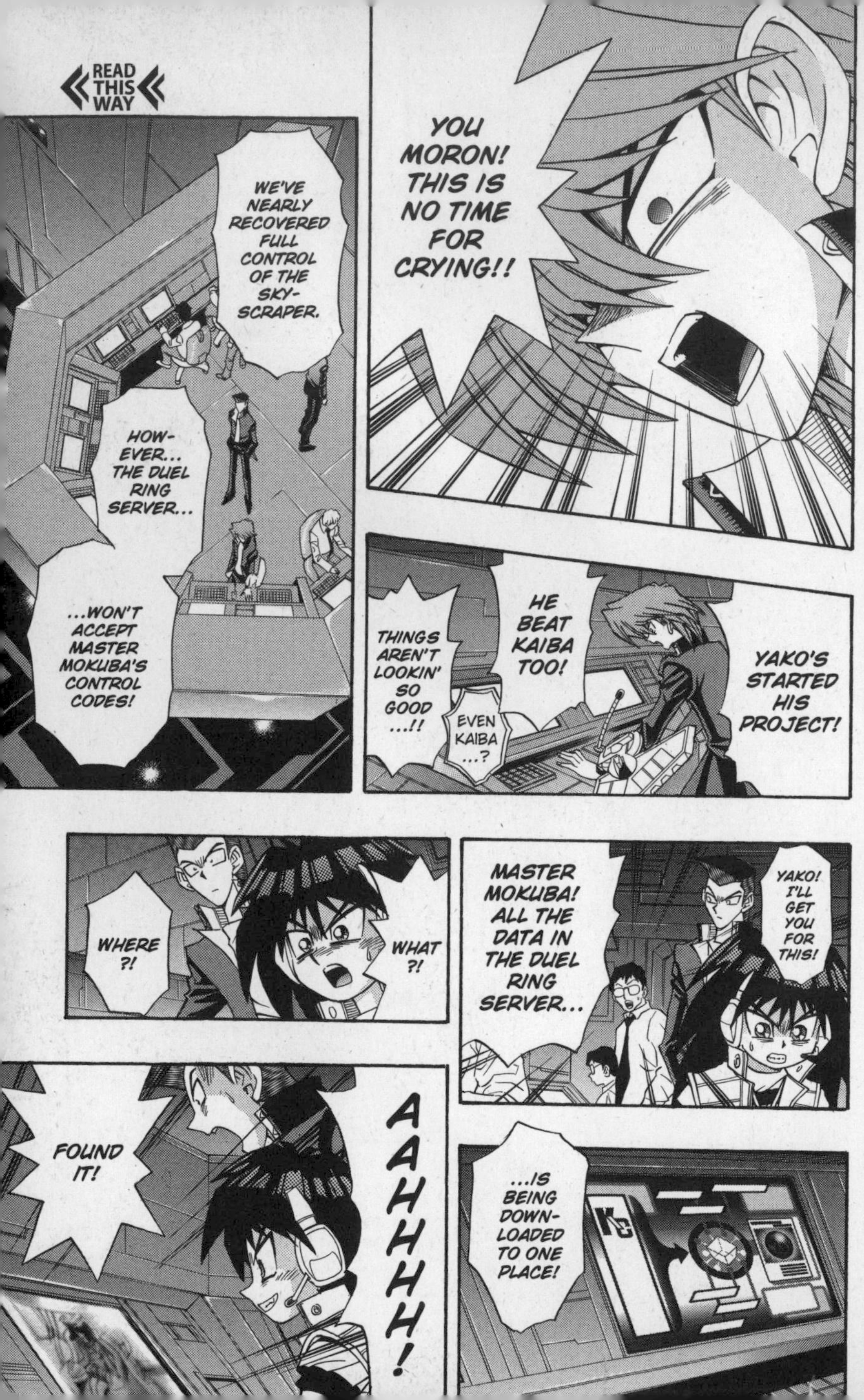
YOU MORON! THIS IS NO TIME FOR CRYING!!
YAKO'S STARTED HIS PROJECT!
HE BEAT KAIBA TOO!
EVEN KAIBA ...?
THINGS AREN'T LOOKIN' SO GOOD ...!!
WE'VE NEARLY RECOVERED FULL CONTROL OF THE SKY-SCRAPER.
HOW-EVER... THE DUEL RING SERVER...
...WON'T ACCEPT MASTER MOKUBA'S CONTROL CODES!
YAKO! I'LL GET YOU FOR THIS!
MASTER MOKUBA! ALL THE DATA IN THE DUEL RING SERVER...
WHAT ?!
WHERE ?!
...IS BEING DOWN-LOADED TO ONE PLACE!
AAHHHHH!
FOUND IT!

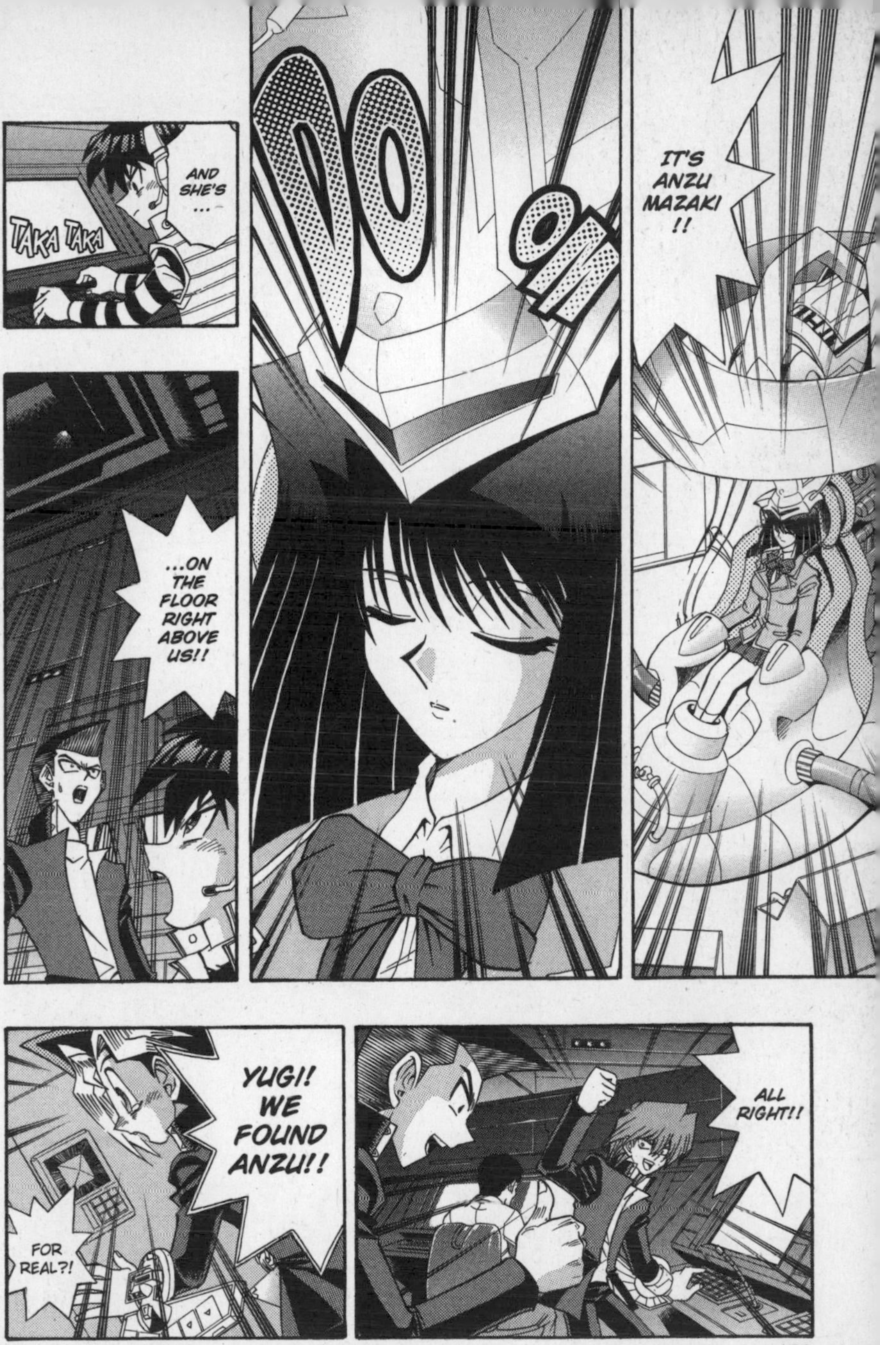
IT'S ANZU MAZAKI!!
AND SHE'S ...
TAKA TAKA
...ON THE FLOOR RIGHT ABOVE US!!
ALL RIGHT!!
YUGI! WE FOUND ANZU!!
FOR REAL?!

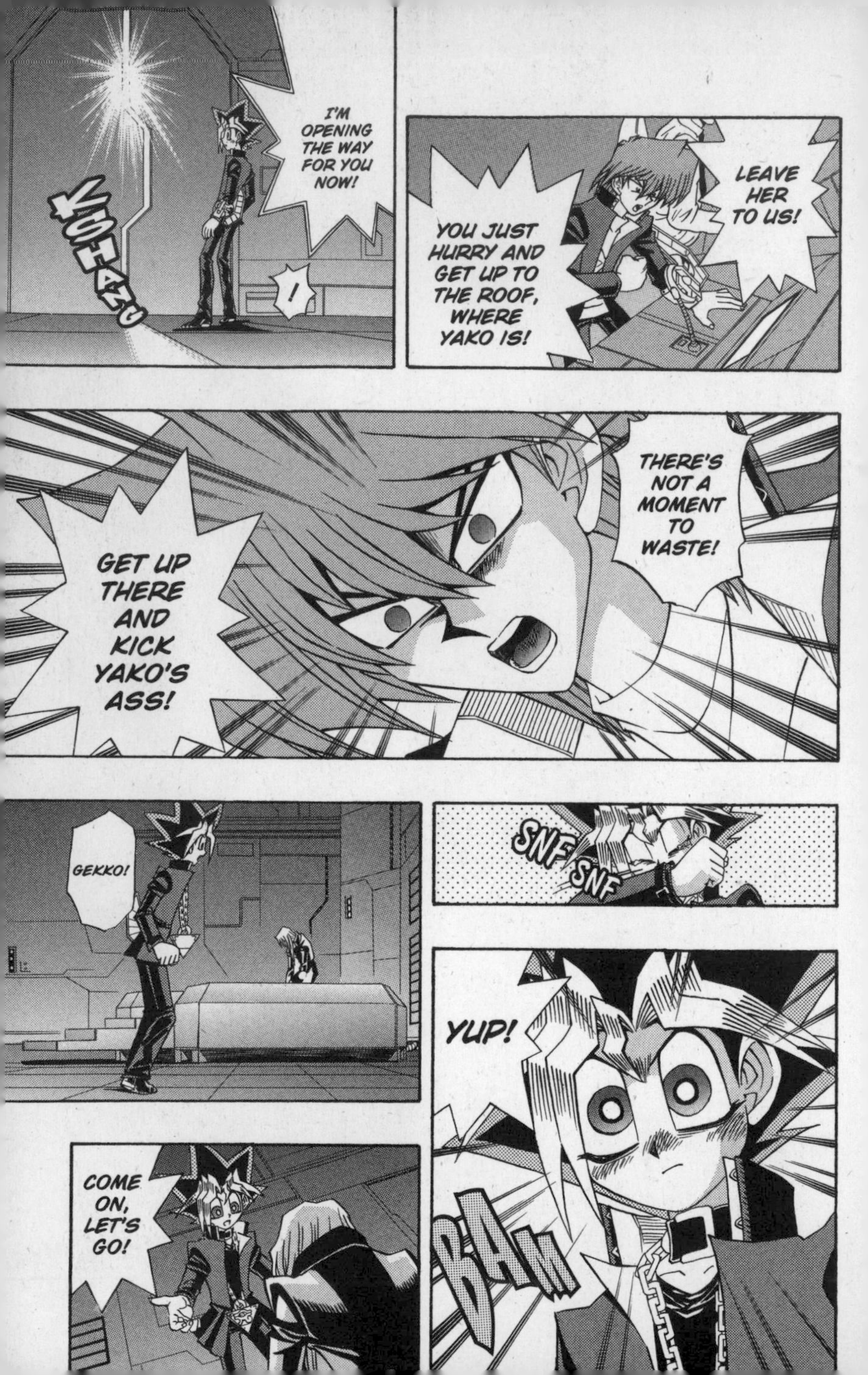
LEAVE HER TO US!
YOU JUST HURRY AND GET UP TO THE ROOF, WHERE YAKO IS!
I'M OPENING THE WAY FOR YOU NOW!
!
KSHANG
THERE'S NOT A MOMENT TO WASTE!
GET UP THERE AND KICK YAKO'S ASS!
SNF SNF
YUP!
BAM
GEKKO!
COME ON, LET'S GO!

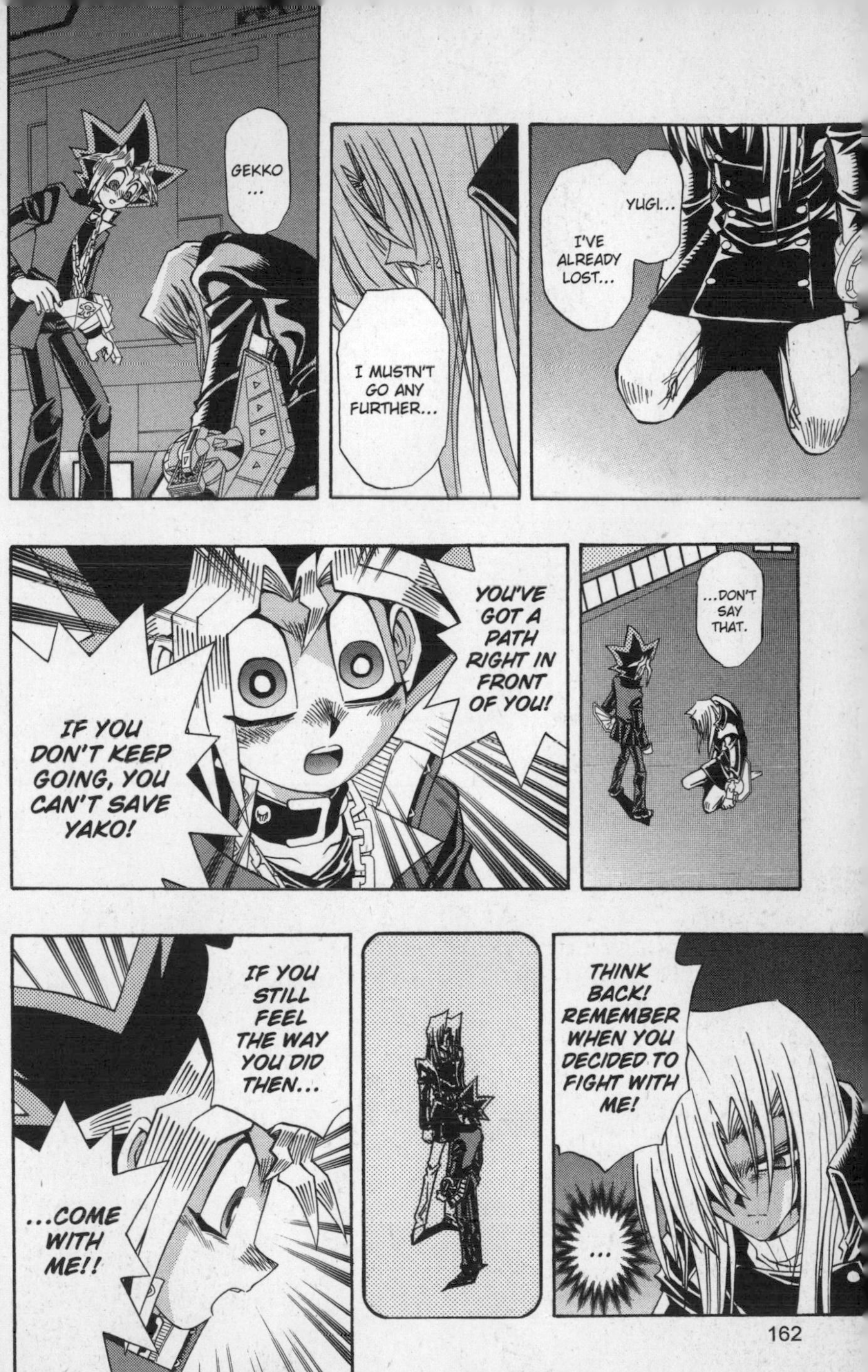
YUGI...
I'VE ALREADY LOST...
I MUSTN'T GO ANY FURTHER...
GEKKO ...
...DON'T SAY THAT.
YOU'VE GOT A PATH RIGHT IN FRONT OF YOU!
IF YOU DON'T KEEP GOING, YOU CAN'T SAVE YAKO!
THINK BACK! REMEMBER WHEN YOU DECIDED TO FIGHT WITH ME!
...
IF YOU STILL FEEL THE WAY YOU DID THEN...
...COME WITH ME!!

READ THIS WAY

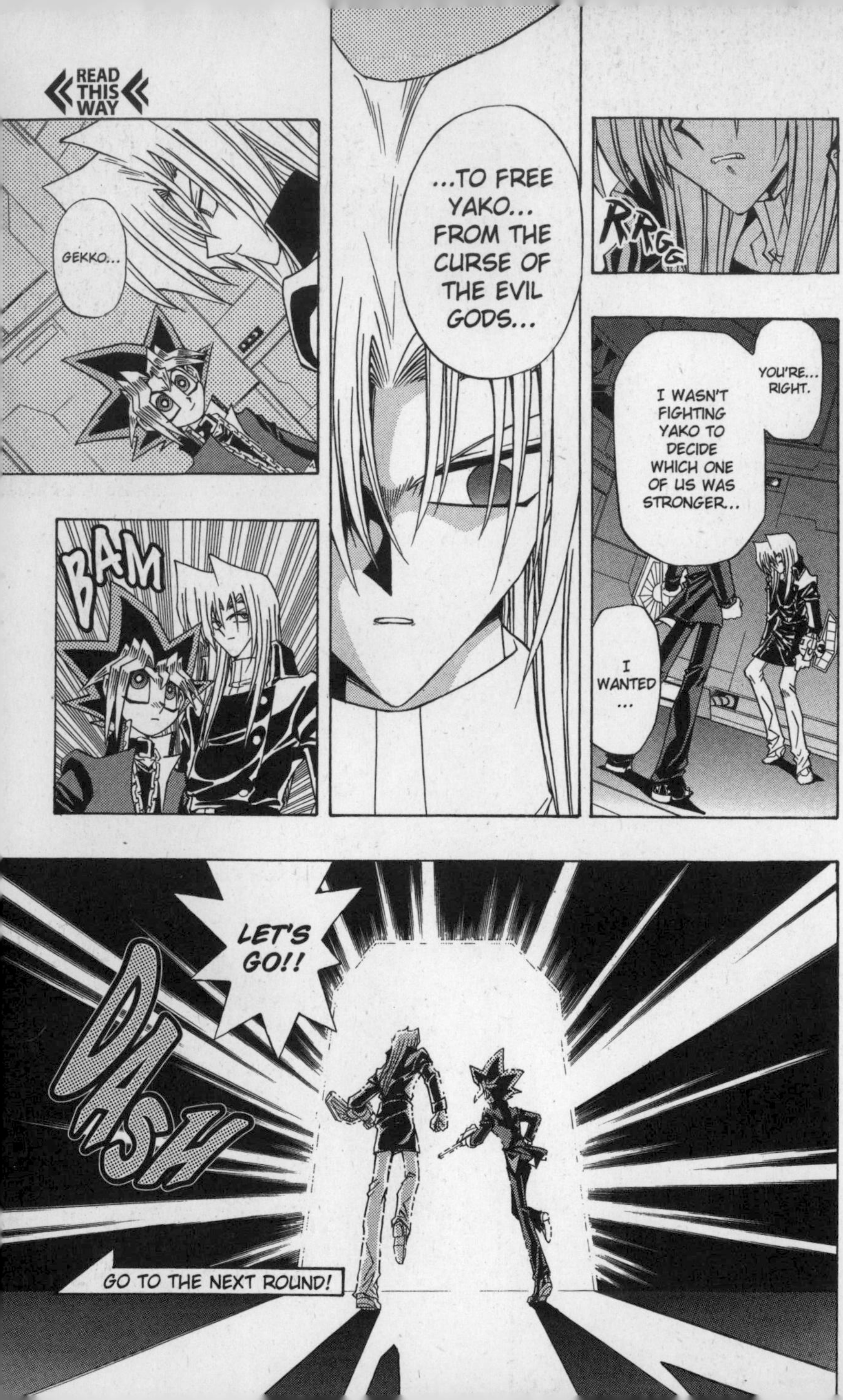
RRGG
YOU'RE... RIGHT.
I WASN'T FIGHTING YAKO TO DECIDE WHICH ONE OF US WAS STRONGER...
I WANTED ...
...TO FREE YAKO... FROM THE CURSE OF THE EVIL GODS...
GEKKO...
BAM
LET'S GO!!
DASH
GO TO THE NEXT ROUND!

Card Professor
Cedar Mill

High-Tech
Marionette
User

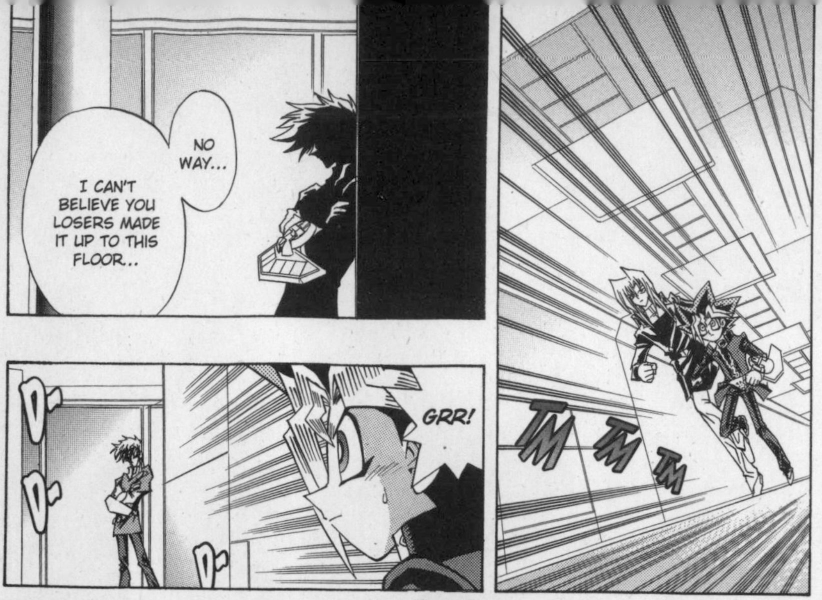
TM
TM
TM
NO WAY...
I CAN'T BELIEVE YOU LOSERS MADE IT UP TO THIS FLOOR...
D-
D-
D-
GRR!

DUEL ROUND 32: THE RESURRECTION OF PEGASUS?!

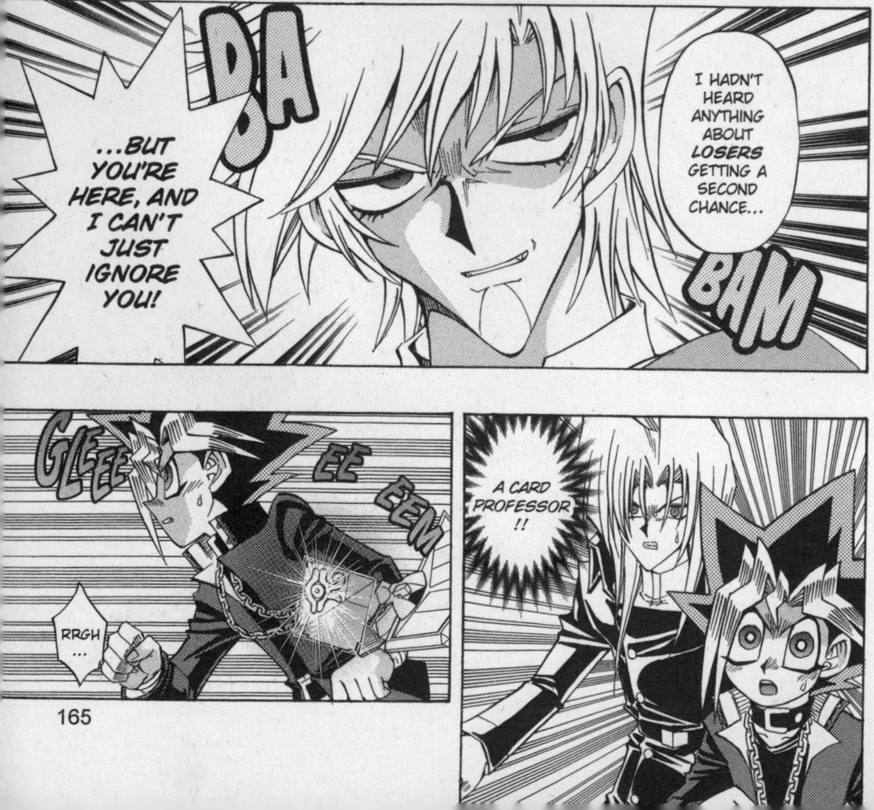
I HADN'T HEARD ANYTHING ABOUT LOSERS GETTING A SECOND CHANCE...
BAM
DA
...BUT YOU'RE HERE, AND I CAN'T JUST IGNORE YOU!
A CARD PROFESSOR !!
GLEEEEEEM
RRGH ...

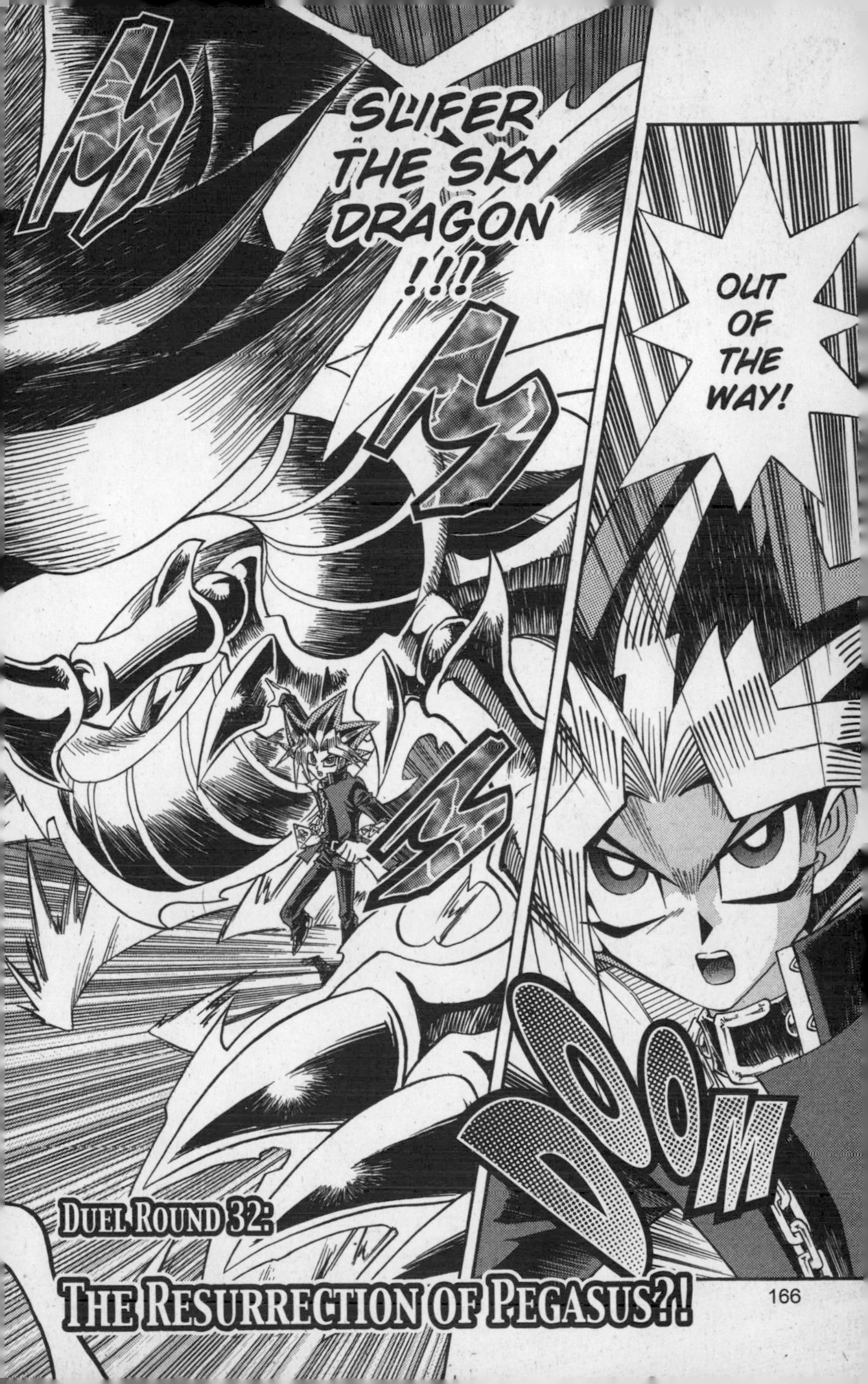
OUT OF THE WAY!
DOOM
SLIFER THE SKY DRAGON!!!
DUEL ROUND 32:
THE RESURRECTION OF PEGASUS?!

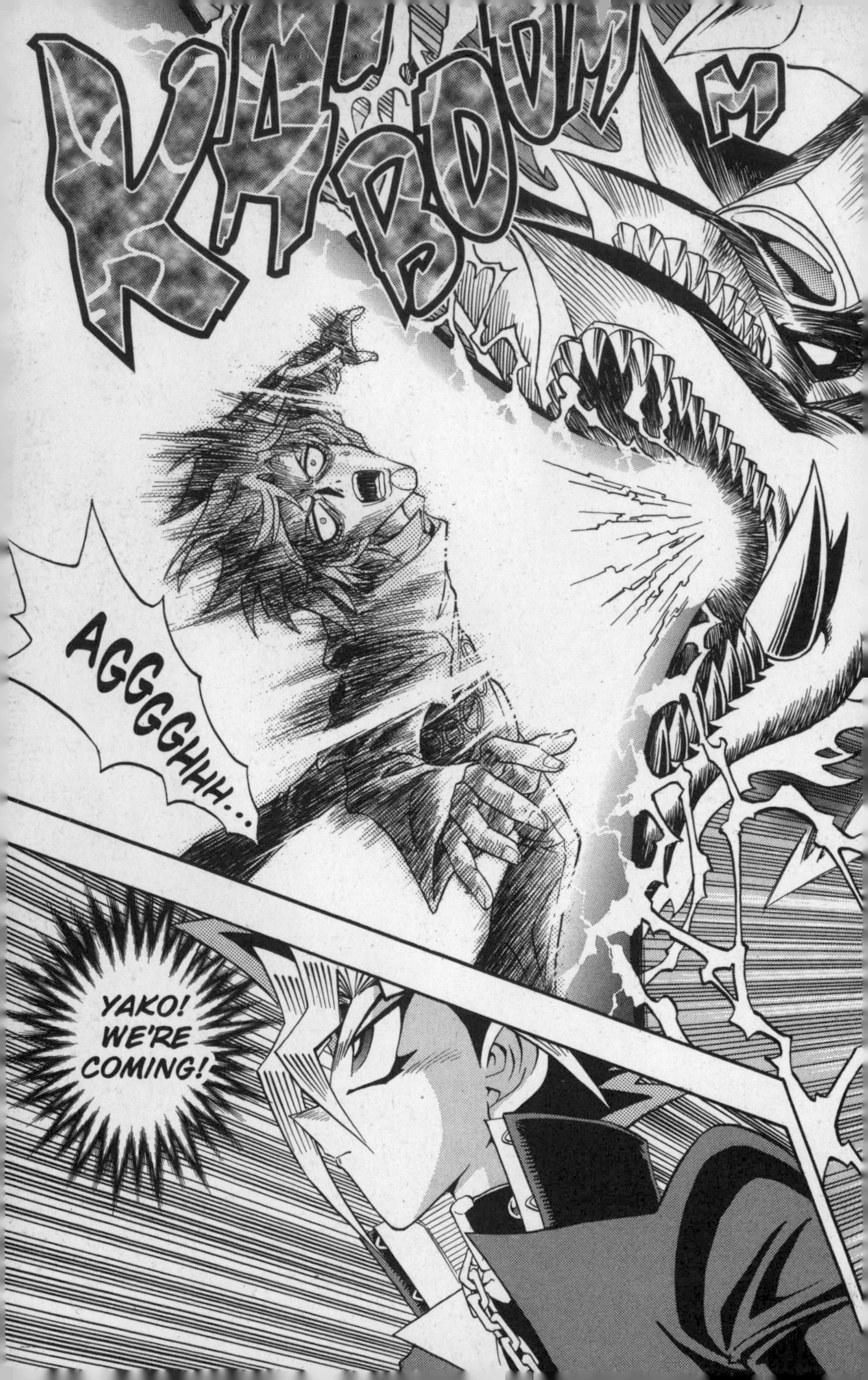
KABOOM
AGGGGHHH...
YAKO! WE'RE COMING!

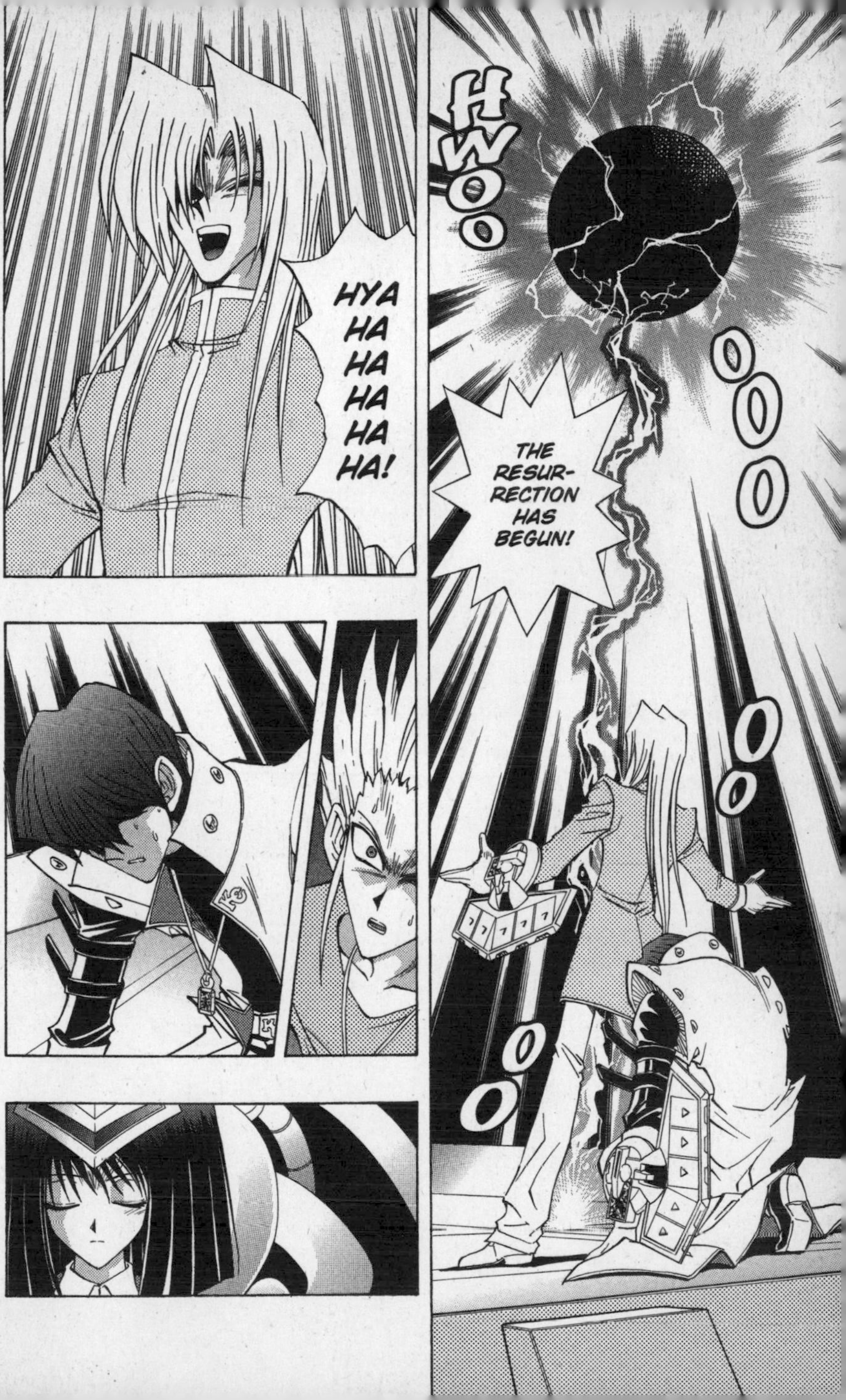
HWOOOOOOOOO
THE RESUR-RECTION HAS BEGUN!
HYA HA HA HA HA HA!

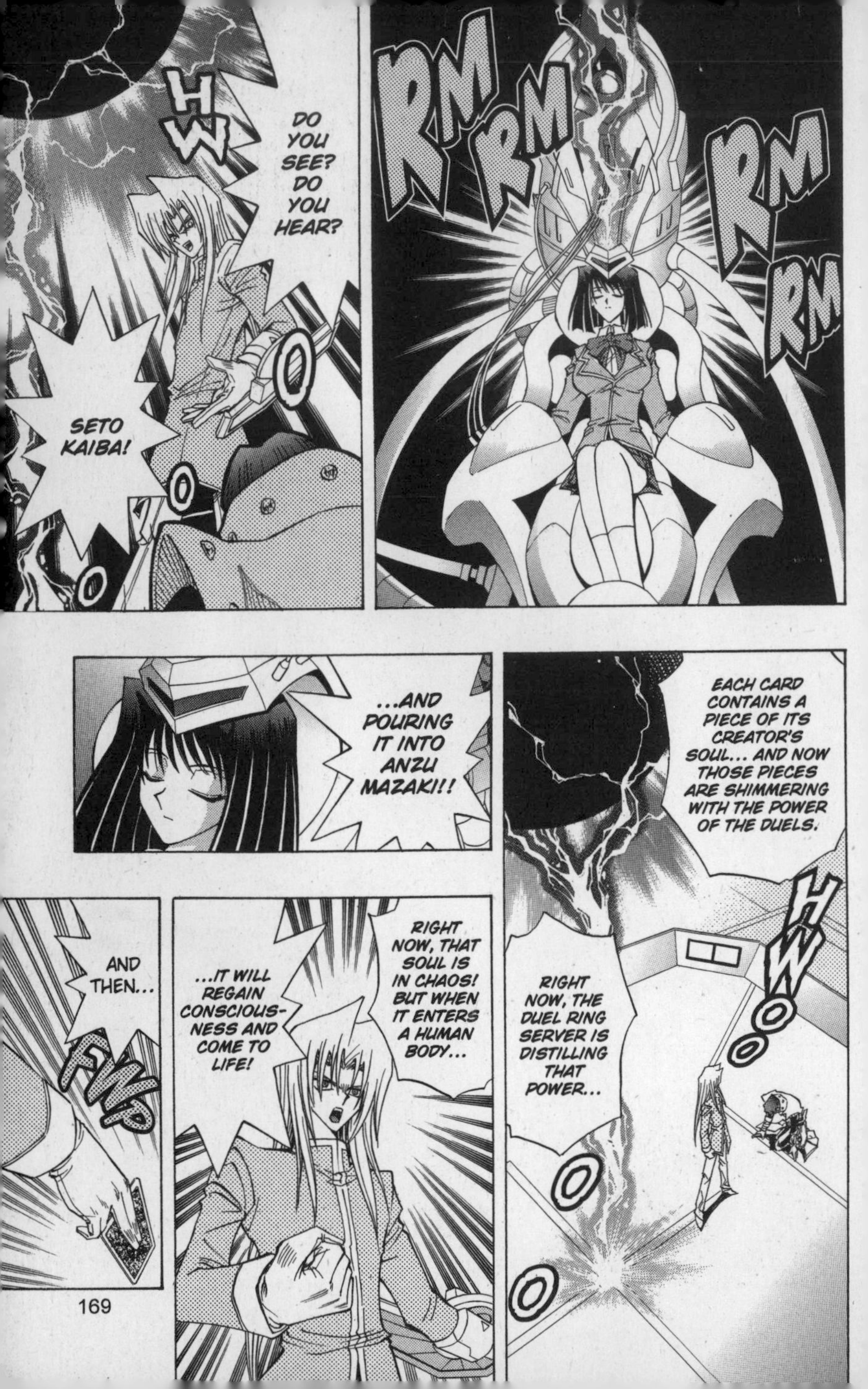
RM RM RM RM RM
HW
DO YOU SEE? DO YOU HEAR?
SETO KAIBA!
O O O
EACH CARD CONTAINS A PIECE OF ITS CREATOR'S SOUL... AND NOW THOSE PIECES ARE SHIMMERING WITH THE POWER OF THE DUELS.
HWOOO
RIGHT NOW, THE DUEL RING SERVER IS DISTILLING THAT POWER...
O O
...AND POURING IT INTO ANZU MAZAKI!!
RIGHT NOW, THAT SOUL IS IN CHAOS! BUT WHEN IT ENTERS A HUMAN BODY...
...IT WILL REGAIN CONSCIOUSNESS AND COME TO LIFE!
AND THEN...
FWP

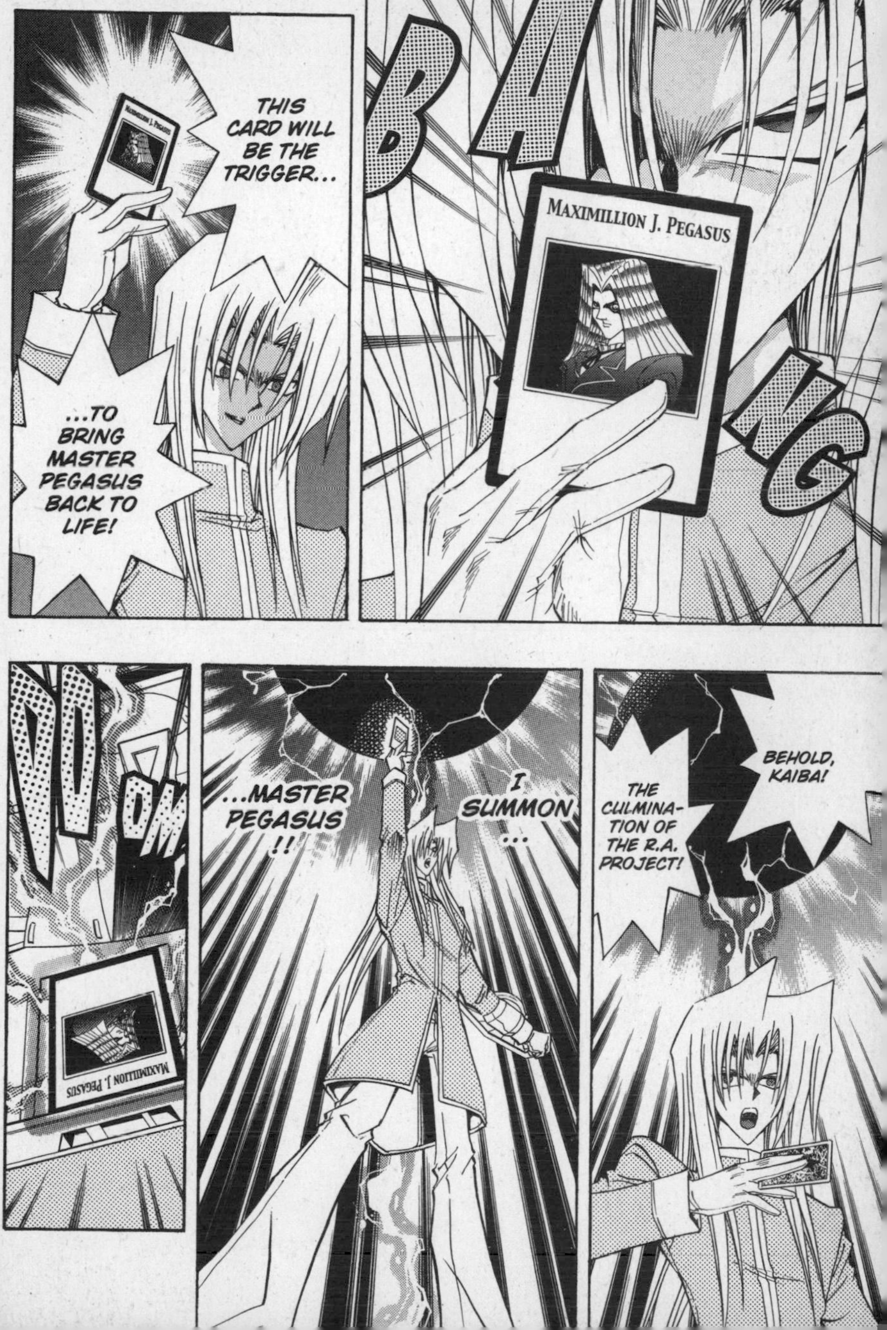
BA
NG
MAXIMILLION J. PEGASUS
THIS CARD WILL BE THE TRIGGER...
...TO BRING MASTER PEGASUS BACK TO LIFE!
BEHOLD, KAIBA!
THE CULMINATION OF THE R.A. PROJECT!
I SUMMON...
...MASTER PEGASUS!!

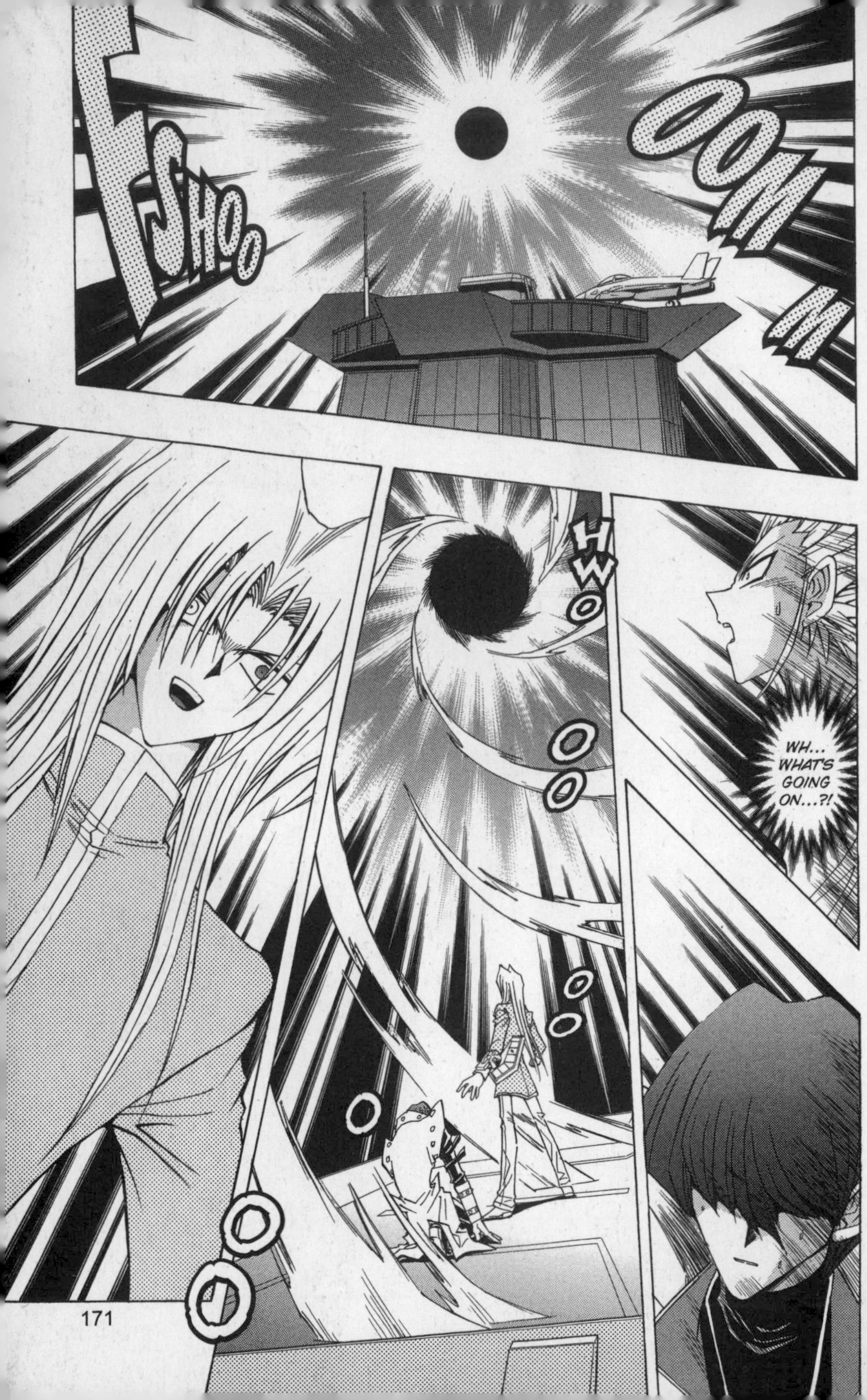

FSHOOO
OOOMM
WH... WHAT'S GOING ON...?!
HWOOOOOOOOO

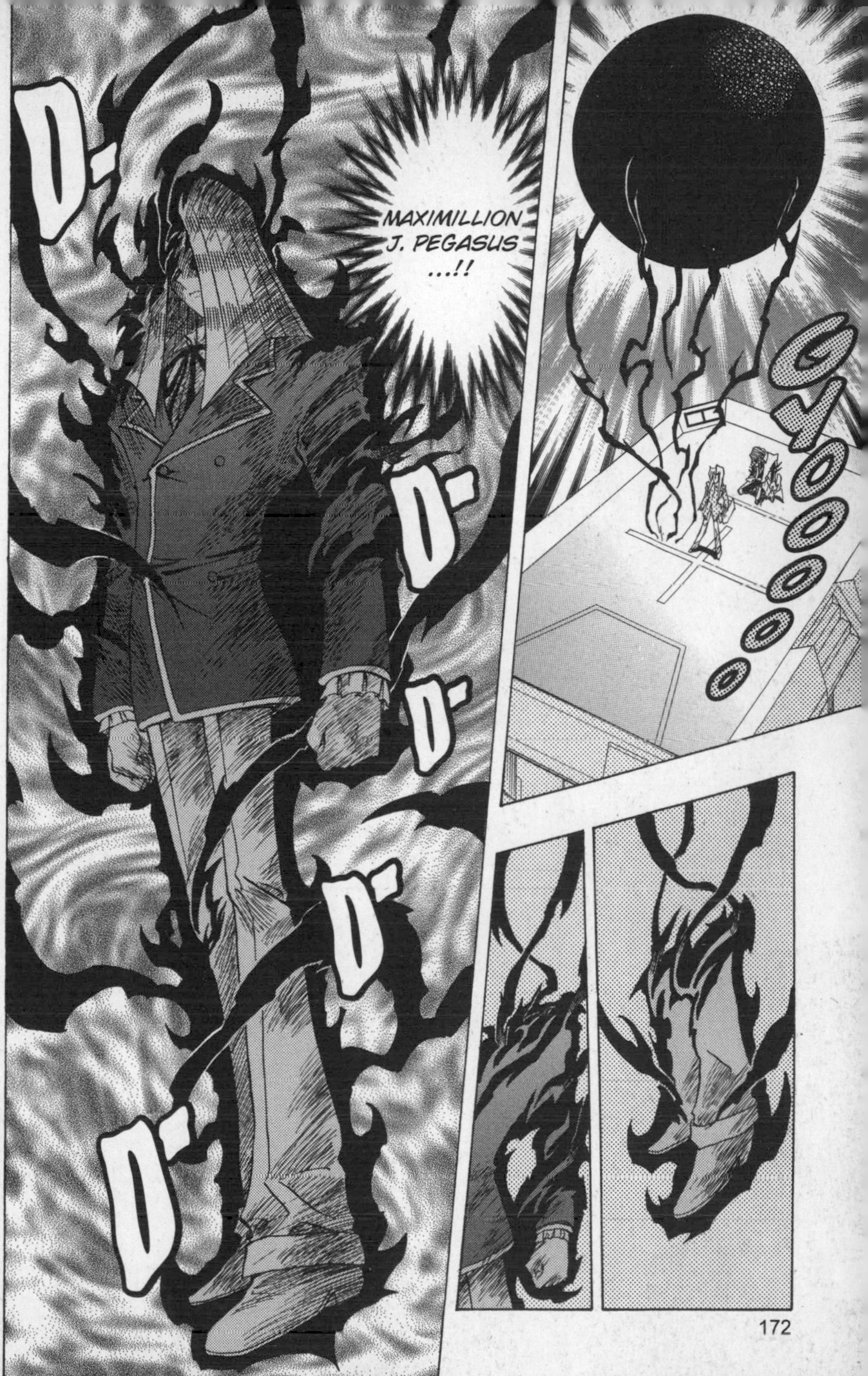
GOOOOOOOO
MAXIMILLION J. PEGASUS ...!!
D-D-D-D-D-

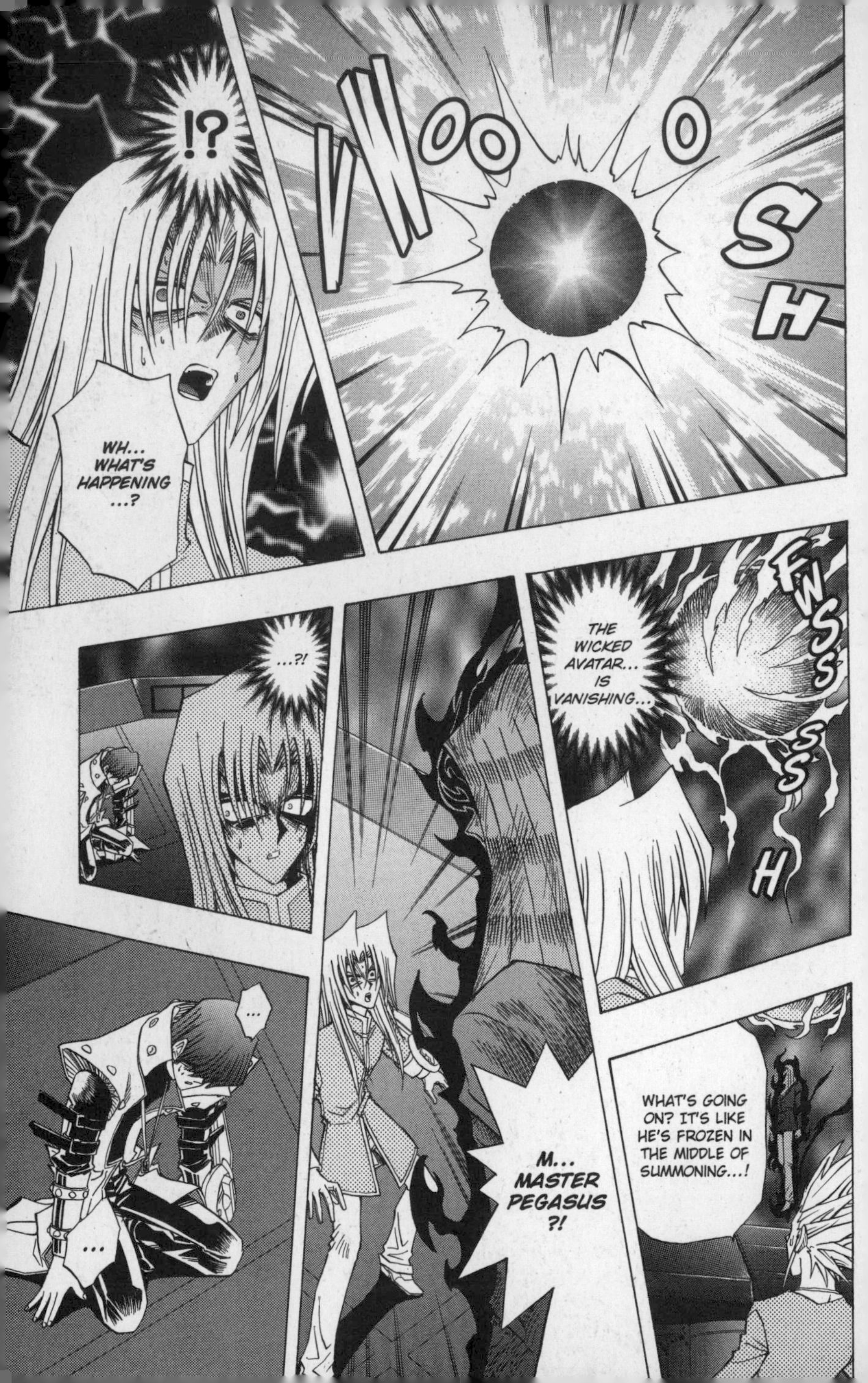
VWOOOSH
!?
WH... WHAT'S HAPPENING...?
THE WICKED AVATAR... IS VANISHING...
FWSSSSSH
WHAT'S GOING ON? IT'S LIKE HE'S FROZEN IN THE MIDDLE OF SUMMONING...!
M... MASTER PEGASUS?!
...?!
...
...

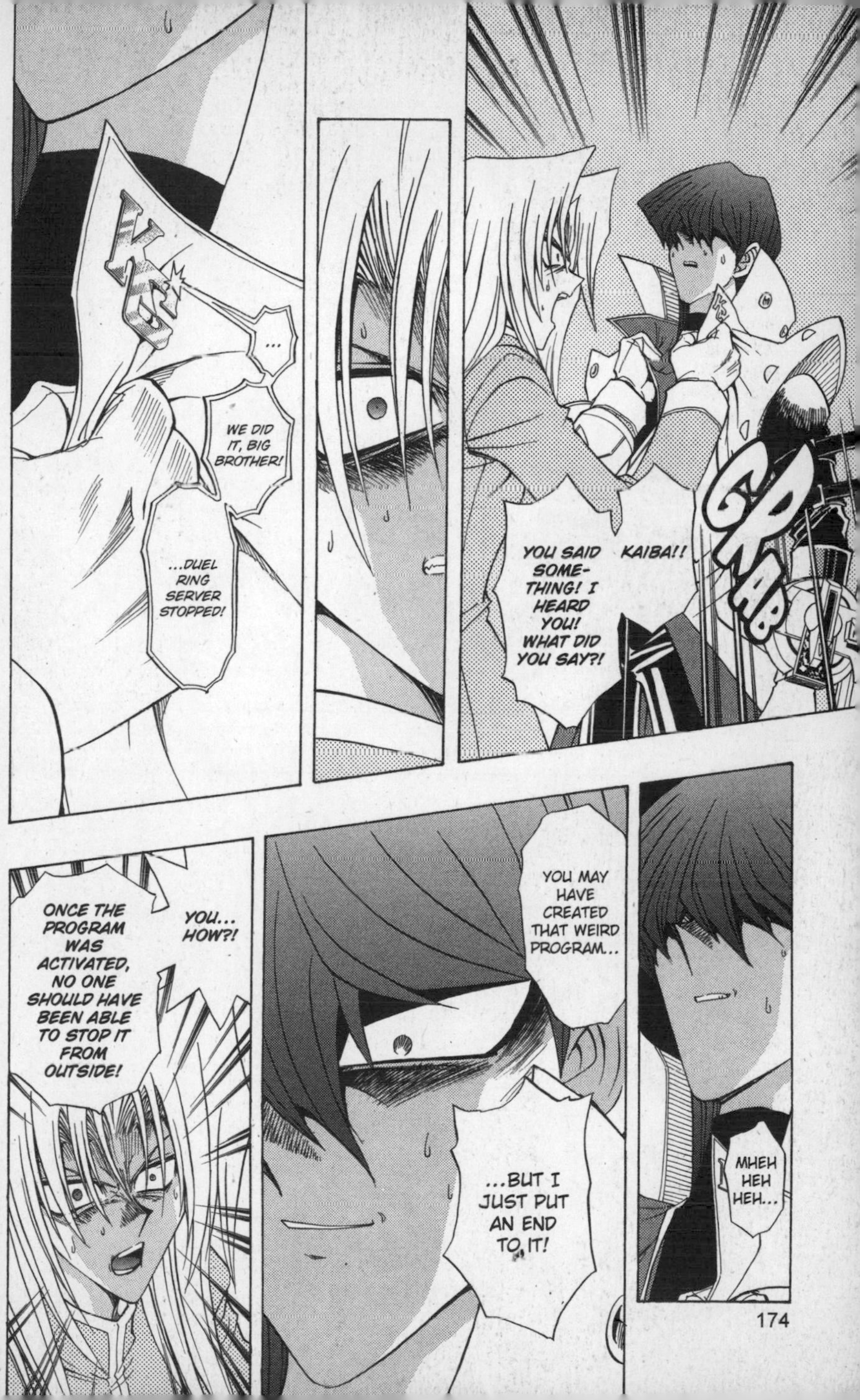
KAIBA!!
YOU SAID SOMETHING! I HEARD YOU! WHAT DID YOU SAY?!
GRAB
...
WE DID IT, BIG BROTHER!
...DUEL RING SERVER STOPPED!
MHEH HEH HEH...
YOU MAY HAVE CREATED THAT WEIRD PROGRAM...
...BUT I JUST PUT AN END TO IT!
YOU... HOW?!
ONCE THE PROGRAM WAS ACTIVATED, NO ONE SHOULD HAVE BEEN ABLE TO STOP IT FROM OUTSIDE!

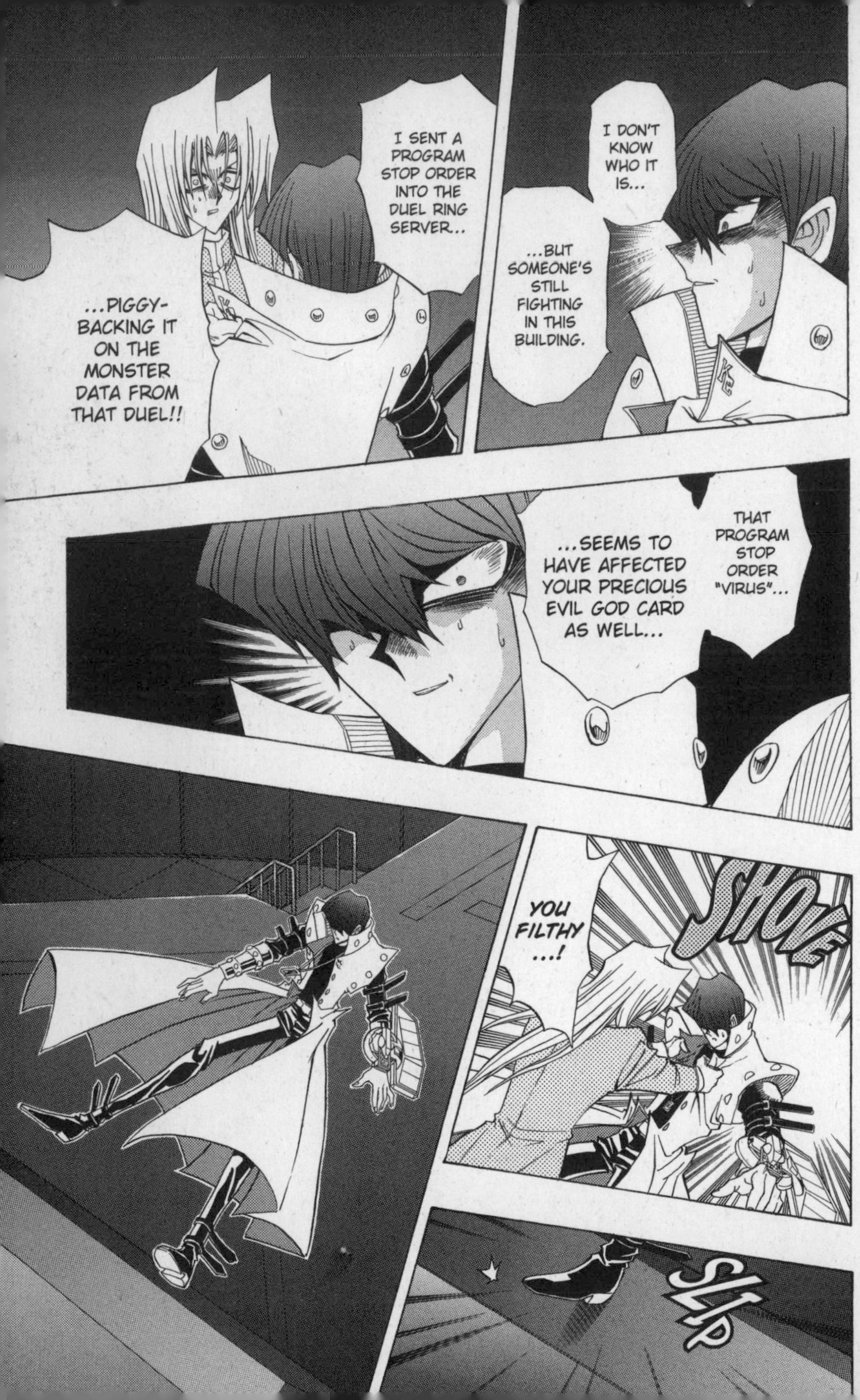

I DON'T KNOW WHO IT IS...
...BUT SOMEONE'S STILL FIGHTING IN THIS BUILDING.
I SENT A PROGRAM STOP ORDER INTO THE DUEL RING SERVER...
...PIGGY-BACKING IT ON THE MONSTER DATA FROM THAT DUEL!!
THAT PROGRAM STOP ORDER "VIRUS"...
...SEEMS TO HAVE AFFECTED YOUR PRECIOUS EVIL GOD CARD AS WELL...
SHOVE
YOU FILTHY ...!
SLIP

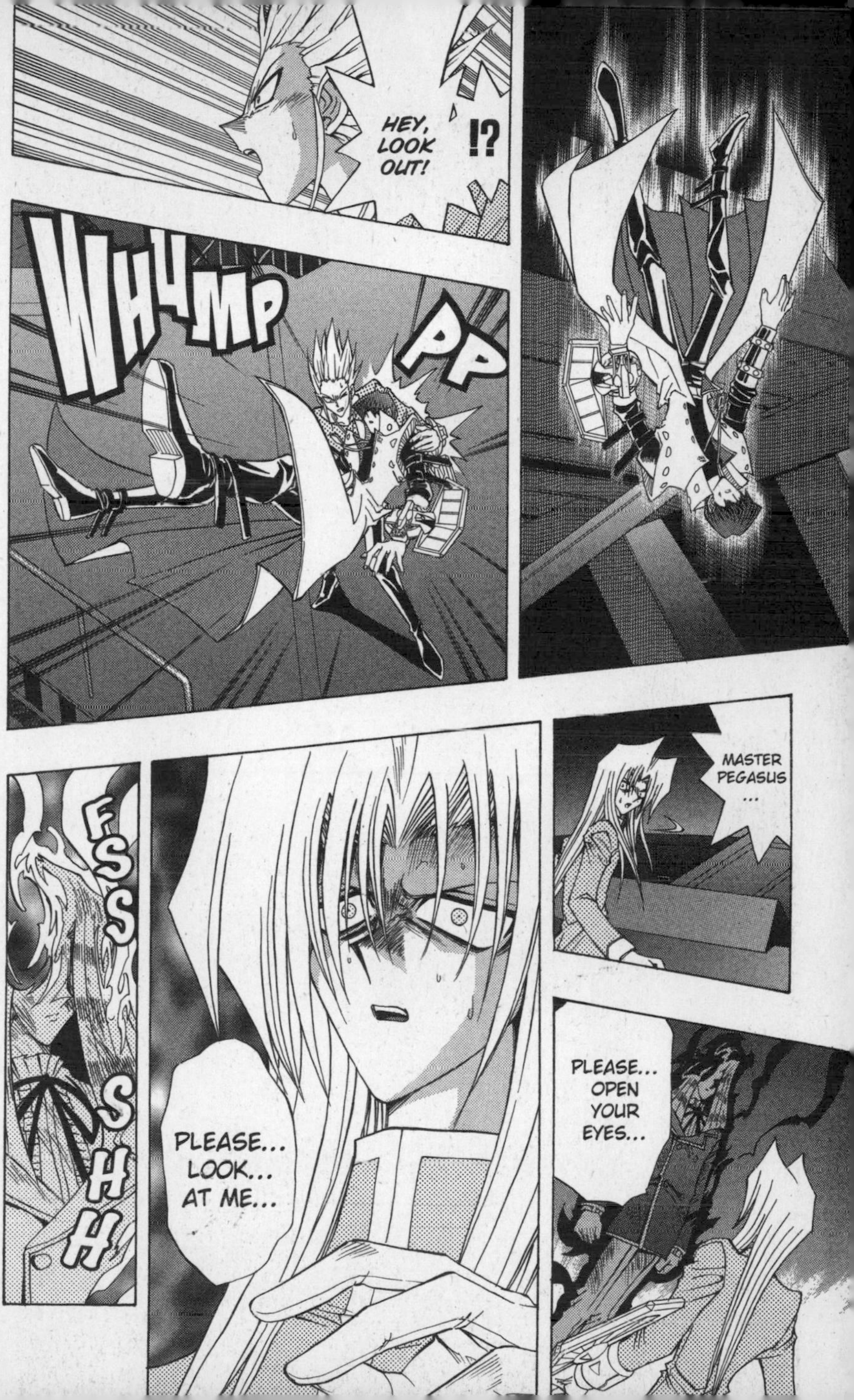
!?
HEY, LOOK OUT!
WHUMPP
MASTER PEGASUS...
PLEASE... OPEN YOUR EYES...
PLEASE... LOOK... AT ME...
FSSSHH

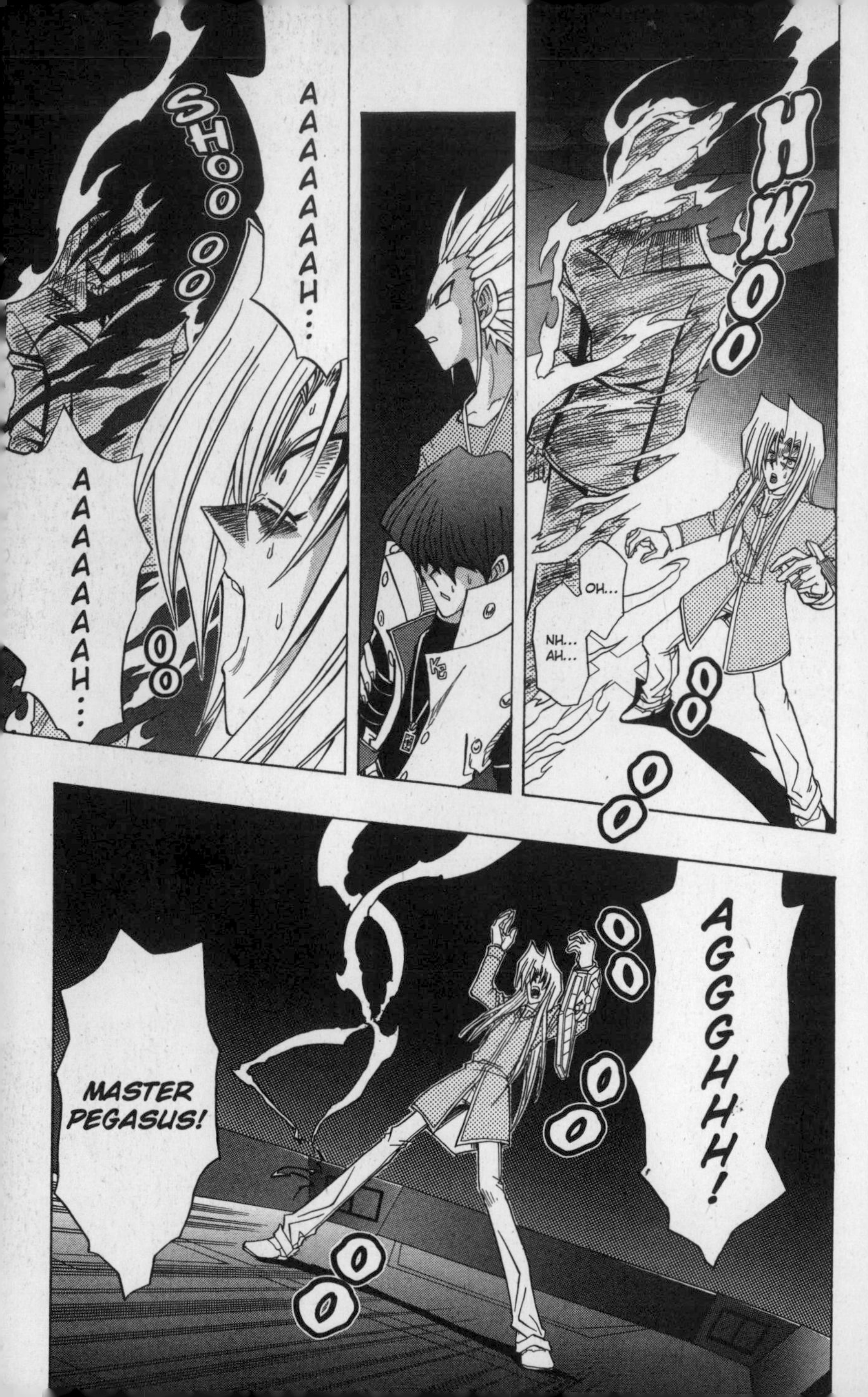
HWOOOOOOOO
OH...
NH... AH...
AAAAAAAAAH...
SHOOOOOO
AAAAAAAAAAAH...
OO
AGGGHHH!
OOOOOOOO
MASTER PEGASUS!

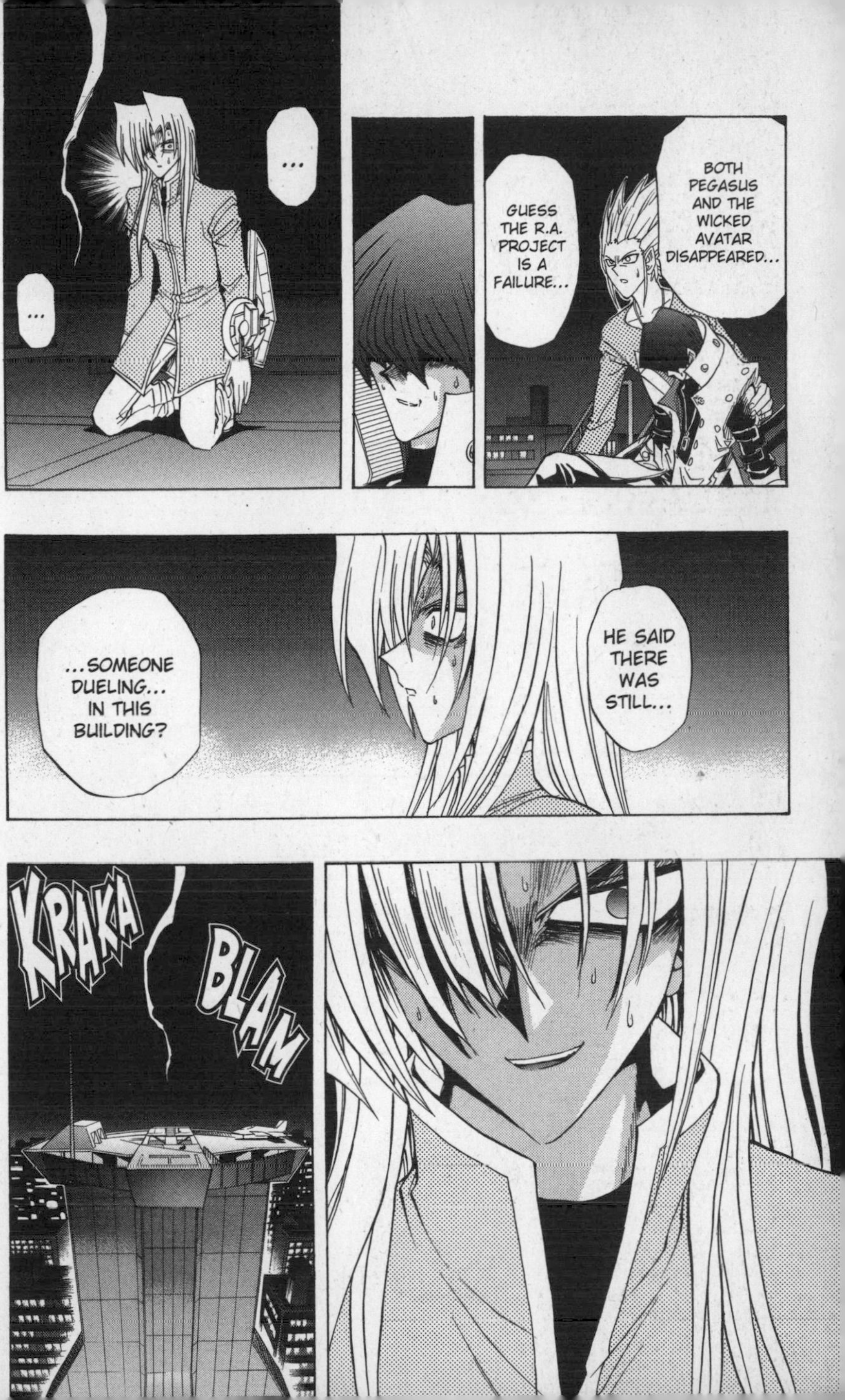
BOTH PEGASUS AND THE WICKED AVATAR DISAPPEARED...
GUESS THE R.A. PROJECT IS A FAILURE...
...
...
HE SAID THERE WAS STILL...
...SOMEONE DUELING... IN THIS BUILDING?
KRAKA
BLAM

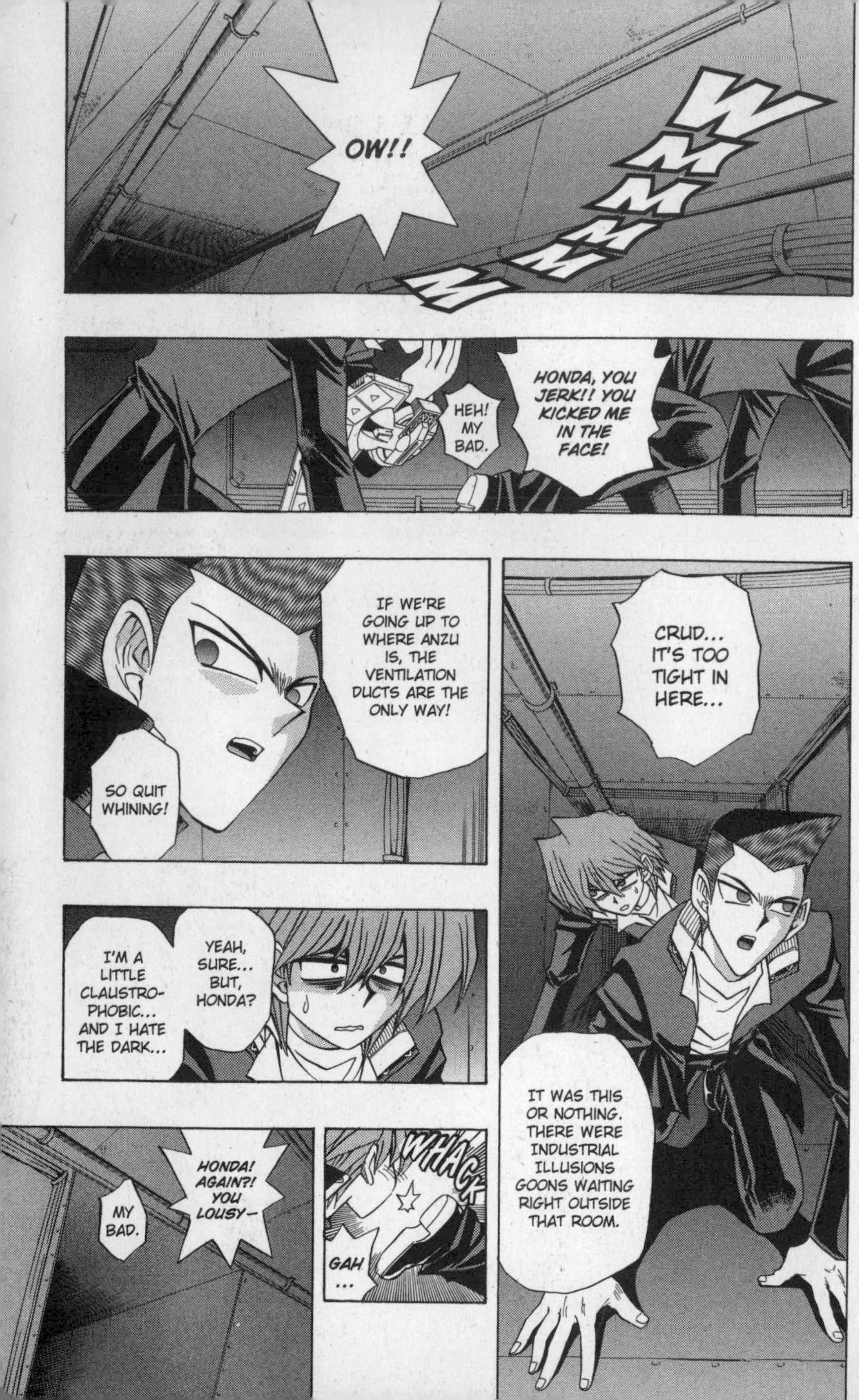
OW!!
WMMMM
HONDA, YOU JERK!! YOU KICKED ME IN THE FACE!
HEH! MY BAD.
CRUD... IT'S TOO TIGHT IN HERE...
IT WAS THIS OR NOTHING. THERE WERE INDUSTRIAL ILLUSIONS GOONS WAITING RIGHT OUTSIDE THAT ROOM.
IF WE'RE GOING UP TO WHERE ANZU IS, THE VENTILATION DUCTS ARE THE ONLY WAY!
SO QUIT WHINING!
YEAH, SURE... BUT, HONDA?
I'M A LITTLE CLAUSTRO-PHOBIC... AND I HATE THE DARK...
WHACK
GAH...
HONDA! AGAIN?! YOU LOUSY—
MY BAD.

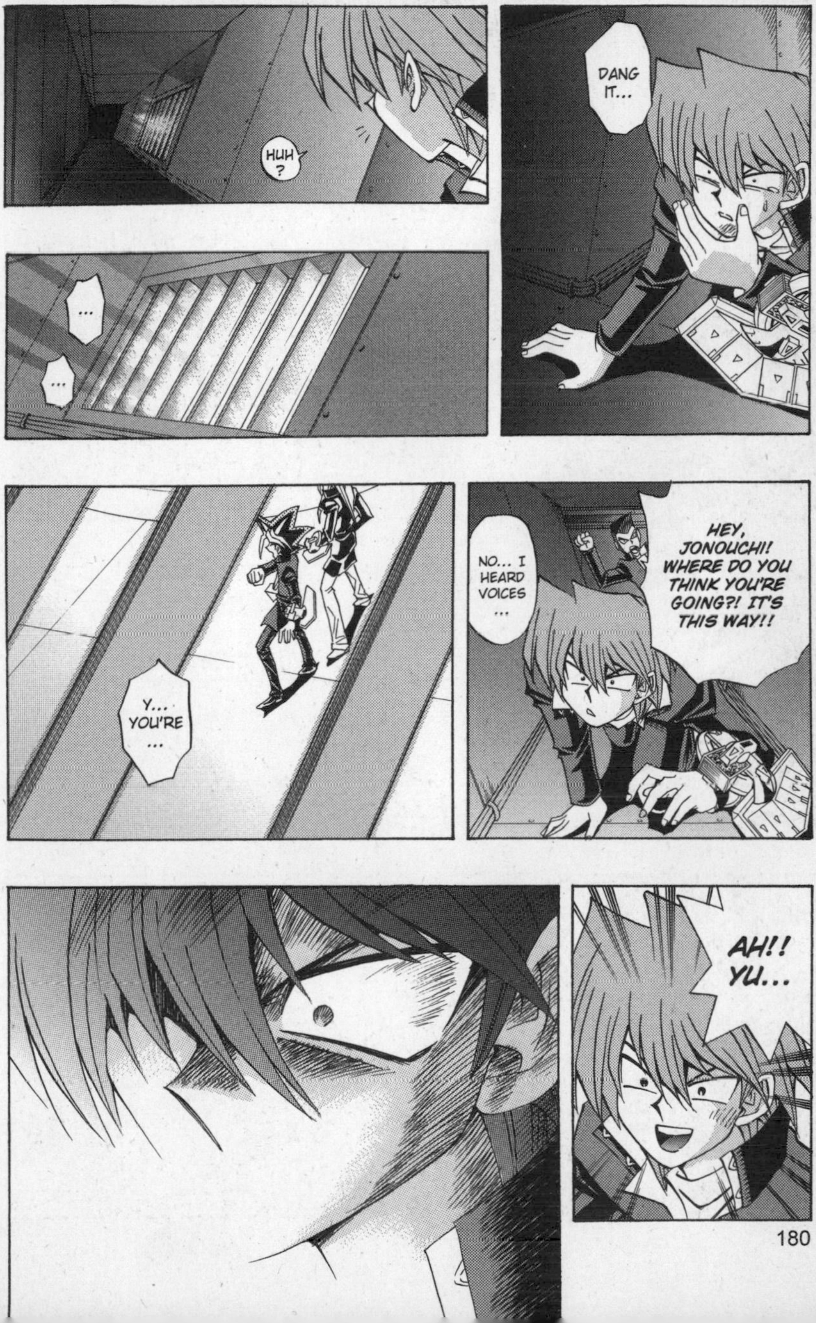
DANG IT...
HUH ?
...
...
HEY, JONOUCHI! WHERE DO YOU THINK YOU'RE GOING?! IT'S THIS WAY!!
NO... I HEARD VOICES ...
Y... YOU'RE ...
AH!! YU...

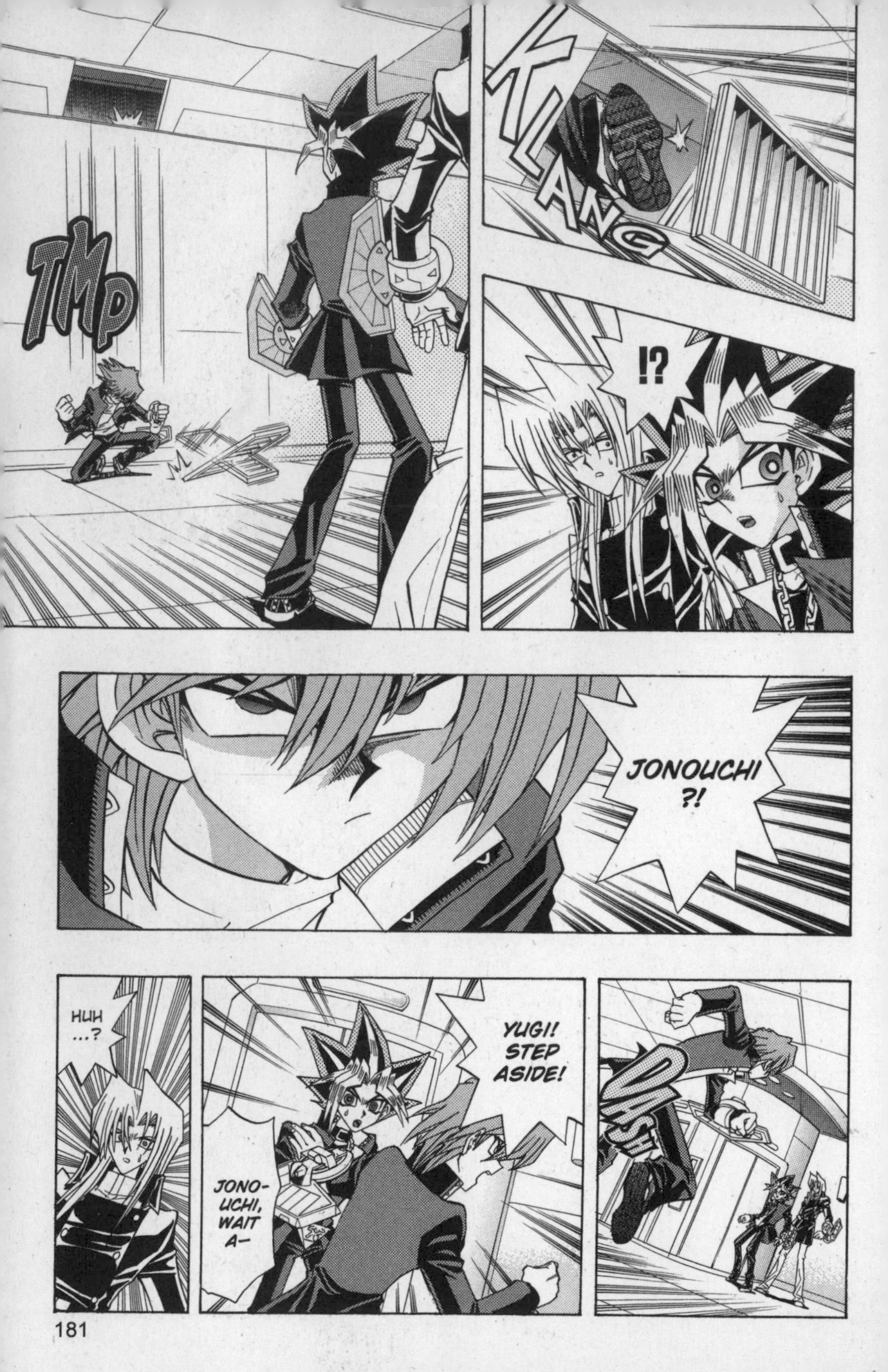
KLANG
!?
TMP
JONOUCHI ?!
YUGI! STEP ASIDE!
JONO-UCHI, WAIT A—
HUH ...?

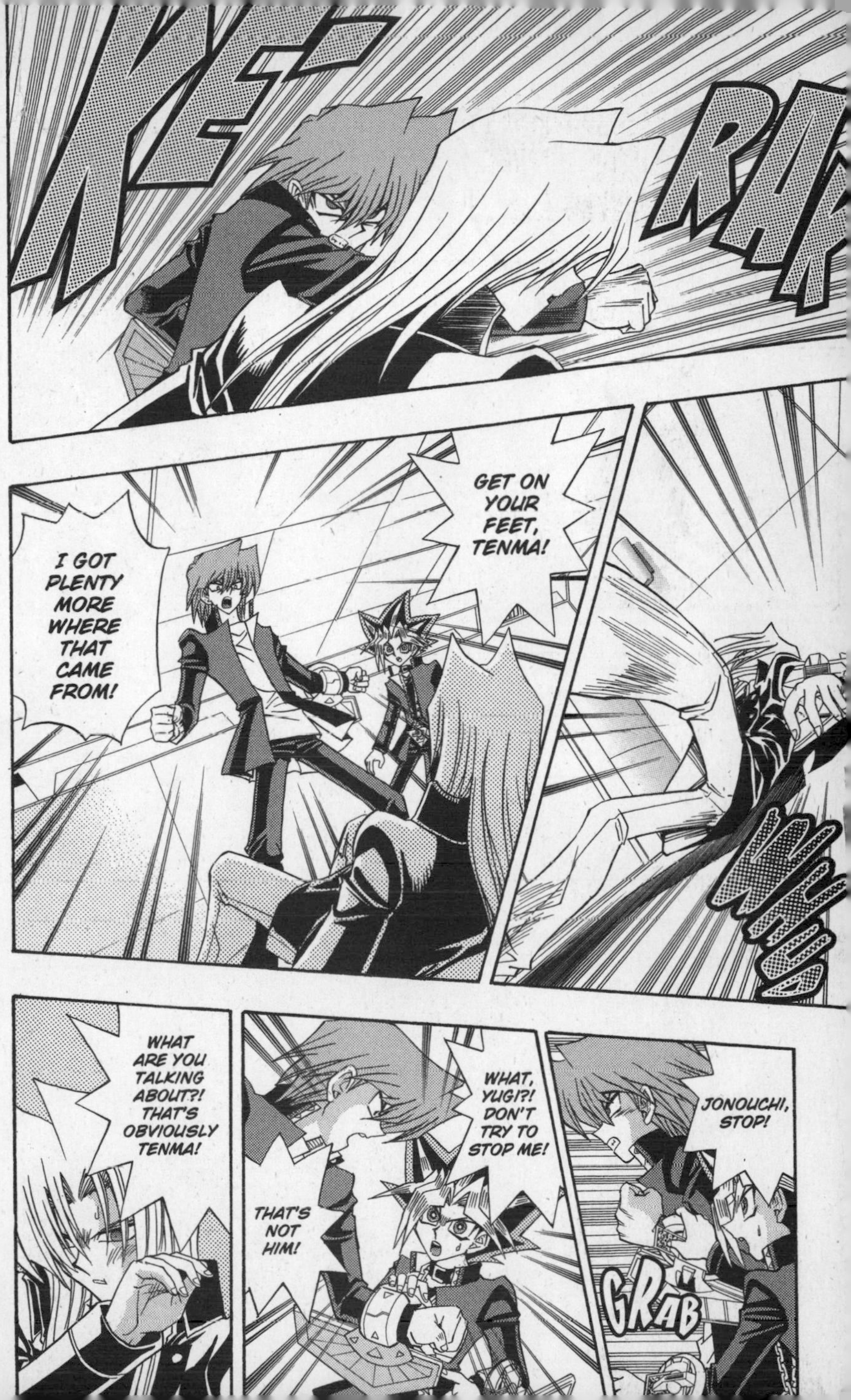
GET ON YOUR FEET, TENMA!
I GOT PLENTY MORE WHERE THAT CAME FROM!
JONOUCHI, STOP!
GRAB
WHAT, YUGI?! DON'T TRY TO STOP ME!
THAT'S NOT HIM!
WHAT ARE YOU TALKING ABOUT?! THAT'S OBVIOUSLY TENMA!

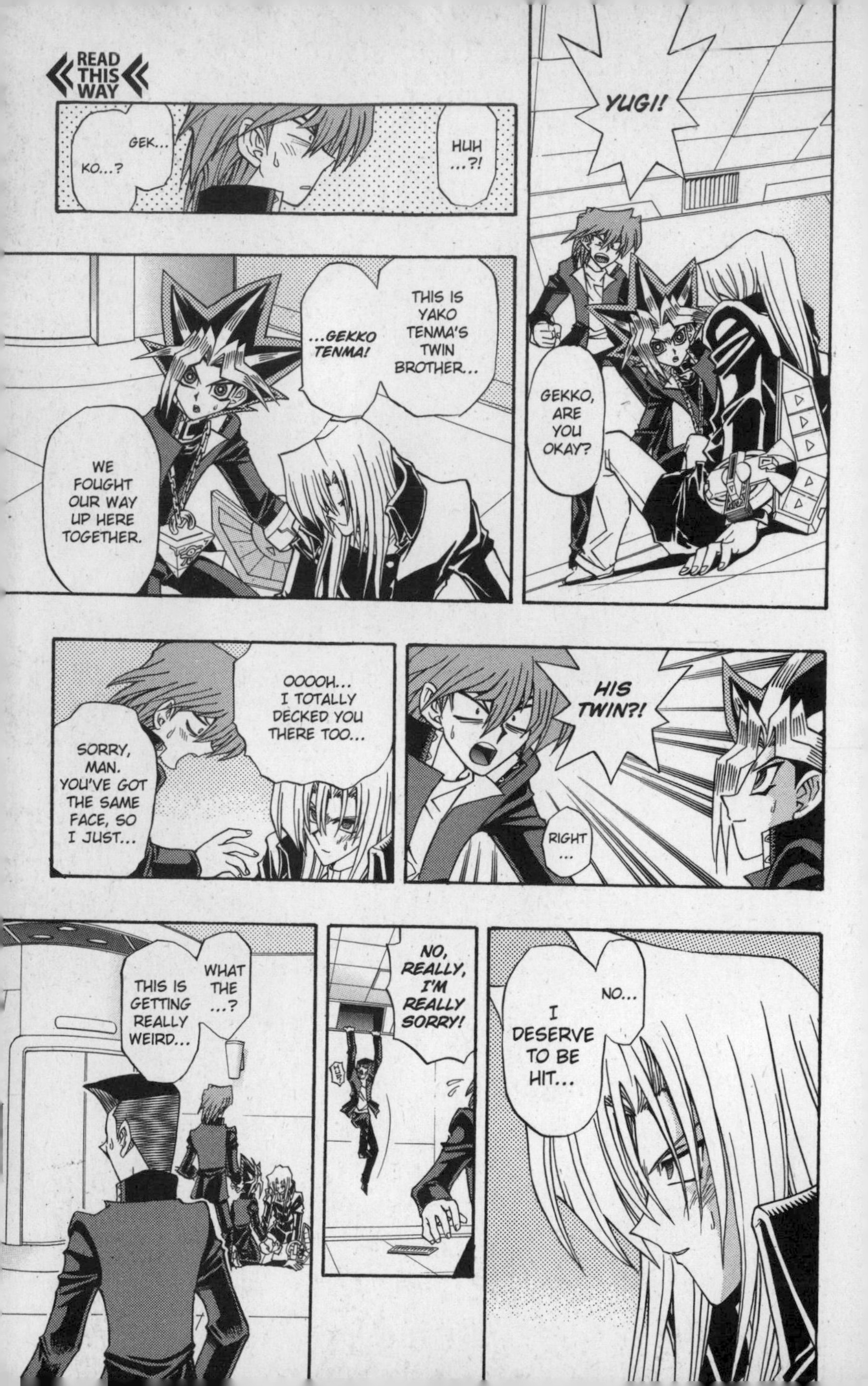
READ THIS WAY
YUGI!
GEKKO, ARE YOU OKAY?
HUH ...?!
GEK... KO...?
THIS IS YAKO TENMA'S TWIN BROTHER...
...GEKKO TENMA!
WE FOUGHT OUR WAY UP HERE TOGETHER.
HIS TWIN?!
RIGHT ...
OOOOH... I TOTALLY DECKED YOU THERE TOO...
SORRY, MAN. YOU'VE GOT THE SAME FACE, SO I JUST...
NO...
I DESERVE TO BE HIT...
NO, REALLY, I'M REALLY SORRY!
WHAT THE ...?
THIS IS GETTING REALLY WEIRD...

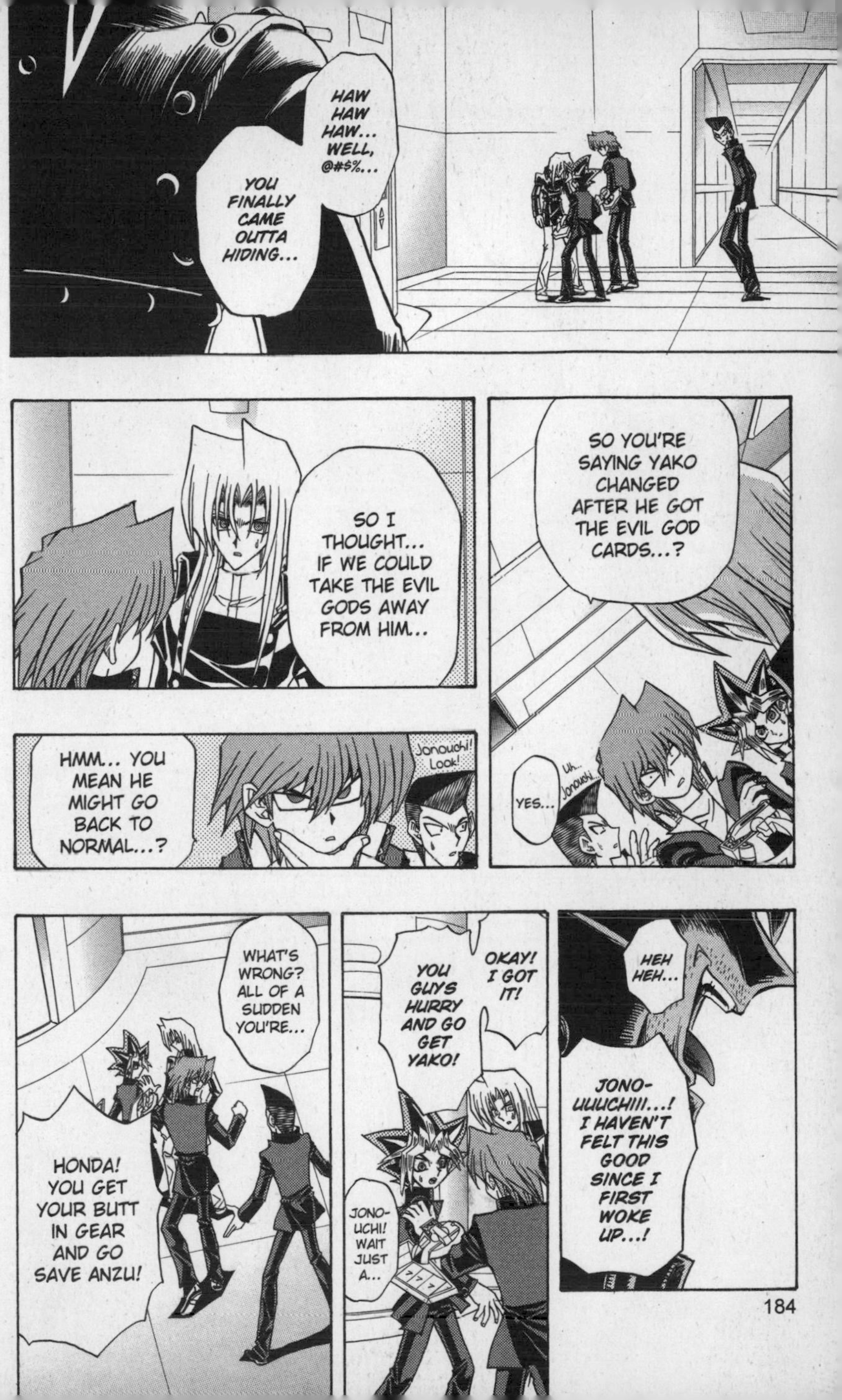
HAW HAW HAW... WELL, @#$%...
YOU FINALLY CAME OUTTA HIDING...
SO YOU'RE SAYING YAKO CHANGED AFTER HE GOT THE EVIL GOD CARDS...?
Uh... Jonouchi...
YES...
SO I THOUGHT... IF WE COULD TAKE THE EVIL GODS AWAY FROM HIM...
HMM... YOU MEAN HE MIGHT GO BACK TO NORMAL...?
Jonouchi! Look!
HEH HEH...
JONO-UUUCHIIII...! I HAVEN'T FELT THIS GOOD SINCE I FIRST WOKE UP...!
OKAY! I GOT IT!
YOU GUYS HURRY AND GO GET YAKO!
JONO-UCHI! WAIT JUST A...
WHAT'S WRONG? ALL OF A SUDDEN YOU'RE...
HONDA! YOU GET YOUR BUTT IN GEAR AND GO SAVE ANZU!

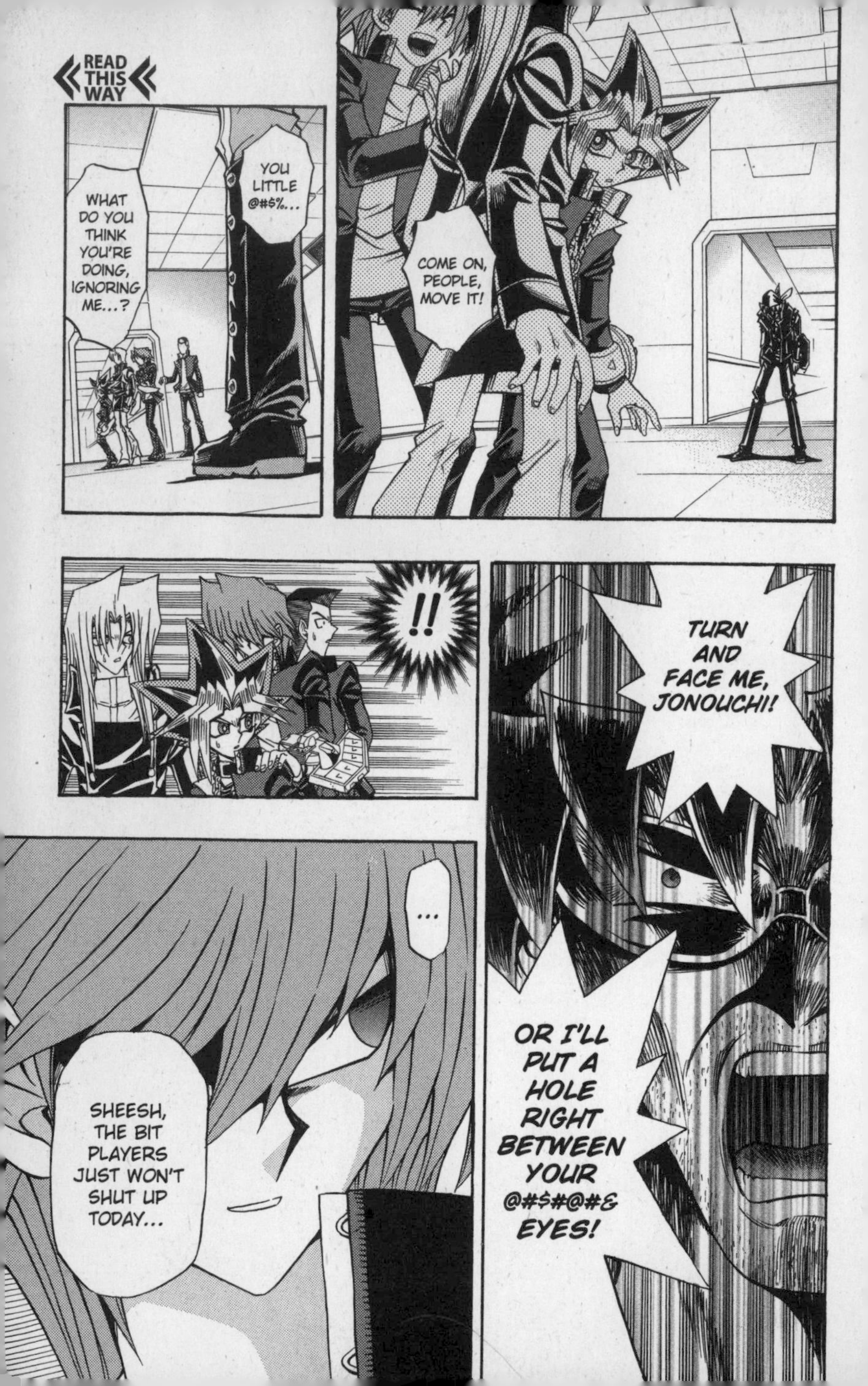
READ THIS WAY
COME ON, PEOPLE, MOVE IT!
YOU LITTLE @#$%...
WHAT DO YOU THINK YOU'RE DOING, IGNORING ME...?
TURN AND FACE ME, JONOUCHI!
OR I'LL PUT A HOLE RIGHT BETWEEN YOUR @#$#@#& EYES!
!!
...
SHEESH, THE BIT PLAYERS JUST WON'T SHUT UP TODAY...

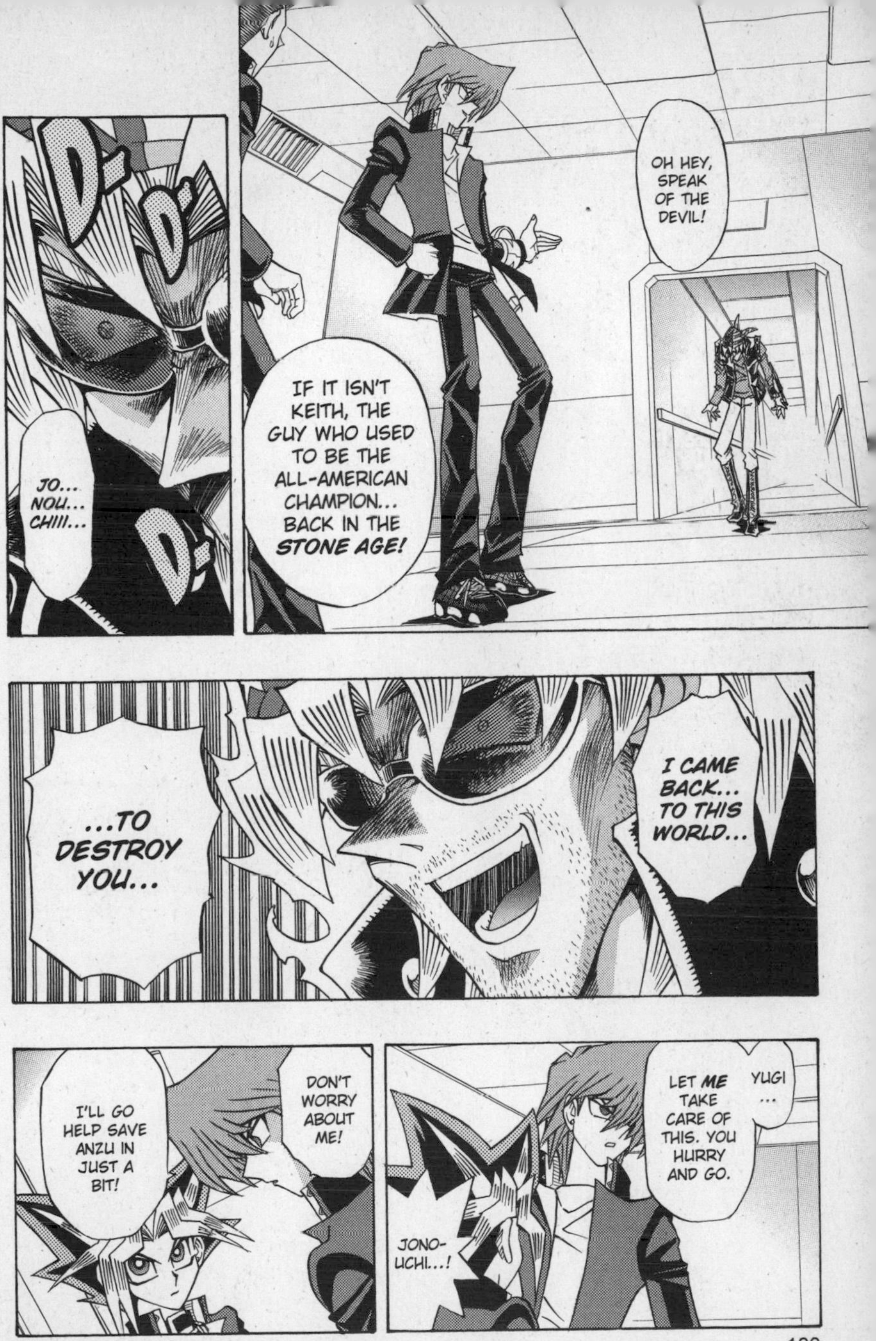
OH HEY, SPEAK OF THE DEVIL!
IF IT ISN'T KEITH, THE GUY WHO USED TO BE THE ALL-AMERICAN CHAMPION... BACK IN THE *STONE AGE!*
JO... NOU... CHIII...
I CAME BACK... TO THIS WORLD...
...TO DESTROY YOU...
YUGI...
LET *ME* TAKE CARE OF THIS. YOU HURRY AND GO.
JONO-UCHI...!
DON'T WORRY ABOUT ME!
I'LL GO HELP SAVE ANZU IN JUST A BIT!

READ THIS WAY

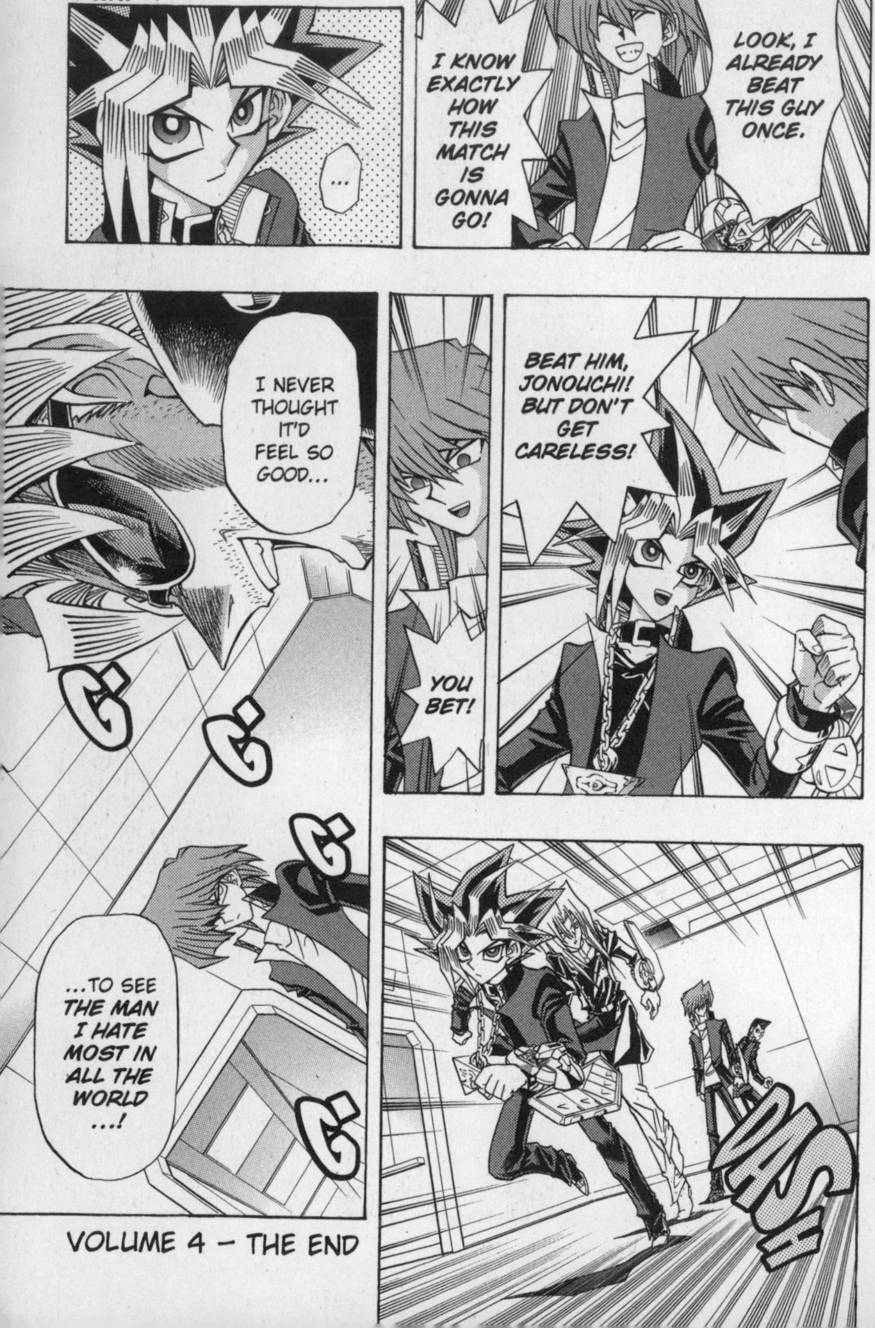

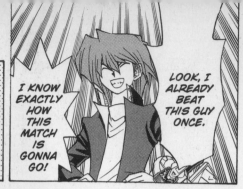

LOOK, I ALREADY BEAT THIS GUY ONCE.
I KNOW EXACTLY HOW THIS MATCH IS GONNA GO!
...
BEAT HIM, JONOUCHI! BUT DON'T GET CARELESS!
YOU BET!
DASH
I NEVER THOUGHT IT'D FEEL SO GOOD...
G
G
G
G
...TO SEE THE MAN I HATE MOST IN ALL THE WORLD ...!

VOLUME 4 – THE END

* Face-down spell cards can be activated whenever the phase changes.

*Face-down trap cards can be activated whenever their trigger event occurs, beginning from the moment they're set on the field.

* Monsters may be summoned in attack mode or in defense mode. In the Official Card Game, monsters can be placed on the field in "reverse defense mode" as well. In this manga, they aren't used that way, but they probably could be. (Although the duelists never do it...)

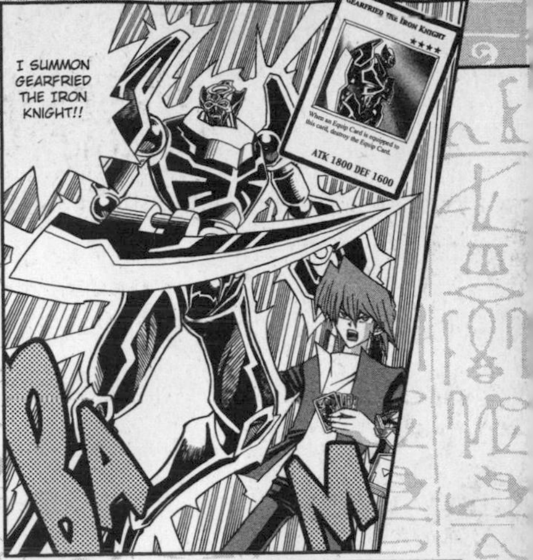
GEARFRIED THE IRON KNIGHT
When an Equip Card is equipped to this card, destroy the Equip Card.
ATK 1800 DEF 1600
I SUMMON GEARFRIED THE IRON KNIGHT!!
BAM

BATTLE PHASE

* When only one monster attacks, everything is the same as it is in the Official Card Game rules, including damage calculation.

* When several monsters attack:

1. Choose which monsters participate in the attack.
2. Choose which of your opponent's monsters each of your monsters will attack.
3. Attack! Begin damage phase.

At this point, all damage to all monsters is dealt with simultaneously. In the manga, it's sometimes drawn as though the damage is dealt in a certain order, but it really happens simultaneously.
For example, in the battle between Yugi and Depre in *Yu-Gi-Oh! R* volume 3, Depre attacks with "Eva Epsilon" and "Greed Quasar." As Yugi takes damage from "Greed Quasar," he activates "Fit of Rage," but when the damage to "Toy Magician" and "Eva Epsilon" is calculated, this isn't reflected.

That's because both the damage to Yugi which triggered "Fit of Rage" and the "Toy Magician" counter-attack were treated as having occurred simultaneously, with "Fit of Rage" applied after the battle phase.

That's basically how I considered things when I was thinking up the duels. Mr. Kageyama from *Yu-Gi-Oh! GX* asked me, "Aren't those rules a little weird?" But these rules are special to *Yu-Gi-Oh! R*, so please just accept them as they are.

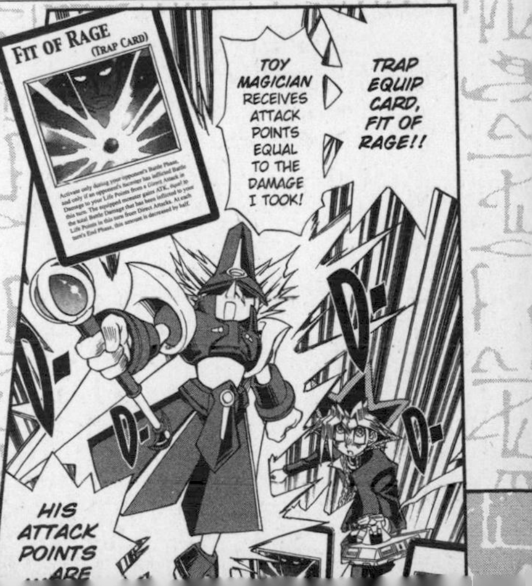
TRAP EQUIP CARD, FIT OF RAGE!!
FIT OF RAGE
(TRAP CARD)
TOY MAGICIAN RECEIVES ATTACK POINTS EQUAL TO THE DAMAGE I TOOK!
HIS ATTACK POINTS ...ARE

YU-GI-OH! R SPECIAL RULES

☆ BY AKIRA ITO ☆

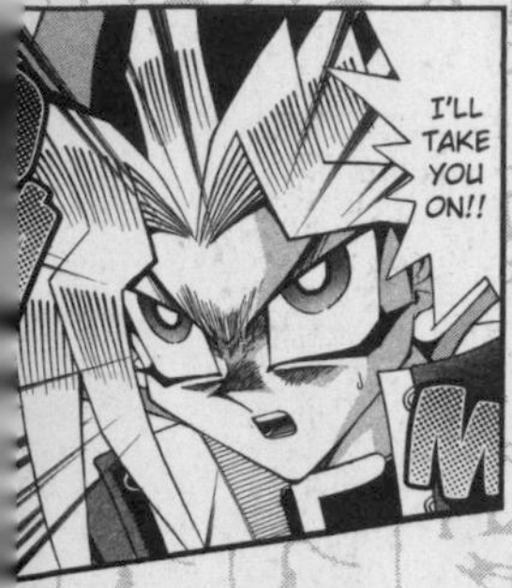
I'LL TAKE YOU ON!!

The duel rules used in *Yu-Gi-Oh! R* are a bit different from the rules in the official card game all of you usually play.

Fundamentally, they're based on the "super expert rules" in the Battle City arc (in *Yu-Gi-Oh! Duelist*) and the ceremonial battle rules in the fight between Yugi and Atem (in *Yu-Gi-Oh! Millennium World*). Since those rules aren't explained in *R*, I'm going to go over them briefly here.

GAME START

* Both players start out with 4000 Life Points.

* Both players draw six cards at the beginning of the duel. On their first turn they draw one card, so each hand has seven cards. It's set up this way because the Ceremonial Battle began with a six-card hand.

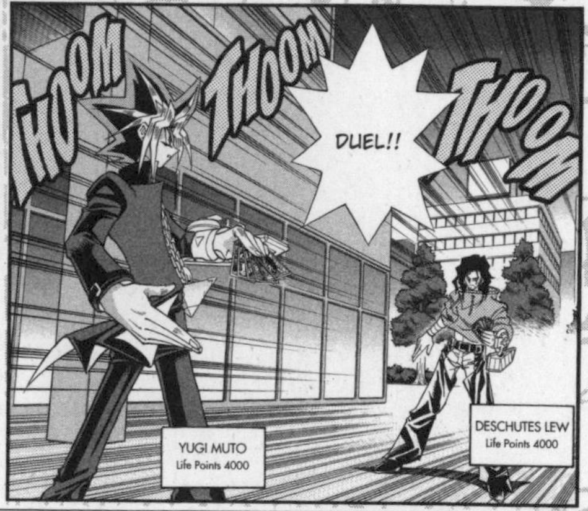
THOOM
THOOM
THOOM
DUEL!!
DESCHUTES LEW
Life Points 4000
YUGI MUTO
Life Points 4000

MAIN PHASE

* On your own turn, you may activate up to one spell card from your hand. Unlike in the Official Card Game rules, you can't activate several at a time when the field is empty.

* You can only place one spell card and one trap card face down during your turn. If you try to cheat and put down two spell cards or something, your duel disk will sound an alarm.

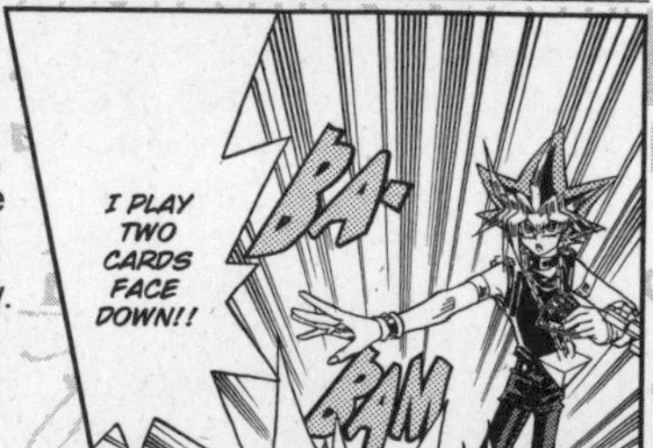
BA-
BAM
I PLAY TWO CARDS FACE DOWN!!

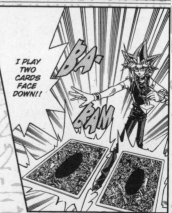

MASTER OF THE CARDS

Yu-Gi-Oh! R is an original story that takes place after *Yu-Gi-Oh!: Duelist* but before *Yu-Gi-Oh!: Millennium World*. It features many new cards never seen before in the manga or anime. As with all original *Yu-Gi-Oh!* cards, names can differ slightly between the Japanese and English versions, so we're showing you both for reference. Plus, we show you the card even if the card itself doesn't show up in the manga but the monster or trap does! And some cards you may have already seen in the original *Yu-Gi-Oh!*, but we still note them the first time they appear in this volume anyway!

EVERY CARD IN THIS VOLUME

First Appearance in This Volume	Japanese Card Name	English Card Name <<!>> = Not yet available in the TCG.
p.8	*The Devils Avatar*	The Wicked Avatar
p.21	*Learning Elf* ラーニング・エルフ	Learning Elf
p.22	*Twin Gunfighter* ツイン・ガンファイター	Twin Gunfighter <<!>>
p.22	*Hanshatate–Reflector* 反射盾―リフレクター	Shield Reflector <<!>>
p.23	*Nigemizu* 逃げ水	Mirage <<!>>
p.32	*Wonderbeat Elf* ワンダービート・エルフ	Wonderbeat Elf <<!>>
p.33	*Gôdatsuben* 強奪鞭	Theft Whip <<!>>
p.39	*Pierce Musketeer* ピアース・マスケッティア	Pierce Musketeer <<!>>
p.40	*Holy Sacrifice* ホーリー・サクリファイス	Holy Sacrifice <<!>>
p.42	*Shoyûsha no Kokuin* 所有者の刻印	Owner's Seal
p.43	*Ikenie no Fukusôhin* 生贄の副葬品	Sacrifice of Grave Goods <<!>>

p.44	*Angel 07* エンジェル07	Angel 07
p.46	*Grenader* グリネイダー	Grenadier <<!>>
p.60	*Genwaku no Senkô* 幻惑の閃光	Dazzling Radiance <<!>>
p.62	*Jiai no Amulet* 慈愛のアミュレット	Amulet of Affection <<!>>
p.63	*Kasumeru Dangan* 掠める弾丸	Grazing Bullet <<!>>
p.82	*Material Bat* マテリアル・バット	Material Bat <<!>>
p.84	*Material Lion* マテリアル・ライオン	Material Lion <<!>>
p.86	*Alpha Ha no Hôsan* α波の放散	Alpha-Wave Emission <<!>>
p.88	*Blue-Eyes White Dragon* 青眼の白龍	Blue-Eyes White Dragon <<!>>
p.88	*Material Scorpion* マテリアル・スコーピオン	Material Scorpion <<!>>
p.89	*Mosaic Manticore* モザイク・マンティコア	Mosaic Manticore
p.91	*Chronic Déjà Vu* クロニック・デジャヴュ	Chronic Déjà Vu <<!>>
p.93	*Vaccine no Sesshu* ワクチンの接種	Vaccination <<!>>
p.95	*Yami no Kôshaku Belial* 闇の侯爵ベリアル	Belial—Marquis of Darkness
p.101	*Holy Doll* ホーリー・ドール	Rogue Doll
p.107	*Agathion* アガシオン	Agathion
p.108	*Cross Shift* クロス・シフト	Cross Shift
p.108	*Lord of Dragon* ロード・オブ・ドラゴン	Lord of D.
p.109	*Dragon • Mezame no Senritsu* ドラゴン・目覚めの旋律	The Melody of Awakening Dragon <<!>>

p.110	*Dragon wo Yobufue* ドラゴンを呼ぶ笛	The Flute of Summoning Dragon
p.113	*Yûgo* 融合	Polymerization
p.114	*Blue-Eyes Ultimate Dragon* 青眼の究極竜	Blue-Eyes Ultimate Dragon
p.116	*Junk Dealer* ジャンク・ディーラー	Junk Dealer <<!>>
p.131	*Comparable Level* カンパラブル・レベル	Comparable Level <<!>>
p.132	*Material Armadillo* マテリアル・アーマディロウ	Material Armadillo <<!>>
p.134	*Angel 01* エンジェル０１	Angel 01 <<!>>
p.136	*The Devils Dread-Root*	The Wicked Dreadroot
p.139	*Chikara no Kekkai* 力の決壊	Power Collapse <<!>>
p.152	*Jashin Eraser* 邪神イレイザー	The Wicked Eraser <<!>>
p.166	*Osiris no Tenkûryû* オシリスの天空竜	Slifer the Sky Dragon
p.170	*Pegasus J. Crawford*	Maximillion J. Pegasus <<!>>

IN THE NEXT VOLUME...

Jonouchi slugs it out with Bandit Keith and his machine monsters in the most brutal rematch in duelist history! Meanwhile, Gekko and Yugi rush to the top of KaibaCorp only to find...what? Was the R.A. Project really a failure? And what about the three evil gods? The answers lie in a duel in the giant 290+ page conclusion!

COMING JUNE 2010!

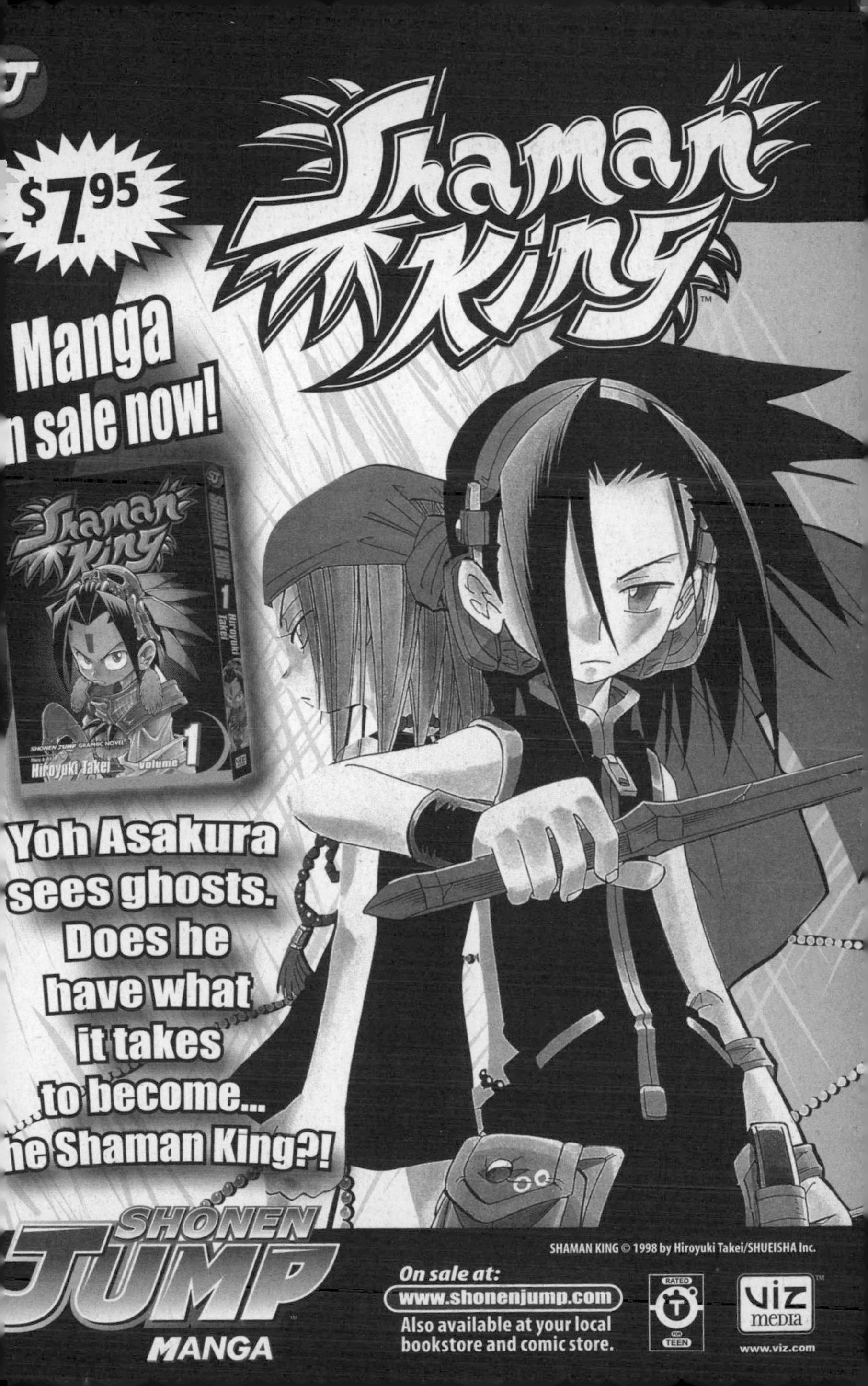
Shaman King
$7.95
Manga
n sale now!
Shaman King
SHAMAN KING 1 Hiroyuki Takei
SHONEN JUMP GRAPHIC NOVEL
Hiroyuki Takei volume 1
Yoh Asakura sees ghosts. Does he have what it takes to become...
he Shaman King?!
SHONEN JUMP MANGA
SHAMAN KING © 1998 by Hiroyuki Takei/SHUEISHA Inc.
On sale at:
www.shonenjump.com
Also available at your local bookstore and comic store.
RATED T FOR TEEN
viz media
www.viz.com

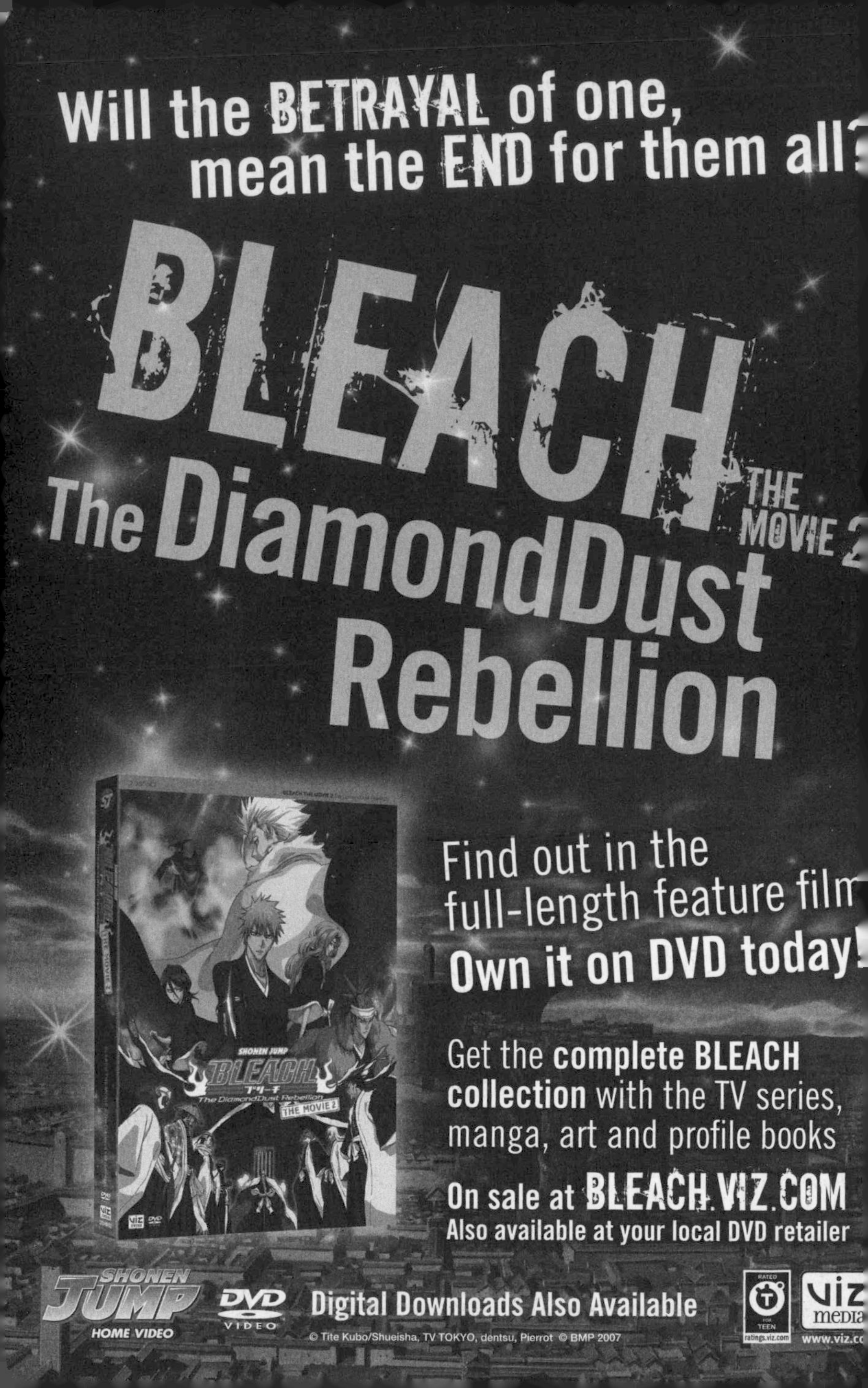
Will the BETRAYAL of one,
mean the END for them all?
BLEACH
THE MOVIE 2
The DiamondDust Rebellion
SHONEN JUMP
BLEACH
The DiamondDust Rebellion
THE MOVIE 2
Find out in the
full-length feature film
Own it on DVD today!
Get the complete BLEACH collection with the TV series, manga, art and profile books
On sale at BLEACH.VIZ.COM
Also available at your local DVD retailer
SHONEN JUMP HOME VIDEO
DVD VIDEO
Digital Downloads Also Available
© Tite Kubo/Shueisha, TV TOKYO, dentsu, Pierrot © BMP 2007
RATED T FOR TEEN
ratings.viz.com
viz media
www.viz.com

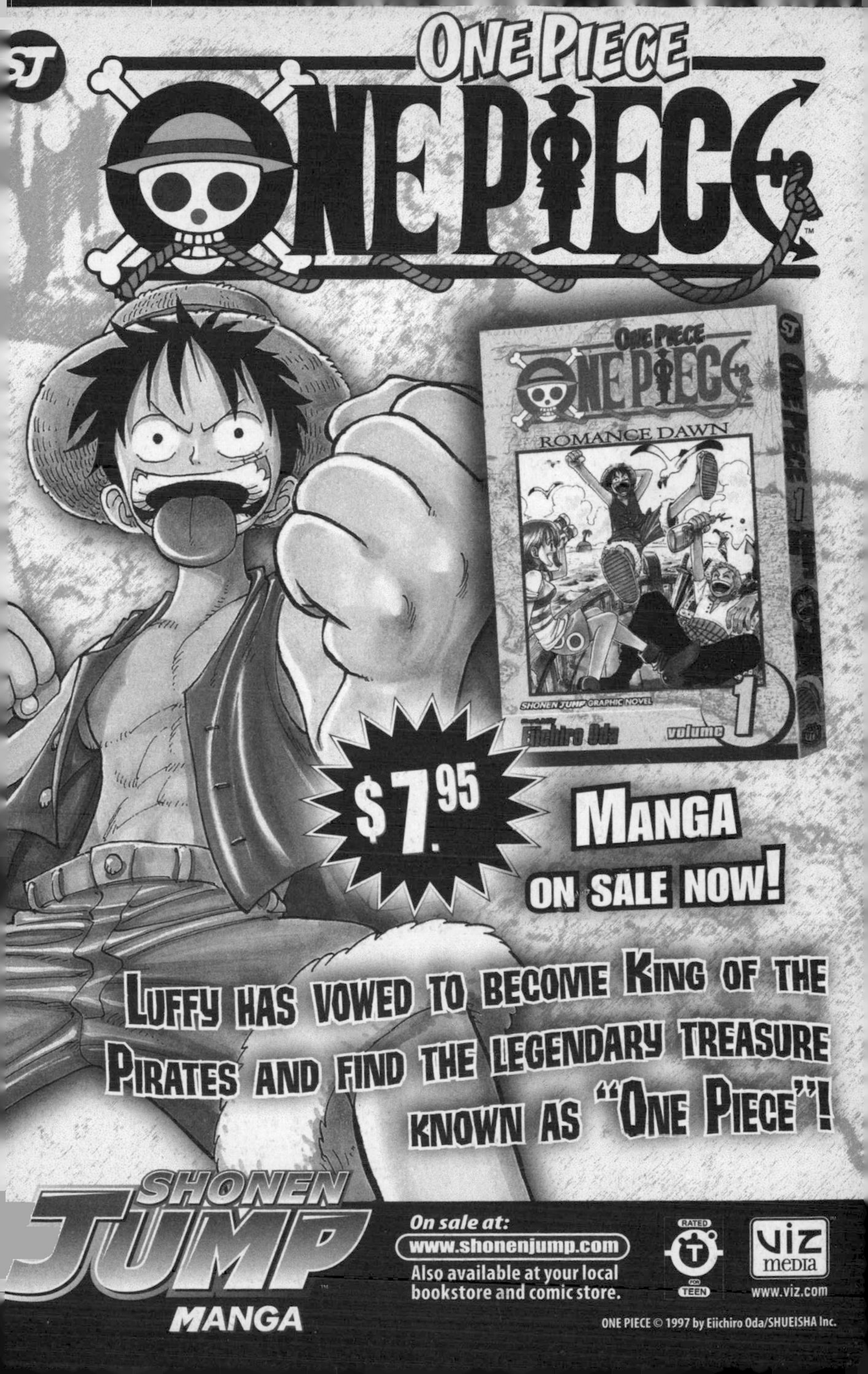
ONE PIECE
ONE PIECE
ONE PIECE
ONE PIECE
ROMANCE DAWN
SHONEN JUMP GRAPHIC NOVEL
Eiichiro Oda
volume 1
ONE PIECE 1
$7.95
MANGA
ON SALE NOW!
LUFFY HAS VOWED TO BECOME KING OF THE PIRATES AND FIND THE LEGENDARY TREASURE KNOWN AS "ONE PIECE"!
SHONEN JUMP
MANGA
On sale at:
www.shonenjump.com
Also available at your local bookstore and comic store.
RATED T FOR TEEN
viz media
www.viz.com
ONE PIECE © 1997 by Eiichiro Oda/SHUEISHA Inc.

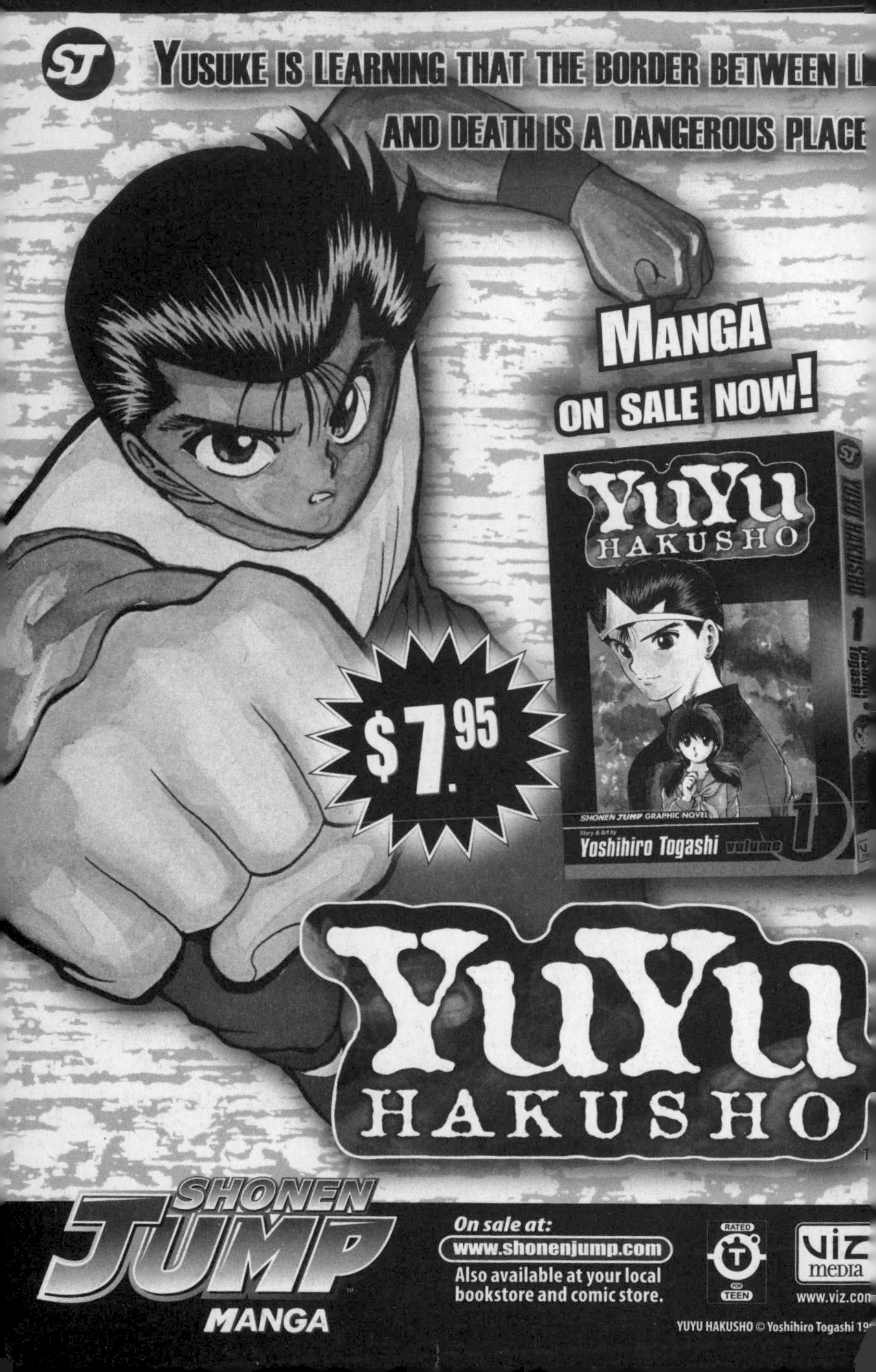
YUSUKE IS LEARNING THAT THE BORDER BETWEEN L
AND DEATH IS A DANGEROUS PLACE
MANGA
ON SALE NOW!
$7.95
YUYU HAKUSHO
SHONEN JUMP GRAPHIC NOVEL
Yoshihiro Togashi volume 1
YUYU HAKUSHO
SHONEN JUMP MANGA
On sale at:
www.shonenjump.com
Also available at your local bookstore and comic store.
RATED T FOR TEEN
VIZ media
www.viz.com
YUYU HAKUSHO © Yoshihiro Togashi 19

SHONEN JUMP

THE WORLD'S MOST POPULAR MANGA

BLEACH
ブリーチ

ONE PIECE

Tegami Bachi
LETTER · BEE

**STORY AND ART BY
TITE KUBO**

**STORY AND ART BY
EIICHIRO ODA**

**STORY AND ART BY
HIROYUKI ASADA**

JUMP INTO THE ACTION BY TELLING US WHAT YOU LOVE (AND WHAT YOU DON'T)

LET YOUR VOICE BE HEARD!

SHONENJUMP.VIZ.COM/MANGASURVEY

HELP US MAKE MORE OF THE WORLD'S MOST POPULAR MANGA!

RATED
T
FOR
TEEN
ratings.viz.com

VIZ
MEDIA
www.viz.com